Jewish Heritage
in Britain and Ireland

An Architectural Guide

Sharman Kadish

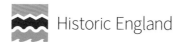
Historic England

Published by Historic England, The Engine House, Fire Fly Avenue,
Swindon SN2 2EH, in conjunction with Jewish Heritage UK
www.HistoricEngland.org.uk

Historic England is a Government service championing England's heritage and giving expert, constructive advice, and the English Heritage Trust is a charity caring for
the National Heritage Collection of more than 400 historic properties and
their collections.

Jewish Heritage UK is dedicated to caring for the synagogues, cemeteries and sites of
Britain's Jewish community
www.jewish-heritage-uk.org

Text © Sharman Kadish 2015
Maps © Barbara Bowman
Images (except as otherwise shown) © Historic England

The views expressed in this book are those of the author and not necessarily those
of Historic England.

First published 2006 by English Heritage ISBN 978-1-90562-428-7
Revised second edition published June 2015
ISBN 978-1-84802-237-9

British Library Cataloguing in Publication data
A CIP catalogue record for this book is available from the British Library.

The right of Sharman Kadish to be identified as author of this work has been
asserted by her in accordance with the Copyright, Designs and Patents Act 1988.

Application for the reproduction of images should be made to Historic England.
Every effort has been made to trace the copyright holders and we apologise in
advance for any unintentional omissions, which we would be pleased to correct in
any subsequent edition of this book.

Historic England holds an unparalleled archive of 12 million photographs, drawings,
reports and publications on England's places. It is one of the largest archives in
the UK, the biggest dedicated to the historic environment, and a priceless resource
for anyone interested in England's buildings, archaeology, landscape and social
history. Viewed collectively, its photographic collections document the changing
face of England from the 1850s to the present day. It is a treasure trove that helps
us understand and interpret the past, informs the present and assists with future
management and appreciation of the historic environment.

For more information about images from the Archive, contact Archives Services
Team, Historic England, The Engine House, Fire Fly Avenue, Swindon SN2 2EH;
telephone (01793) 414600.

Brought to publication by Sarah Enticknap, Publishing, Historic England

Typeset in Plantin 8pt

Edited by Patricia Briggs
Indexed by Alan Rutter
Page layout by Francis & Partners

Printed in Belgium by DeckersSnoeck

Contents

JEWISH HERITAGE UK

To Syd, my husband, whose family
set me on this path of discovery

In 2006 this project was made possible through the generous support of:

ENGLISH HERITAGE

Arts & Humanities
Research Council

The Pilgrim Trust

The British Academy

The R M Burton Charitable Trust

Hanadiv Charitable Foundation

The Royal Institute of British Architects

The Paul Mellon Centre for Studies in British Art

The Aurelius Charitable Trust

The Trustees of Notting Hill Synagogue

Bevis Marks Synagogue Trust

The Sternberg Charitable Foundation

Michael & Ilse Katz Foundation

The Victor Mishcon Charitable Trust

The Center for Jewish Art, Jerusalem

Mr Anton Felton

Anonymous

Note on Dating

The heading for each site entry includes a date in all cases where this has been established with certainty from primary sources.

Civil Dates

For *synagogues:* the year or years given in the heading generally refer to the laying of the foundation stone and/or the official opening of the building.

For *burial grounds:* the year given is preferably that in which the first burial took place. In cases, particularly of older burial grounds, where this information is not available (because burial registers are lost or incomplete), alternatives may include either the date of the acquisition of the site (usually from an extant lease or title deed) or the date of the consecration of the ground (often from a press report). An explanation of any problems with dating is given in the text.

Researchers interested in the primary sources used in the preparation of this guidebook may apply to consult the *Survey of the Jewish Built Heritage* Database, Archive and Image Library that are being deposited at Historic England Archives in Swindon.

Hebrew Dates

The Jewish year starts in September/October. This means that there is a discrepancy of approximately three months between Hebrew and 'English' (*i.e.* Gregorian) dates. In the case of sites where the Hebrew year has been established (usually from an inscription on a date stone or derived from a chronogram) – but not the exact day or month – then the corresponding civil year given refers to the period from January to September/October of the quoted year. However, the Hebrew date actually covers the period from September/October of the previous year to September/October of the quoted year. For example: 5775 corresponds roughly to '2015', but it really covers the period September/October 2014 to September/October 2015.

Preface to the Second Edition

This guidebook is a new and expanded edition of *Jewish Heritage in England*, which came out back in 2006, to coincide with the 350th Anniversary of the Resettlement of the Jewish community in England (1656–2006). Publishers English Heritage were astounded at the interest that it generated. The first print-run sold out within three months and the book has since gone out of print. Consequently, in the summer of 2011, I was approached by John Hudson, Head of Publishing at English Heritage, to revise and update the text. The first thing that we did was to revise the title, better to reflect the contents of the book. Although it is now a Historic England imprint, it gives due weight to all parts of the British Isles, including the Irish Republic and off-shore islands (Jersey and the Isle of Man) that are not technically part of the United Kingdom. 'Anglo'-Jewry – with all its increasing internal diversity – remains a distinct cultural minority within the entirety of these shores, irrespective of the legal and political framework. Jews in England, Wales, Scotland and Ireland (north and south) share a common history and heritage that justifies holistic treatment.

The bulk of the rewriting was carried out over the summer and autumn of 2013. By way of contrast with the original Survey of the Jewish Built Heritage,[1] the preparation of this new edition did not necessitate revisiting all of the synagogues, cemeteries and other sites that have entries in the book. Certainly, in the intervening years, I have returned to some of them (indeed, some, many times), in my capacity as Director of Jewish Heritage UK. This has usually been in order to check on changes in their physical condition and to provide support for small communities who are struggling to look after their historic properties. In 2009, together with my longstanding colleague architect Barbara Bowman, I visited all of the listed synagogues currently in use for the Synagogues at Risk survey commissioned by English Heritage as part of their wider Places of Worship at Risk programme. The findings of that survey, which assessed each synagogue on a scale of 'risk' in terms both of the 'condition' of the fabric and the level of 'usage' of the building (or lack of it) by the Jewish community, were published in a report the following year.[2]

Barbara retired at the end of 2012 after 15 years as fieldworker with our Survey and as principal consultant architect to Jewish Heritage. Among her final tasks was, where necessary, to revise the excellent heritage trail maps that she drew for the first edition. These have been complimented for their clarity. In the case of the maps, I decided that it was necessary to retrace all of the walks on the ground in each featured location. This we did during the spring and summer of 2012. Barbara once again accompanied me around the East End of London and in Manchester (Cheetham). Architect Viorica Feler-Morgan came to Birmingham and Brighton. I would like to thank them both, and Barbara especially for her caring and conscientious contribution and sound advice over many years.

We did not undertake site visits to the majority of the sites included in the second edition. Instead, I have travelled the length and breadth of the country from my desk courtesy of Google Earth, Google Maps and Google Streetview. When we embarked on the original Survey site visits back in the 1990s we had to go to the library to read 6- or 10-figure coordinates off Ordnance Survey maps, and to photocopy pages from the *A to Z* street map series. We would highlight our sites and the best routes for reaching them with a luminous marker pen, make contact and warn keyholders by telephone that we were coming, and then set out and hope for the best. Now we have SatNav and the Internet!

In many ways technology makes the task much easier. It certainly cuts down on the legwork – in terms of visiting not only the sites themselves but also the libraries, archives and local record offices, in order to carry out the background research. To take just one example: 30 years ago, researching Anglo-Jewish history meant humping down from the shelf hefty bound volumes of the *Jewish Chronicle* (*JC*), and leafing through them by hand. This (physical) exercise was replaced by microfiche machines and reels of microfilm, which sometimes snapped or got rewound back-to-front. Now every copy of the *JC* since it was first published in 1841 has been scanned and can be searched far more easily than was ever previously possible through the *JC* Archive online (so long as you pay your subscription!). Thanks to the *JC* Archive, for this new edition I have been able to locate a number of references that have long eluded me, and to clear up some queries regarding the dating of some of the more obscure sites – and even, in a few cases, to identify their architects and designers for certain.[3]

The Internet has made direct engagement with primary sources easy; it has enabled the researcher to trawl through far larger quantities of data far more quickly than ever before, and

thereby it has enhanced the possibilities of scholarship. However, we have been made increasingly aware of the downside: the proliferation of online 'resources' that are not based on genuine primary research, that feed off one another, have specific agendas and biases, amplify inaccuracies and, worse, disseminate them globally. Even the most successful work in print cannot hope to reach the readership available online through all the electronic media now available to us on our latest laptops, tablet computers, e-readers ('Kindles') and mobile phones.

Most websites and online databases cannot be classed as primary sources and should not be treated as such. They mediate between the reader and the archives that are the building blocks of history, ie letters, diaries, printed books and newspapers etc produced at the time an event took place. For the architectural historian, architects' plans, building contracts, conveyances, old drawings, photographs and maps, and contemporary architectural journals, are essential research materials.

On the Web, it is necessary to distinguish between primary and secondary sources, just as it is when dealing with traditional paper records. To take our previous example, the *Jewish Chronicle* scanned is a primary source made widely available and much more accessible by the provision of an electronic search facility. In contrast, online databases, especially of burial records, have been created from data contained in original registers, allowing for human error to creep into transcription (especially when it comes to Hebrew inscriptions) and data entry. This is not to deny the usefulness of these ever-growing resources, nor the tremendous labours that have gone into their creation. Of most interest to readers of this guidebook who are tracing their family trees are JCR-UK, the Jewish Communities and Records Database (www.jewishgen.org/databases/

UK)[4] and Cemetery Scribes (www. cemeteryscribes.com). However, we do need to remind ourselves that such resources may not be 100 per cent accurate and can never entirely replace the original documents that must be conserved and protected in a secure place. (In the long run, the existence of digital records will help preserve the fragile paper records by reducing the wear and tear on them by users.)

Of course, errors do occur in printed books, but the well-established processes of peer review, editing, copyediting and proofreading usually ensure that these remain minimal. As predicted, a few errors and omissions occurred in the first edition of this guidebook. Although none was serious, I am delighted now to have the opportunity to rectify them. I am very grateful to all the people who have pointed out errors and/or provided updates or the findings of new research for the second edition. Dr David Graham kindly provided updated Jewish population statistics from the 2011 Census. For specific sites, I would like to thank the following (not an exhaustive list; others are mentioned in the footnotes): Charles Tucker (London cemeteries); David Garrard (English Heritage) (Nuevo Cemetery); Bryan Diamond (Liberal Jewish Synagogue and Cemetery); Prof Benny Chain (Golders Green Synagogue); Ivor Nadel (Hampstead Synagogue); Michael Woolfson (Aldershot); Simon Gingold (Birmingham); Gordon Franks, Godfrey Gould (Brighton); Alex Schlesinger (Bristol); Mark Harris, Trevor Marcuson (Cambridge); Alan and Jennifer Silverston (Cheltenham); Anthony Fagin, Leslie Lipert, Keith Pearce, Susan Soyinka (Falmouth and Penzance); Rabbi Shlomo Katanka, Dovid Pruim, Shlomo Schleider (Gateshead); Leo Solomon (Grimsby); Max Gold (Hull); Alan Coleman, Sarah Margittai, Elizabeth Sugarman (Ipswich); Malcolm Sender (Leeds); Alaster Burman, Arnold Lewis, Saul Marks, Jeff Shulkind (Liverpool); Sam Portnoy[5] (Manchester); David Gradus (Margate); Jackie and David Slesenger (Newcastle); Jerry Sibley (Plymouth); Mark Drukker (Reading); Martin Morris (Stoke-on-Trent); Martin Rispin (Wolverhampton); Ron Black, David Factor, Judge Anthony Morris; Cai Morgan Parry-Jones, Prof Harold Pollins (Wales); Harvey Kaplan, Fiona Frank, Paul O'Cuinn (Scotland); Steve Jaffe, Freddie Rosehill, Stuart Rosenblatt (Ireland); Malcolm Shifrin (*mikvaot*); Adina Hoenicker (stained glass). It is particularly gratifying to hear from younger-generation doctoral students whose research topics have been inspired by my work (in Adina's case on David Hillman; Cai's on Welsh synagogues).

Much effort has gone into checking and cross-checking to ensure complete accuracy, as far as is possible, in this new edition. The book reflects the changing face of technology, as discussed above, by including for the first time Web addresses as well as up-to-date telephone contacts for all sites that have them. It also cites a full five-, six- or seven-digit postcode for every site entry in the UK (so far, the Irish Republic has not adopted this system), given the new-found faith in our SatNavs (GPS satellite navigation systems).

However, a word of caution here about the pitfalls of postcodes. They were invented for the purpose of helping postmen do their rounds on foot in our cities, not for pinpointing sites, especially those in isolated locations, with precision. As I have discovered, the postcode system is not scientific; the combination of numbers and letters in the second sequence of three digits has no obvious logic akin to the Ordnance Survey's northings and eastings. Postcodes are not generally unique. They usually apply to a block of houses. Some streets have one code down one side (odd numbers) and another down the other (even numbers). Some sites occupy street corners or junctions.

They may even have two sets of postcodes, for the main entrance and for the door to the office (through which letters are posted) on the other side of the building. This is especially true in the case of a number of large London synagogues. In one case, the postcode given on their website took me to their mail box (POB) at the local post office – great if you want to send a letter but not if you want directions to the actual building!

Then there was the challenge posed by cemeteries (or other monuments) that have no living residents to whom you could send a letter! In some cases, especially municipal cemeteries that contain a Jewish plot, the problem was solved by the presence of a cemetery office or caretaker's lodge. However, thanks to local government cuts, there are fewer of these than there used to be (except in Scotland where the condition of many cemeteries has greatly improved in recent years). In other cases, I have simply had to take an editorial decision: to use the postcode of the nearest house, block of flats, shop, factory or office. Google Streetview itself carries a warning to the effect that images and addresses do not always coincide. Sometimes I had to resort to zooming in onto front doors – or even onto wheelie-bins – in order to track down a legible house number to use! The next stage was to go to the Royal Mail postcode-finder website and obtain the code for that address, or for others nearby; finally, to return to Google Maps and/or satellite mode and key in the alternative postcodes (sometimes as many as ten) in order to find the one that takes you closest on the ground to the site in question. I hope that this painstaking and at times frustrating process has paid off and will get you to your destination without hitch, however you choose to travel, on foot, by car or by public transport. If not, please do let me know (although neither I nor my publishers can be held liable for any financial losses incurred thereby)!

In addition to five-, six- or seven-digit postcodes, in the new edition, I have endeavoured to include more precise directions to help the visitor locate a site, especially where the street layout, or perhaps the interior layout of a big cemetery, appears confusing on the ground.

There are some other differences between the new edition and the old. This edition remains a 'heritage' guide in that it is still largely confined to sites that date from before the Second World War (1939). In the case of small and isolated communities, I have always tried to include the address of the sole remaining, current synagogue, even if it was opened after 1945, to help visitors to make contact with the local Jewish community. I have also made mention of some burial grounds opened since 1940 where these are direct successors to earlier grounds, now full, that have entries in the guidebook. Post-war cemeteries are also referred to in the context of smaller communities that managed to build a synagogue before the war, but not to establish a burial ground until sometime later. A good example is Cambridge where the first Jewish cemetery was actually opened during the war, in 1941. However, the inclusion of post-war Jewish plots cannot claim to be comprehensive, especially regarding Reform plots found usually in municipal cemeteries. Many Reform communities did not really become established until after 1945 and so really lie beyond the concern of this book.

Given the passage of time, the heritage protection agencies nationally have begun to assess the long-term importance of buildings erected over 30 years ago. Accordingly, I have now included the first post-war listed synagogue, Carmel College, and have occasionally drawn attention to other interesting or influential modern synagogues such as Belfast and Dundee or the Liberal Jewish Synagogue in London. I have also featured examples of mid-20th-century stained glass by David Hillman and Nehemiah Azaz.

A more subtle expansion of editorial boundaries has allowed the inclusion of a few more current synagogues founded before the war in converted buildings, Ealing being a good example, and listed buildings built for other purposes that have become home to synagogues since the war, such as Elstree Liberal Synagogue, a former Church of England schoolhouse.

However, the editorial policy has been adhered to of excluding almost all[6] buildings that were used as synagogues at some time in their history, but were neither built as synagogues, nor remained so subsequently. The use of converted spaces, whether rooms in, or built onto private houses, or former churches and chapels, schools and workshops, or even theatres and public houses, was a characteristic pattern of worship in the late 19th and early 20th century, particularly in large cities that hosted poor Jewish immigrants from eastern Europe. *Hevrot* (prayer circles) and Hasidic *shtieblekh* (conventicles) proliferated in the East End of London, just as they did on the Lower East Side of New York City, and as they do again today in resurgent Orthodox communities. The difference is that now such accommodation is often a matter of choice rather than the result of limited means.

Sometimes it has not been easy to determine whether a synagogue was purpose-built or not. The case of the North Manchester Synagogue may serve to illustrate the challenges presented to the researcher. When they heard about our project, native-born Mancunians confidently informed us that this former synagogue was still standing. We checked, and indeed the two-storey, red-brick Manchester *palazzo*-style warehouse building identified as the synagogue (at 28 Bury New Road, M8 8EL, on the corner with Jury Street), was identical to archive photographs published in local history books.[7] This synagogue was known as the 'Broyder' because, like many immigrant congregations, it was a *landsmanschaft* from the Galician border town of Brody. The *minyan* was founded in 1891 in a bedroom and then moved to a hired room that could accommodate 300 people in Waterloo Road. The 'North Manchester Synagogue and Beth Hamedrash' opened on the Bury New Road site in 1899 and remained there until 1944. However, further investigations established that the purported 'synagogue' was in fact used as the Beth HaMedrash from 1899. The synagogue itself stood next door to it, at north, and has been demolished. Moreover, neither building started life in Jewish use. The demolished 'synagogue', that had boasted a classical portico, was in fact the former Salem Chapel, built in the 1850s by a Methodist sect called the 'New Connexion'. In 1899 the growing Broyder Shul, with some 800 members, acquired on a long lease both the chapel and its separate hall and schools next door and turned the *latter* building into the Beth HaMedrash. Thus the building that is extant on Bury New Road does not qualify for an entry in this guidebook, based on the criteria that we have set.[8]

I have also added a handful of buildings previously presumed 'lost': for example the former Sunderland Beth HaMedrash in Villiers Street, recovered thanks to research for a conservation appraisal by Sunderland City Council. Stoke-on-Trent's synagogue in Hanley was still standing empty in 2013, although it had been expected that it would be demolished after the tiny congregation vacated the building in 2006. Fixtures and fittings, including the Minton tile *Magen David* over the entrance, were salvaged with the help of a Heritage Lottery Fund grant.

Nevertheless, since the last edition was published, a few site entries have had to be removed, thanks to demolition and redevelopment. These included, in London, Clapton Federation Synagogue, which was in process of demolition while the first edition was in press. In the East End, 'Mother Levy's' Jewish Maternity Home in Underwood Street, E1, was the subject of a big planning battle late in 2011 and was finally reduced to rubble by the Peabody Trust in January 2012 in the face of strenuous local protests and a petition signed by 750 people. Around the country, Birmingham's Progressive Synagogue in Sheepcote Street, a modernist building designed by Ernest Joseph in 1938, had already had to be 'pulled' from the first edition when it was sacrificed to the developers in February 2006;[9] Manchester's Sha'are Sedek Synagogue in Didsbury was demolished in 2010; and the fascinating Bright Family Mausolea at Rodmoor outside Sheffield were deliberately bulldozed on the eve of the Christmas holidays in December 2011. Descriptions of other sites have had to be rewritten to reflect the fact that they have badly deteriorated through redundancy, neglect or vandalism. Probably the worst case in this category is Sunderland's attractive art deco Grade II listed synagogue, the lead site for the North-East Region.

A comparison with the first edition will show that the book has undergone some design changes, although the convenient pocket-guide format has been retained. I am indebted to Historic England Publishing Project Manager Sarah Enticknap, who worked very hard to bring this second edition to press. We have never met, but have spent many creative hours on the telephone discussing design and layout and improvements to both. She also obtained a number of photographs from outside sources, and must therefore share credit for the attractive look of the book. The 'non-England' sections, previously confined to a final chapter, have been considerably expanded and enhanced with photographs.[10] New publication-standard photography was carried out for my 'big' book, *The Synagogues of Britain and Ireland: An Architectural and Social History*,[11] published by Yale University Press in 2011. Only a tiny number of the images were then used and so we had a wealth of visual material to draw upon for the revised guidebook. Of course, a seismic shift in photographic technology has taken place, from print to digital formats. (In fact, the output of our Survey documents this shift. Our archive includes negatives, prints and slides as well as digital images that were originally stored on floppy disks, ZIP, JAZ disks, CDs and DVDs. Storage has now progressed to external hard drives and memory sticks – and no doubt we will all end up in the Cloud!) The Royal Commission on the Ancient and Historical Monuments of Scotland (Edinburgh) took and kindly allowed use of their photographs of Glasgow synagogues. The Royal Commission on the Ancient and Historical Monuments of Wales (Aberystwyth) provided the same service, and thanks go to Stephen Hughes for arranging for photographer Iain Wright to go out and take the pictures of Welsh synagogues and cemeteries. Ex-English Heritage photographer Nigel Corrie made a special trip for us to his native Ireland to cover sites in Dublin, Cork and Limerick. I am very grateful to him[12] and to all the other English Heritage photographers listed in the acknowledgements for the first edition (alas, many of whom no longer work for the organisation), without whose efforts this book and its predecessors would not have been possible. Steve Cole and Charles Walker were responsible for coordinating the teams. Nigel Corrie and Derek Kendall were commissioned to take brand new photographs of Bevis Marks and Hampstead synagogues in London, on account of changes to the appearance and/or siting of these buildings since their previous assignments. James O Davies, now head of Photography at Historic England, kindly visited Southport Synagogue on very short notice in early 2015. Thanks also to independent Leeds-based photographer Ruth Baumberg who kindly donated several images of Princes Road Synagogue that enhance the text.

Inevitably, things change, and I have found out a lot about the subsequent fate of Jewish buildings that have gone out of Jewish hands simply by 'googling' them. I have already mentioned redundancy and demolition. Since 2006, there have been some good-news stories too. Not all new owners and users rip out and remodel former synagogues or obliterate their history (although it is still true that many do). Some show great respect and cherish their building as part of the town's heritage. Wolverhampton's former synagogue now regularly participates in Heritage Open Days in the guise of 'St Silas's Church', while others are proud to be known as the 'Old Synagogue', and/or sport new heritage plaques proclaiming their former identity. This has even become a selling point, as demonstrated by the case of the flats constructed inside Brighton's Regency synagogue at Devonshire Place. As for burial grounds, a number of Friends Groups have emerged over the past decade and have set about improving the condition of sites, most successfully at Deane Road in Liverpool, thanks to securing Lottery funding. Not all of these groups were created by members of the Jewish community; at Bath, for instance, local residents regularly go into the old cemetery to garden.

Some threatened synagogues have been saved from sale out of the Jewish community, have become listed or upgraded through the initiative of concerned members. Some have secured public grant aid through the Repair Grant Scheme for Listed Places of Worship and/or other programmes now run by the Heritage Lottery Fund. Good examples include Bradford, Bristol, Leicester and Golders Green. Others are experiencing regeneration or a resurgence of members, especially true of some big Victorian so-called 'cathedral synagogues' that were written off 20 years ago as old fashioned, such as Birmingham's Singers Hill and Hampstead's Dennington Park. At Jewish Heritage, we view such outcomes with satisfaction, while continuing to 'look out' for the welfare of these buildings. We hope that this new edition of *Jewish Heritage in Britain and Ireland* will further raise awareness of the vulnerability of our Jewish architectural heritage and the necessity of protecting it for the benefit of future generations.

March 2015/Adar 5775

Acknowledgements for the First Edition (2006)

This guidebook is based on material gathered by the Survey of the Jewish Built Heritage in the UK and Ireland. The contribution of Survey fieldworkers, architect Barbara Bowman and archaeologist Andrew Petersen, cannot be overstated. Together we drove all over England, Wales and Scotland, as well as visiting Jersey in the Channel Islands and the Isle of Man, photographing and documenting over 350 sites of Jewish interest. In addition Barbara has made measured survey drawings of selected historic synagogues, and she drew all of the Heritage Trail maps in this guidebook.

Jewish Heritage Trails were pioneered in the late 1970s and early 1980s by the two Bills: Bill Fishman in the East End of London[1] and Bill Williams at the Manchester Jewish Museum. The East End and Cheetham Heritage Trails presented in this guidebook are indebted to them. Other walks are entirely new: I developed these with Barbara and we *shlepped* around Birmingham and Brighton on foot in temperatures of 30°C in the summer of 2005 to ensure that the trails actually work on the ground.

We expect that the Anglo-Jewish Heritage Trails and 'top ten' heritage sites that lead each chapter in this guidebook (plus Garnethill Synagogue in Glasgow) will be incorporated into the *European Routes of Jewish Culture* currently under development across the continent. This will undoubtedly put Britain on the Jewish heritage tourism map internationally. The part played by Barbara Nathan and Valerie Bello of B'nai Brith UK in bringing the annual European Jewish Heritage Day to Britain has been crucial: since 2000 it has become an annual event in the Anglo-Jewish calendar, attracting on average 10,000 visitors to Jewish sites on the first Sunday in September.[2]

I am grateful for the professional support for this project on the part of staff at English Heritage. Most of the photographs in this guidebook have been taken by English Heritage's photographic units around the country, which have generously put their resources at our disposal. In particular, I wish to thank Derek Kendall and Bob Skingle, and also Keith Buck, Steve Cole, Nigel Corrie, Michael Hesketh-Roberts, James O Davies and Peter Williams. Encouragement and technical advice have been freely given. I must single out the contribution of Susie Barson of the London Division, who more than anyone else made English Heritage 'synagogue friendly' in the late 1980s. I am also indebted to Dr John Bold of the former Royal Commission on the Historical Monuments of England (now part of English Heritage), who 'got the ball rolling' by investing vital seed-money in the Survey back in 1995. Also, I value the support shown by Bob Hook, original chairman of the Survey Steering Group, and Colum Giles, the Heritage Lottery Fund-appointed project monitor, as well as his predecessors Hugh Richmond and Dr Ann Robey; also John Schofield and Humphrey Welfare. Sarah Brown, who has special responsibility for places of worship, continues to be a great support, as does Dr Robin Taylor, who enthusiastically backed publication by

English Heritage from the conception of the guidebook idea.

We are grateful too for the support of Geoffrey Stell, formerly of the Royal Commission on the Ancient and Historical Monuments of Scotland (Edinburgh), for making available resources, including photographs, to the Survey, and to the staff of the Royal Commission on the Ancient and Historical Monuments of Wales in Aberystwyth for similar co-operation. In Ireland, Gerry Browner and Brendon Pocock of Dúchas, the Irish Heritage Service, and David Griffin of the Irish Architectural Archive (Dublin), plus Ken Neill and Marion Meek of the Department of the Environment (Belfast), have also provided assistance.

The Survey is indebted to a large number of other people who have granted us access to their buildings and sites. Numerous synagogue secretaries, officials, caretakers and sextons have shown great enthusiasm for and appreciation of our work. Keyholders and local historians in many parts of the country have generously given of their time to meet us and to give us impromptu guided tours of sites in their area, thus making the job of finding our way around a strange town easier. Access to archives has been granted and the Survey has sometimes assisted on the spot with the sorting and boxing of collections of papers. It is appropriate here to make special mention of the kindness and hospitality of our hosts and their families, particularly in the regions, who provided accommodation, meals and/or *Shabbat* hospitality in the following towns and cities: Belfast, Cyril Rosenberg and Gail Taylor; Birmingham, Dr Anthony Joseph and Judy Joseph; Brighton, Myrna Carlebach; Bristol, Prof Raphael Emanuel; Cardiff, Dr Ralph Cantor; Cork: Fred Rosehill; Edinburgh: Bill and Valerie Simpson; Gateshead, the Orshansky and Pruim families; Glasgow, Dr Kenneth Collins and Dianne Wolfson; Hull, Max Gold; Leeds, Suzanne Ziff; Liverpool, the late Dr Mervyn Goodman; Manchester, Dr Neville and Ruth Berlyne; Norwich, Karl Wolf; Portsmouth, Julius Klein. In London, my mother, Renée Kadish, and my sisters Helen Lamb and Diane Gholam, have played the same essential role, while Evelyn Bacharach's private B & B in Belsize Park has been invaluable to my colleague Barbara Bowman.

Included in the Survey are many synagogues that have undergone change of use. They have been converted into places of worship for other faith communities – churches, mosques or temples. Synagogues have also passed into secular use (some uses being more appropriate than others), such as theatres, gymnasia, warehouses or business centres. Very often current owners and tenants, when faced with an unexpected visit from the Survey, have shown great interest in the past history of the building that they occupy.

Several academic institutions have assisted us in various ways. My student Rhona Beenstock, who has published on Manchester architect Edward Salomons, acted as volunteer research assistant in the north-west. In 1996 Dr Boris Leker of the Center for Jewish Art at the Hebrew University of Jerusalem accompanied me on the RIBA-sponsored pilot project in the East End of London. In 1998 Rachel Bonner, a student under Philip Grover at Oxford Brookes University, acted as photographer during initial fieldwork in Birmingham. As part of their final year projects in 1998 and 1999, students of the Department of Architecture at the University of Huddersfield, under course tutor Helen Price, took photographs and made measured drawings of Sheffield and Bradford synagogues for the Survey. Latterly, Prof Philip Alexander crucially backed our successful bids to the British Academy and the Arts & Humanities Research Council, which established the link between the Survey and the Centre for Jewish Studies at the University of Manchester.

The Survey has liaised with the staff of the new *Buildings of England*, now renamed *Pevsner Architectural Guides*, to ensure that Jewish buildings are properly represented. This cooperation has proved to be of mutual benefit and, in this connection, I would like to thank former editor Bridget Cherry, current editor Simon Bradley, Charles O'Brien (east London), Clare Hartwell (Manchester), Joseph Sharples (Liverpool), John Minnis (Leeds) and Andy Foster (Birmingham).

Individual researchers, academics and local historians have generously shared material, in some cases coming forward with vital information. They include, on London buildings, Clive Bettington, Dr Stanley Cohen, Maya Donelan, Peter Guillery (English Heritage), Dr V J Hammond, Marc Michaels, Joseph (Simon) Mirwitch, Hedy Parry-Davies and Isobel Watson; on the regions, Judith Samuel (Bath), Barry Goodstone (Blackpool), Kenneth Fabian (Bradford), Martyn Cooperman, Gordon Franks, Godfrey Gould, the late David Spector (Brighton), Alan Tobias, Mr S A Silverman (Bristol), Hilary and Marie Halpern, Gabriel Lancaster (Chatham), Michael Webber (Cheltenham), Leslie Brown, Stuart Rosenblatt (Dublin), the late Harold Gillis (Dundee), Sonia Foder, Frank Gent (Exeter), Eric Dawkins, Dave Hooley (English Heritage) (Falmouth), Rabbi Nathaniel Lieberman (Gateshead), Bernard Greenberg (Grimsby), Martin Levinson (Hartlepool), Barrie Donn, Michael Westerman (Hull), Alan Coleman (Ipswich), Murray Freedman (Leeds), Denis M Leonard (Limerick Civic Trust), Dr Cecil Moss (Liverpool), Denis Coberman (Margate), Joe Gellert, Bernard Lewis (Newcastle upon Tyne), Avraham Davidson, the late Mr I Rocker (Newport), Dr Michael Jolles (Northampton), Barry and Maureen Leveton (Norwich), Keith Pearce (Penzance), Miriam Aggiss (Plymouth), Neville Ballin, John Samuels (Sheffield), Sidney Ferder, Martyn Rose (Southampton), Harold Meek (Southport), Sydney Morris (Stoke-on-Trent); on Scotland, Dr Philip Mason (Edinburgh), Harvey Kaplan (Scottish Jewish Archives Centre, Glasgow); on Wales, the late Dorene Jacobs (Cardiff), Harry Sherman (Swansea); Revd Geoff Breffitt (Isle of Man); and Freddie Cohen (Jersey).

Libraries and record offices are essential to a project such as this. I am grateful to the many archivists who have kindly made their collections accessible to the Survey team, either in personal visits or through correspondence. Thank you to the *Jewish Chronicle*'s librarian, Anna Charin, for digging out rare photographs of old synagogues for digitising for the Survey Image Library. Archaeology units and local authority cemetery departments and conservation officers have been generous with their time and have looked up their records and retrieved old plans for us, in some cases thereby saving these from destruction. I must particularly thank Toni Demidowicz (Birmingham City Council), Michael Stead (Bournemouth Borough Council), Sue Whitehouse (Wolverhampton City Council), Joe Martin (Salford City Council) and especially David Hilton, Plan Keeper at the City Architects' Department, Manchester City Council, for sharing his prodigious knowledge of Manchester's buildings with me.

A special thank you to Charles Tucker, archivist to the Office of the Chief Rabbi, who fired my interest in Jewish funerary architecture over 20 years ago. He was a founder member of the original Working Party of Jewish Monuments that I set up back in 1991 to lobby on Jewish heritage issues. Other members who have contributed over the years are Michael Harris (Board of Deputies of British Jews), Evelyn

Friedlander, David Jacobs, Jennifer Marin, Stephen Rosenberg, Revd Malcolm Weisman (Minister to Small Communities, Jewish Memorial Council), Kitty Green (secretary) and the late Edward Jamilly, who was chairman from 1994 until his death in 2003. I would also like to remember two other people who are no longer here to see this guidebook published, but who were, in the years that I was privileged to know and work with them, a source of inspiration: Rabbi Dr Bernard Susser, historian of the Jewish communities of south-west England, and Alec Israel, literary editor of the *Jerusalem Post*. *Zikhronom l'Vrakhah* ('May their memory be for a blessing').

Colleagues overseas have been a source of encouragement, especially Dr Sam Gruber and Prof Carol Krinsky in the USA, Prof Avraham Greenbaum and Dr Serge Kravtsov in Israel (the latter at the Center for Jewish Art, where I spent three years between 1994 and 1997) and Prof Dominique Jarrassé in France. It was a revelation to discover in 1995 that he was engaged in exactly parallel activity to my own on the other side of the English Channel! Thanks to his efforts, France is at least 10 years ahead of Britain in research and publication on synagogue architecture.

We are grateful to all of our sponsors listed on the Donors' Page for making this project possible. The Jewish Memorial Council played a crucial financial role by advancing funds to the Survey of the Jewish Built Heritage before money came through from the Heritage Lottery Fund. I must acknowledge the role of the JMC's Honorary Treasurer, the late Alex Rosenzweig, and Administrator, the late Joseph Zaltzman, in this regard. I would also like to thank both Dr Jeremy Schonfield and Isaac Zekaria for their assistance with fundraising. Thanks are also due to Anthony (Tony) Lerman, Chief Executive of Hanadiv Charitable Foundation, for facilitating financial support for Jewish Heritage UK, which was set up in 2004 to care for the Jewish community's historic buildings and sites. Mention should be made too of the other members of the Jewish Heritage UK Advisory Committee: Sarah Brown (again), Peter Halban and Prof Tony Kushner.

Finally, this guidebook is dedicated to my husband, Dr Sydney (Syd) Greenberg, who has never ceased to encourage me through bad times as well as good in bringing this project to fruition. He has acted (often unpaid) as database designer, computer consultant, technical support, accountant, bookkeeper, and chief cook and bottle-washer to the Survey.

Manchester, January 2006/Tevet 5766

Introduction

In 1656 Jews returned to England after an absence of nearly 400 years, since the medieval expulsion under Edward I in 1290. Jews from Amsterdam came back in the wake of Rabbi Menasseh Ben Israel's petition to Oliver Cromwell, during the brief period when England was a republic. The Jewish community has enjoyed a history of continuous settlement in Britain since 1656,[1] a record unmatched anywhere else in Europe.

Today, Anglo-Jewry, a small community that has never numbered more than about 450,000 people, is the oldest non-Christian minority in Britain. For the first time, *Jewish Heritage in Britain and Ireland* celebrates in full colour the undiscovered architectural heritage of Anglo-Jewry. This guidebook contains information on some 350 Jewish buildings and sites organised on a country and region-by-region basis. Each chapter leads with the 'must-see' Jewish landmark in the region, ranging from Britain's oldest synagogue, Bevis Marks Synagogue in the City of London, through the Georgian gems of the West Country, to the splendid High Victorian 'cathedral synagogues' of Birmingham, Brighton, Liverpool and Glasgow that reflected the confidence of the newly emancipated Jewish community in the Victorian era. Interesting Victorian, Edwardian and art deco synagogues are to be found in unexpected places, while family history enthusiasts will especially welcome the listings of Jewish burial grounds around

the country. The West Country, for example, is rich in Georgian Jewish cemeteries, while two of the oldest Jewish cemeteries are located outside England, on the South Wales coast at Swansea and in the Irish Republic's capital Dublin. Funerary architectural curiosities are stumbled upon, such as a romantic gateway and column marking the entrance to the Jews' Enclosure in Glasgow's Necropolis, Sir Moses Montefiore's last resting place in Ramsgate, and the Sassoon Mausoleum in Brighton, whose eccentric dome competes with the Royal Pavilion itself. Other oddities not to be missed include a 19th-century private penthouse synagogue, also in Brighton, and an Egyptian-style *mikveh* (ritual bath) in Canterbury. This guide is intended to appeal to the specialist and the tourist alike.

Featured here are Heritage Trails around former Jewish quarters of Britain's major cities, including the East End of London, Manchester, Birmingham and Brighton. Relics of Anglo-Jewry's medieval past are explored in Lincoln, Norwich and York. The medieval Jewry arrived from Normandy with William the Conqueror after 1066 and ended with the expulsion under Edward I in 1290. England has the dubious distinction of being the first recorded country in Europe to expel its Jewish community during the Middle Ages.

A word on what is not included in this guidebook. It mostly[2] covers buildings and sites that date from before the Second World War, including, as just mentioned, a handful of sites associated

Detail of Ark and East Window at Princes Road Synagogue in Liverpool (Ruth Baumberg)

with the medieval period. However, to qualify for inclusion, a synagogue had to be purpose-built as such. If it was not originally built as a synagogue (and we have cases of churches and chapels converted into synagogues), then the adaptation of the building must have taken place prior to 1939. Hence, Sandys Row Synagogue and the former Spitalfields Great Synagogue in the East End of London are included, even though both started life in the 18th century as Huguenot churches. The latter building is now the London Jamia Mosque, but we decided to include it because it is such a well-known landmark. Home, in succession, to Christians, Jews and Muslims, this building encapsulates on a single site the immigrant history of east London.

On the other hand, *shtieblekh* and *hevrot* – prayer rooms, the former specifically Hasidic, inside private dwellings or workplaces – are not in general included here. Such small 'synagogues' once proliferated in the East End of London and in other urban centres where Jewish immigrants congregated, and still do so today in Orthodox communities, in Stamford Hill and Golders Green in London, or Broughton Park and Prestwich in north Manchester. However, *shtieblekh* are not usually of much architectural interest to the outside visitor.

Former synagogues, built as such but which are no longer in use for their original purpose, are included. Examples range from the mid-Victorian Spanish and Portuguese Synagogue, now happily converted into the Manchester Jewish Museum, and the 1930s Leeds New Synagogue, with its huge 'Byzantine' dome, now the Northern School of Contemporary Dance. Former synagogues have become places of worship serving other faiths: churches, mosques, mandirs and gurdwaras. Others have been less fortunate, now factories, warehouses, gymnasia or pubs. Still others stand derelict and vandalised.

Buildings erected by the Jewish community to serve a communal purpose, such as Jewish schools, hospitals, trades union headquarters and soup kitchens, are also covered by this guidebook. Many of these buildings were erected in the great age of Victorian philanthropy and have now gone out of use, for example the Westminster Jews' Free School of 1882–3 or the Leeds Jewish Tailors' building of 1910. However, excluded from this category are buildings designed by Jewish architects for use by non-Jews, as well as domestic architecture, principally private residences built for wealthy Jews, such as the Rothschilds. Waddesdon Manor, which has published its own superb catalogue of its great art collection, comes immediately to mind.

Houses occupied by prominent Jews at some point in their history could also not be included: for example, in London, the 17th-century Cromwell House in Highgate, the home of the *converso* Da Costa family from 1675, or no. 6 Bloomsbury Square, once the home of the Disraelis and in use recently as the headquarters of the Board of Deputies of British Jews.

Public sculpture is largely excluded, except for the occasional memorial or fountain commemorating a particular Jewish philanthropist or civic dignitary. The custom of erecting sculptures of famous people is alien to Jewish tradition with its well-known inhibitions about figurative art, especially in three dimensions. Thus you will not find mention here of statues of famous men or women of Jewish origin, such as Prime Minister Benjamin Disraeli, nor of blue plaques marking the places where they lived or worked.

Bear in mind that the sole criterion for an entry here is architectural interest. After all, this book is 'an *architectural* guide'. This distinguishes it from popular guidebooks, trails, tours and websites[3] that are now becoming increasingly available, where the main

Blessing of welcome in floor tiling at entrance to Princes Road Synagogue, Liverpool. Hebrew text is from **Deuteronomy 28:6** (Ruth Baumberg)

emphasis is on social history and the association of places with personalities. By contrast, *Jewish Heritage in Britain and Ireland* deals with physical sites that still exist – actual *sights* that can be seen, visited and experienced.

Of the sites listed here, 99 per cent have been visited by the author personally, at least once, the bulk of them originally during fieldwork for the Survey of the Jewish Built Heritage mainly between 1998 and 2001. The Survey was set up in 1997 with the support of English Heritage and the Heritage Lottery Fund to research and record the vanishing architectural heritage of the Jewish communities of Britain and Ireland. Inevitably, over time some sites listed in this guidebook will undergo changes of use or will disappear altogether.

The population of British Jewry has declined, currently standing at 269,568 (according to the 2011 national Census),[4] having fallen from a post-war peak of *c* 450,000. However, recent indicators reveal that this trend could be reversed in the future, owing to the booming birthrate among *Haredi* (strictly Orthodox) Jews, although this is currently limited to specific enclaves.

Indeed, the Jewish community is becoming a tale of two cities: London and Manchester. Even here Jews are no longer much encountered in inner-city areas of primary settlement colonised by earlier immigrant generations, such as the East End of London or Red Bank and Cheetham in Manchester. British Jewry has become a largely suburban phenomenon. Left behind were historic synagogues that are too far to reach on foot on the Sabbath, when travelling is prohibited in the Orthodox Jewish tradition.

The publication of *Jewish Heritage in Britain and Ireland* is designed to make the unique architectural heritage of Anglo-Jewry accessible for the first time to the general public. Every effort has been made to ensure that information given is up to date at the time of going to press. The author would, of course, be grateful to be informed of any errors, omissions or updates.

March 2015/Adar 5775

Notes for Visitors

If you have never visited a synagogue before you may want some background information on the building type and on how it functions as the Jewish place of worship. Space here does not permit the inclusion of a 'recommended reading' list, or even a list of informative websites. However, I will draw attention to one handy little source (since I wrote it myself!),[1] available on the *Pevsner Architectural Guides'* excellent website: www.lookingatbuildings.org.uk/types/religious/other/synagogues.html.

Practical information of value to the tourist is available from many other sources. The annual Anglo *Jewish Year Book* and *Jewish Travel Guide*, both published by Vallentine Mitchell, will assist you in planning your trip. Be aware that printed information can get out of date quickly. However, Jewish communal and tourist information websites now proliferate on the Internet and in many cases are frequently updated. It would be foolhardy to try to list any here – save (naturally) Jewish Heritage UK's own website at www.jewish-heritage-uk.org. It is aimed chiefly at architectural and conservation specialists and enthusiasts and has links to other websites with similar interests.

Internet sources are also best consulted for essential information on food and hotels. Jewish visitors are often concerned to locate kosher food suppliers. A word of warning: there are few kosher outlets in England, once you get outside London. Even in London such facilities are largely confined to specific neighbourhoods: mainly Stamford Hill in north London, at points 'up the north-west passage', Golders Green, Hendon and Edgware, and increasingly in South Hertfordshire, Borehamwood, Radlett and Bushey. There is a dearth of supervised kosher eateries in central London. I will permit here only mention of the erratic existence of a restaurant[2] at the historic Bevis Marks Synagogue, the oldest synagogue in Britain, a convenient and smart venue for lunch during your tour of the City of London. In general, it pays to telephone restaurants to check opening hours, book tables and even to find out if they are still in business before making your, invariably hungry, journey there!

In the regions, make for Manchester. However, even in England's second Jewish city there are no kosher restaurants in the city centre, only in the northern suburbs. Even relatively large Jewish communities don't necessarily support a kosher deli, let alone a butcher or baker. Kosher hotels are few, confined to Golders Green and Stamford Hill in London. There is one kosher hotel in Manchester. Even those that once proliferated in seaside towns popular with Jewish holidaymakers have mostly closed down. At time of writing, only one is left in Bournemouth[3] on the south coast. These days, observant Jewish families (especially large ones) prefer self-catering holidays when holidaying in the UK – and find it cheaper than staying in hotels.

Visitors being shown the Ark at London's New West End Synagogue (DP102199)

This guidebook makes no attempt to include detailed information on routes, transport or opening hours. We simply indicate whether or not a given site is open to the public, at least occasionally, for example on Heritage Open Days in September. Historic synagogues are not generally open to the public, although Bevis Marks in the City of London does have regular opening times, as does the former Spanish and Portuguese Synagogue in Manchester, which is now the city's Jewish Museum. Most synagogues, like churches, are not normally kept open, for security reasons. Historic synagogues in particular welcome tourists who telephone first to make an appointment to view the building. Wherever possible we have supplied a telephone number. However, do bear in mind that tiny communities may not be able to support a synagogue secretary, let alone an office, and a handful don't even possess a landline in the building! You should at least be able to leave a recorded voicemail message or send a text, even if you can't obtain an instant reply by telephone. As a rule, we have avoided giving home numbers of individual members or rabbis, and never mobile numbers, because these are apt to change.

Instead, we have provided Web addresses for all synagogues that have them (now the vast majority[4]) through which you can make contact by email. Some small communities can be surprisingly active in the virtual world of social media, possessing Facebook pages or Twitter accounts, or even posting videos on YouTube, so you should be able to elicit a response by one of an increasing range of methods. Always make a point of somehow getting in touch in advance if you wish to bring a group. (Do not phone Friday afternoon or Saturday – *Shabbat* – as you will only reach an answering service!) Jewish visitors are always welcome to attend services, especially in small communities that struggle to raise a *minyan*. You are advised first to check days and times of services with the congregation. Small communities may manage to hold services only on *Shabbat*, often just on Saturday morning. Nowadays, many synagogues post times of services on their websites.

Regarding Jewish burial grounds, we indicate whether a site is generally accessible or, as may often be the case, locked up or difficult to reach. When cemeteries that are privately administered by the Jewish community are stated to be 'open' on a 'daily basis', this always means from Sunday to Thursday, or Friday morning; you will find them closed on *Shabbat*. Don't visit a Jewish-owned cemetery on a Friday afternoon in the winter, or on a Saturday. On the other hand, many Jewish plots are located within the boundaries of municipal cemeteries and are therefore open (or at least the key is available) during general cemetery hours.

Sadly, vandalism, whether simply malicious or racist in intent, is a fact of life (and of Jewish life in particular, even in Britain). Making Jewish sites better known and attracting more visitors to them is probably the best antidote. Neglected sites – those that nobody apparently cares about – are the most vulnerable to attack. In cases where a cemetery is locked, we have wherever possible tried to supply a telephone number for the keyholder (an office or institution, never an individual) plus basic directions for reaching the cemetery, and the Jewish plot inside it, especially if it is not in an obvious location or is not marked on the map.[5]

The thrust of our research in documentary and other sources, such as historical maps and plans, for this architectural guide has been towards establishing the age, location and extent of Jewish burial grounds, not to record the inscriptions on individual gravestones, a task best left to local and family historians. However, for the benefit of the latter, we have tried, wherever possible, to indicate whether or not original burial records exist for a particular site. Genealogists will want to supplement this information with research on the Internet. The best starting points are the website of the Jewish Genealogical Society of Great Britain (www.jgsgb.org.uk) and of its American equivalent (www.jewishgen. org). Online databases of burial records continue to grow. Users should always be aware that such secondary sources may not always be reliable or accurate.[6]

Lack of space means that we have not included detailed footnotes giving the exact sources on which our entries are based. Academics and other researchers will want to consult my monograph, *The Synagogues of Britain and Ireland: An Architectural and Social History*, which was published with the support of The Paul Mellon Centre for Studies in British Art by Yale University Press in 2011. Whereas this guidebook contains entries for synagogue buildings that are extant, *The Synagogues of Britain and Ireland* in addition recovers the history (and most importantly – where possible – the appearance) of lost synagogues through extensive archival research. On cemeteries and Jewish funerary architecture, readers seeking further information are referred to articles that I have published in the *Transactions of the Ancient Monuments Society* (2005) and *Jewish Historical Studies* (2011).[7] For more literature, see our website (www.jewish-heritage-uk.org) and click on 'Publications'. Unpublished material is contained in the Survey of the Jewish Built Heritage's database, which is being deposited at Historic England Archives. The Survey's paper archives and photographic and digital output may be examined in person on written request.

CONDUCT AT JEWISH SITES

Most of the sites listed in this guidebook are sacred places and, as such, should be treated with appropriate respect in matters relating to behaviour and dress.

Please be kind enough to dress modestly when visiting a synagogue or Jewish cemetery. Less Orthodox congregations, and those belonging to the Reform and Liberal movements, may take a more relaxed attitude, but it is always best to err on the side of caution.[8]

Men: please wear a head covering inside the building or grounds, long sleeves and trousers, not shorts.

Women: married women should cover their heads. Wear long sleeves and skirts below the knee and, preferably, no trousers or jeans that are not considered suitable clothing for synagogue visits.

It is forbidden to eat, drink or smoke in the synagogue proper or in a Jewish burial ground. Please do not bring food or drink onto synagogue premises, nor inside a cemetery. Always go out for refreshments. However, you may by all means accept the hospitality of the synagogue secretary or other official for tea or coffee in the office.

The Torah Ark (*Aron HaKodesh*) *in a synagogue*: this is the focal point of the synagogue because it houses the *Sifrei Torah* (the 'Scrolls of the Law'), which are the most sacred objects in the possession of the congregation. Usually, the Ark is kept locked when not in use, for security. Never try to open the Ark, or attempt to remove a Torah scroll from the Ark. If you wish to take photographs, ask for permission. Photography is not permitted on *Shabbat*.

In a cemetery: it is strictly forbidden to walk over or step on any grave. It is the custom among Jews to wash their hands on leaving a cemetery. However, running water is not always available at older burial grounds.

Thank you for your consideration.

Regional Distribution of Jewish Sites in the UK

SCOTLAND

North East

North West

Isle of Man

Yorkshire & Humberside

IRELAND

Midlands

Lincoln & East Anglia

WALES

South East

London

West Country

South

Jersey

FRANCE

Distribution of Jewish Sites in London (by Borough)

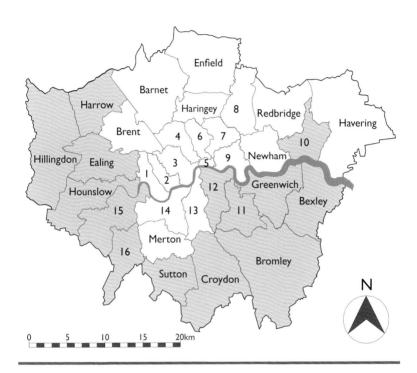

Boroughs coloured cream have extant
pre-1939 Jewish sites (featured in the Guidebook)

1	Hammersmith & Fulham	9	Tower Hamlets
2	Kensington & Chelsea	10	Barking & Dagenham
3	Westminster	11	Lewisham
4	Camden	12	Southwark
5	City	13	Lambeth
6	Islington	14	Wandsworth
7	Hackney	15	Richmond upon Thames
8	Waltham Forest	16	Kingston upon Thames

LONDON

ONDON HAS BEEN HOME to about two-thirds of the Jewish community throughout the modern period. The Jewish population of London today stands at roughly 180,000 (2011 Census).[1] The proportion of the community that has resided in London has remained fairly constant. Consequently, London has always had more synagogues and other Jewish buildings and sites than anywhere else in Britain.

Even in the Middle Ages the City of London acted as an economic magnet. Jews first arrived from Rouen with William of Normandy, the 'Conqueror'. The Jewish community clustered in protective proximity to the **Guildhall**. The Wren church of **St Lawrence Jewry** (1671–80, bombed 1940, remodelled 1954–7 *plaque*) in the **Guildhall Yard** is a reminder of the well-documented medieval 'Jewry' that existed from the Norman Conquest (1066) until the Expulsion under Edward I (1290). In fact, the Jewry was located on the other (east) side of **Gresham Street**, as attested by the names of both the Wren church of **St Olave Jewry** (1671–9; mostly demolished) and the street **Old Jewry**,[2] where (on the east side) there is a ceramic Corporation of London plaque that reads: THE GREAT SYNAGOGUE STOOD NEAR THIS SITE UNTIL 1272.

Although no above-ground physical remains of the Jewish quarter (it was never a ghetto) of Old London survive, some archaeological discoveries have been made. In 2001 a flurry of excitement accompanied the unearthing of a medieval *mikveh*, a purpose-built Jewish ritual bath, in a rescue dig during redevelopment of a site bounded by **Milk Street** and Gresham Street. This *mikveh*, dating from the 13th century, was meticulously dismantled by the Museum of London Archaeology Service and can now be seen on display in the recently enlarged **Jewish Museum** in Camden (*see* p 54).

The Milk Street *mikveh* is of great significance, providing for the first time real material evidence of the presence of Jews in medieval London. (The excavations of the site of the medieval Jewish cemetery at **Cripplegate**, just outside the northern end of the **City of London Wall**, in 1949 and 1961 yielded no significant remains.) Indeed, the *mikveh* is the *only* uniquely Jewish building type, the discovery of which, even in the absence of small finds or inscriptions, is incontrovertible evidence of the presence of Jews. Thus London's medieval *mikveh* compares in importance with more famous examples from the Rhineland, the heartland of medieval Ashkenaz.

The first synagogue of the Resettlement after 1656 was located not very far from Gresham Street in **Creechurch Lane**. It is commemorated in a *plaque* on the wall of the building that today occupies the site (Cunard Place). Its successor, the Spanish and Portuguese Synagogue, is around the corner in **Bevis Marks**, today the oldest synagogue in Britain. The Ashkenazi Great Synagogue in **Duke's Place** (rebuilt by *James Spiller* in 1790; marked by another Corporation of London *plaque*) was bombed during the Second World War. **Aldgate** and **Houndsditch**, on the limits of the

City of London,[3] in which Jews were officially debarred from owning freehold property, was the historic centre of Anglo-Jewry until the Blitz.

In the 19th century Jewish settlement radiated eastwards along the Whitechapel and Commercial Roads. Given its proximity to the Port of London, the East End was the point of arrival for upwards of 100,000 Jewish refugees from persecution in Tsarist Russia (the so-called 'Pale of Settlement' that included a large part of Poland, Lithuania, Belarus and Ukraine) and other parts of eastern Europe (especially Austrian Galicia and Rumania), mainly between 1881 and the outbreak of the First World War in 1914. The vast majority of today's Jewish community are descendants of these immigrants.

The tiny privileged elite of Anglo-Jewry, the so-called 'Cousinhood' of families, both Sephardi and Ashkenazi (Montefiores and Mocattas, Rothschilds and Goldsmids and so on) had already in the 18th century begun to migrate westwards to classier districts, such as Belgravia and Bayswater, and some even had country retreats in Surrey or Buckinghamshire. 'West End' Jewry by and large looked askance at the

'East End', with its foreign ways, religious piety (or radical socialism) and vibrant Yiddish cultural life.

Dispersal from the East End was a gradual process, which was largely completed after the Second World War. Suburbanisation was in two main directions, northwards to Hackney, Stamford Hill and Tottenham, once lined with middle-class Victorian villas, or 'up the north-west passage', following the new Northern Underground Line to Golders Green (nicknamed 'Goldberg's Green' by many London Jews on account of the enduring popularity of the neighbourhood) and beyond. Today's major London Jewish communities in the Borough of Barnet

(Golders Green, Hendon and Edgware) and Hertsmere, South Hertfordshire (Borehamwood, Elstree and Radlett) are largely a third- and fourth-generation phenomenon, the grandchildren and great-grandchildren of the Jewish East End.

Jewish settlement south of the River Thames has always been sparse, perhaps because it lacked the driving force of the development of the Underground. The only substantial purpose-built synagogues built in Victorian and Edwardian South London, the Borough Synagogue (Albion Place, Walworth, *H H Collins* 1867) and South East London Synagogue (New Cross, *Delissa Joseph* 1904–5) are long demolished, the latter a victim of the Blitz. The growth of today's suburban communities in Surrey, such as Richmond, Kingston upon Thames and Sutton, was largely stimulated by wartime evacuation.

אנכי ה׳
לא יהיה
לא תשא
זכור את
כבד את

לא תרצח
לא תנאף
לא תגנב
לא תענה
לא תחמד

The *Ehal* (Ark) (BB95/11789)

Bevis Marks Synagogue

Bevis Marks, EC3A 5DQ[4] / Joseph Avis, 1699–1701, Grade I

A hidden gem in the City of London, Britain's oldest synagogue is over 300 years old

Bevis Marks Synagogue can be easily missed. It stands within a quiet courtyard behind an arched Victorian gateway on Bevis Marks. The simple building is constructed of typical London red brick with Portland stone dressings and plain parapet. The keystone above the classical entrance bears the date in English: A.M. 5461. 1701. However, the Hebrew *inscription* in the tympanum above commemorates the actual opening of the building on the eve of the Jewish New Year 5462 (=30 September 1701). A decorative wrought-iron lamp hangs over the entrance and, at either side, there are matching foot-wipers. The clock above is Victorian, inscribed with the date 5618/1858.

The architect of Bevis Marks was a master builder, *Joseph Avis*, a Quaker carpenter, 'Cittizen and merchant taylor of London', who had previously worked for *Christopher Wren*. Perhaps Avis got the commission because, unlike Wren himself, he and the Jews were not part of the Anglican establishment.

Two traditions are attached to the opening of the synagogue, both of which lack documentary proof. When Avis found that he had not entirely used up his budget of £2,650 (a not inconsiderable sum, about half of which had been raised from members of the congregation)

he returned the surplus on the principle that he refused to profit from the building of a house of God. The other legend is that Queen Anne herself, as Princess Anne, presented an oak beam from one of the ships of the Royal Navy to be used in the roof of the synagogue. Certainly, some of the hefty ceiling beams are in secondary use, lending possible weight to this story.

The dignified architectural style of Bevis Marks shares features in common with both contemporary Wren churches in London and the larger Nonconformist

The courtyard

The doorcase (BB95/11783)

meeting houses. Once inside, the striking resemblance becomes apparent to the 17th-century Portuguese Great Synagogue of Amsterdam (*Elias Bouwman* 1674–5), the mother congregation of Bevis Marks. On closer inspection, however, there are significant differences between the two buildings, not least in scale: Bevis Marks measures only 24m by 15m (80ft by 50ft).[5]

INTERIOR: The interior of the prayer hall is approached through a small panelled vestibule with smaller side draught lobbies. The generous, deeply recessed, clear glazed and leaded windows flood the interior with natural light. The windows on the east wall were decorated with a dark blue border, probably Victorian, now replaced with reproduction glass.

Good lighting is essential in the synagogue, where reading from the *Torah* scrolls is central to many services. Hence, too, there is an abundant provision of massive brass ball chandeliers, seven in all, low-slung over the *tevah* (reading platform). In addition, there are 10 candlesticks to light both *Ehal* and *tevah*. Some of this brass-work was donated by the parent synagogue in Amsterdam, probably the great central chandelier over the *tevah* and the four

lamp stands before the *Ehal* inscribed with the name of the donors: P.M. & R. PEREIRA D.KS. Although electric lighting was installed in 1929, it was designed only to supplement the wax candles and not to supersede them. The chandeliers are still lit by hand for special occasions.

The ceiling is flat with a plaster cornice and a series of rosettes from which are suspended low over the space the seven brass chandeliers. The gallery runs around three sides supported on Tuscan columns, of timber painted to look like marble. The gallery is screened by a high wooden trellis-work *mehitzah*. The original access to the gallery is via the staircase from the men's section to the right (south-west) of the main entrance. Much of the timber floor has been replaced.

FURNISHINGS: The arrangement of the furnishings conforms with the Sephardi liturgical tradition. The *Ehal*, which houses the *Sifrei Torah*, the focal point of the synagogue, is placed on the east wall, roughly in the direction of Jerusalem. The *tevah* is slightly displaced towards the west, with the majority of the fixed benches facing inwards, running longitudinally through the space.

The fine seating is mostly original early 18th century and includes several free-standing forms at the back of the main prayer hall that are probably among those known to have been brought from Creechurch Lane. An unusual feature is the canopied wardens' pew, or *banca*, set along the north wall, a Sephardi custom imported from Amsterdam and not found elsewhere in Britain.

The wooden Ark cabinet is in the shape of a reredos, reminiscent of a late Renaissance church front, because its two storeys are connected by scrolls. Altar screens of similar design are to be seen in Wren City churches.

The oak *Ehal* actually consists of three separate Ark cupboards, divided by

fluted Corinthian pilasters under a continuous entablature. The entablature carries a second tier, with broken pediment and carved scrolls, which contains the *Luhot* inscribed in gold Hebrew block. The painted Hebrew inscription above is one frequently found over synagogue Arks: 'Know before Whom you stand'.[6] The apex and main entablature are completed by carved vase finials, five in all. The *Ehal* is richly carved, painted and gilded.

The silver oil *ner tamid* hanging over the Ark was presented by a member of the congregation in 1876, and Bevis Marks owns rare 17th- and 18th-century *Sifrei Torah*, ritual silver and textiles, some of which may sometimes be on display.

The chandeliers (BB95/11797)

Of particular interest are the old timber boards hanging on the walls, especially in the gallery. In addition to *Omer* calendars, some of these boards contain special prayers, while others list names of donors and past officials of the synagogue. The wooden charity boxes with iron straps are also mainly original.

The most famous worshipper at Bevis Marks was undoubtedly Sir Moses Montefiore (1784–1885), a member of the Stock Exchange and a Sheriff of the City of London. He devoted much of his 100-year-long life to philanthropic work for his fellow Jews, and was created a baronet by Queen Victoria. He occupied a front seat (no. 354), with its own movable footrest, nearest to the *Ehal*. A less respected but even better known son of Bevis Marks was Prime Minister Benjamin Disraeli, whose father Isaac D'Israeli left the congregation after a row with the *Mahamad* (synagogue council) and subsequently had his children baptised.

In the modern basement communal hall adjoining hangs a 17th-century painting of Moses and Aaron with the Ten Commandments, in Hebrew and Portuguese, by one *Aaron de Chaves*, which previously probably hung over the Ark at Creechurch Lane. In the synagogue's tercentenary year (2001) the discreet new extension (by *Thomas Ford & Partners*), which housed the restaurant, was opened.

Bevis Marks survived the Blitz unscathed. The synagogue had had a narrow escape in the 1880s in redevelopment schemes hatched by its own congregation, who wanted to build themselves a new synagogue convenient to their homes in leafy Maida Vale. Thanks to the efforts of the Bevis Marks Anti-Demolition League and the intervention of William Morris's Society for the Protection of Ancient Buildings (SPAB), Bevis Marks was saved. On 10 April 1992 and again on 24 April 1993 the synagogue was damaged by massive IRA bombs that rocked the City of London. The bombsite, just around the corner, is now marked by *Sir Norman Foster's* curvilinear 'Gherkin' (the former **Swiss Re Building**, 30 St Mary Axe), which has become a modern landmark on the London skyline.

OPENING HOURS: *Shabbat* and weekday services. Heritage Open Days (September). Regularly open to visitors. National Trust 'partner' site. Admission charge. To check times and for group bookings: tel 020 7626 1274 and/or 020 7621 1188 (office) www.bevismarks.org.uk and www.sandp.org

Discover the Jewish East End

Given the distances and number of sites involved, it is recommended that the Jewish East End Heritage Trail is divided into two, three, or even four parts:

1 The City Limits and Spitalfields
(4km; approx. 2 hours, without entry into sites)

2 Whitechapel to Stepney Green
(1.5km; 2 hours, without entry into sites)

3 Stepney Green
(1.5km; 1 hour)

4 Mile End: The Jewish Burial Grounds of the Resettlement
(4.25km; 1½ hours)

These walks are on the level, without any steps. Longer and shorter routes are suggested along the way, and use may also be made of the regular no. 25 bus along the Whitechapel Road.

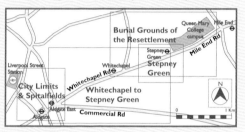

Numbers refer to Jewish sites on the Heritage Trail maps. Letters refer to general landmarks. Extant Jewish sites are indicated in bold in the text.

---

1 THE CITY LIMITS AND SPITALFIELDS
LONDON EAST END HERITAGE TRAIL

● *Start from the* **Kindertransport Memorials at Liverpool Street Station ①**.

There are two memorials within the station complex. To see the first of these, stand on the main concourse and locate the main entrance to the Underground station – the sculpture is just to its left: **Für das Kind – Displaced** *by Flor Kent (2011).*

For the second memorial, make for the Liverpool Street exit, on the south-west side of the station. Climb the stairs to the upper level to the small 'Hope Square', usually crowded with commuters, in the middle of which you will spot the

sculpture: **Children of the Kindertransport** *by Frank Meisler and Arie Ovadia (2006).*

Both memorials are bronze figures on Portland stone plinths. Touchingly realistic, they portray refugee children, carrying their suitcases and toys, arriving at Liverpool Street on the eve of the Second World War from Germany, Austria and Czechoslovakia. Approximately 10,000 Jewish youngsters, fortunate enough to have been sponsored, were

hurriedly brought to England by train and boat in 1938–9. The majority never saw their families again: the families perished in the death camps during the Nazi Holocaust. The memorials refer to the cities in Central Europe whence the children hailed, especially the capitals Berlin, Vienna and Prague, whose main railway stations are home to reciprocal memorials. At Liverpool Street, the Israeli sculptor *Frank Meisler*, himself a *kinder*, and best known for his sentimental figurines, was commissioned by the Association of Jewish Refugees and the Central British Fund for World Jewish Relief, while the Venezuelan *Flor Kent's* similar sculpture replaced a less conventional glass box that contained original artefacts in a changing exhibition, first installed in 2003.

● *Leave the station at left and turn left onto* **Liverpool Street.** *Cross over* **Bishopsgate** *into* **Houndsditch** *(noting* **St Botolph's Church**, **Bishopsgate** *on your right). Turn right into* **Bevis Marks**. *The synagogue is on the right, hidden away in a gated courtyard behind* **no. 14 Bevis Marks**.

On leaving **Bevis Marks Synagogue ②** *turn right on Bevis Marks and first right into* **Creechurch Lane.**

The '**Site of First Synagogue after the Resettlement 1657–1701**' is marked by a ceramic *plaque* ❸ on the corner of **Creechurch Lane** and **Bury Street**. This is located on the wall of the

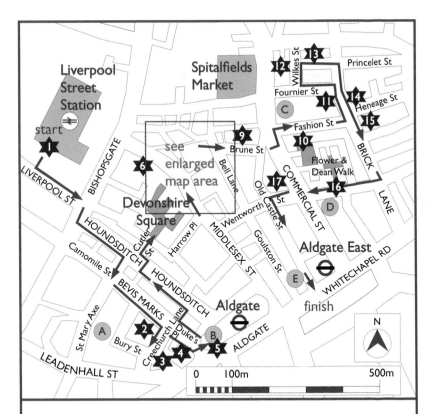

Jewish Sites of Interest

1 Liverpool Street Station –
   Kindertransport memorials
2 Bevis Marks Synagogue
3 *site of* first Resettlement Synagogue
4 *site of* London Great Synagogue
5 Mocatta Memorial Fountain
6 *former* Jewish Board of Guardians offices
7 Sandys Row Synagogue
8 *former* Ein Ya'akov Synagogue
9 *former* Jewish Soup Kitchen
10 *former* Emporium
11 *former* Spitalfields Great Synagogue
12 *former* Warsaw Lodge Synagogue
13 *former* Princes Street Synagogue
14 Katz shop front
15 *former* Ezras Haim Synagogue
16 Rothschild Buildings Archway
17 *former* Jews' Infant School

Other Sites of Interest

A No 30 St Mary Axe ("The Gherkin")
B St Botolph's Church, Aldgate
C Christ Church, Spitalfields
D Toynbee Hall
E *former* Whitechapel Baths

yellow-brick new-build
Cunard House. The
Spanish and Portuguese
**Creechurch Lane
Synagogue** was the
predecessor of Bevis
Marks.

❹ *Return to* **Bevis Marks** *(the
street) and turn right.*

Another *plaque* ❹, this time
an old Corporation of
London metal one, marks
the site of the Ashkenazi
**London Great
Synagogue** on the corner
of **Duke's Place** and
St James's Passage. The
Great Synagogue of 1690

was extended by *George Dance the Elder* in 1765–6 and rebuilt by *James Spiller* in Adam style in 1790. It was bombed in September 1941.

◐ *Cross at lights to **St Botolph's Church, Aldgate (B)**.*

St Botolph's Church, Aldgate,[7] constructed between 1741 and 1744, was designed by *George Dance the Elder* – who was also responsible for the lost Great Synagogue across the road. On the railings in front of St Botolph's is the **Mocatta Memorial Fountain ❾**. This stone fountain, made by *J Whitehead and Sons*, was erected in 1906 to the memory of Frederic David Mocatta (1828–1905). Mocatta was a moving force in the affairs of the Jewish Board of Guardians and in the Four Per Cent Industrial Dwellings Company (more of which below). The Metropolitan Drinking Fountain and Cattle Trough Association was a most progressive organisation, active in an age when clean running water on tap was almost unknown.

◐ *Retrace your steps back down **Duke's Place**, cross at lights and walk right down the **east side of Creechurch Lane**. Turn left into **Houndsditch**. Cross again and turn right into **Cutler Street**, scene of the Houndsditch Murders in 1910, in which Russian Jewish anarchists were allegedly involved. Turn right again into **Devonshire Square**, left into **Harrow Place** and thence into **Middlesex Street**. Middlesex Street marks the official border between the City and the East End – the E1 postcode area.*

Middlesex Street is better known as 'Petticoat Lane'

The Ark and *Bimah* at Sandys Row Synagogue (E030015)

because of the famous Sunday street market, where mostly clothing is sold. The traders were once predominantly Jewish, the *Shmatteh* (rag) trade being the staple industry of the Jewish East End. Come on a Sunday if you want to do some shopping!

◐ *Turn left (north) and walk up Petticoat Lane to the junction with **Widegate Street**.*

Former **Jewish Board of Guardians' Offices ❻**

125–9 Middlesex Street, E1 7JF
Davis & Emanuel, 1896

This is a red-brick L-shaped mansion block converted into flats (Astral House) and The Shooting Star pub. Designed *gratis*

by *Barrow Emanuel* of *Davis & Emanuel* for Anglo-Jewry's foremost charitable institution, founded in 1859. Now 'Jewish Care', the charity moved from the East End in 1982. *Plaque*.

◐ *Almost doubling back, turn to the right down **Widegate Street** and then left into **Sandys Row** (signposted). The synagogue is on the right-hand side.*

Sandys Row Synagogue ❼

4A Sandys Row, E1 7HW, Grade II

Sandys Row Synagogue is one of the earliest surviving examples of a chapel conversion for Jewish worship in Britain. The building started life as a Huguenot church, L'Eglise

de l'Artillerie, in 1766.
From the Huguenots, the church passed through a series of other Protestant groups – the Universalist Baptists, the Unitarian Baptists, the Scottish Baptists and the Salem Chapel – before it reached the Hevrat Menahem Avelim Hesed v'Emet ('Comforters of the Mourners Kindness and Truth Society') in 1867. This friendly society had been set up in 1853 and consisted mostly of Dutch Ashkenazi workingmen, cigar makers, diamond cutters and fruit traders. They were a fiercely independent lot and defied the centralising tendencies of the United Synagogue that was created in 1870.

They found an unexpected champion in *Nathan Solomon Joseph*, the architect, who, as brother-in-law of the Chief Rabbi, later carried out many large-scale synagogue commissions for the United Synagogue.

It is perhaps surprising that the future architect to the United Synagogue backed the independence of the immigrant *hevrot* in the East End against the big City synagogues that sought to absorb them. In 1870 Joseph wrote to the *Jewish Chronicle* strongly defending the rights of the so-called 'minor synagogues'. He attacked the patronising snobbery of the City synagogues, which were prepared to bestow free seats on poor Jews. 'This will not do', he protested. 'In such a synagogue, all men would be equal in the sight of God, but not in the sight of the beadle.'[8]

For the Dutch Jews Joseph remodelled the French chapel in Parliament Court, which, like other Nonconformist churches, was suitable for conversion into a synagogue, as it possessed a gallery. However, the orientation was wrong: the street entrance was on the south-east wall on **Parliament Court**. *Walk around the back.* Joseph blocked up the original entrance in order to accommodate the Ark correctly aligned in the direction of Jerusalem. He opened a new street entrance on the opposite, north-west side, as approached today from Sandys Row.

INTERIOR: Modelled on the Ashkenazi Great Synagogue in Duke's Place, especially the classical Ark (1904) built into an apse, the coved ceiling, cornice and groined clerestory windows. The *bimah* and pews were replaced in the 1950s, made by congregant *Louis Brookarsh*, an engineer.[9]

OPENING HOURS: Lunchtime services (*Minha*) during the week. Heritage Open Days (September). Tours and occasional exhibitions: tel 020 7377 6196; www.sandysrow.org.uk

◗ Continue (northwards) to the end of **Parliament Court** or **Sandys Row** itself and turn right into **Artillery Lane**. Follow the road as it bends right and **Dome House** is on the right–hand (south) side.

Former **Ein Ya'akov ('Well of Jacob') Synagogue** ❽

Dome House, 48 Artillery Lane, E1 7LS

A mid-18th-century chapel occupied by the Jewish congregation Ein Ya'akov between 1896 and 1948, the lightly painted stuccoed building retains the recognisable arrangement of doors and windows typical of 18th-century meeting houses, but has been much rebuilt. The roof dome and lantern, heavily restored (*Lawrence Law & Associates*, 1991), have given the interior office development its current name of Dome House.

◗ Artillery Lane bears left, but turn right to detour through narrow **Artillery Passage** to appreciate a rare survival of Old London. Note the rare Georgian box shopfronts

Sandys Row Synagogue (DP094479)

The Jewish Soup Kitchen, Brune Street (DP045024)

on the corner (**56–8 Artillery Lane**). Return to **Artillery Lane** and turn right into **Bell Lane**. The Jews' Free School, the largest Jewish school in Britain, founded in 1817, was situated in Bell Lane, on the corner with the redeveloped **Frying Pan Alley** (on your right), in a building designed by **Nathan Solomon Joseph**, from 1883 until it was bombed during the Second World War. Cross over and take the first left, **Brune Street**, formerly called Butler Street. On the left (north) side is the next site.

Former **Soup Kitchen for the Jewish Poor** ❾

17–19 Brune Street, E1 7NZ, Grade II

Lewis Solomon, 1902

The Soup Kitchen was established in Leman Street in 1854, preceding the foundation of the Jewish Board of Guardians by five years, to provide food for poverty-stricken Jews, especially during the 'slack' trade months each winter. It moved via Black Horse Yard to Fashion Street where, after a fire, purpose-built premises were erected, designed by *H H Collins* in 1868, and

replaced in 1902 by the red-brick and buff terracotta premises in Butler Street (now Brune Street) by *Lewis Solomon*. A florid pediment with conch-shell design serves as the background for a soup tureen in relief, once dubbed the 'Apotheosis of Soup'. A terracotta band, which forms a frieze connecting the doorways, contains an *inscription* declaring the date and purpose of the building, the whole with a distinctly Arts and Craft feel. It was closed in 1992 and converted into flats by *City Space Makers* (1998).

❯ Walk to the end of **Brune Street**, turning slightly left via **Toynbee Street**, and cross busy **Commercial Street**. Opposite, a little to your left (north) over the road is Nicholas Hawksmoor's splendid **Christ Church, Spitalfields (C)** (1714–29). Turn down **Fashion Street** immediately opposite.

Former **Emporium** ❿

10–48 Fashion Street, E1 6PX, Grade II

Abraham Davis, 1905

Almost the length of the south side of this street (mentioned by Israel Zangwill in the opening chapter of his novel *Children of the Ghetto*, 1892), is occupied by the curious Moorish frontage of a short-lived shopping arcade of 1905 by East End Jewish builder *Abraham Davis*, a failed speculative development. Despite the horseshoe arches, *Davis Bros.* are not known to have built any synagogues, in 'orientalist' style or otherwise. It was restored and converted into up-market office units in 2003–4.

❯ Turn left into **Brick Lane**. The former **Spitalfields Great Synagogue** is on the next corner to your left (north) with **Fournier Street**.

Detail of the frieze, Jewish Soup Kitchen, Brune Street (DP045026, DP045027)

Former **Spitalfields Great Synagogue (Mahzikei Hadas)** ⓫

Brick Lane Jamme Masjid
(Mosque)

59 Brick Lane, E1 6QL, Grade II*

In 1897 the strictly Orthodox Lithuanian *kehillah* called Mahzikei Hadas ('Strengtheners of the Faith') moved into the former Neuve Eglise or New French Church, which had been built on the corner of Brick Lane and Fournier Street, in the heart of Spitalfields, in 1742–3. The simple but elegant brick church, with large round-headed windows, was designed by *Thomas Stubbs* (or *Stibbs*) in the style of 18th-century meeting houses, the sundial on its south gable (Fournier Street side, originally the main front) being its chief distinguishing feature.

In common with Sandys Row, this building had not passed directly to the Jews, but was first occupied by Wesleyan Methodists. In fact, between 1809 and 1819 the property was leased out, as their original headquarters, to the London Society for Promoting Christianity among the Jews. This, the largest and most active missionary society in east London, had been set up in 1809 by Joseph Frey, a German Jewish convert. The London Society was afterwards based in purpose-built premises in Bethnal Green, with the appropriate address of 'Palestine Place'. Their original baptismal font, especially for converting

Jews, is preserved at Christ Church, Spitalfields. It appears that later in the century the Brick Lane church was once again used as a centre for missionary activity, then being known as the 'Mission House for Converting Jews'. The church was used in turn by the East London Wesleyan Mission and the Jewish Evangelical Society, the latter run by an apostate called Mr Ashkenazi, for proselytising among the growing Jewish population of the neighbourhood.

Evidently, the evangelist societies did not prosper. In 1898 the former chapel became the Spitalfields Great Synagogue and the self-styled 'fortress' of religious Orthodoxy in Anglo-Jewry. Based on the rigorous Lithuanian

tradition of intense Jewish learning, the Mahzikei Hadas was famed for its continuous *minyanim*. Its most celebrated rabbi was Rav Kook who was stranded in London during the First World War and afterwards became Ashkenazi Chief Rabbi of Palestine under the British Mandate.

Today, the Mahzikei Hadas, once a Huguenot church, then a synagogue, is the London Jamme Masjid Mosque serving the Bangladeshi Muslims, the latest arrivals in the neighbourhood.

Former Spitalfields Great Synagogue (Mahzikei Hadas)
(K040854)

The interior has been completely stripped of what remained of the 18th-century woodwork and galleries. However, the Jews had begun the work of dismantling the interior, when part of the fine oak gallery on the east wall was removed to make room for the Ark. This created a *halakhically* acceptable synagogue while destroying the classical symmetry of the original building.

In the street outside, a freestanding tall, steel 'minaret' (*DGA Architects* 2009), topped by the Islamic Crescent, now accents the presence of the mosque.

The former Spitalfields Great Synagogue is the best example of the recycling of a place of worship in Britain. It has been occupied by Christians, Jews and Muslims in succession and encapsulates on a single site the immigrant history of east London.

◑ *Turn left and walk down* **Fournier Street**. *You are now in the heart of Georgian Spitalfields.*

The gracious terraced townhouses were built for prosperous Huguenot silk weavers, those Protestants who fled Catholic France when Louis XIV revoked the Edict of Nantes in 1685. Looking around at the beautifully restored and highly sought-after properties, it is hard to recall that this area was saved from wholesale demolition in the 1970s and 1980s. We owe *The Saving of Spitalfields* (1989) to the late Raphael Samuel (of 'History Workshop' fame), and to architectural

Former Princes Street Synagogue (K041039)

historians Mark Girouard and (TV presenter) Dan Cruikshank, who lives in the neighbourhood.

◑ *Turn right into* **Wilkes Street**.

Former **Warsaw Lodge Synagogue** ⓬

17 Wilkes Street, E1 6QF

A synagogue for Polish Jews was built in the backyard of this Georgian house (*Marmaduke Smith c* 1723–4) in 1925. Until the 1950s the house was subdivided into offices and flats occupied by Jewish families. Private residence.

◑ *Turn right into* **Princelet Street** *directly opposite.*

Former **Princes Street Synagogue** ⓭

19 Princelet Street, E1 6QH, Grade II*

A much better-known example of a synagogue built onto the back of a

Georgian house, this was added in 1870 to a former Huguenot master silk weaver's house of 1718–19, designed by *Samuel Worrall*, which was once occupied by an ancestor of the Courtaulds textile family. The weaver's loft and many original 18th-century fittings, panelling, mouldings, fireplaces and the weavers' attic (note the continuous window lights on the roof) remain intact. The long, narrow synagogue, with a gallery, was constructed in the back yard between what was then Princes Street and Hanbury Street, to serve a Polish *hevrah*, the Loyal United Friends (*Hevrat Nidvat Khen*) friendly society. Like many East End synagogues, Princes Street was lit from above through a glass leylight, in this instance decorated with tinted glass. Like others, too, restrictions of space meant that the Ark was wrongly oriented, being on the north rather than on the east or south-east wall. The architect was a 'Mr Hudson', probably, *John Hudson*, who had a large practice operating from Leman Street. It was altered and the façade partially rusticated by *Lewis Solomon* in 1892–3.

Since 1980 various attempts have been made to rescue the building, which came to national attention thanks to Rachel Lichtenstein's *Rodinsky's Room* (1999). Her 'Jewish roots' tale is based on the story of Princelet Street's last reclusive tenant, who mysteriously disappeared from the garret, leaving behind his effects, frozen in time.

A slightly inaccurate *blue plaque* next door commemorates Miriam Moses (1885–1965), Mayor of Stepney in 1931 and the first Jewish woman mayor in Britain. She was for 33 years warden of the **Brady Girls' Club** close by in Hanbury Street (*see* below).

OPENING HOURS: Occasional, tel 020 7247 5352; www.19princeletstreet.org. uk

○ *Return to* **Brick Lane**. *If you wish, take a detour along the continuation of Princelet Street (east side) to visit the following additional sites:*

Former **Brady Clubs and Settlement**

192–6 Hanbury Street, E1 5HU

Ernest Joseph, 1935

Now the Brady Arts Centre. Founded in 1896, the Brady Street Clubs were the prototype Jewish youth clubs in the East End. Very 1930s, with faience cladding and 'Crittall' windows. *Foundation stones.* Later additions and alterations.

○ *Situated at the eastern end of Hanbury Street (south side); alternatively, accessed via the cycle lane from* **Vallance Road**. *Signage on Whitechapel High Street and Vallance Road.*

Former **Great Garden Street Synagogue**

7–15 Greatorex Street, E1 5NF

Lewis Solomon, 1896

Situated behind the post-war façades (nos. 7–15 at the corner of Old Montague Street, renumbered from nos. 9–11) of the former headquarters of the Federation of Synagogues, abandoned in the 1990s – together with the famous Kosher Luncheon Club next door – and gutted to create office space (*Ankur Architects*, 1999), currently used by the Spitalfields Small Business Association. In a small courtyard (ask for access at reception), pleasantly furnished with pot plants and garden furniture, are displayed a series of memorial stones including the original *foundation stones*, made by East End stonemasons *Harris & Son*. The top-lit well is a reminder of the skylights that were a feature of East End synagogues, which were often built on confined sites where light and air were at a premium.

○ *Back on* **Brick Lane**, *go down (south) towards* **Heneage Street**, *passing no. 92.*

Ch N Katz shop front ⓮

92 Brick Lane, E1 6RL

Katz rope-makers were the last surviving Jewish business in Brick Lane, closing in the 1990s. The late Victorian red- and yellow-brick frontage has recently been restored and is now a gallery.

○ *Turn into* **Heneage Street**: *no. 2 is on the right (south) side.*

Former **Ezras Haim Synagogue** ⓯

2 Heneage Street, E1 5LJ

Another house-synagogue, of *c* 1902, this time inside the building – with the gallery formed by knocking a hole in the first-floor ceiling – rather than a rear extension. Converted into flats. An upstairs two-bedroom 'duplex' apartment, featuring the 'original wood ceiling beams' – vestiges of the prayer hall – was being marketed for a cool £950,000 in 2013.

○ *Return to* **Brick Lane**. *Continue down (south) to* **Wentworth Street**, *on the way passing* **Flower and Dean Walk**, *once the heartland of 'The Rookeries' – the 'no-go area' of the 19th-century East End. Turn right into* **Wentworth Street** *and walk towards busy* **Commercial Street**.

Rothschild Buildings Archway ⓰

Toynbee Estate, E1

Situated at the entrance to the Toynbee Estate (1984) from Wentworth Street.

This red-brick and terracotta arch is all that remains of *N S Joseph*'s model social housing project, Rothschild

Buildings. The arch was salvaged from demolition in 1972. As the *inscription* declares, the Charlotte de Rothschild Dwellings were erected as the first project of the Four Per Cent Industrial Dwellings Company in 1886. The block was six storeys high with a semi-basement built around a courtyard between Flower and Dean, Lolesworth and Thrawl streets. Read Jerry White's *Rothschild Buildings* (1980) for a vivid picture of life in 'The Buildings' as experienced by Jewish immigrant families.

❍ *Stop on the corner of* ***Commercial Street****. To your left (south) at no. 28 is the collegiate-style* ***Toynbee Hall (D)*** *(Elijah Hoole, 1884–5, some decor by C R Ashbee), founded by Samuel, afterwards Canon, Barnett and his wife Henrietta Octavia (Rowland) Barnett, as the first East End 'Settlement'. Look up the street in the other direction (north) to see the next site, on the opposite side of the road.*

Former **Jews' Infant School** ❼

Commercial House,
43A Commercial Street, E1 6BD,
Grade II

Tillot & Chamberlain, 1858,
extended by Davis & Emanuel, 1885

The Jews' Infant School was founded in a warehouse in Houndsditch in September 1841. The premises were enlarged in 1853 to accommodate the growing numbers of Jewish children in the area. In 1858[10] the purpose-built school was erected in Commercial Street, on land leased from the Public Works' Commissioners. The building itself cost nearly £5,000. The city-based architects (based in Gresham Street) had previously carried out work (in 1848 and 1855) at the senior Jews' Free School in Bell Lane (*see* p 13). In 1885 an extension was built on the corner with Tenter Street by *Davis & Emanuel*.[11]

At its peak the school accommodated 1,500 pupils between the ages of 3 and 8. The surviving building forms part of the terrace, is classical in style, of greying yellow brick with stucco dressings, parapet and a deep cornice. Five double-height round-headed windows originally lit the two large classrooms upstairs. Now in commercial use, the ground floor is disfigured by modern shop-fronts.

Former **Jewish Model Dwellings**

Norvin House,
45–55 Commercial Street,
E1 6BD (next door)

H H Collins (1862–3), partially rebuilt.

❍ *Cross* ***Commercial Street*** *and continue along* ***Wentworth Street****. This end of the road has an excellent textile market, formerly predominantly Jewish, now Asian and African. Turn left into* ***Old Castle Street****. The next site is further up, to the right.*

Former **Whitechapel Baths (E)**

25 Old Castle Street, E1 7NT
cr Goulston Street

Price Pritchard Baly, 1847,
modernised by John Hudson, 1878

This was the first 'model bathhouse' funded by local government in London, built under the Public Baths and Washhouses Act (Dukinsfield's Act) 1846 – a major piece of sanitary legislation in the age of 'the great unwashed' when very few people had private access to clean running water, let alone a bathroom. With two-thirds of the facilities originally priced at one penny (1d), Goulston Street was clearly aimed at the poorest end of the market and was well frequented on Friday afternoons ahead of *Shabbat* by East End Jews. In 1896 a swimming pool was added. The derelict mainly 1960s Whitechapel Amenity Complex was redeveloped in 2000–1 as the Women's Library (formerly the Fawcett Library) by architects *Wright & Wright*. The Old Castle Street façade with its original *inscription* WASH HOUSES 1846 was retained and incorporated into the highly praised building. Unfortunately, in 2012, the library closed, amid protests, and the collection was relocated to the London School of Economics. The future of the Old Castle Street building is unknown.

❍ *Return to Commercial Street. To your right is* ***Aldgate East Underground Station****, marking the end of the walk. Bring a picnic or check if there is now a kosher restaurant in the area for a more substantial lunch. Sadly, 'Blooms' on Whitechapel Road, famous for its hot salt-beef sandwiches, closed during the 1990s.*

This walk basically follows the Whitechapel Road, one of the two main commercial arteries that run east from the City at Aldgate. The other is the Commercial Road, which diverges to the south-east. Use may be made of the no. 25 bus along Whitechapel Road.

○ Start from **Aldgate East Underground Station**. NB From

the Underground platform, take the **west** exit, marked 'Toynbee Hall'. This brings you up on the **north** side of **Whitechapel Road** on the **corner of Commercial Street**. Walk **east** along **Whitechapel High Street** away from the City of London.

First stop, just beyond the narrow Dickensian alleyway called **Gunthorpe Street**, look up to see the **shop-sign**

over 'Albert's' menswear shop at **88 Whitechapel High Street** (Grade II). This marked the former **offices of *Der Post* (*Jewish Daily Post*) ○**, a short-lived rival of the Yiddish-language *Di Tsayt* (*Jewish Times*) in the 1930s. The cast-iron and gold-painted relief above the entrance was designed by *Arthur Szyk* in 1934–5,

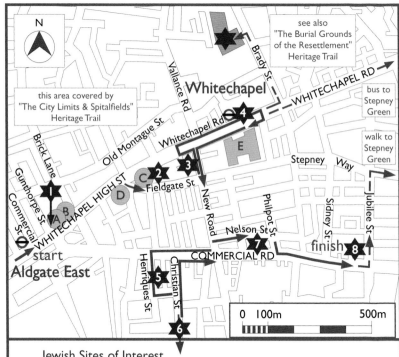

Jewish Sites of Interest

1 *former* offices of *Der Post*
2 *former* Fieldgate Street Synagogue
3 *former* Vine Court Synagogue
4 Whitechapel Drinking Fountain
5 *former* Bernhard Baron Settlement

6 to *former* Talmud Torah school,
   now Markazi Masjid (Mosque)
   approx 200m south
7 East London Central Synagogue
8 Congregation of Jacob Synagogue

Other Sites of Interest

A White Hart public house
B Whitechapel Art Gallery
C London Muslim Centre

D Whitechapel Bell Foundry
E Royal London Hospital

Jewish Daily Post sign by Arthur Szyk above no. 88 Whitechapel Road
(BB for SJBH)

Mosque with its prominent dome and minaret – visible only if you carry straight on. At the junction with Fieldgate Street, note the **'Fieldgate Oasis'** (2009), complete with palm tree in a container decorated with religious symbolism representing the presence of Christianity (crosses and bells), Judaism (Star of David) and Islam (Crescent), in the neighbourhood. It stands in front of the historic **Whitechapel Bell Foundry (D)** (south side). Follow Fieldgate Street round until you reach the small synagogue situated (north side) right behind the mosque.

before the Polish-born artist, illustrator, and anti-Nazi political cartoonist made a name for himself in America. If you can gain access, another sign, the only one to survive inside, marks the lift entrance on the first floor. This sign, also full of Jewish symbolism, is in relief, heavily over-painted in white. The heraldic motif is akin to decorative *Torah* Arks found in East End synagogues, which consist of a pair of Lions of Judah protecting the *Luhot* topped with a crown (*Keter Torah*).

Just to the right of Albert's is the **White Hart (A)** pub, reputedly the location of one of Jack the Ripper's murders.

By the east exit of Aldgate East Station is the glazed terracotta Arts & Crafts façade of the **Whitechapel Art Gallery (B)** (*Charles Harrison Townsend*, 1898–1901) and the former **Whitechapel Library (B)** (*Potts, Son & Hennings*, 1891–6) next door. The gallery was a venue for exhibitions by first-generation Jewish immigrant artists including *Mark Gertler* and *David Bomberg*, while the *blue plaque* on the wall of the library commemorates the First World War Jewish artist and poet *Isaac Rosenberg*. The horizons of many East End Jews were broadened by the existence of these two cultural institutions, which often functioned as a route to social 'betterment'. A £3.5 million Lottery grant in 2005 secured the future of the library building, reprieved from demolition and successfully integrated as an extension to the gallery in a project designed by Belgian practice *Robbrecht en Daem Architecten*.

❍ Detour up narrow **Angel Alley** by the side of the art gallery to visit the **Freedom Press** and its **Anarchist Bookshop**, reminders of the radical politics that once flowered in the Jewish East End. Then continue east along the **Whitechapel Road**. Cross over and turn into **Fieldgate Street**, which runs behind the **London Muslim Centre (C)** (completed 2004) and **East London**

Former **Fieldgate Street Synagogue** ❷

41 Fieldgate Street, E1 1JU
William Whiddington, 1899

Dwarfed by the dome and minaret of the East London Mosque behind it on Whitechapel Road, and now hemmed in by tall new housing blocks built for the London Muslim Centre, Fieldgate Street 'Great' Synagogue (there were once at least three other synagogues in this street[12]) was one of the last remaining examples of a Federation 'model' synagogue. The 'model' synagogues were premises deemed 'suitable' for poor new arrivals, which were funded after 1888 by the East End-based Federation of Synagogues. Unlike many of the others, this synagogue was purpose-built, designed in 1899 by a little-known City-based architect *William Whiddington*. However, he managed to place the Ark wrongly on the north wall. Fieldgate Street Great Synagogue was badly damaged during the Blitz. Grodzinski, the kosher

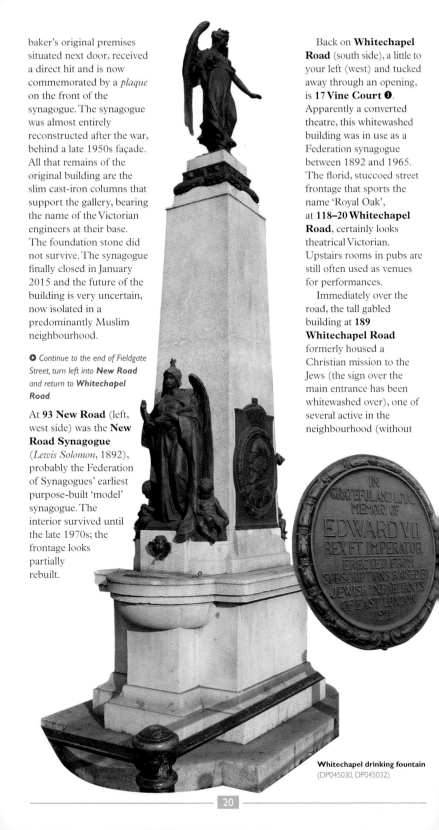

baker's original premises situated next door, received a direct hit and is now commemorated by a *plaque* on the front of the synagogue. The synagogue was almost entirely reconstructed after the war, behind a late 1950s façade. All that remains of the original building are the slim cast-iron columns that support the gallery, bearing the name of the Victorian engineers at their base. The foundation stone did not survive. The synagogue finally closed in January 2015 and the future of the building is very uncertain, now isolated in a predominantly Muslim neighbourhood.

⚫ *Continue to the end of Fieldgate Street, turn left into* **New Road** *and return to* **Whitechapel Road**.

At **93 New Road** (left, west side) was the **New Road Synagogue** (*Lewis Solomon*, 1892), probably the Federation of Synagogues' earliest purpose-built 'model' synagogue. The interior survived until the late 1970s; the frontage looks partially rebuilt.

Back on **Whitechapel Road** (south side), a little to your left (west) and tucked away through an opening, is **17 Vine Court ❸**. Apparently a converted theatre, this whitewashed building was in use as a Federation synagogue between 1892 and 1965. The florid, stuccoed street frontage that sports the name 'Royal Oak', at **118–20 Whitechapel Road**, certainly looks theatrical Victorian. Upstairs rooms in pubs are still often used as venues for performances.

Immediately over the road, the tall gabled building at **189 Whitechapel Road** formerly housed a Christian mission to the Jews (the sign over the main entrance has been whitewashed over), one of several active in the neighbourhood (without

IN
GRATEFUL AND LOYAL
MEMORY OF
EDWARD VII
REX ET IMPERATOR
ERECTED FROM
SUBSCRIPTIONS RAISED BY
JEWISH INHABITANTS
OF EAST LONDON
1911

Whitechapel drinking fountain
(DP045030, DP045032)

appreciable success). Next door once stood the Pavilion Theatre, Britain's premier Yiddish theatre from 1906 until the mid 1930s.

○ *Cross over the busy road. Continue **east** along the **north** side of Whitechapel Road. (NB If you lose your bearings, make sure that the towers of the 'downtown' City of London – NatWest, Lloyds Building, Norman Foster's 'Gherkin', etc. – are **behind** you.)*

Among the market stalls lining Whitechapel Road, right opposite the **Royal London Hospital (E)** is the **Whitechapel Drinking Fountain ○** (*W S Frith*, 1911, Grade II). As the *inscription* on one of the four faces of the stone obelisk states, this was erected as a memorial to King Edward VII, whose portrait in bronze relief is shown on one side, funded FROM SUBSCRIPTIONS RAISED BY JEWISH INHABITANTS OF EAST LONDON. It features also the female figure of JUSTICE and sculpted cherub faces on the taps. A bronze angel stands atop.

○ *At this point you have walked about 1.5km. Here you can take a **detour** up Brady Street to see the **Brady Street Cemetery**, the first stop on the **Burial Grounds of the Resettlement Heritage Trail** (0.75km).*
    Return to Whitechapel Road. At this point, you have several alternatives, depending on the amount of time – or energy – that you have.
    *You can **walk or take the no. 25 bus** straight along **Whitechapel Road** to Stepney **Green Underground Station** (1km), which can be the starting point for **Trail No. 3: Stepney Green** (see pp 25–6) or for the completion of **Trail No. 4: Jewish Burial Grounds of the Resettlement** (see p 27).*

*Or return to New Road in order to continue the present walk, either by following the **longer route**, which takes in a couple of sites **south of Commercial Road**, or the **shorter route** to take in two still-functioning East End synagogues, on the way to linking up with the start of the **Stepney Green Heritage Trail (No. 3)**. The latter option is probably best reserved for Heritage Open Days when the two synagogues are likely to be open to visitors (check beforehand).*

*Walk southwards down **New Road** until you reach **Commercial Road**. In order to explore two more sites on the **south side** of this busy main road, turn right, back in the direction of the City (west), cross over and walk down **Henriques Street**.*

Former **Bernhard Baron Settlement ○**

Bernhard Baron House, 71 Henriques (formerly 33 Berner) Street, E1 1LZ

Hodben & Porri, 1929

The former headquarters of the Oxford & St George's Club, these are now Housing Association flats. Basil Henriques came down from Oxford to the East End in 1913 and founded his settlement in the parish of St George's in the East. Known as 'The Gaffer', Henriques was an imposing figure, over 1.8m (6ft) tall, with a distinguished military record. His approach to Jewish youth work was strongly influenced by Baden-Powell.

○ *Walk around the block (eastwards) until you hit **Christian Street**, almost at the bottom of which, just before you reach the railway bridge, is located the next site.*

Former **Commercial Road Talmud Torah School ○**

9–11 Christian Street, *cr* Pinchin Street, E1 1SE, 1934[13]

This red-brick building towards the bottom of Christian Street (west side) is now the rear of the Markazi Masjid (Mosque). The Hebrew inscriptions over the entrance have been obliterated. The architect remains unidentified. The Christian Street School, opposite, a typical Victorian elementary school that was 99 per cent Jewish in the 1930s (when my mother was a pupil), was demolished in the 2000s. This whole neighbourhood is undergoing extensive redevelopment.

Wall tablets, Bernhard Baron Settlement (DP021609 (top) and DP021610)

◐ *Continue up Christian Street to **Commercial Road**, cross back and return to **New Road**. The first turning on your right (east side) is **Nelson Street**. Walk along until you see the next site situated on the south side of the street.*

East London Central Synagogue ❼

30–40 Nelson Street, E1 2DE

Lewis Solomon & Son (Digby), 1922–3

NELSON STREET SFARDISH SYNAGOGUE, as it says over the doorway, began life as a *hevrah*, a *landsmanschaft* from Berdichev in Poland. The congregation still worships according to *Nusah Sephard* (the Sephardic rite, but *not* Sephardi), suggesting Hasidic origin. The plain red-brick façade belies a modest but dignified neo-classical interior.

INTERIOR: Now painted in the ubiquitous pastel blue and white favoured by both the United Synagogue and the Federation after the establishment of the State of Israel. Architect Edward Jamilly once described such Federation interiors as possessing 'a tinselly feel' with their crudely painted and gilded columns and cut-out wooden lions surmounting the Ark. At Nelson Street the unfluted giant Ionic columns are hollow, concealing iron shafts. The Ark is set in an apse

Congregation of Jacob Synagogue, the Ark wall (E020044)

within a simplified Palladian arch and the pews are of oak. The space is well lit by natural light from large round-headed metal-framed windows filled with frosted glass, and by clerestory fanlights, cut into the coved ceiling above a deep moulded cornice – features that are ultimately derived from *James Spiller*'s Adamesque Great Synagogue in Duke's Place of 1790.

OPENING HOURS: *Shabbat* and festival services: tel 020 7790 9809.

❍ *Walk almost to the end of Nelson Street and turn right into* **Philpot Street**. *Philpot Street was once home to the* **Philpot Street 'Great' Synagogue**, *a Methodist chapel with classical portico, converted in 1908 by Lewis Solomon, and to the* **Philpot Street Sfardish Synagogue** *(1911) housed in the former Methodist school house opposite, both bombed in the Second World War. Turn right into the main* **Commercial Road**. *Carry on along the north side of the street, passing the end of* **Sidney Street**, *scene of the famous Siege, at no. 100, a stand-off between Home Secretary Winston Churchill and Russian (Jewish) anarchists in 1911. You can see the square tower of Canary Wharf ahead of you to the south.*

Congregation of Jacob Synagogue (Kehillas Ya'akov) ❽

351–3 Commercial Road, E1 2PS

Lewis Solomon & Son (Digby), 1920–1

Date stone '1921' in the gable. The wrong orientation of the main internal space, where the Ark is on the north wall, suggests a conversion, if not an almost complete rebuild by *Lewis Solomon*'s

son *Digby*, who succeeded his father as honorary architect to the Federation and continued to build in the 'model' style developed by him.

INTERIOR: Inside, the largely Hasidic community created for themselves in the heart of East London an inner space strongly redolent of the world of eastern European Jewry that they had left behind. Note the skylight, a feature that we have seen elsewhere in East End synagogues, an import from eastern Europe. The Ark is surmounted by a heavily gilded, but crudely carved, pair of heraldic Lions of Judah flanking the *Luhot*. Behind is a painted panel featuring traditional iconographical elements often encountered in eastern European Jewish art: the seven-branched *menorah*, the *arba minim* ('Four Species': palm, citron, myrtle, willow) associated with the festival of *Succot* (Tabernacles), the Seven Species of fruits and grains from the Land of Israel and musical instruments played in the Jerusalem Temple. Research has revealed that this panel is of comparatively recent date, probably created in the 1950s when the rear wall was repaired after sustaining bomb damage during the Blitz. The artist, Dr *Philip Steinberg*, was a member of the congregation. Nevertheless, both the style and content are throwbacks to an earlier era. Decorative woodcarving and wallpainting in folk-art style was a characteristic

of synagogue-building, particularly in Poland, the Ukraine and Rumania. Perhaps Kehillas Ya'akov was once a riot of colourful wall paintings. The rest of the panels have long since been obliterated by plain blue paint. Currently this synagogue is undergoing a revival with a new, younger congregation. Restored with the help of the World Monuments Fund.

OPENING HOURS: *Shabbat* and festival services. Heritage Open Days (September). Other times by appointment: tel 020 7790 2874; www.congregationofjacob.org

❍ *On leaving the Congregation of Jacob, continue along* **Commercial Road**. *Turn left up* **Jubilee Street** *and then right into* **Stepney Way**, *this neighbourhood being largely post-war housing. A gate in the railings on the left-hand side leads you into* **Stepney Green Park**. *Head diagonally across the park towards the* **Clock Tower** *on* **Stepney Green** *itself. Exit through the park gates onto the green, to join the southern end of the* **Stepney Green Trail (No. 3)**.

Wall painting over the Ark at Congregation of Jacob Synagogue (E020043)

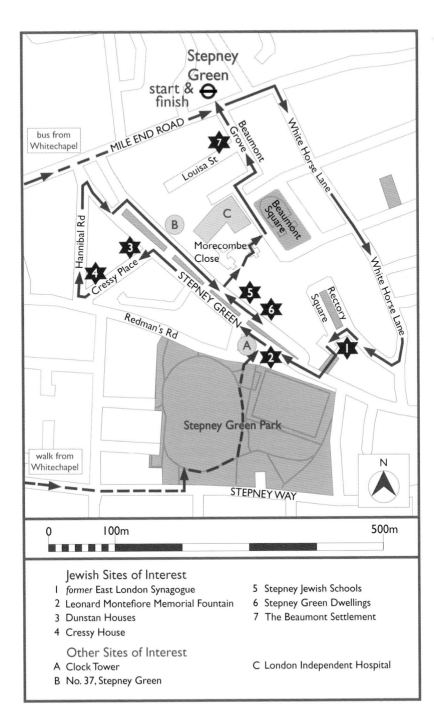

Jewish Sites of Interest

1 *former* East London Synagogue
2 Leonard Montefiore Memorial Fountain
3 Dunstan Houses
4 Cressy House
5 Stepney Jewish Schools
6 Stepney Green Dwellings
7 The Beaumont Settlement

Other Sites of Interest

A Clock Tower
B No. 37, Stepney Green
C London Independent Hospital

An unexpectedly attractive oasis, today Stepney Green has regained the appeal that it had in the 19th century. In 1873 the *Jewish Chronicle* endorsed the aim of communal leaders: 'to encourage the settlement of the Jewish industrial population in this wholesome and airy district [Stepney Green] as far as possible from the restricted and confined so-called Jewish quarters, the lanes, courts and alleys of Middlesex Street, Houndsditch and Spitalfields.'[14]

This was largely achieved through the erection by the newly established United Synagogue of the **East London Synagogue** in **Rectory Square**, on the far (east) side of Stepney Green. The East London was the only example of the grand 'West End' 'cathedral-synagogue' type ever built east of Aldgate. Situated beyond the heart of the 'ghetto' of Whitechapel, it was a deliberate piece of social engineering and good strategic planning. The synagogue was built just before the mass influx of Jews from eastern Europe after 1881.

○ Start the walk from **Stepney Green Underground Station**. *Cross over the* **Mile End Road** *and walk all the way down* **White Horse Lane**. *Before you reach* **Ben Jonson Road** *and the medieval parish church of* **St Dunstan's** *beyond, turn right into* **Rectory Square**.

Former **East London Synagogue** ❶

Temple Court, 52 Rectory Square, E1 3NU

Davis & Emanuel, 1876–7, Grade II

The shell is all that is left of one of the finest Victorian synagogues in London, abandoned in 1987, subjected to arson, flooded and vandalised until finally converted by *Arc Architects* into up-market flats in 1996. The *foundation stone* is *in situ* to the right of the south entrance (now the rear). If you can get inside the gated complex, see vestiges of the east wall in the 'atrium' and some more *inscriptions* displayed upstairs. However, to the outsider, even the identity of the synagogue has been all but obliterated in the name 'Temple Court'. 'Synagogue Court' might not have been so saleable. It would have been kinder to demolish.

○ *Walk all the way around the building, which is in the middle of a small housing estate. Walk through the brick archway to your left, past the rear (south) entrance of the former synagogue, through a small green area, down a brick pathway and exit through the* **gate** *onto* **Stepney Green**. *Stand in Stepney Green.*

At the **south end** of the Green, facing the **Clock Tower (A)** (1913, Grade II) is the very neglected red granite **Leonard Montefiore Memorial Fountain** ❷ (1884, Grade II).

○ *Walk northwards up on the left (west) side of* **Stepney Green**

towards the main **Mile End Road**. *On your left are examples of late Victorian model dwellings, built in red brick and terracotta.*

Dunstan Houses ❸, with the distinctive copper-clad corner turret, was a social housing project carried out by *Davis & Emanuel* in 1899 for the East End Dwellings Co, as is stated on the gilded *inscription* on the wall. It is best known for its anarchist residents, including Rudolph Rocker, who lived in flat no. 33 (see William J Fishman's classic book *East End Jewish Radicals*, London: Duckworth, 1975).

○ *Turn left into* **Cressy Place** *and walk around the triangular block via* **Hannibal Road** *to view* **Cressy House** ❹, *also by Davis & Emanuel (1894), on the corner angle with* **Hannibal Road**. *Return to Stepney Green and walk south down the* **other (east) side** *of the street.*

Note the delightful Queen Anne house at **37 Stepney Green (B)** (Grade II★). In the past used as a Home for Aged Jews and later on as extra space for the **Stepney Jewish Schools** (*see* below) and as a doctor's surgery, the house has more recently been the home of a chief executive of English Heritage.

○ *Continue down.*

Pass the former **Stepney Orthodox Synagogue**, now the **Rosalind Green Hall**, a 1950s rebuild of the bombed breakaway from East London Synagogue, formed in 1896 in protest at the introduction of a mixed choir. The Ark wall survives inside the building, which is used as a sports club.

Further down, at **no. 71**, are the red-brick and terracotta former **Stepney Jewish Schools** ❺ (Grade II). *Davis & Emanuel* designed the main buildings, including the charming headmaster's house with its porte-cochère, in 1872. An additional floor and a new wing were added by *Ernest Joseph* in 1906–7. The schools were founded in the 1860s and pioneered 'muscular Judaism' through their athletics programme and associated Stepney Jewish Lads' Club. The Revd J F Stern, minister of East London Synagogue, who sported bishop's gaiters, took a close interest in the spiritual life of the club. The schools moved to Ilford in the 1970s. Note the faded *inscription* on the gable and the initials SJS worked into the original ornamental school gates.

Stepney Green Dwellings ❻, all red-brick and stucco decoration, with a stepped gable, were designed in 1896 by the rival firm of *N S Joseph* for the Four Per Cent Industrial Dwellings Co (renamed Stepney Green 'Court').

❍ *Retrace your steps, walking back (north) to the **Stepney Jewish Schools**. Take the pathway that runs at the side of the schools, through **Morecombe Close** estate into **Beaumont Square**.*

Beaumont Square, now entirely redeveloped except for the far north-west corner (Victorian Tudor-style terrace), was once

Stepney Jewish Schools (DP045028)

occupied by better-off Jewish families.

❍ *Stay on the same side of the square and turn left (north) past the **London Independent Hospital (C)**.*

This was the site of the former **London Jewish Hospital** (*Edwin T & E Stanley Hall*, 1915–19), funded by penny subscriptions from the poor Jews of the East End. The buildings, including the hospital synagogue designed by *Ernst Freud* in 1958, were demolished in the 1980s to make way for the new private hospital.

❍ *Turn right into **Beaumont Grove** and follow the road around to the left passing **Louisa Street**.*

The Beaumont Settlement ❼

2–8 Beaumont Grove, E1 4NQ
cr Louisa Street
Cecil J Eprile & P V Burnett, 1938

This is the last outpost of the Jewish East End. It still operates a friendship and luncheon club (Stepney Jewish Community Centre).

The remnants of Basil Henriques' Settlement Synagogue has merged with the South West Essex Reform Synagogue. Although the neighbouring 1950s Hillel Jewish student house has been sold off, the 'Settlement' is still home to the Alice Model Nursery, named after the pioneering midwife, affectionately known as 'Mother Levy', who ran the demolished (2012) Jewish Maternity Home at nos. 24–26 Underwood Road (off Vallance Road).[15]

Now called **Phyllis Gerson House**, after a long-serving warden, the original 1938 clubhouse of the Stepney Jewish Girls' Club & Settlement is on the other (north) corner with Louisa Street. Note the *foundation stone* low on the wall, whitewashed over.

❍ *Come out on **Mile End Road**. A no. 25 bus stop (direction: The City) is immediately in front of you, and **Stepney Green Underground Station** is across the road. End of the walk.*

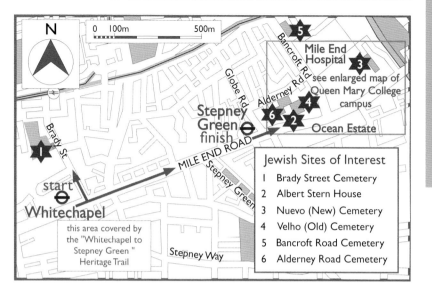

Jewish Sites of Interest

1 Brady Street Cemetery
2 Albert Stern House
3 Nuevo (New) Cemetery
4 Velho (Old) Cemetery
5 Bancroft Road Cemetery
6 Alderney Road Cemetery

Most of the sites on this route are not normally open to the public. You will need to telephone ahead in order to arrange access. Contact numbers are provided.

⊙ Start from **Whitechapel Underground Station.** Turn left (east) along the **Mile End Road** and left again up **Brady Street.** The burial ground is towards the top of the road, on the left-hand side (west).

Brady Street Jewish Cemetery ❶

This is the burial ground of the **London New Synagogue,** founded in 1761. Later shared with the **Ashkenazi Great Synagogue, Duke's Place,** the site was in use until 1858. The 1780–1 *ohel* by *James Campling* has long gone from the site, then quaintly known as 'Tuck and Pan Lane'. Land

on the west side of 'Ducking Pond Lane' was added when the freehold was acquired in 1795.

This extensive walled cemetery is an unexpected oasis of green in the heart of the East End, with well-trimmed grass, mature trees, fruit trees and shrubs. It contains over 3,000 tombstones, with many more layered burials in the large central mound,

a feature otherwise unique in Britain (think of Prague). Many Georgian tombstones survive but most are illegible.

There are some interesting memorials of distinguished Victorian Jews, including those to NATHAN MAYER (1777–1836) and HANNAH ROTHSCHILD (1783–1850), a pair of chest tombs with classical pediments.

Brady Street Cemetery (DP021634)

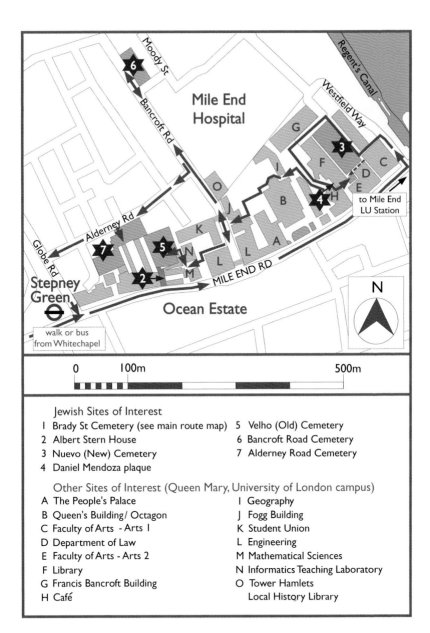

Jewish Sites of Interest

1 Brady St Cemetery (see main route map)
2 Albert Stern House
3 Nuevo (New) Cemetery
4 Daniel Mendoza plaque
5 Velho (Old) Cemetery
6 Bancroft Road Cemetery
7 Alderney Road Cemetery

Other Sites of Interest (Queen Mary, University of London campus)

A The People's Palace
B Queen's Building/ Octagon
C Faculty of Arts - Arts 1
D Department of Law
E Faculty of Arts - Arts 2
F Library
G Francis Bancroft Building
H Café
I Geography
J Fogg Building
K Student Union
L Engineering
M Mathematical Sciences
N Informatics Teaching Laboratory
O Tower Hamlets
  Local History Library

New marble plaques have been affixed. Nathan was the founder of the British branch of the famous banking house. SOLOMON HIRSCHELL (1762–1842), Chief Rabbi, has a memorial in the form of an obelisk.

In the middle of the cemetery, close to the mound, is a very rare Jewish example of a bust of a woman: MIRIAM, wife of MOSES LEVY, identified as MIRIAM LEVEY (1801–1856), a welfare worker who opened the first soup kitchens in the East End. Her tomb is in the form of a square obelisk with four faces decorated with figurative reliefs.

ACCESS: United Synagogue Burial Society (based at Bushey Cemetery): tel 020 8950 7767; www.theus.org.uk

Mocatta House, *Joseph & Smithem* 1905, occupies

**Memorial to Miriam Levy
in Brady Street Cemetery**
(DP021636, DP021635)

the south-eastern corner of
the cemetery, a distinctive
mansion block of red brick
with yellow-stone dressings
and decorative ironwork
balconies. Tapered brick
pylons flank the entrance in
art nouveau style.

*❍ Return to Mile End Road and
walk on towards Stepney Green,
or take the no. 25 bus and alight at
'Ocean Estate' stop, just past the
Underground station. This bus stop is
right outside the next site on this trail.*

Albert Stern House,
former **Spanish and
Portuguese Bet
Holim ('Lying-in'
Hospital and
Sephardi
Almshouses)** ❷

253 Mile End Road, E1 4BJ

Manuel Nunes Costello,
1912–13, Grade II

Behind these well-built
mock Queen Anne style
houses lies the oldest
Jewish burial ground in
Britain. Before the First
World War, Sephardi
architect *Manuel Nunes
Costello*, funded by Ella
Mocatta, demolished the
previous terraced building
(1851) of the Sephardi
community's maternity
hospital, known simply
as *Bet Holim* (hospital).
This institution had its
origins in the 17th century
Gemilut Hasadim or 'Help
Society' (1665), and had
operated from premises
in Leman Street from
1747–8[16] before moving
to the present site in Mile
End in 1790.

In addition to the
decorative 'Wrenaissance'
terrace, Costello replaced
a separate 'Asylum for the
Aged', at the rear, by
almshouses for married
pensioners. These were
plainly built in an L-shape,
linked by a veranda (much
reconstructed), forming a
pleasant grassy courtyard
around the Sephardi old
cemetery, the **Velho**. In
1977 the *Bet Holim*, now
just a home for the elderly,
removed to Forty Avenue,
Wembley. As well as the
foundation stone and
(inaccurate) historical
plaque on the wall of the
façade, look out for

another *plaque* on the
cottages, once you get
inside the courtyard.
However, this is accessible
only via the burial ground
through the campus of
**Queen Mary University
of London**.

*❍ With the exception of Brady
Street, all of the remaining historic
Jewish cemeteries in the East End
are situated in or close to the
University campus. The best route
through the campus is described
below and shown on the Campus Map.*
   *Continue along the Mile End
Road to the far end of the
campus. You will retrace your steps
back through the campus from
east to west. Pass the (New)
People's Palace (A), a favourite
venue for performances attended
by many East End Jews in the
1930s, and the Queen's Building
(B). Turn left into Westfield Way.
This area consists of new halls of
residence backing on to the
Regent's Canal. Turn to the left
behind the new-build brick Arts
1 Building (C) and bear left until
you see the next site.*
   *Before viewing the cemetery
itself, enter the new-build Arts 2
Building (E) in order to view
a section of the Georgian
Boundary Wall that has been
incorporated under glass into
the floor.*

Nuevo or 'Novo'
(New) Cemetery
of the Spanish and
Portuguese Jews ❸

Old Section: 1733, Grade II
(plaque and boundary wall)

New Section: 1855, P & G Grade II

Part of the Victorian
section (1849–53) with its
typical Sephardi flat stones,
is, in fact, all that remains
of the newly styled NOVO
CEMETERY 1733. The lost
Georgian part was in use
from 1733 until *c* 1836.
The original Portland stone
consecration *plaque*[17] dated

17 Nisan 5493 (= April 1733) has been relocated to the wall of the Victorian section. Despite losing its pediment, this scrolled tablet has now been listed in its own right (2014), considering its antiquity. A later *plaque* attests to the fact that the new section was in use from July 1855. The *ohel* that stood at the street entrance was demolished in 1922. About 200 graves were damaged and 80 tombstones were destroyed across the entire cemetery in strafe bombing in September 1940. This explains the raised circular memorial decorated with a *Magen David* towards the rear. The oldest extant stones are along the back wall. The names and inscriptions attest to the Iberian origins of those interred here, and their 'global reach', with places of birth, residence and death ranging from Europe through the Middle East and north Africa, to the Caribbean and the Americas as far as Australia.[18]

In a scandal that still reverberates, most of the cemetery, which originally extended to the west and south right down to the Mile End Road, was dug up in 1974 when land was sold to Queen Mary College. Most of the remains, over 7,000 bodies, were reinterred in a field provided by the University in **Brentwood, Essex** (*see* below) in what looks more like a mass grave. Other than the graves of a handful of prominent rabbis and their families, who were reinterred at the successor cemetery at **Hoop Lane, Golders Green**, no individual tombstones were salvaged or recorded.[19] The Victorian section was handed over to the University on a 999-year lease, under which the latter took over responsibility for basic maintenance. This section contains over 2,000 graves, of which 400 were found to be at least partially legible in 2011.

In March 2012 the Victorian section was reconsecrated, after a major landscaping project undertaken by *Seth Stein Architects*. This project formed part of the ongoing redevelopment of the campus. The freehold of the old, narrow access path behind the **Department of Law (D)** was rumoured to have been sold to the University for £1 million. The path was widened and a raised walkway built around the southern side of the cemetery to ease circulation through the campus. This bridge provides an excellent viewing platform for both students and visitors. It was also designed to avoid half a dozen graves on the very edge of the cemetery. New signage and interpretation boards were installed. In another trade-off, the University was allowed to build a raised concrete 'piazza' over a small railed grassed plot that had hitherto marked the only portion of the Georgian section that had survived after 1974. This part of the project attracted the particular opprobrium of strictly Orthodox Jews because, formerly, a sign placed on the railings by the Spanish and Portuguese, referred to this plot as 'consecrated ground'. Recent archaeology and research[20] using old maps of the area (dating back to 1703) seem to suggest that there may never have been any burials in this area. From 1746, at least, various buildings occupied the southern and western corners of the site fronting the Mile End Road, including a 'mortuary chapel' and probably also a 'watch house' or caretaker's house that later had a garden. These buildings had all disappeared by the early 1960s, although the surviving lengths of the listed Georgian brick boundary walls, which have escaped demolition or incorporation into later buildings, are well preserved.

ACCESS: The key can be obtained from the Security Lodge on the ground floor of the **Queen's Building (B)** (Reception) on Mile End Road. Telephone bookings in advance are required (especially for large groups): tel 020 7882 5000.

❍ *After viewing the cemetery, continue around the boundary of the* **Nuevo** *at the back of the Library (F). Bear left and follow round past the* **Francis Bancroft Building (G)** *and back in front of the* **Library (F)** *to the* **Café (H)**. *Affixed to the wall of the Library (south-west corner) is the* **Daniel Mendoza plaque** ❍ *L Soloway, 2008.*

Daniel Mendoza (1764–1836), the famous Jewish pugilist, THE FATHER OF SCIENTIFIC BOXING was indeed BURIED IN A SPOT NEARBY as the inscription reads. However, his was one of the *c* 7,000 bodies unceremoniously dug up and sent to **Brentwood** in 1974. The bronze plaque based on the well-known illustration by Gillray, which depicts him in the boxing ring, was unveiled by boxer Henry Cooper in 2008.

◗ *Back-track and walk through the passage between* **The Octagon (B)** *(to your left) and* **Geography (I)** *(to your right) towards the green-and-yellow* **Fogg Building (J)** *and out of the gate onto* **Bancroft Road** *opposite the* **Student Union (K)**. *Turn left back into the campus, then right, and follow round behind* **Engineering (L)**, *between* **Mathematical Sciences (M)** *and the* **Informatics Teaching Laboratory (N)**. *The entrance to the* **Velho ❺** *is through a pointed brick archway in the wall around the back (left) of this building.*

General view of the Velho, the oldest Jewish cemetery in Britain (AA020546)

Velho [Old] Cemetery of the Spanish and Portuguese Jews ❺

1657, Grade II

The aptly named Velho is the oldest post-Resettlement Jewish burial ground in Britain. A small plot was acquired leasehold in February 1657. At this early date, the right of Jews under English law to own land and real estate had not been fully determined. Both the site and the lease were extended incrementally until in 1737 the freehold was finally secured by **Bevis Marks Synagogue**. The first burial was that of Judith de Brito, the wife of one of the signatories to the Jews' Petition to Oliver Cromwell in 1656. The cemetery was situated at Mile End, well beyond the eastern wall of the City of London, in accordance with Jewish law.

Wall tablet at the Velho Cemetery. Note the inscription in Portuguese and the cherubim (AA020549)

The rural character of Mile End, a tiny hamlet among gardens and orchards, is evident from *J Gasgoyne's Map*, published in 1703, where the cemetery is clearly labelled 'the Jews Burying Place'. It was in continuous use until 1742 and became contiguous with the oldest Ashkenazi

ground at **Alderney Road**, which was not opened until almost 40 years after the Velho. Therefore a few Ashkenazim are buried in the Velho. In the early 20th century the cemetery became enclosed on two sides by the **Sephardi Almshouses**, forming a pleasant courtyard for the residents (note the *inscription* on the wall).

The oldest boundary wall at the rear (north) of the cemetery also has a stone *inscription*, here dating back to 1684 (probably the year in which the wall was built), that gives the names of the founders in Portuguese. This tablet, heavily restored, is decorated with a winged cherub in relief. Look carefully to see more faces of cherubim on children's graves (there are hundreds of these, many unmarked, as well as unmarked graves thought to be of victims of the Great Plague of 1665), some weathered Sephardi family crests, and skull and crossbones on the small number of chest tombs clustered against the back wall. The chest tomb of Don Isaac Lindo of Campo Mayor in Portugal, d 18 March 1712 is of particular interest

(tombstone restored, 1924). Candles are lit by *Hasidim* on the restored slabs to **Bevis Marks'** revered rabbi, Venetian-born Haham David Nieto (1654–1728), and of one of his successors, Haham Raphael Meldola, whose request one hundred years later, in 1828, to be buried at the feet of his master was honoured. Otherwise, approximately 700 gravestones, mainly of limestone, are plain and flat, in the Sephardi style and most are illegible. Early inscriptions were in Portuguese, as well as Hebrew and, later on, English. There is nothing here to compare with the famous baroque figurative reliefs of the Dutch Sephardim at Ouderkerk-aam-de-Amstel near Amsterdam.

ACCESS: As for the Nuevo above.

● *Return to **Bancroft Road** and walk all the way up (north-west), away from the Mile End Road, passing the **Tower Hamlets Local History Library (O)** on your right (east). **Bancroft Road Cemetery** is also on the right at the corner with **Moody Street**.*

18th-century chest tombs in Velho Cemetery featuring the skull and crossbones
(AA020550)

Bancroft Road Jewish Cemetery ●

Through the railings you can view the disused cemetery founded by the defunct Maiden Lane Synagogue, which started life as a breakaway from the Westminster (later called the Western) Synagogue (Ashkenazi) in *c* 1810. In 1811 the congregation acquired 'Globe Fields' – this area is still called Globe Town by locals. By 1896 the ground was almost full and fast falling into neglect; it was closed in 1907 when the Maiden Lane Synagogue, as it was called from 1829, remerged with the Western. There are thought to be about 500 burials at Bancroft Road but the vast majority of the tombstones have toppled or disappeared. The site suffered some bomb damage during the Second World War. Today, the abandoned cemetery is in the trusteeship of the Board of Deputies. The records have disappeared.

ACCESS: Locked. United Synagogue Burial Society (based at Bushey Cemetery): tel 020 8950 7767. Appointments in advance only, by permission of the Board of Deputies of British Jews.

🔵 Retrace your steps down **Bancroft Road** and turn right (west) into **Alderney Road**. The entrance to the cemetery is on your left (south side of the street).

Alderney Road Jewish Cemetery 🔟

Grade II

A peaceful garden cemetery hidden behind a high wall, this is the oldest Ashkenazi burial ground in Britain, dating from 1696–7. The original plot, which you enter first, was purchased on a 999-year lease for the sum of £190 by Benjamin Levy, one of the 12 'Jew Brokers' then permitted to trade on the London Stock Exchange. The owner was a 'gentleman' called Captain Nathaniell Owen, described as being of 'Mile End Green in the Parish of Stebunheath at Stepney in the County of Middlesex'. The site, which adjoined the Sephardi **Velho** at the south-east corner, had already been enclosed with 'Brickwalls' and included a dwelling house at the north-west corner.

Today, the site retains its original character as a 'Garden Ground'. Horse chestnut, elderberry and plum trees all grow there and there is even a fig tree in the middle. The boundary wall is mainly of brick, in parts buttressed and rendered with cement. Some 18th- or early 19th-century brickwork survives. The house was clearly indicated on both editions of *R Horwood's Map* of London (1799, 1819). However, the present caretaker's house at **no. 27 Alderney Road**, which

Modern memorial stone at Alderney Road (DP021625)

you pass on the way in, stands on a slightly different axis and further to the east. It seems that the house was rebuilt in 1890–1 by N S Joseph.[21]

There are two distinct sections. The oldest part, immediately behind Alderney Road, contains the chest tombs of notables including Chief Rabbi David Tevele Schiff and the Cabbalist Rabbi Samuel Falk, the 'Ba'al Shem' of London. His tomb, near the east wall, has latterly become a place for prayer by London *Hasidim*. It bears a *plaque* (1 June 1997). Iconography includes skull and cross-bones in relief, very rare in an Anglo-Jewish burial ground, let alone in an Ashkenazi one (but see above on the **Velho**).

The later section to the south-west, purchased freehold in 1749, is reached

along the meandering central pathway that takes you through a narrow opening. An unusual Georgian tombstone (here the tombstones are generally upright in the Ashkenazi tradition) bears the face of a cherub, a figurative motif unique among Anglo-Ashkenazi cemeteries (but *see* above on the **Velho**). The cemetery was closed in 1853.

A full illustrated survey was undertaken in 1993, organised by the present writer, edited by the late Rabbi Dr Bernard Susser and published to mark the tercentenary of this cemetery: Susser B (ed) 1997 *Alderney Road Jewish Cemetery London E1, 1697–1853*. London: United Synagogue.

ACCESS: United Synagogue Burial Society (based at Bushey Cemetery): tel 020 8950 7767; www.theus.org.uk

🔵 Continue to the end of **Alderney Road** and turn left into **Globe Road**, which comes out on the side of **Stepney Green Underground Station**. The walk ends here.

Tomb of Rabbi Samuel Falk, d 4 Iyar 5542 [=17 April 1782] (DP021629)

HACKNEY

Former **Hackney Synagogue**

20 Brenthouse Road, E9 6QG,

Delissa Joseph, 1897, extended by Cecil J Eprile, 1936, Grade II

Now wrongly considered as 'the East End', Hackney, with its long rows of terraced houses, represented at the end of the 19th century the achievement of lower-middle-class respectability. Built for the United Synagogue, the former South Hackney Synagogue has a single plain red-brick elevation along the street (north) side, seamlessly extended to the west by *Eprile*. In 2009 the building was sold to a Brazilian Pentecostalist church (UCKG) for £2 million. The *Luhot* remain over the main entrance.

INTERIOR: The Ark, *bimah* and pulpit were originally grouped at the east end with seating facing, in the Reform manner, an arrangement pioneered in acculturated 'Orthodox' synagogues by *Delissa Joseph*. *Cecil Eprile* returned to tradition with a central art deco *bimah* in 1936 but *Joseph*'s clever visual conceit, an unusual convex Ark, rather than the expected coffered apse, was retained. The Ark has been stripped out and the *bimah* completely removed, despite the Grade II listing. The church refurbished the basement

as a modern worship space – and even installed a baptismal pool. Meanwhile, the rest of the building appeared neglected.

Former **Montague Road Beth HaMedrash**

Montague Court,
62A Montague Road, E8 2HW

Lewis Solomon & Son, 1934

For the Federation of Synagogues. Closed 1980. Set well back from the street behind gates, the red-brick building has artificial stone dressings and is slightly Italianate in style, with a triple-arcaded open porch and a parapet with balusters. It was subdivided into 11 upmarket flats by developer *City Build London* in 2001. The *foundation stone* (legible in 2000) seems to have survived, but the Hebrew name under the roofline has been painted over, and the domed ceiling has probably disappeared.

Former **Stoke Newington Synagogue**

UK Turkish Islamic Trust Mosque,
9–15 Shacklewell Lane,
E8 2DA

Lewis Solomon, 1902–3

On a prominent site; by Federation standards of the period a large building. The red-brick façade with glazed terracotta door cases is reminiscent of *Solomon*'s **Jewish Soup Kitchen** in the East End, opened the previous year. The dome

was added on conversion into a Turkish mosque in 1977. The light interior, with the Ark made into a *mihrab*, the *bimah* and pews removed, had been tastefully decorated in 1998, but in 2000 was gutted by a firebomb. Kurdish separatists were suspected.

Ohel Ya'akov ('Tent of Jacob') or **Springfield Synagogue**

202 Upper Clapton Road,
Clapton Common, E5 9DH

A 1929 house conversion for the Federation, it is still in use, but most of the fixtures and fittings are post-war. The original Ark was donated to Hitching *yeshivah* and was later destroyed by fire. The upstairs of the two-storey Victorian house retains its original cornices, fireplaces and leaded lights over the stairwell.

OPENING HOURS: *Shabbat* and weekday services: tel 020 8806 3167.

BURIAL GROUND IN HACKNEY

Hackney Jewish Cemetery

103 Lauriston Road, E9 7HJ

1788

The second cemetery (after **Hoxton**: *see* West Ham, below) of the former Hambro Synagogue (1707), Magpie Alley, Fenchurch Street. Once known as Grove Road, it was used from 1788 to 1886. The site was extended at the front (north-west) in 1852, and thoroughly overhauled and landscaped in 1869–70 thanks to a generous donation from Mrs Flatou of the Hambro in memory of her husband.

H H Collins 'partly pulled down and partially rebuilt'[22] the dilapidated Georgian *bet taharah* in Italianate style, now long gone. At the same time he designed the Lodge, at **no. 103**, with deep Queen Anne cornice and ironwork porch.

Behind the ornamental gateway and railings (also dating from 1869 to 1870) can be viewed the pleasant garden cemetery, neatly kept, with short grass and fruit trees. The tombstones face west; many of the 18th-century ones towards the rear are illegible, although still standing, made of limestone and some of slate. A group of Victorian memorials are clustered to the left of the central path, notably to the Magnus family, and include chest tombs, one in the shape of a coffin. The last funeral at Lauriston Road took place in 2003, the interment of the cemetery's last caretaker, the long-serving Janet Samson.

LOCATION: South end of Lauriston Road, opposite Rutland Road.

ACCESS: United Synagogue Burial Society (based at Bushey Cemetery): tel 020 8950 7767; www.theus.org.uk

Hasidim at Egerton Road Synagogue

Knightland Road Synagogue

50 Knightland Road, E5 9HS

J Falkender Parker, 1930–1

Built for successful manufacturer Sender Herman behind his home 'Shalva'. The *mikveh* at the rear was the first in the Stamford Hill Jewish community. A plain single-storey brick-built synagogue with no vestibule, the only architectural feature of interest it has is the shallow dome in front of the Ark, reputedly inspired by the so-called 'Hurvah' Synagogue (1858–64, demolished in 1948 and rebuilt in 2010) in the Old City of Jerusalem, seen by Reb Sender. However, the recently opened (1928) **Stamford Hill Beth HaMedrash** (*see* below) also had a saucer-domed ceiling, while the barrel vault at the contemporary **Clapton Federation Synagogue (Sha'are Shamayim)**, 47 Lea Bridge Road, E5 (*Marcus*

Kenneth Glass, 1931–2, demolished 2006)[23] was painted as a starry sky, as was originally the case at Knightland Road. Kitted up in intimate Stamford Hill *shtiebl* style, from 1938 (after *Kristallnacht*) this synagogue hosted German refugees from 'Schneider's', Rabbi Moses Schneider's *yeshivah* in Frankfurt. A souvenir of this period is a *Sefer* (religious book) with pages cut and defaced with a swastika.

LOCATION: At the Warwick Grove end of Knightland Road, set back behind houses down a passageway, marked no. 50 on the gate.

OPENING HOURS: *Shabbat* and weekday services.

The New Synagogue

Bobover Synagogue and Beth HaMedrash, Egerton Road, N16 6UB

Joseph & Smithem, 1915, Grade II

After some 15 years, this synagogue was rescued in 2007 from the Heritage at Risk Register and was

converted into the *Bobover Shul*, the largest Hasidic synagogue in London. The red-brick and stone-turreted Edwardian baroque exterior by *Ernest Joseph* belies greater historical significance within.

INTERIOR: The interior is a partial replica of the previous New Synagogue (*John Davies*, 1837–8) in Great St Helen's, Bishopsgate, in the City, demolished by Marcus Samuel, later Lord Bearsted, in 1912 to make way for the company headquarters of Shell Petroleum. The style chosen was Italianate with an inbuilt Ark in a semi-circular apse with a coffered ceiling. The columns flanking the Ark and that carry the gallery are Corinthian above, superimposed on Tuscan Doric below, all with gilded capitals. The clerestory windows were retained but, instead of a flat ceiling, the rebuilt version has a shallow barrel vault and the galleries are tiered and were open, the heavy brass-work lattices obscuring the women from view having been dispensed with

(a high timber lattice *mehitzah* has been reinstated by the Bobovers). The concave mahogany Ark with its sliding doors was brought in its entirety from Bishopsgate. It was inspired by that of *James Spiller*'s Great Synagogue in Duke's Place and in turn influenced those of a number of other synagogues including **Sandys Row** and Birmingham's **Singers Hill**. Three surviving massive candlesticks that now stand in front of the Ark were removed from the *bimah*, which has been dispensed with. Heavily lacquered, these are the original 1830s brass work.[24]

STAINED GLASS: The rear (north) window is thought to be the earliest (*c* 1957) stained glass window in a British synagogue depicting the emblem of the State of Israel, a view of the Citadel and the Rebuilt Jerusalem. Dedicatory *inscription* in Hebrew and English to the memory of long-serving minister REV SOLOMON LEVY.

OPENING HOURS: *Shabbat* and festival services. Other times by appointment,

through the office of the Bobover Talmud Torah ('Bobov Foundation Primary School'), 84–7 Egerton Road, N16 6UE: tel 020 8880 1425 (opposite, upstairs on the left-hand side of the yard).

Former **Stamford Hill Beth HaMedrash,** now **Vishnitz Talmud Torah**

26 Lampard Grove, N16 6XB

George Coles, 1928

Formerly known as Grove Lane Beth HaMedrash, affiliated to the Federation of Synagogues, this institution has always been a bastion of Orthodoxy, once Lithuanian, but since 1986 Hasidic. It is a substantial two-storey red-brick building in stripped classical style with concrete dressings and a hipped slate roof. *Foundation stones.*

INTERIOR: Galleried with a shallow domed ceiling, now the school hall, with classrooms inserted around the sides. The architect was better known for cinemas.

ACCESS: School office: tel 020 8806 0898.

Walford Road Synagogue

99 Walford Road, N16 8EF

This was a brick Wesleyan chapel (1865) converted into the 'Sha'are Mazel Tov' ('Gates of Good Fortune') Synagogue in 1920 for an independent Jewish congregation that had begun life in a house at no. 99 Belgrade Road in

The former Stamford Hill Beth HaMedrash, now the Vishnitz Talmud Torah school (E020053)

The doorway at South Tottenham Synagogue (AP for SJBH)

1912. It was extensively rebuilt in 1931. The interior, with painted donors' boards decorating the gallery fronts, is reminiscent of earlier East End synagogues, such as **Princelet Street**, although here there is a shallow barrel-vaulted ceiling rather than a skylight.

LOCATION: Corner Nevill Road.

OPENING HOURS: *Shabbat* and festival services. Tel 020 7249 1599; www. walfordroadsynagogue.org

South Tottenham Synagogue

111 Crowland Road, N15 6UR

Richard Seifert, 1938

The only known synagogue designed by *Richard* (born *Reuben*) *Seifert* (1910–2001) before he 'made it' after the Second World War as architect of high-rise office blocks such as Centre Point (1966) and the NatWest Tower (1981). He was a self-made Swiss-born Jewish immigrant who

grew up in a family of 10 in the East End. A modest single-storey red-brick central range is jazzed up with a massive deco doorway. The hall (*Norman Green*, 1978) bore the brunt of a serious arson attack in 2004. The interior of the synagogue has been much modernised.

LOCATION: Set back behind houses opposite Elm Park Avenue.

OPENING HOURS: *Shabbat* and weekday services: tel 020 8880 2731.

Adath Yisroel *Bet Taharah* (Mortuary)

Burma Road, N16 9BJ

All that remains of the substantial Adath Yisroel Synagogue (*S Clifford Tee*, 1911) at 125–6 Green Lanes. This strictly Orthodox community, modelled on the lines of the separatist *Austrittsgemeinden* in Germany, had started life as the Tottenham Beth HaMedrash at 127 Newington Green Road in 1886. Their synagogue was built on a square with a dome, a plan very fashionable in Germany before the First World War. This was the only *bet taharah* built within the curtilage of a synagogue and right in a residential neighbourhood (next door to the Burma Road Estate). It was in use until *c* 2009.

LOCATION: Close to Burma Road Estate. Redevelopment likely.

Former **Tottenham Jewish Home and Hospital**

Sycamore Gardens, 295 Tottenham High Road, N15 4RQ

H H & M E Collins, 1899–1901, synagogue c 1913–15

This began life as the 'Jewish Home for Incurables' in 1889. *Marcus E Collins*, son of *Hyman Henry Collins*, was winner of a limited competition in 1899 in which six Jewish architects participated. Fashionable red-brick and terracotta mock Jacobean sporting a series of curly Dutch-style gables and barley-sugar chimneys. A synagogue, also by *Marcus Collins*, formed part of the 1913–15 extension. On closure in 1996 the high-quality carved oak fittings, including panelling and the Ark, were rescued and recycled at the **Sukkat Shalom Reform Synagogue** in Wanstead (*see* below). A sensitive conversion of the former Home and Hospital into Housing Association flats, the buildings are set back from the busy street behind the original spearhead railings and leafy London plane trees. An outhouse to the north was formerly the hospital mortuary.

LOCATION: West side, next door to the College of North East London.

Across the road at **366A Tottenham High Road** is the former home (1910–2003) of the **Tottenham Hebrew Congregation** (Federation), which had begun as a *minyan* in the Tottenham Jewish Home and Hospital in 1904.

The building itself was originally the Clarion Workingmen's Club, much altered.

BURIAL GROUNDS IN ENFIELD

Edmonton Western Cemetery

Montagu Road, Angel Road, Lower Edmonton, N18 2NF

1886

Acquired in 1884; first interment 1886, after the official closure of **Fulham Road** (*see* below), the original burial ground of the defunct Western Synagogue, whose building in Alfred Place (*Claude Waterlow Ferrier*, 1915–18) was bombed in 1941. The salvaged doors, with their decorative metalwork, were reused for the large two-storey *ohel*-cum-caretaker's flat in the forecourt. *Date stones.* Adath Yisroel section (C) opened in 1909.

ACCESS: Separate entrance from Federation cemetery on Montagu Road. Sunday to Thursday, Friday morning. Closed *Shabbat* and festivals. Western Marble Arch Synagogue Burial Society: tel 020 7724 7702.

NB The Western acquired a new site at **Cheshunt**, Bullscross Ride, EN7 5HT (1967–8). On-site office: tel 01992 717 820; shared with the Jewish Joint Burial Society of the Reform and Liberal synagogues: tel 020 8989 5252; www.jjbs.org.uk

Enfield *Ohel*
(AP for SJBH)

Edmonton Federation Cemetery

Montagu Road, Angel Road, Lower Edmonton, N18 2NF

1890

A grim urban site containing at least 10,000 graves, situated in a run-down inner-city residential area overlooked by tower blocks. The original land was acquired in 1889 from the contiguous **Western Synagogue Cemetery** by Samuel Montagu, the 1st Lord Swaythling, the founder of the Federation. He paid for later extensions. The street outside was renamed after him (formerly Jeremy's Green Lane), as were some others in the neighbourhood (eg Swaythling Close), as well as the local school. The earliest tombstone can be found in block A, row 1, no. 1: Esther, daughter of Philip and Eva Marchinski d 16 April and buried 18 April 1890. As well as Jewish communal notables such as Samuel Montagu, and his rebellious daughter Lily Montagu, a founder of Liberal Judaism, a number

of Hasidic *rebbes* were buried at Edmonton before the opening of the Adath cemetery down the road at **Enfield.** Small *ohalim* were erected for leaders of Belz, Sassov and Dzikov Hasidim, plus a stripped classical *ohel* in memory of *HaGaon* ('the great sage') Rabbi Eleazer Gordon, the Telzer *Rav*. He was born near Vilna, Lithuania, and died while on a fundraising trip to England in 1910.

ACCESS: Sunday to Thursdays, Friday morning. Closed *Shabbat* and Jewish holidays. Office: tel 020 8807 2268; www.federationofsynagogues.com/burial-society/

Enfield Jewish Cemetery

246 Carterhatch Lane, EN1 4BG

1925

Plans were approved and the site was purchased in 1924 by the Adath Yisroel and Union of Orthodox Hebrew Congregations under the spiritual leadership of Rabbi Victor (Avigdor) Schonfeld. The **Spitalfields Great Synagogue** (*see* above)

Chest tomb of Sir Isaac Lyon Goldmid at the West London Reform Cemetery (AP for SJBH)

had its own plot from 1932 in a hedged section located at the southern corner. The unusual white-glazed brick-fronted *ohel* by *Hamilton* (1937) has hexagonal corner turrets, slit windows and shallow domes. The oldest grave (1925) is situated in the far corner, in the second row, at the end of the western boundary wall (plot A, row 1, grave 1); the English name of the deceased, Myer Rosenthal, like the inscriptions on every tombstone in this strictly Orthodox cemetery, is given on the back of the upright stone which is otherwise entirely in Hebrew. *Ohalim* to eastern European Hasidic *rebbes* who settled in London sport candles and lanterns lit according to Hasidic custom. The *ohel* over the *kever* of the Shatzer Rebbe (Rabbi Shulim Moshovitz, 1878–1958), with pious extracts from his long 'Ethical Will and

Testament' hand-painted on the walls, was burnt down and rebuilt in the 1990s, the fire probably caused by the candles.

ACCESS: Sunday to Thursday, Friday morning. Closed *Shabbat* and Jewish holidays. Adath Yisroel Burial Society: tel 020 8802 6262.

NB The Adath opened a successor cemetery at **Silver Street**, Goffs Oak, Hertfordshire, EN7 5JE in 1963.

BOROUGH OF ISLINGTON

West London Reform Cemetery

Kingsbury Road, N1 4AW

1843

Also known as Balls Pond Road, off which lies Kingsbury Road; the earliest Reform cemetery in the country, which was opened in 1843 and was in regular use until the opening of **Golders Green** in 1895 (*see* below).

Reserved plots were taken up until 1952. It was saved from destruction in 1995 thanks to a campaign mounted by the Jewish Genealogical Society of Great Britain with the support of English Heritage, and declared a Conservation Area. Under an 'enabling development' compromise, construction of Peabody Housing Association flats was permitted on an unused section. There are a number of elaborate Victorian memorials in Portland stone, granite and marble, including those of the emancipationist Isaac Lyon Goldsmid, Joseph (Levy) Lawson, the founder of the *Daily Telegraph* and the first Anglo-Jewish architect, *David Mocatta*. The styles employed and the liberal use of English inscriptions indicate the acculturation of a certain section of the Jewish elite in 19th-century England, while the mixture of upright Ashkenazi and flat Sephardi stones reflects the cultural mix of the early founders of the Reform movement. The old lodge has completely disappeared.

ACCESS: By appointment via West London Synagogue: tel 020 7723 4404.

BOROUGH OF NEWHAM

Former **Upton Park Synagogue**

56 Tudor Road, E6 1DR

1923

Upton Park was admitted to the United Synagogue as an 'Associate' synagogue in 1923. In the same year, this purpose-built synagogue was quickly run up; the foundation stone was laid in June and the consecration ceremony was held in September.[25] The identity of the architect remains an enigma – perhaps *Cecil Eprile*. The simple gallery-less single-storey yellow-brick building had a low-slung pitched roof. Such a profile would have been familiar from *Der Heym* (the 'Old Country') to the eastern European parents of the mainly British-born congregation who had moved out of the East End proper. The synagogue became a full 'Constituent' of the United in 1937, and closed in 1972.

The building was being used as a Morman church *c* 2000 but in *c* 2011 became an Almadiyya Muslim movement mosque. It has been considerably spruced up with a new extension and has been rendered and whitewashed. New signage in smart chrome-coloured lettering on the gable proudly announces its latest incarnation.

LOCATION: Best viewed from the east (rear), Tudor Road side.

Former **East Ham and Manor Park Synagogue**

26–8 Carlyle Road, Manor Park, E12 6BN

Cecil J Eprile, 1926–7

For the United Synagogue. Closed 1978 and now a Sikh Gurdwara and community centre (Ravidassia community). The plain pinkish-grey brickwork of the synagogue, another one with traditional baroque gable, has since 2000 been rendered and painted in a pale pink. The still yellow-brick hall has a flat gable. It is most unusual to see the *date* of opening embossed in relief on the drainpipe hoppers.

NB The former Federation **Leyton and Walthamstow Synagogue** at 79 Queens Road, E17 8QR, corner with Chelmsford Road (1937, architect not identified), was also heavily rendered and whitewashed, with a steeply pitched and gabled roof (with a segmental pediment). It became the Masjid-e-Umer Mosque, which has a reputation for radical Islam. The old building has now (since 2006) disappeared, replaced by a brand new mosque.

BURIAL GROUNDS IN NEWHAM

Three large Jewish cemeteries, all administered by the United Synagogue, are situated quite close to one another in the Borough of Newham. All are forbidding places, with ranks of graves, mostly conventional upright

memorials made of York stone or white marble unrelieved by grass and flowerbeds. Urban foxes prowl around. So do vandals. An anti-Semitic outrage took place at West Ham in the summer of 2005.

ACCESS: The caretaker is based at East Ham – the only one of the three cemeteries which is still open: Sunday to Thursday, Friday morning. Closed *Shabbat* and Jewish holidays. Parking is available inside Plashet.

CONTACT: United Synagogue Burial Society (based at Bushey Cemetery): tel 020 8950 7767; www.theus.org.uk

West Ham Jewish Cemetery

Buckingham Road, E15 1SP

1856

Acquired by the **New Synagogue** (Great St Helen's) because **Brady Street** had been closed under the 1853 Burial Act, and soon shared with the Great Synagogue (Duke's Place). *H H Collins* designed all the buildings on site, including a 'large mortuary hall [*ohel*]' and 'a proper lavatory for efficiently washing the dead [*bet taharah*]' as well as the keeper's 'retiring rooms' [a flat over the *ohel*], 'a tool house, &c for keeping the biers' and 'a watch house' (to guard against grave robbers) – none of which survive today.[26]

This bleak site is dominated by the elegant marble Renaissance

The Rothschild Mausoleum by Matthew Digby Wyatt (K031465)

rotunda of the **Rothschild Mausoleum** by *Matthew Digby Wyatt* (1866, Grade II). Commissioned by Ferdinand de Rothschild (1839–98) of Waddesdon in memory of his young wife 'Eva' Evelina de Rothschild (1839–66) who died in childbirth aged 27. Both are buried inside in a pair of marble chest tombs, behind ornamental gates, flanked by urns and replete with foot-scrapers. Carved *inscriptions* feature the entwined initials of the deceased.

Located in two strips behind the Rothschild Mausoleum towards the back (north) wall and marked by modern *plaques* are remains from the former **Hoxton** burial ground, of the defunct Hambro Synagogue (Magpie Alley, Fenchurch Street, 1707–1878). These were reinterred at West Ham in 1960 when the United Synagogue, with the agreement of the Chief Rabbi (Israel Brodie),[27] allowed the Hoxton site to be destroyed for redevelopment by the London County Council. A row of surviving 18th-century tombstones can be seen to the right of the path that runs behind the mausoleum, one clearly dated 1794.

Plashet Jewish Cemetery

High Street North, E12 6PQ
1896

Purchased 1888 but not used until 1896 because **West Ham** was becoming full. It has an ornamental entrance gateway on Plashet High Street (west

side), but the Victorian caretaker's house at **no. 361** has been sold off and much altered. The red-brick *ohel* by *N S Joseph*, with arched doorway, is at the rear of a courtyard immediately behind the main gates. An extensive L-shaped site.

East Ham Jewish Cemetery

Marlow Road, High Street South, E6 3QG
1919

The whitewashed *ohel* (1924) by *H W Ford* in the middle dominates the grim site, with paths radiating from it dividing the cemetery into four main blocks. The oldest tombstone (G 11, to the right of the path leading from the main gate), is easily spotted by its neatly kept privet surround, and the poignant inscription reads:
ERECTED BY THE BURIAL SOCIETY OF THE UNITED SYNAGOGUE TO ABLE SEAMAN JACOB EMANUEL [JOHN KELLY] WHO DIED ON JANUARY 6TH WHILST ON ACTIVE SERVICE, AND WAS THE FIRST TO BE INTERRED WITHIN THIS CEMETERY ON JANUARY 12TH 1919 AGED 25.

Highams Park and Chingford Synagogue

81A Marlborough Road, E4 9AJ
Israel Schultz, 1937

Plain modernist synagogue with a flat roof in buff brick with a single-storey

faience-clad entrance, designed for the United Synagogue by *Israel Schultz (Ivor Shaw, c* 1905–33). The low foyer has rounded corners, 1937; classrooms at the rear 1953; and the matching hall was added next door in 1968–9. Spot the join. *Foundation stones.*

INTERIOR: Strangely, the Ark faces north. Without a gallery, has art deco upholstered, tip-up seats salvaged from a local cinema. On display is an illuminated bound history of the congregation.

OPENING HOURS: *Shabbat* and festivals. Tel 020 8523 1609; www.hpcshul. For any changes check the 'Local Communities' pages of the United Synagogue website: www.theus.org.uk

Sukkat Shalom Reform Synagogue

Victory Road, Hermon Hill, E11 1UL

Housed in the Venetian Gothic former Merchant Seaman's Orphan Asylum (*George Somers Clarke Senior,* 1861–3, Grade II★), latterly part of Wanstead Hospital. In 1994–6 the redundant building was acquired by the new Jewish congregation, who restored and provided a home to the magnificent Ark and panelling rescued from the **Tottenham Jewish Home and Hospital** (*see* above), with the support of the Heritage Lottery Fund. It reopened as a synagogue in 2000. A model conservation project by *Ronald Wylde Associates.*

OPENING HOURS: *Shabbat* morning services and

The Ark from the Tottenham Jewish Home and Hospital installed at Sukkat Shalom Reform Synagogue
(AP for SJBH)

festivals. Heritage Open Days (September). Other times and groups by appointment: tel 020 8530 3345; www.sukkatshalom.org.uk

Rainham Federation Cemetery

416 Upminster Road North, RM13 9SB

1938

The successor to **Edmonton** occupies a very extensive, flat, open site. The red-brick Italianate *ohel* complex, with curved covered arcades, and gateway on the road to match, was designed by Federation architect *Digby Lewis Solomon* of *Lewis Solomon*

& Son. Foundation stone. The buildings were consecrated on 20 February 1938, and the first burial (in block A, row 10, no. 10) of Nathan Weitzen (d 20 February 1938, aged 53) took place on the same day. The cemetery is laid out in four basic blocks, largely full on the east but empty on the west. Holocaust memorial by *Jackie King-Clyne* (2002).

ACCESS: Sunday to Thursday, Friday morning. Closed *Shabbat* and Jewish holidays. On-site office: tel 01708 552 825; www.federationofsynagogues.com/burial-society/

Brentwood Sephardi Cemetery

Dytchleys, Coxtie Green, Brentwood, CM14

Remains of some 7,500 burials from the Georgian (1733) part of the **Mile End Nuevo** (*see* above) were controversially reinterred here in 1974 in the manner of a mass war grave. No tombstones. *Plaques.* The land was donated by Queen Mary, University of London in a lucrative development deal struck with the Spanish and Portuguese Jews' Congregation, which was achieved through the passage of a private Act of Parliament.

LOCATION: Not easy to find! Open gate located on south side of Coxtie Green Road, between Weald Park Hotel & Golf Club (CM14 5RJ) and Oakhurst Farm (CM14 5QB).

Former **Southend and Westcliff-on-Sea Hebrew Congregation**

99 Alexandra Road, Southend, SS1 1HD

Parkes & Evans, 1911–12

Built for the Jewish East End overspill and holiday-makers. Essentially an Edwardian orientalist building, with a pleasing if unadventurous red-brick and stone façade, a pair of little turrets, a curved gable and floral leaded lights. But it masks the forward-looking use of new building technology: reinforced concrete for the floors and gallery, and partial steel framing. The slender columns under the cantilevered gallery were hardly structural, but do qualify Alexandra Road as probably the oldest synagogue in the country tentatively to employ this new technology before the First World War. It closed in 2001 and in 2002 became a children's nursery, as it says on the new sign that covers up the Hebrew inscription on the pediment (Genesis 28:17). *Foundation stone.*

The current **Southend and Westcliff-on-Sea Hebrew Congregation** is at **Finchley Road**, Westcliff, SS0 8AD (*Norman Green*, 1967). A typically 1960s wood-panelled interior, but chiefly remarkable for the panoramic stained-glass window dominating the first-floor landing, visible from the street, which depicts the topography of Jerusalem.

Installed after the Six Day War. Glassmaker unidentified.

OPENING HOURS: *Shabbat* and festival services: tel 01702 344 900.

NB **Southend and Westcliff Jewish Cemetery,** Stock Road SS2 5QF (1962), adjoins Sutton Road municipal cemetery. Sutton Road contains a Reform section with its own gate further round on Stock Road.

The former Southend and Westcliff-on-Sea Hebrew Congregation building (AA060826)

שמע ישראל יהוה אלהינו יהוה אחד

The lavish interior of the New West End Synagogue (E030009)

The New West End Synagogue

St Petersburgh Place, Bayswater, W2 4LB
(Postal address: St Petersburgh Mews, W2 4JT)
George Audsley with N S Joseph, 1877–9, Grade I

London's most splendid synagogue interior, rich in High Victorian 'orientalist' opulence

Younger 'sister' of **Princes Road Synagogue** in **Liverpool**, the New West End was essentially the work of the same Liverpool architect, *George Audsley* (1838–1925). Audsley, in keeping with his total-design philosophy, designed the Ark, *bimah*, original pulpit and even the gaslight fittings himself, and engaged other craftsmen to execute the pieces, including some of the same Liverpool firms who had worked on Princes Road. Not surprisingly, the two buildings have much in common. Both were upgraded in 2007–8, bringing them into line with **Bevis Marks** as the only Grade I listed synagogues in England.[28]

The *foundation stone* was laid on 7 June 1877 (unfortunately it is now hidden inside the back office). The good site, a short distance from the Bayswater Road, was purchased with the help of the Rothschilds and a loan from the United Synagogue. The synagogue was consecrated by the Chief Rabbi on 30 March 1879. It stood along the street from the new Greek church (later Cathedral) of St Sophia in Moscow Road, which was built at exactly the same time (1878–9) in a neighbourhood stuffed with lavish churches. The social elite of West End Jewry had also arrived!

The synagogue has an imposing tripartite front elevation with corner turrets. It is of red brick with Mansfield stone and terracotta dressings. An enormous wheel window is set within a cusped horseshoe arch, and a cusped horseshoe-shaped portal dominates the façade. Immediately above the main entrance, with its massive teak doors on wrought iron hinges, are placed the *Luhot* that discreetly hint at the identity of the building. As at Liverpool, the style is eclectic, combining Gothic, Romanesque, Assyrian and Moorish elements.

INTERIOR: Inside 'orientalism' predominates. The gallery of the basilica-shaped prayer hall is carried on horseshoe arches and octagonal columns. The gilded and turreted Ark, Assyrian in inspiration, is set beneath a large horseshoe arch, the arch being repeated at the other end of the space. The choir loft behind the Ark has an elaborate grille. In the vestibule hangs a delightful clock with Hebrew face, the shape of which is modelled on the Ark.

The grand vestibule, currently whitewashed, was originally much more richly treated, while the interior of the prayer hall itself was once plainer than it is today. The present colour scheme of alabaster, green and gold, inspired by the Ark, was carried out in 1895, when the costly marble cladding of the columns and walls was also introduced (see the various donors' *plaques* in the vestibule, gallery and adjoining hall). The new interior design, using a mixture of English, Irish and continental (mainly Italian and Swiss Cipollino) marbles, was supervised by Sir Isidore Spielmann, the noted impresario, exhibition organiser and art critic of late Victorian and Edwardian London. The arabesque decoration in the arch spandrels also dates from this period, each of a different design, for which alternative stylistic references were claimed, variously derived from Constantinople and Ravenna.

The gallery fronts, made of pine, are exceptionally richly panelled with carved ebony pilasters to form a blind balustrade, painted and gilded with a low open ornamental brass railing. Hebrew *inscriptions* in gilded brass tracery run around the bottom of the gallery fronts and high up on the walls, a rare example of the decorative use of Hebrew calligraphy in an English synagogue, comparable with the

synagogues of medieval Spain. The texts, mainly from the Psalms, were chosen by the Revd Simeon Singer, the New West End's most eminent minister, translator of the eponymous *Authorised Daily Prayer Book* (the 'Singer's *Siddur*') of the United Synagogue since 1890. (His portrait by *Solomon J Solomon* hangs over the mantlepiece in the synagogue hall.) The inscriptions were designed by the East End stonemasons *Harris & Son*, and made by *Shirley & Co.* The lettering is joined by elaborate scrollwork,

Street elevation of New West End Synagogue
(DP021640)

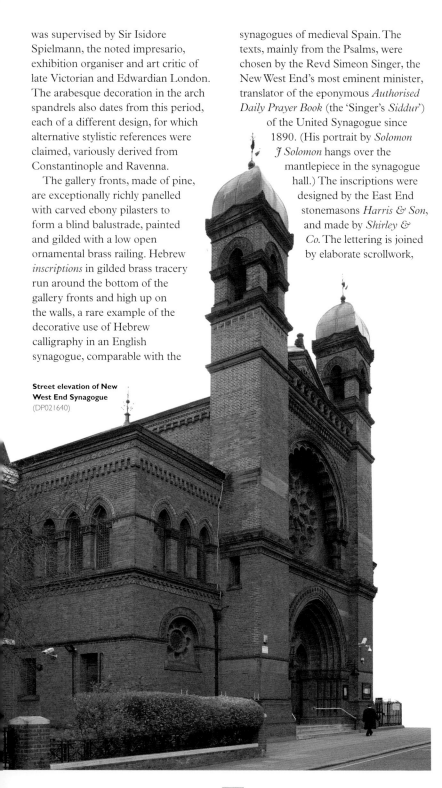

View from the gallery (E030025)

embossed and cut from a single sheet of metal.

The plush *bimah* is slightly displaced to the rear, although this is an Ashkenazi synagogue. The alabaster and marble pulpit, with its 1m (3ft) high plinth, was, like the Ark and *bimah*, made by *Norbury, Upton & Paterson* of Liverpool, but was not designed by *Audsley* nor installed until 1907.

STAINED GLASS: Most of the stained glass at St Petersburgh Place was commissioned from *Nathaniel H J Westlake* between 1905 and 1907 so was not part of the original scheme. The west wheel window was made by *R B Edmundson* of Manchester. The rose window over the Ark is by the Hungarian Jewish refugee glassmaker *Erwin Bossanyi*, commissioned in 1935 by Rozsica Rothschild, née

Wertheimstein, a fellow Hungarian emigré. It incorporates classic Jewish symbols such as a *Sefer Torah, Luhot, menorah, shofar,* spice box, *lulav* and more. The window is signed in the bottom right-hand corner by the artist.

The interior of the synagogue, darkened by the arrival of the stained glass, was originally lit by gas, but converted to electricity in 1894. A variety of exotic light fittings survive in the building, both rare gasoliers made to *Audsley*'s design by *Hart Son Peard & Co* (London) and later electroliers, ascribed to *Sir George Aitchison* (the architect of Leighton House in nearby Holland Park).

OPENING HOURS: *Shabbat* and festival services. Heritage Open Days (September). Other times and group bookings by appointment: tel 020 7229 2631; www.newwestend.org.uk

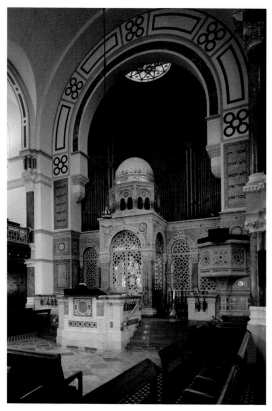

West London's pipe organ is the only example in a synagogue in Britain, forming the backdrop to the magnificent Ark and *Bimah*, combined in the Reform manner (J030141)

West London Synagogue

34 Upper Berkeley Street,
W1H 5QE

(Postal address: 33 Seymour Place, W1H 5AU)

Davis & Emanuel, 1869–70, Grade II

The 'cathedral' of Reform Judaism in Britain. The breakaway 'West London Congregation of British Jews' had been founded in 1840 but was devoid of the radical reforming zeal of classical Reform Judaism as it developed in German-speaking lands from the early 19th century. 'Upper Berkeley Street' retained a central *bimah* until 1897,[29]

when today's strongly eastern axis of Ark, *bimah* and pulpit – the arrangement typical of Reform – was created. Moreover, West London was built with a gallery that was reserved for women well into the 20th century. Over its doorways are *inscriptions* in Hebrew: the opening and closing verses of *Eshet Hayil*, 'A Woman of Worth', the traditional hymn praising the Jewish wife, sung at the dinner table on *Shabbat* eve (Proverbs 31:10–31). The organ, by contrast, was an innovation. West London is the only synagogue in Britain that possesses an

integrated pipe organ. The *Davis & Emanuel* practice designed the panelled circular choir and organ chamber behind the Ark in 1908. The organ case was by *Gray & Davison*, 1869, rebuilt 1908 by *Harrison & Harrison* of Durham, who also made the organs at Westminster Abbey and the Royal Albert Hall.

The narrow street frontage is of Portland stone, predominantly Romanesque in style with orientalising hints, corner buttresses but no proper turrets. Behind lies a roomy complex. The fine double-flight staircase at the end of a long panelled north–south vestibule sports a pair of bronze lamps inscribed on their bases: PRESENTED A.M. 5609 [=1849] – that is, these were brought from the previous Reform synagogue at 50 Margaret Street, Cavendish Square (*David Mocatta*, 1849).

INTERIOR: A cavernous domed space, which is an exact square, 21m by 21m (70ft by 70ft). The ceiling is supported on massive marble clustered columns at each corner. It lost its elaborate mosaic and gilding to bomb damage during the Second World War, but the Hebrew *inscriptions* in gilded mosaic survived. The bronze gallery fronts are of open lattice-work *mashrabiya*, derived from Egyptian mosques, and match the choir screens and grille over the orientalist-inspired Ark. The freestanding form of this Ark, made of white stone, richly decorated with inlaid marbles and covered

Ceiling light, West London Synagogue
(BB for SJBH)

with an octagonal drum and gilded dome – combined with the visibility of the *Sifrei Torah* inside – is highly unconventional even in a Reform synagogue. The massive hexagonal pulpit is raised on 10 steps, built of white stone with inlaid marbles to match the Ark. The brass *hanukiah* was brought from Margaret Street. Adjoining hall on Seymour Place by *Mewes & Davis* 1933–4, and 1974 wing by *Julian Sofaer*.

OPENING HOURS: *Shabbat* and festival services. Heritage Open Days (September). Other times and group visits by appointment: tel 020 7723 4404; www.wls.org.uk

Old **Central** **Synagogue**

36–40 Hallam Street, W1W 6NW

N S Joseph, 1869–70

London's Central Synagogue was the first thoroughly oriental-style synagogue, both inside and out, constructed in Britain.

It was bombed during the Blitz. However, if you walk around to the office at the back of the rebuild on **Great Portland Street** (by *C Edmund Wilford & Son*, 1956–8), you will see that the yellow-brick rear wall of Joseph's original building has survived. Note the attractive interlaced horseshoe windows on the balconies with their Moorish red-and-white striped heads.

OPENING HOURS: *Shabbat* and weekday services. Tel 020 7580 1355; www. centralsynagogue.org.uk

Former **Westminster Jews' Free School**

5 Hanway Place, W1T 1HD

H H Collins, 1882–3

Only the frontage now survives, forming the rear wall of the Sainsbury's supermarket on Tottenham Court Road and as part of the 'Hanway Place' residential development (2000). Institution founded 1811. Of yellow-and-red brick with terracotta band, with an *inscription* proclaiming the building's date and function.

Woburn House, former **Jewish Community Offices**

20 Tavistock Square, WC1H 9HQ

Messrs Joseph (Ernest Joseph), 1930–2

A strongly articulated 1930s office block, eight storeys high, of red brick with stone facing at street level. Has a spacious basement, upstairs meeting hall, mezzanine and mansard roof with dormers. Much variety in the window openings. The headquarters of British Jewry until 1996, including offices of the Board of Deputies, the United Synagogue, the Office of the Chief Rabbi and London Beth Din, and the Adler Hall was a popular venue for functions. The University of London acquired the, by then, dreary building, widely nicknamed 'Wobegone House' and spruced it up; now transformed into the 'Woburn House Conference Centre'. Meanwhile, Anglo-Jewry has lost its collective central London base.

LOCATION: At the north-east corner of the square, opposite the British Medical Association (site of the first suicide bombing of a London bus, 7 July 2005).

NB Woburn House was also home to the **Jewish Museum** until it moved to Camden Town in 1994.

Spanish and Portuguese Jews' Congregation

9 Lauderdale Road, Maida Vale, W9 1LT

(Postal address: 2 Ashworth Gardens, W9 1JY)

Davis & Emanuel, 1896, Grade II

Intended successor to **Bevis Marks** in the City. A splendid 'Byzantine' edifice for the wealthy Sephardim who had moved west to leafy Maida Vale. Of red brick with stone and concrete dressings and a copper-covered dome on a glazed drum. The dome is topped by a lantern, cupola and ball finial.

INTERIOR: The ceiling dome is pierced by 12 roundels, and is carried on substantial Swedish polished granite piers with carved capitals. A light, airy and uncluttered space lit from the beginning by electricity; the original light fittings still survive. The orientalist-inspired *Ehal* – the original was replaced soon after the synagogue was built – fails to match up to the strength of the interior. Elsewhere in the complex the modern *succah* (1998) features Islamic-style blue-and-white tiling. Incongruously, the modern library and reading room are outfitted in plush *Country Life* style.

OPENING HOURS: *Shabbat* and festival services (weekdays in *Bet Midrash*). Heritage Open Days (September). Other times and group bookings by appointment: tel 020 7289 2573; www. lauderdaleroadsynagogue. org and www.sandp.org

BOROUGH OF
KENSINGTON & CHELSEA

Holland Park Synagogue

8 St James's Gardens, W11 4RB

S B Pritlove and Manuel Nunes Costello, 1928

At the south-west corner of an elegant square that was originally laid out as a housing development in 1847. An appropriately 'Byzantine' copper-domed synagogue for a congregation (1910) predominantly of wealthy carpet merchants from the former Ottoman Empire, especially Salonika (Thessaloniki) and Smyrna (Izmir). But a precedent lay closer to home at **Lauderdale Road**.

INTERIOR: Pleasant and light with classical dark oak Ark and oval-shaped *tevah* slightly displaced to the rear in the Sephardi tradition. Notice the charming pair of *Omer* calendars flanking the *Ehal*, which are carved and gilded to match. Hebrew *date stone* in lozenge over main entrance (down side of building) and *foundation stones*. Hall by *Henry Darsa* (1951–3).

OPENING HOURS: *Shabbat* and festival services. Other times by appointment.

Spanish and Portuguese Synagogue, Maida Vale (J030136)

Tel 020 7603 7961; www.
hollandparksynagogue.com
and www.sandp.org

Former **Notting Hill Synagogue**

206–8 Kensington Park Road,
W11 1NR

Heavily rendered and
whitewashed former chapel
and Sunday school
converted for the
Federation of Synagogues
by *Lewis Solomon* in 1900.
Triple-window arcade over
the entrance. Closed and
sold in 2000. Used as a
restaurant (2006) and now
a Montessori school.

Former **Fulham and West Kensington Synagogue and Talmud Torah**

259 Lillie Road, SW6 7LL

Lewis Solomon & Son (Digby),
1926–7

According to the once
legible but painted-out *date
stone* on the lintel, this
synagogue was FOUNDED
1926–5687. Admitted to
the Federation in 1929;
absorbed by **Shepherd's
Bush** in 1959.
Undistinguished
whitewashed building with
a Baroque curved and
stepped roofline and
segmental gable. Now the
Fulham Seventh Day
Adventist Church.

BURIAL GROUND IN
CHELSEA

Western Synagogue Cemetery

Queen's Elm Parade,
Fulham Road, SW3 6EJ

1815

A tranquil and secluded
spot behind high brick

**Omer Calendar in Holland
Park Synagogue**
(BB for SJBH)

walls off the busy Fulham
Road. The Queen in
question was Elizabeth I
and this area is also
associated with silk making,
being formerly dotted with
mulberry trees. Opened in
1815 adjoining the Chelsea
Hospital for Women,
now the Royal Marsden
Hospital. In use until the
Home Office ordered its
closure in 1886, forcing
the Western Synagogue to
start to use **Edmonton.**
Reserved plots were
exempted, hence the burial
of the Dowager Dame
Cecilia Salomons, next to
her first husband, in 1892.
Her second husband was
Sir David Salomons, first
Jewish Lord Mayor of
London in 1855. The
ohel and office have
disappeared, but otherwise
it is a well-preserved, if
rather overgrown, cemetery
with some mature trees.
There is a square obelisk
(near the south-west
corner) to SOLOMON
ALEXANDER HART R.A.
PROFESSOR OF PAINTING &
LIBRARIAN TO THE ROYAL

ACADEMY, d 11 June 1881,
aged 75. Hart was the
earliest Anglo-Jewish Royal
Academician.

ACCESS: Locked. Western
Marble Arch Synagogue
Burial Society: tel 020
7724 7702.

Former **Hammersmith and West Kensington Synagogue**

69–71 Brook Green, W6 7BE

Delissa Joseph, 1890–6

Situated on a prime site
overlooking leafy Brook
Green, this red-brick
building with clerestory
closed in 2001 and
underwent transformation
into the Chinese Church in
London. This was *Delissa
Joseph*'s local synagogue
and he wasted no time in
extending it (opened 1890,
extended 1896) and in
introducing a combined
Ark and *bimah*
arrangement on the east
wall. The swept scrolled
double-flight staircase,
massive pulpit and flanking
art nouveau stained glass,
designed by *Percy L Marks*
and made by *Campbell &
Christmas* (1911), have all
now disappeared.[30] Ditto
the verses from the
Scriptures painted in gold-
shadowed Hebrew around
the walls at cornice level by
Moritz Beyl (1896). The
pews have been removed.
Only the empty Ark niche
survives, and a few leaded
lights and the ironwork
gallery supports. English,
Cantonese and Mandarin
church services are all now
available at this former
United synagogue.

Former Shepherd's Bush Synagogue

1A Poplar Grove, W6 7RF

Henry Darsa, 1938–9

For a congregation founded in 1913 and which joined the Federation. A smooth whitewashed stucco façade, lined out to resemble ashlar, possibly an existing building merely remodelled by an obscure architect, *Henry Darsa*. Closed 1989. The Ark finished up at **Notting Hill** until that synagogue also closed, in 2000. The mansard roof and dormers were added by the Jehovah's Witnesses who took over the building. Note the one remaining, rather deco, window with inverted curves at the left of the front door. The other one on the right has been knocked through to create a subsidiary entrance. However, the pair of original lantern bracket lamps survive. The two *foundation stones* were only barely legible back in 2000.

Ealing Synagogue

15 Grange Road, W5 5QN

The extension of the District line westwards in 1903 led to the development of the smart London suburbs of Ealing and Acton. An informal *minyan* reorganised itself into a congregation in 1919 and the large Victorian House in Grange Road became their synagogue (United) in 1923. A gallery was created, and the prayer hall was fitted out with the original convex Ark by *Delissa Joseph* that came from **Hampstead Synagogue**.

The importance of this Ark has increased on account of the damage recently sustained by **Hackney**'s and the complete loss of **Cardiff**'s, which were of almost identical design. Ealing have preserved this Ark in the small synagogue created in the communal hall (*W S Blount*, 1938) in 2011. The fine panelled doors remain. Unfortunately, the height and depth have been reduced to fit the lower ceiling height. Six large stained and leaded windows, and two small *Magen David* hexagons made for the original synagogue (these look 1920s) are mounted on the blind walls in light boxes. Consent was refused to demolish and redevelop the old house as flats; instead it has been leased to a children's nursery. The *inscription* in relief EALING & ACTON DISTRICT SYNAGOGUE 5684 – 1923 on the pointed arch and column capitals of the whitewashed main entrance was still legible in 2012.

ACCESS: 020 8579 4894; www.ealingsynagogue.org.uk

Liberal Jewish Synagogue

28 St John's Wood Road, NW8 7HA

Messrs Joseph (Ernest Joseph), 1925

Completely rebuilt with adjoining flats in 1989–91 by *Preston Rubins Associates*, with *The Fitzroy Robinson Partnership* (exterior), *Koski Solomon* and *Cantor Schwartz* (interior) behind *Ernest Joseph*'s original Greek Revival Portland stone portico. With its giant order of six Ionic columns, the portico was dismantled and reconstructed, slightly altered in scale in the process, by *Stonewest Cox* stonemasons.

The Liberal Jewish Synagogue had evolved out of the Jewish Religious Union (1902). The new purpose-built synagogue 'On the Lord's side' of St John's Wood Road (ie the cricket ground) was the successor to a converted (1911) chapel in Hill Street, Marylebone. New *foundation stone*; the old ones are preserved at the **Liberal Jewish Cemetery** (see below).

INTERIOR: State-of-the-art galleried auditorium based on an octagon. Fine acoustic space enhanced by an electronic sound system and subtle lighting control. A measure of natural light is let into the enclosed space through a slatted ceiling lantern. Organ by *Copeman Hart*. The American cherrywood seating (by *Bob Pulley*) is disposed around the polished oak platform that serves as both *bimah* and pulpit. The Ark surround is a curved screen clad in Jerusalem limestone, to recall the Western Wall. This sets off the Ark doors, which are framed in bronze and made of copper basketwork and metallic mesh in a diaper pattern (Ark and *ner tamid* by *Amit Schur*). *Inscription*: Psalm 100:2. A Holocaust memorial of Kilkerry limestone by *Anish Kapoor* (1996) is located in the old vestibule immediately behind the Ark. From here, note the slit window set in a wall made of deep red crushed marble under a sweeping archway of Jerusalem stone. The slit is aligned on an axis with the Ark, which can be glimpsed through it. Other artwork in the building by *Hans Feibusch*, *Frank Meisler* and *William Utermohlen*.

OPENING HOURS: *Shabbat* and festival services. Heritage Open Days (September). Other times and groups by appointment: tel 020 7286 5181; www.ljs.org. Guidebook available.

New London Synagogue

33 Abbey Road, St John's Wood, NW8 0AT

H H Collins 1880–2, Grade II

In 1965 the former home of St John's Wood United Synagogue was rescued from demolition by architect and pioneer marine archaeologist *Alexander Flinder* (1921– 2001). While the United moved around the corner to a vast new edifice (*T P Bennett & Son*, 1962–4) on Grove End Road, *H H Collins'* red-brick and terracotta Italianate building became the refuge for Rabbi Dr Louis Jacobs (1920–2006) and what developed into the *Masorti* (traditionalist, that is, conservative) Jewish

Interior, looking toward the rear, New London Synagogue (J020235)

The Jewish Museum

Raymond Burton House,
129–31 Albert Street,
NW1 7NB

The richest collection of high-art Judaica in the country, dating back to 1932. Housed in a pair of houses in an early Victorian terrace (Grade II) since 1994, the museum expanded into a former Victorian piano factory behind, helped by a grant of £4.2 million from the Heritage Lottery Fund (2005). Reopened in 2010, the permanent collection now includes the medieval **Milk Street Mikveh**, but the museum is situated in an area of London that has more connections with Irish than Jewish history.

OPENING HOURS: Sunday to Thursday, Friday morning. Closed Saturday and Jewish festivals. Open public holidays (except 25, 26 December). Changing special exhibitions. Admission charge. Guidebook, shop, café (kosher): tel 020 7284 7384; www.jewishmuseum.org.uk
⊖ Camden Town.

The British Library

96 Euston Road, NW1 2DB

World-class collection of Hebrew illuminated manuscripts, incunabula and printed books, a selection of which are on permanent display in the Sir John Ritblat Gallery.

OPENING HOURS: Daily. Free admission to exhibition area; charge for special exhibitions. Admission to the library restricted to ticket-holders or by special appointment. Tel 0330 333 1144 (switchboard); www.bl.uk/onlinegallery
⊖ Euston or King's Cross.

The British Museum

Great Russell Street, WC1 3DG

Look out for the showcase on 'Judaism' in the 'Enlightenment' Gallery (Gallery 1) as soon as you enter this vast national museum. It features Georgian silver sold by **Plymouth Synagogue** in 2009.

OPENING HOURS: Daily. Free admission; charge for special exhibitions. Tel 020 7323 8000 (switchboard); www.britishmuseum.org
⊖ Goodge Street, Tottenham Court Road, Russell Square.

Ben Uri Gallery

108A Boundary Road,
St John's Wood, NW8 0RH

The Ben Uri Art Society was established in 1915 to encourage contemporary Anglo-Jewish artists. Changing exhibitions from its own and other collections. Free.

OPENING HOURS: Sunday, Monday afternoons; Tuesday, Wednesday, Thursday 10.00 to 17.30; Friday in winter 10.00 to 15.30; closed Saturday and Jewish festivals. Tel 020 7604 3991; www.benuri.org.uk
⊖ St John's Wood or Swiss Cottage (10–15 minute walk). Buses 31, 139, 189.

Czech Memorial Scrolls Museum

Westminster Synagogue,
Kent House, Rutland Gardens,
Knightsbridge, SW7 1BX

Third floor of this refurbished mansion of 1870, which also houses the independent progressive **Westminster Synagogue** (since 1960–3) and banqueting and conference rooms. Collection of more than 1,500 *Sifrei Torah*, rescued in 1964 from destroyed communities in Bohemia, Moravia and Slovakia, repaired and redistributed to new Jewish communities around the world. Museum display created by *Fritz Armbruster* in 2008.

'Mount Zion' window by Maurice Sochachewsky at Hampstead Synagogue

OPENING HOURS: For times and appointments: tel 020 7584 3741; www.czechmemorial scrollstrust.org

⊖ Knightsbridge.

Victoria & Albert Museum

Cromwell Road, South Kensington, SW7 2RL

Permanent display (installed 2005) of Jewish sacred silver and stained glass in London's world-famous museum of the decorative arts: galleries 83 and 84 on Level 3 and objects viewable on the website.

OPENING HOURS: Daily (except 24, 25, 26 December). Free admission; charge for special exhibitions. Tel 020 7942 2000; www.vam.ac.uk

⊖ South Kensington.

Imperial War Museum

Lambeth Road, SE1 6HZ

Includes state-of-the-art Holocaust Gallery.

OPENING HOURS: Daily (except 24, 25, 26 December). Free. Tel 020 7416 5000; www.iwm.org.uk

⊖ Lambeth North, or bus from Waterloo.

Check websites for details and changes to opening times and for information about special exhibitions.

movement. Jacobs had effectively been sacked from the pulpit of the **New West End Synagogue** following the controversy in 1964 surrounding his book *We Have Reason to Believe*. He had been a candidate for the chief rabbinate.

INTERIOR: Notable use of structural cast-iron 'railway station' style in the supporting columns, spandrels to the arches and gallery fronts; original pendant light fittings and a deep coved cornice. The decor was redesigned in beige and brown by *Misha Black*, who also retained the classical timber Ark, now misleadingly painted white like stone, under a semicircular archway. The Ark doors are hidden from view behind a full-length pink velvet 'stage' curtain that serves as the *parohet*. *Foundation stones* are to be found on the rear wall (no longer external) behind the Ark – which faces the wrong way (west). In the courtyard: a bronze Holocaust memorial by *Naomi Black*.

OPENING HOURS: *Shabbat* and festival services. Heritage Open Days (September). Other times and groups by appointment: tel 020 7328 1026; www.newlondon.org.uk

Former **North West London Synagogue**

69 Caversham Road, Kentish Town, NW5 2DR

A Schonfield & Co, 1900

This modest red-brick structure has big round-

arched windows. Built on a square plan, it has lost its pyramid roof and square dome – *à la* Rome Synagogue that was then in planning (*Costa & Armanni*, 1899–1904). Closed *c* 1975 and acquired by *David Stern*, architect of several post-war synagogues, who added the mansard roof and continuous glazing. Later additions. Now used as a recording studio.

Hampstead Synagogue

1 Dennington Park Road, West Hampstead, NW6 1AX

Delissa Joseph 1892–1901, Grade II*

A monumental dark red brick exterior in eclectic Romanesque style with a prominent square tower decorated with small octagonal orientalist turrets.

INTERIOR: The exterior hides a vast and cavernous prayer hall, built on a central plan and then awkwardly extended (hence the elongated barrel-vaulted Ark), in 1900–1, and topped by an octagonal steel-ribbed dome and lantern well. In 2009–11 the decor was sensitively restored, at a cost of £2.3 million, much closer to the original white – a radical scheme by 1890s standards. At the same time, a central *bimah* was introduced, Hampstead having been the first 'Orthodox' synagogue in the country built with a Reform-inspired combined Ark and *bimah* (here at south) – although this arrangement never sat well with the central plan. The classical red-veined

Hampstead Synagogue

marble Ark, with matching screen, balustraded choir balcony and semi-circular pulpit in front, was installed 1923–4, probably by *Ernest Joseph*, given the resemblance to **Golders Green**. A plethora of *stained glass* of differing periods, including the vivid modern series 'Six Days of Creation' in the dome lunettes and the 'Mount Zion' rear window by *Maurice Sochachewsky*, date from the 1960s.

The impressive vestibule features elaborate marble war memorials. The art deco Children's Synagogue by *Ernest Joseph* (1935) was demolished in the course of the redevelopment of the rear of the site as flats in 2009–11. However, the proceeds helped finance the major repairs to the synagogue itself.

LOCATION: Close to the junction with West End Lane (B510).

OPENING TIMES: *Shabbat* and festival services. Visitors and groups by appointment: tel 020 7435 1518; www.hampsteadshul.org.uk

Once home to no fewer that four substantial purpose-built synagogues, built in the first three decades of the 20th century and all now closed. Ironically, the neighbourhood has become fashionable once again among young Jews and a new **Brondesbury Park Synagogue** now occupies the hall (*Shaw Lloyd*, 1960) of the former **Willesden Synagogue**. They have fitted up the interior with the art deco Ark and some of the fine stained glass by *David Hillman* that came from the former **Cricklewood Synagogue**.

Former **Brondesbury Synagogue**

Chevening Road, NW6 6TN

Frederick W Marks, 1904–5

The only synagogue built for the United by this talented but little-known Australian-born Jewish architect (1858–1922). Closed 1974, and in 1993

acquired by the Al-Khoei Foundation. With its copper-covered onion domes and horseshoe arcades, the building is well suited to its new role as 'the premier Shi'a mosque in the city'.[31]

LOCATION: South side of Chevening Road, at junction with Carlisle Road.

Former **Cricklewood Synagogue**

Gerard Court, 131 Walm Lane, NW2 3AU

Cecil J Eprile, 1930–1

Built for the United Synagogue. Converted into flats by *Rosenberg & Gentle* (1989), who also turned the hall next door (west) into a small synagogue, now closed. Brick and Portland stone dressings

mask structural steelwork and reinforced concrete. *David Hillman*, who was then a member of the congregation, designed 67 stained-glass windows as an integral part of the building, and worked on them over a 30-year period. The Cricklewood windows constituted the earliest set of Hillman synagogue glass in the country. They were dispersed in 2005 when the congregation was finally wound up. Fortunately, some can now be seen at the new **Brondesbury Park Synagogue** (see below).

LOCATION: East side A407 at junction with continuation of Walm Lane. The main A407 becomes Chichele Road at this point.

The former Brondesbury Synagogue has found an appropriate new use as a mosque (DP021613)

'Halleluya' window (Psalm 150), St John's Wood Synagogue (DP042770)

David Hillman (1894–1974) was Britain's most prolific designer and maker of stained glass for synagogues.

Born in Riga, the capital of Latvia, he grew up in Glasgow and was among the first students at the Glasgow School of Art. He also became a rabbi in compliance with his father's wishes.[32]

His distinctive stained glass repays close scrutiny. It is always in vivid jewel colours and is full of original detail, steeped in Jewish symbolism and accompanied by Hebrew texts drawn from biblical sources. Many of his images evoke comfortable suburban domesticity. He also dared to push at the frontiers of what was deemed permissible in the synagogue context. He included partial depictions of people by using devices such as outstretched arms, human shadows, back views or obscured profiles.

David Hillman's brother-in-law was Rabbi Isaac Herzog, Chief Rabbi of Ireland and afterwards of Palestine under the British Mandate, and thus he was also uncle of President Chaim Herzog of Israel. His good family connections may well have helped him land commissions for stained glass at prestigious London synagogues, mainly for the United Synagogue.

WHERE TO SEE HIS WINDOWS TODAY

A lot of Hillman's glass has been relocated from the synagogues for which it was originally made. Much can still be seen in the capital, as well as in **Leeds** (and at Hechal Shlomo, the seat of the chief rabbinate in Jerusalem).

'By the Rivers of Babylon' (Psalm 137) originally at Cricklewood Synagogue

St John's Wood Synagogue (United)

37–41 Grove End Road, London, NW8 9NG

T P Bennett & Son, 1962–4

This was Hillman's own *shul*[33] and today is the largest repository of his glass in the country, with a staggering total of 110 panels, each one composed of several lights. The collection incorporates the 24 windows on *Shabbat* and festival themes Hillman made for **Abbey Road** in 1954, brought to the successor synagogue around the corner. An assortment of designs, where dated, from 1964 to 1979.[34]

CONTACT: tel 020 7286 3838 www.shulinthewood.com

Central Synagogue, Great Portland Street

36–40 Hallam Street, London, W1W 6NW

C Edmund Wilford & Son, 1956–8

Hillman designed all the windows for the main prayer hall of this synagogue, rebuilt by Sir Isaac Wolfson after *N S Joseph's* Moorish 1870 Central was bombed during the Second World War.

CONTACT: tel 020 7580 1355 www.centralsynagogue.org.uk

'The righteous shall spring up like a Palm tree. He shall grow up like a cedar in Lebanon' (Psalm 92) at St John's Wood Synagogue (DP042774)

Western-Marble Arch Synagogue

32 Great Cumberland Place, London, W1H 7TN

T P Bennett & Son, 1961–2 , Grade II

These windows mainly date from 1957 to 1959, brought (1993) from the defunct independent **Western Synagogue**'s last home, **12 Crawford Place**, W1H 5JE,[35] just off the Edgware Road. Themes include Months of the Year, the Twelve Tribes of Israel and, unusually, the Matriarchs. Some are in the main Marble Arch Synagogue, flanking the Ark, plus four festival panels in the rear gallery.[36] Others are displayed in the upstairs vestibule (some in light boxes) and in the dedicated *Bet Midrash*.

CONTACT: tel 020 7723 9333; www.marblearch. org.uk

Brondesbury Park Synagogue

143–5 Brondesbury Park Road, London, NW2 5JL

Home to a number of the windows made for **Cricklewood**, including the scroll-edged centrepiece: 'By the Rivers of Babylon'. Here Hillman depicts the *kinor* – the Biblical lyre – in various forms, hung from the trees in a traditional interpretation of Psalm 137 found in eastern European Jewish folk art. Musical instruments of all types, ancient and modern, often appear in his windows. Other panels from Cricklewood are at **Hendon Synagogue**.

CONTACT: tel 020 8459 1083; www.bpark.org

Leeds United Hebrew Congregation

151 Shadwell Lane, Leeds, LS17 8DW

Peter Langtry-Langton, 1983–7

In the *Bet Midrash* see six Hillman windows including his triple-panel King George V Silver Jubilee window (1935–7) that attractively combines Jewish and English symbolism. The 'Lion of Judah' has been transformed into a bright red heraldic lion, akin to an English pub sign (see book cover). Originally made for the **Leeds New Synagogue**, Chapeltown Road (*see* p 205–6).

CONTACT: tel 0113 269 6141; www.uhcleeds.com

Smaller selections of Hillman windows can be seen at some other London synagogues, including **Hampstead** and **Hendon**.

'Peace' window, St John's Wood Synagogue (DP042845)

Former **Willesden Synagogue**

17 Heathfield Park, NW2 5JE

Fritz Landauer for Wills & Kaula, 1936–7

A rare example of direct continental modernist influence on synagogue architecture in London. *Fritz Landauer* (1883–1968), born in Augsburg and who practised in Munich, arrived as a refugee from Nazism in the 1930s. At Willesden, he used the corner site that closes the cul-de-sac to striking advantage, in terms of both plan and section, treating the forecourt as a segment of a circle and setting within it the façade angled in the shape of a chevron. The reverse-angle cantilevered space over the entrance he filled with a large window, whose grille work incorporated a Hebrew text (Genesis 28:17) and stylised *menorah* and crescent motifs.

INTERIOR: The exposed brick walls were reminiscent of Landauer's highly praised work at Plauen Reform Synagogue, Saxony (1928–30, destroyed). His reputation was hardly appreciated by his English clients at the Federation and United Synagogue (which took over the project when the congregation got into debt). At Willesden the interior was afterwards plastered and the Ark bastardised. Poor old Landauer, reduced to working as a stonemason, died almost penniless in Hampstead.[37] On closure in 2000 the interior was stripped out, even down to Landauer's distinctive light fittings and, worse, the whole frontage with its attractive banded brickwork, disappeared under a coat of dark red paint – an inexcusable act of vandalism in a Conservation Area.[38] Now the façade has been toned down by a coat of whitewash, a doubtful improvement; the windows and their lovely grille work have entirely disappeared. Willesden was bought by the same Brazilian Pentecostalist church (UCKG) that more recently acquired the listed **Hackney Synagogue** with similar dire results.

Former **Dollis Hill Synagogue**

Torah Temimah School, Parkside, Dollis Hill Lane, NW2 6RJ

Evan Owen Williams, 1937–8, Grade II

With its cantilevered reinforced concrete walls, this is the only really radical modernist synagogue in England. Traditional Jewish symbolism was incorporated into the iron railings on the street (stylised *menorah* design), and in the windows: hexagonal shapes based on the *Magen David* and U-shaped based on the *menorah*. The building technology employed was as innovative as the form, cast *in situ* using state-of-the-art 'folded plate' construction. The pioneer architect-engineer *Owen Williams* (1890–1969) designed the nearby Wembley Arena and Empire Pool in 1933–4. Although the famous twin towers of Wembley Stadium (demolished 2002) were designed by *Maxwell Ayrton* (1921–4), they were translated into concrete reality by Williams' engineering skill.

Never much loved by its congregation, the synagogue's stark interior was badly compromised by the application of wood panelling in the 1950s. In 1996 it was divided up into classroom space for the Torah Temimah Jewish primary school now housed in the building. Fortunately, externally, the

The once daring Dollis Hill Synagogue now serves as a Jewish primary school (E020054)

Grade II-listed building retains its powerful design integrity. It is frequently in need of a coat of whitewash.

LOCATION: Almost at the end of Parkside (west side) facing Gladstone Park.

BURIAL GROUNDS IN BRENT

Willesden Jewish Cemetery

Beaconsfield Road, NW10 2JE
N S Joseph, 1873

The first cemetery of the newly formed United Synagogue (1870), as successor to **West Ham**, was then situated in the 'rural village' of Willesden. Considerable care was taken in the planting of evergreens, such as laurel and fir, cedar, yew, holly and cypress, an unusual level of landscaping in a Jewish cemetery to rival the best of the new public cemeteries. Today, the impression is rather bare, with gravel paths, a tarmac road, and tightly packed graves laid out on a grid system. But Willesden contains some of the finest Jewish memorials in the country, many belonging to the 'Cousinhood' of leading families, such as the Rothschilds, Waley-Cohens and Beddingtons, some with their own family enclosures. Nevertheless, in terms of both scale and grandeur, London's Willesden cannot compete with Berlin's Weissensee Jewish cemetery.

N S Joseph's Gothic *ohel* complex is built of Kentish ragstone with Bath and Mansfield stone dressings, with diamond leaded windows of tinted cathedral glass. The roofs are covered in green-and-purple fishtail slates with red tile crestings.

The oldest sections are east and west of the central path leading south from the *ohel*, with later extensions southwards. The earliest burial: SAMUEL MOSES JP (block L, Row A, No. 1), a chest tomb by the path, which, like many of the early memorials, gives his full address: 119 YORK TERRACE, REGENTS PARK AND BOA VISTA, TASMANIA, d 2 October 1873, aged 66. He was buried on the day (5 October) that the cemetery was consecrated by the Chief Rabbi. Near him lies the artist SOLOMON J. SOLOMON d 22 July 1927. The pre-Raphaelite *Simeon Solomon's* neglected grave was given a new slab in 2014, carved by *Joss Nankoo*, thanks to a fundraising campaign led by art-lover Frank Vigon. Interesting memorials can be found mostly either side of the central path, including, to the right (west):

- Rothschild family enclosure with four granite pillars, including graves of NATHANIEL MEYER (1840–1915), 1st Baron Rothschild, and that of HANNAH, LADY ROSEBERY (1851–90), a finely carved enclosure in white marble featuring her initials, reminiscent of the **Rothschild Mausoleum** at **West Ham**.
- Rosenberg family enclosure, a series of four grey granite obelisks with aediculae.
- *Nathan Solomon Joseph* (1834–1909), architect of the cemetery and of numerous synagogues,

a grey granite memorial with two identical ones either side to commemorate his two wives, ALICE (d 1879) and LIZZIE (1859–99).

- EDGAR family, paired Corinthian columns supporting an entablature (in the north-west extension).
- ISRAEL GOLLANCZ (1863–1930) a large, well-weathered rock with an inscription taken from Beowulf (in the south-east extension).

Look out for the graves of successive Chief Rabbis NATHAN and HERMANN ADLER, J. H. HERTZ, ISRAEL BRODIE – situated to the left (east) of the path near the *ohalim* – and the great and good of Anglo-Jewry: WALEY-COHENS, MARCUS SAMUEL, LORD BEARSTED, SIR GEORGE JESSEL. The Adolf Tuck family enclosure contains cremations – although this was an 'Orthodox' cemetery. Look out too for some fine artwork: a series of terracotta memorials by *Mary Seeton Watts* and an elegant headstone designed by *Eric Gill*.

Only burials of the privileged and of those with reserved plots still take place at Willesden. After the Second World War two more large cemeteries to serve London Jewry were opened by the United Synagogue: in 1947 at **Bushey**, Little Bushey Lane, Hertfordshire, WD23 3TP, tel 020 8950 7767, and in 1960 at **Waltham Abbey**, Skillet Hill, Honey Lane, Waltham Abbey, Essex, EN9 3QS, tel 01992 714 492.

LOCATION: Entrance on Glebe Road. Contiguous with the general Willesden Cemetery and with the Liberal Jewish Cemetery, to the rear, on Pound Lane.

ACCESS: Sunday to Thursday, Friday morning. On-site office. Guided walk Heritage Open Days (September). United Synagogue Burial Society (based at Bushey Cemetery): tel 020 8950 7767. They offer a free search service for all their cemeteries on their online database; www.theus.org.uk

Liberal Jewish Cemetery

Pound Lane, Harlesden Road, NW10 2HG

1914

Adjacent to the United Synagogue cemetery but entirely separate. A unique elaborate columbarium complete with urns stored in niches can be found right inside the *ohel*, which is by *Ernest Joseph*. There is an additional columbarium wall outside. Generally, the almost complete absence of Hebrew within the cemetery and designs, including figurative sculpture, speaks of a high degree of cultural assimilation. Resistance to the plastic arts, especially to sculpted likenesses of the deceased, endured in Britain's Jewish community, which remained overwhelmingly Orthodox throughout the 19th century, nominally at least. Interesting memorials include:

• Sculptor BENNO ELKAN (1877–1960) and his wife HEDWIG. Crouching and weeping woman, in

bronze, on a granite plinth (north-west side of path).[39] Elkan had developed this design for war memorials while still in Germany, notably a work (entitled *Trauernde* and inscribed *Allen Opfern*) he made in 1925 for the cemetery in Völklingen in the Saarland. The original was destroyed in 1935.[40]

• BERNHARD BARON (1850–1929), benefactor of the **Bernhard Baron Settlement**, a granite chest tomb with Egyptian features (north-west side of path).

Memorial to Hedwig and Benno Elkan (BB for SJBH)

IN MEMORY OF
HEDWIG AND BENNO
ELKAN

FORTITER   FIDELITER
FELICITER

• Illegible but distinctive circular tomb carried on tortoises with Latin inscription TUTUS AD ICTUS, alluding either to the classical myth that the (flat) world is carried on the back of tortoises, or to the 'tortoise' formation of Roman legions with interlocking shields held over their heads for protection from missiles; either way, an unexpected encounter in a Jewish cemetery (south-east side of path).

• GEORGE NATHAN d 1 June 1927 aged 32. In Gothic script 'AND WAS LAID TO REST TO THE SOUND OF THE LAST POST IN THE UNIFORM OF THE REGIMENT HE LOVED' (north-west side of path, near the *ohel*).

This cemetery has a Portland stone war memorial plus one of the earliest Holocaust memorials in Britain, erected TISHA B'AV [6 August] 1957. *Foundation stones* from the **Liberal Jewish Synagogue** (*see above*) are located outside the *ohel*.

ACCESS: Sunday to Friday. On-site office: tel 020 8459 1635; www.ljs.org

Golders Green Synagogue

41 Dunstan Road, NW11 8AE

Lewis Solomon & Son (Digby), 1921–2, enlarged by Messrs Joseph, 1927, Grade II

A polite red-brick neo-Georgian façade with stone dressings that blends in with the genteel suburban surroundings. Yet it masks transitional building technology. *Digby Solomon's* original portion utilised steel construction but retained the column supports under the gallery, which *Ernest Joseph* had painted black to reduce their visibility. The traditional round-headed windows are set in a mixture of timber and metal frames, the latter associated more with 1930s buildings. Joseph's additions created a T-shaped, almost cruciform, plan and he added the circular ceiling lantern and Portland stone Tuscan porch, Golders Green being a contemporary of his **Liberal Jewish Synagogue**. *Foundation stones.*

INTERIOR: When *Joseph* extended the building through the Ark wall (almost doubling the size to nearly 1,000 seats), he designed a combined Ark and *bimah*, with classical oak screen and choir gallery above. Reordered in a more Orthodox direction with a central *bimah* by *Winston Newman* in 1978. However, the imposing semicircular pulpit remains, placed centrally in front of the Ark between a pair of curved red-veined Sienna marble stairs.

The conservative Italianate interior is ultimately derived from *James Spiller's* **London Great Synagogue**, Duke's Place, of 1790. This in turn influenced *John Davies's* Bishopsgate **New Synagogue** (1837–8), as reinterpreted by *Ernest Joseph* in Stamford Hill. The barrel-vaulted ceiling and clerestory lunette windows are very reminiscent of Egerton Road. Much *stained glass*, unsigned, mainly on biblical themes. Of particular interest, a window on the north wall shows a domed building labelled THE HEBREW UNIVERSITY JERUSALEM, recognisable as *Patrick* *Geddes's* unexecuted design (1919) for the Mount Scopus campus that opened in 1925, the same date as this window. Hebrew text with English translation: Isaiah 2:3: 'FOR OUT OF ZION SHALL GO FORTH THE LAW AND THE WORD OF THE LORD FROM JERUSALEM.' New *ner tamid* and *parohet* by *Michael Gore*, 2013.

In 2007 the neglected synagogue was saved from sale, demolition and replacement by lucrative flats, thanks to a Grade II listing, apparently on the initiative of a dissatisfied member of the congregation. An English Heritage/Heritage Lottery Fund repair grant for the roof followed in 2011. In 2012 *The Times*[41] reported that the congregation had raised £1 million for the redevelopment project. Some pews have been removed from the rear of the prayer hall and (reversible) partitions installed to subdivide the space, in a bid to render this large synagogue fashionable once again in London's premier Jewish neighbourhood, which has become increasingly dominated by Hasidic-style *shtieblekh*.

Behind the synagogue, ancillary halls by *R J Hersch* (1939) and *Ivor Warner* (1958) have been demolished to make way for the new-build Rimon Jewish Primary School (*c* 2012).

OPENING HOURS: *Shabbat* and weekday services. Other times and groups by appointment: tel 020 8455 2460; www.golders greenshul.org.uk

Golders Green, the Ark

North Western Reform Synagogue

Alyth Gardens, NW11 7EN

Fritz Landauer, 1935–6

Closes the cul-de-sac of Alyth Gardens, which gives the congregation its popular name. The horizontality of Landauer's red-brick façade, with Crittall-style windows, disappeared behind a new porch in 2004. It was not as original as *Landauer*'s work at **Willesden**. *Foundation stones* including a bronze plaque by *Benno Elkan*, can now be found inside the porch. Extensive later additions.

INTERIOR: The original open-plan space, with exposed roof beams, exposed brick walls and parquet flooring, has lost much of its austerity, although the 1930s movable seating has been retained. Unusual direct access from the back of the prayer hall to the gallery above the vestibule, but being a Reform synagogue, the gallery was probably never intended to be reserved for women. Bold vertical panels of stained and pot glass in bronze cames by *Roman Halter* (1983), supplemented by his son *Ardyn Halter*'s lunar cycle in 2006–7. Ark end remodelled. Copper *Luhot* and Holocaust memorial in vestibule by *Fred Kormis*, copper *hanukiah* by *Benno Elkan*, textiles by *Kathryn Salomons*.

OPENING HOURS: *Shabbat* and festival services. Heritage Open Days (September). Other times and groups by appointment: tel 020 8455 6763; www.alyth.org.uk

The frontage of Hendon's 1930s suburban synagogue (E020055)

Hendon Synagogue

18 Raleigh Close, Hendon, NW4 2TA

Cecil J Eprile, 1934–5

A red-brick modernist synagogue massed behind a tripartite cubic façade on a generous suburban site. The brick hides a steel-framed and cantilevered reinforced concrete construction. The building is flat roofed and features vertical slit windows. The big window above the porch has a metal grille in the form of a stylised *menorah*. The flat-headed *Luhot* that flank the brickwork *Magen David* in the central gable are a later addition. *Foundation stones*.

INTERIOR: A clean, light 'Cunard' feel with a gallery on three sides with curved concrete corners and clerestory glazing. The original brass wall-lights on the gallery brackets reflect the simple design motifs in the leaded lights: *menorah, Magen David, Luhot*, open *Sefer Torah*. The prayer hall is 20m (65ft) square – more conducive to the present central *bimah* than the original layout with combined Ark-*bimah*, reordered by *Joseph Fiszpan* in 1963.

STAINED GLASS: Four mounted and back-lit panels on the ground floor by *David Hillman* were brought from **Cricklewood Synagogue**.

OPENING HOURS: *Shabbat* and weekday services. Heritage Open Day (September). Other times and groups by appointment: tel 020 8202 6924; www.hendon synagogue.com

Old **Edgware United Synagogue**

Mowbray Road, Edgware, Middlesex, HA8 8JL

Cecil J Eprile, 1934

This is the modest single-storey brick predecessor of the present Edgware United Synagogue (*Hans Sigmund Jaretzki*, 1955–1960).[42] It has gable ends with a small Ark apse at the east; the main entrance is in the long north wall. Modern glazing has been added to the later two-storey, red-brick hall behind. The Rosh Pinah Primary School opened in the hall in January 1956, before the synagogue itself had transferred to Parnell Close (off Edgware Way, HA8 8YE).[43] In the 1990s the school moved to a brand new building in Glengall Road, leaving behind its nursery division for which the old synagogue served as its hall until 2014, when the building was taken over by a *Haredi* congregation.

BURIAL GROUND IN BARNET

Golders Green Jewish Cemetery

1 Hoop Lane, NW11 7NL

1897

In 1894 the **West London Synagogue** acquired land in Golders Green for £3,000. In 1896 they sold eight acres to the **Spanish and Portuguese Jews' Congregation**, thus creating the arrangement of sharing cemetery space between the Reform and the Sephardim that has persisted into the 21st century (*see* below).[44] In the 1930s **Alyth** was built on another part of the site.

The imposing *ohel* complex was designed in Romanesque style by *Davis & Emanuel*. A barrel-vaulted porte-cochère spans the main access road and connects the *ohalim* of the two congregations, that of the Spanish and Portuguese to the east, Reform to the west. Of red brick and terracotta with bands of sandstone, external buttresses, and a deep 'Rosemary' clay-tiled roof. Beyond, the access road bisects the cemetery, the

two halves of which are each of very different character. The Sephardi plot, with characteristic flat stones, is tightly packed with gravel underfoot. The larger Reform section, with more grass and planting, extends to the rear of the **North Western Reform Synagogue** on Alyth Gardens.

Of interest is the oldest headstone, just behind the lodge: FRANCES, WIFE OF CHARLES K SALAMAN, ELDEST DAUGHTER OF THE LATE ISAAC SIMON OF MONTEGO BAY, JAMAICA AND REBECCA OROBIO, HIS WIFE, b Jamaica 27 June 1817, d London 6 May 1897, THE FIRST INTERMENT IN THIS CEMETERY. A refreshing variety in the design of headstones and tombs. Celebrities buried in the Reform section include JACQUELINE DU PRE, MARJORIE PROOPS, JOE COLLINS (father of the glamorous sisters Jackie and Joan, and a distant cousin of synagogue architect *H H Collins*) and RABBI HUGO GRYN. Inside the Reform *ohel* are more interesting memorial plaques attesting to the international connections of some of Britain's leading

Jewish families, and a First World War roll of honour. Open-air columbaria in the Reform section. Cremations take place across the road in the **Golders Green Crematorium**. The pop singer Amy Winehouse was cremated there in 2011, although the funeral service and the interment of her ashes (2012) took place at the successor (1973) **Edgwarebury Cemetery**, Edgwarebury Lane, Edgware, Middlesex, HA8 8QP, tel 020 8958 3388; www.edgwareburycemetery.org.uk). This is, once again, shared between the Joint Jewish Burial Society (Reform and Liberals) and the Spanish and Portuguese.

ACCESS: Sunday to Friday. Closes two hours before *Shabbat* on winter Fridays: tel 020 8958 3388 (Edgwarebury); www.hooplanecemetery.org.uk, where a downloadable site guide is available: Epstein, J and Jacobs, D 2006 *Rabbis and Teachers Buried at Hoop Lane Cemetery*. London: Reform Judaism. See also www.sandp.org; www.wls.org.uk; www.ljs.org

The *Ohel* at Golders Green Jewish Cemetery (BB for SJBH)

Former **Brixton** Synagogue

Eurolink Business Centre,
49 Effra Road, SW2 1BZ

Cecil Masey, 1921–6

Closed 1981: the fussy
stuccoed and whitewashed
classical façade is
admirably well suited to its
afterlife as a 1980s-era
business centre, in classic
retail park style.
Completely rebuilt behind
(*Paul Straupmanis*, 1992).

South London Liberal Synagogue

1 Prentis Road, Streatham,
SW16 1ZW

One of the earliest Liberal
congregations in the
country, South London
was founded in 1929. In
1938 they moved into a
former girls' school, whose
patron, Amy Tate, (see the
foundation stone) was the
daughter of the sugar
magnate Henry Tate, the
founder of the Tate Gallery
(now Tate Britain) on
Millbank. The architect of

the 1908 Queen Anne
Revival building was
Sidney E J Smith. The
barrel-vaulted school hall
serves as the prayer hall,
with a modern Ark on the
stage. The pews look older.

OPENING HOURS: *Shabbat*
morning service. Heritage
Open Days (September).
Other times and groups
by appointment:
tel 020 8769 4787;
www.southlondon.org

Lodge of former Norwood Orphanage

The Lodge, 38 Knights Hill,
West Norwood, SE27 0JD

Tillot & Chamberlain, 1861–3

The red-brick lodge with
its Jacobean gables is all
that remains of the Jews'
Hospital and Orphan
Asylum built in 1859–62,
known as 'Norwood'. This
was the successor to the
Spanish and Portuguese
Jews' Hospital, Mile End
(*c* 1806, enlarged *c* 1818).
Architects *James Tillot* and
Thomas Chamberlain won
the design competition in
1859, fresh from their work
on the **Jews' Infant
School**, in Commercial
Street, E1.

REFERENCE: Norwood
Archives, 80–82 The
Broadway, Stanmore,
Middlesex, HA7 4HB,
tel 020 8809 8809;
www.norwood.org.uk

Former **South West London Synagogue**

104 Bolingbroke Grove,
Battersea, SW11 1DA

Charles Living Jnr, 1927

Built onto the rear of
a Victorian house on
Bolingbroke Grove, which
was purchased by the
congregation in 1915 and
then given a facelift. The
red-brick ground floor and
front boundary wall are
very inter-war modernist,
especially the stepped
surround to the square
doorway and elongated
Crittall windows, with bold
diamond-pattern glazing
bars. A *Magen David*
roundel is visible in the
block to the side. The
synagogue itself is best
viewed from the rear in
Chivalry Road, opposite
Battersea Cemetery.
It was an unremarkable

The former Brixton Synagogue tranformed into a convincing 1980s-era business centre (F040127)

Street frontage of former South West London Synagogue
(VFM for SJBH)

two-storey yellow-brick prayer hall, with red-brick dressings and pitched roof. Closed in 1997, by the time our Survey got there in 2000 the building was derelict and we were unable to gain access. The original leaded lights in a *Magen David* design survived on the long walls. These have now been replaced with clear glazing, the synagogue having been converted into a private house.

Nightingale House

101–5 Nightingale Lane, SW12 8NB

'Ferndale', a fine yellow-brick mid-Victorian house with extensive gardens, was donated by the philanthropist and Liberal MP Sydney James Stern, Lord Wandsworth (1844–1912), in 1906 for use by the Home for Aged Jews, founded in Stepney Green in 1876. New frontage and extension by the society architect *William Flockhart* (1906). There are several *plaques* including an English Heritage *blue*

plaque to the champion boxer Ted 'Kid' Lewis (1893–1970) who died at the home. The original *foundation stone* for Nightingale now forms part of a freestanding garden feature.

Accretions and rebuilding have taken place over the years and have been integrated into a seamless complex with peaceful garden and manicured lawns to the rear. Back in 2000, the red-brick turrets and hipped slate roof of the original synagogue (1910?, architect unknown; refurbished 1981) were just visible from the garden, on your left as you faced the main range. It had a barrel-vaulted ceiling with large segmental windows with leaded lights at either end. Poor disability access was the cause of its demolition as part of a new phase of redevelopment in 2010. However, the dark wood interior fittings, panels of donor boards, light-fittings and even the gable windows and doors, with leaded half-glazing, were installed in the rebuilt synagogue.

OPENING HOURS:
During visiting hours: tel 020 8673 3495; www.nightingale.org.uk

BOROUGH OF MERTON

Streatham Jewish Cemetery

Rowan Road, Greyhound Lane, SW16 5JF

1915

The only London Jewish cemetery south of the river was established in

1915 by a Polish burial society Hesed V'Emet ('Kindness and Truth'), of what in 1949 became known as the **West End Great Synagogue**. This congregation's last independent premises in an office block at **21 Dean Street**, Soho (*Joseph Fiszpan*, 1962) were sold in the 1990s and, like the former **Western Synagogue**, they moved to **Marble Arch Synagogue**. The cemetery was consecrated on 14 November 1915 and *foundation stones* (extant) were laid for an *ohel*. However, the current *ohel* is dated 1932 on its prominent whitewashed gable with pediment-shaped top.

This is quite a big site divided by a central pathway, tightly packed with tombstones of conventional form. The cemetery has been severely treated with weed-killer and gravel, rendering it a depressing contrast to the municipal cemetery next door, whose trees soften the overall effect.

ACCESS: Adjoining Streatham Park Cemetery, but with a separate entrance. Open Sunday to Friday morning. On-site caretaker. Western Marble Arch Synagogue Burial Society: tel 020 7724 7702.

NB Since 1968 South London Liberal Synagogue burials have taken place in a corner of a plot (no. 25 in west corner) within Streatham Park Cemetery.

SOUTH-EAST ENGLAND

THE SOUTH-EAST, dominated by London, is the most heavily populated corner of England. London, as we have seen, has always been the capital of Anglo-Jewry. So it is not surprising that urban Jews have sought to escape from the city to the suburbs and beyond, a trend that continues today; South Hertfordshire is the fastest growing Jewish area in the country. Young families are moving beyond the reach of the London Underground network to Borehamwood and **Elstree**, Radlett and Bushey, in an attempt to escape the inflated house prices of the north-west London suburbs.

In the 18th and 19th centuries wealthy West End Jews had country estates in the London hinterland, in Surrey and Kent – 'the garden of England'. The Rothschilds preferred Buckinghamshire: Waddesdon and Tring.

Sir Moses Montefiore took up residence by the sea at **Ramsgate**. In the 18th century, Jewish communities had formed in coastal towns, on the **Medway** and at **Dover**, associated with the Royal Navy.

Margate and Cliftonville were popular seaside holiday destinations for London Jewish families after the First World War, but the advent of cheap foreign holidays has led to their decline. The cathedral town of **Canterbury**, seat of the Church of England, boasts a little-known Georgian Jewish cemetery and an Egyptian-revival synagogue built in the 1840s. The only other extant example of a synagogue in this style is on the other side of the globe at Hobart in Tasmania, built during the same period (1843) by Jewish settlers from Europe.

Today, small Jewish communities are scattered around Kent; see www.jewishkent.org.uk for contact details.

The Thanet & District Reform Synagogue, 293A Margate Road, Ramsgate CT12 6TE regularly participates in Heritage Open Days (September).

Interior of the Montefiore Synagogue at Ramsgate (E020069)

The Montefiore Synagogue and Mausoleum

Honeysuckle Road, Ramsgate, Kent, CT11 8AA/B[1]

Synagogue by David Mocatta, 1831–3; Mausoleum, 1862, Grade II★

A Regency-style synagogue and the curious last resting place of Sir Moses and Lady Judith

This is all that remains[2] of the seaside estate (East Cliff) owned by Anglo-Jewry's most celebrated 19th-century philanthropist, Sir Moses Montefiore (1784–1885), who died at the age of 101. In the manner of an English aristocrat, the Sephardi grandee built his own private 'chapel' in reticent neo-classical style, utilising the skills of his cousin *David Mocatta* (1806–82), the first Anglo-Jewish architect,[3] a former pupil of *Sir John Soane*. Ramsgate has the distinction of being the first purpose-built synagogue in

Britain designed by a Jewish architect. The simple building is based on a rectangular plan with canted corners plus a semi-circular apse at the back to accommodate the Ark. It has whitewashed stucco walls and a lead roof. The clock on the façade, an unusual feature of synagogues (the most famous clock being that on Prague's baroque Jewish town hall), is inscribed in English

The Montefiore Synagogue at Ramsgate
(E020066)

The Montefiore Synagogue gallery (E020071)

with the motto: TIME FLIES, VIRTUE ALONE REMAINS. The clock once chimed, the only example of one in an English synagogue. There was no Hebrew, nor any Jewish symbolism, to identify the building's function. The worn *plaque* bearing Sir Moses Montefiore's coat of arms was affixed to the wall later. It was rescued from the demolition of the Judith, Lady Montefiore Theological College (*yeshivah*) built in memory of his wife in 1865–9 (architect: *Henry David Davis* of *Davis & Emanuel*). This was an attractive crescent in mock Tudor style located near the synagogue. The coat of arms features a lion and a deer with a

pendant containing an *inscription*, the Hebrew place name for 'Jerusalem'.

INTERIOR: Semicircular stone steps (at north) lead to a tiny vestibule with a marble washstand. The interior of the small prayer hall was originally dimly lit from above by an octagonal dome and lantern of frosted and red glass, a feature typical of the Regency, and by a tiny window over the Ark (*Ehal*), now filled with stained-glass *Luhot*. Only later were windows introduced at gallery level. The classicism of the tapering Ark is modified by the lotus-bud capitals to the columns, which give it a slightly Egyptian feel.

Other alterations to the interior of the Ramsgate Synagogue have somewhat compromised the restrained neoclassicism: the cream, pink and grey granite and marble lining the walls (in 1912), replacement and rearrangement of the furniture (by oak in 1933; the *tevah* is now in the centre) and the introduction of iron gallery supports and stained glass (also in 1933). Nevertheless, the synagogue, in common with its parent **Bevis Marks** (both follow the Spanish and Portuguese rite), is still lit by candles in their original brass chandeliers. As at Bevis Marks, you can still see Sir Moses' own seat by the Ark, as well as Lady Judith's in the gallery (no. 3). The gallery faces the Ark along the rear (west) wall and has a traditional high latticework *mehitzah*.

The synagogue possesses rare silver and textiles presented by various members of the Montefiore family, some of which are sometimes on display. In 1933 the original timber Royal Family prayer board was replaced. It can now be seen at **Bristol Synagogue**.

The Montefiore Mausoleum

Sir Moses Montefiore travelled widely during his long life and visited the Land of Israel seven times. He left a distinctly English mark on the architectural development of modern Jerusalem in the shape of the Mishkenot Sha'ananim almshouses and the Montefiore windmill, both situated in what was later (1890s) to become the Yemin Moshe quarter, named in his honour. 'Yemin Moshe', a Biblical allusion, means 'The right hand of Moses' [that is, Montefiore] and was one of the first Jewish neighbourhoods to be built outside the walls of the Old City.

The almshouses were designed by English architect *William Edward Smith* in 1855–60. He utilised decorative 'railway station' ironwork specially imported from *G S Culver*'s East Kent Metalwork factory – in Ramsgate – while the landmark windmill (1857) was based on prototypes in Kent, including the Hereson flourmill that was actually located on the East Cliff estate.

The Jerusalem version was constructed

The Montefiore Synagogue and Mausoleum at Ramsgate (E020065)

The Montefiore Mausoleum at Ramsgate (E020067)

side by side in brick vaults covered by identical chest tombs of Aberdeen marble. As is traditional Jewish practice, the tombs face the east (towards Jerusalem) under a small stained-glass skylight. There is no other decoration inside the mausoleum. The floor is of Minton tile. The porch is filled with iron grilles in a Moresque fretwork pattern. The *inscription* over the entrance is from the last verse of the Hebrew hymn *Adon Olam*, 'Master of the Universe'.

Behind the mausoleum is a short stone pillar on a plinth. It perhaps alludes to the *matzevah* erected by the Patriarch Jacob over his dead wife's grave. Reputedly brought back by Sir Moses from the Land of Israel, the dark weathered stone is porphyry which was used throughout the Roman world.[4] The Ramsgate Synagogue and Mausoleum are of international significance as physical expression of the imperial link between Britain and the Holy Land in the 19th century.

LOCATION: Well hidden. Of the two entrances to Honeysuckle Road, on the east side of Hereson Road, take the southernmost one. The street opens out in front of The Honeysuckle public house, splitting in two. Public parking is in this area. Take the left (north) turn and then right (east) past gateposts with bollards obstructing unauthorised vehicular traffic. Continue up this unmarked lane, which then swings to the left (north), and the synagogue and mausoleum are 50m further on, behind railings and a gate.

OPENING HOURS: Occasional services, including an annual memorial service in July/August to mark the *Yahrzeit* or Hebrew anniversary of Montefiore's death (16th Av). Heritage Open Days (September). Other times by appointment via the Spanish and Portuguese Jews' Congregation, Lauderdale Road, 2 Ashworth Road, Maida Vale, London, W9 1JY; tel 020 7289 2573; www.montefioreendowment.org.uk

by *Messrs Holman*, engineers and millwrights, of Canterbury. The machinery was imported from England via Jaffa, and 4 months, a fleet of camels and 40 men were required to bring it to Jerusalem.

The Ramsgate Mausoleum, next door to the synagogue, is testament to the reciprocal attachment of Sir Moses to the Land of Israel. It is basically a replica of Rachel's Tomb, on the road from Jerusalem to Bethlehem, a traditional place of pilgrimage for both Jews and Muslims. It is reputedly the site where the Matriarch Rachel was buried by her husband Jacob after dying in childbirth with her younger son, Benjamin (Genesis 35:19–20). The fascimile was commissioned by Sir Moses as an appropriate memorial to his childless wife, who predeceased him. The couple had visited Rachel's Tomb in 1839 and had paid for its repair. The Ramsgate Mausoleum is stuccoed and rusticated, unlike the stone prototype with its distinctive dome on a square, which is thought to date back to the Crusader period and was rebuilt by the Muslims in the 15th century.

Lady Judith died on 24 September 1862 and Sir Moses died on 28 July 1885. The Montefiores were laid to rest

East Cliff Lodge was purchased by Moses Montefiore in 1830–1. Designed by *Boncey* of Margate (1794–9), the house itself was demolished in 1954. The land became the **King George VI Memorial Park**. The **glasshouses** that Sir Moses renovated and Lady Judith tended, remain. Perhaps dating from the time the house was built, these important glasshouses are Grade II* listed. The **gate house** and **old stable block**, Montefiore Avenue, CT11 8BD, were both by *Boncey* (1794, Grade II) in Regency Gothic style with a crenellated roofline, to match the main house. *Private*. The stables once housed the well-travelled Montefiore carriage, painted with the family crest. A replica is now on display in Yemin Moshe in Jerusalem, after the original was destroyed in a fire in 1986. The **walls** and surviving main entrance **gates** to the lodge are also listed (Grade II).

Surrounding the synagogue complex, their ornamental Victorian **gates** and piers, and the brick and flint **boundary walls** are likewise listed. So too, much to the amusement of the Jewish press,[5] are the **gentlemen's toilets** built in the grounds of the synagogue in coordinating Regency style. In the 2000s, the site of the former **Judith, Lady Montefiore College**, demolished in 1964/5, was the focus of a protracted planning battle between local residents and Thanet District Council, which had acquired it from the Spanish and Portuguese. Thanet Council in turn sold off part of the land for construction of the private **Montefiore Medical Centre** (Dumpton Park Drive, CT11 8AD). In return, in 2011 they presented an adjacent unkempt piece of woodland to Ramsgate Town Council. The plot was designated as the **Montefiore Woodland** and a Friends Group (2012) was set up to manage the site as a nature reserve, encouraging a diversity of wildlife, birds, butterflies and wild flowers (volunteers welcome, see www.montefiorewoodland.org.uk). Sir Moses has given his name elsewhere in the town, to Montefiore Avenue, Montefiore Arms public house, Montefiore Bowls and Games Centre and the electoral Montefiore Ward for Thanet District Council. To mark the incorporation of the town in 1884, the year before his death, Sir Moses presented the mayoral chain still worn by Ramsgate's Town Mayor. It is made from links in the shape of the Hebrew letter *mem*, standing for the initials of Moses Montefiore. In 2012, Ramsgate had a Jewish mayor, Cllr David Green.

In 1887, Manuel Nunes Costello[6] laid the foundation stone of **Florry Cottages**, 91–101, Hereson Road, CT11 7DU. This terrace of estate-worker cottages was named after Sarah Floretta, the youngest daughter of Sir Moses' nephew and heir Joseph Sebag-Montefiore (1822–1903). The terrace has been much 'improved', but still bears the Moses Montefiore coat of arms, the family motto THINK AND THANK, and the word JERUSALEM in Hebrew script. The cottages were finished in 1888 as indicated by the Hebrew date 5648 in the *inscription*.

NB Not to be confused with the Dutch gables of the **Lazarus Hart Havens of Rest** at The Havens, 1–10 Thanet Road, CT11 8EL (1917–22, Grade II), built on the proceeds of a legacy from Lazarus Hart, a hardware merchant and the first Jewish mayor of Ramsgate. He donated £10,000 for these almshouses to be shared by Jews and Gentiles. *Private*.

GUIDED WALK: Ramsgate Montefiore Heritage (established 2012) runs a Ramsgate Montefiore Town Trail. This runs parallel to the Pugin Trail, and explores the local connections between the Montefiore and Pugin heritage in Ramsgate. For times, enquire at The Custom House, Harbour Parade, CT11 8LP. Leaflet available. www.ramsgatemontefioreheritage.org.uk

Ramsgate Jewish Cemetery

Upper Dumpton Park Road, CT11 7PG

1872, Grade II

Established privately in 1872 by Benjamin Norden in order to bury his wife, and given to the Jewish community of Ramsgate – who were not as privileged as the Montefiores. Jews were resident in the town from 1786 but were hitherto buried at **Mile End** (in the case of Sephardim) or at **Canterbury**. Administered by the Spanish and Portuguese since 1887 and extended in 1931. A mixture of flat Sephardi and upright Ashkenazi stones are arranged in neat grassy rows. The oldest identifiable tombstone (the registers have not been located), of flaking sandstone, is in the central section running back from the *ohel*: MOSES MAYERS 'OF MIDDLESEX, LONDON', who died 22 August 5633 [=1873].

Nowadays, you enter through the simple brick *ohel* in the high boundary wall on Upper Dumpton Road. The *ohel* and the attached sections of the brick and flint boundary wall are listed. The Hebrew *inscription* translates roughly as 'The dead will the Lord make live', derived from the daily liturgy.

LOCATION: At the corner of College Road and Cecilia Road.

ACCESS: Locked. Contact the Spanish and Portuguese Jews' Congregation, Lauderdale Road, 2 Ashworth Road, Maida Vale, London, W9 1JY; tel 020 7289 2573.

OTHER JEWISH SITES IN KENT

CANTERBURY

The Old Synagogue

King Street, CT1 2AJ/2AR[7]

Hezekiah Marshall, 1847–8, Grade II

Ironically, built on the site of a hospice of the medieval Knights Templar and adjoining Edward, the Black Prince's Chantry – all inveterate anti-Semites. Remnants of medieval masonry may be seen in the listed garden walls. *Plaque*. This ancient cathedral town, seat of the Archbishop of Canterbury, had an important Jewish community in the Middle Ages. **Jewry Lane**, the site of the Jewish quarter, still exists to the south-west of the High Street, and a few minutes' walk from the Old Synagogue.

The synagogue is set discreetly back from King Street in a leafy garden. The Ark wall (south-east), which faces the street, is an early example of the use of cement-render on the façade of the striped brick-built synagogue. Moreover, Canterbury is the only example of a thorough-going Egyptian-revival-style synagogue in Britain, and one of only two extant anywhere in the world. Its counterpart is Hobart Synagogue, Tasmania, designed by ex-convict Scotsman *James Alexander Thomson*, 1843–5.[8] In the 1840s convict ships moored in the Medway ports set sail bound for Australia, raising the intriguing possibility of a maritime link between Canterbury and Hobart.

The Egyptian-revival façade of Canterbury's Old Synagogue (DP047122)

The Ark (DP047118)

Canterbury's architect was a little-known local man who we know was instructed by his Jewish clients to avoid the Gothic style because of its unhappy associations with persecution by the medieval church. The fashion for neo-Egyptian was inspired by Napoleon's Egyptian campaign (1798) and archaeological excavations in the Orient. Its application to synagogue architecture was a bit bizarre: the ancient Israelites were 'slaves unto Pharaoh in Egypt'. Nevertheless, reconstructions of

Solomon's Temple drawn by Christians in the 1820s and 1830s were based on Egyptian prototypes. There is no evidence that such depictions directly influenced synagogue design, having rather more effect on the architecture of Freemasonry.

The east wall is dominated by a pair of pilasters with lotus-leaf capitals, a design that is repeated on the Ark surround that survives inside. The whole building tapers to the roof and employs Egyptian motifs such as pylons, obelisks, angular window heads and palmettes, even on such details as the gate posts, rear gallery front (which was once latticed) and gallery pews (the only original furnishings that remain). Restored 1889; closed 1931. Sympathetic restoration (1982) by *Anthony Moubray-Janowski* of the *Lee Evans Partnership* of Canterbury; landscaping by *Clare Shaw*. Despite change of use – it is now the King's School Recital Room – the synagogue retains complete design integrity. Indeed, its

restrained character appears almost modern: the art deco of the 1930s also owed something to Egyptian inspiration.

Modern *parohet* by *Betty Myerscough.*

The Old *Mikveh*

Next door. Built in matching Egyptian style in 1851, and paid for by the La Mert brothers in memory of their mother. The *inscription* in the gable is neither original nor accurate. The genuine consecration tablet can be seen on the wall at the **Whitstable Road** cemetery (*see* below). The actual pool has long since been covered in, and the room is now used as rehearsal space.

OPENING HOURS: Occasional services (Reform style) are held by the reconstituted Canterbury & District Jewish Community (see www.jewishkent.org.uk); concerts; Heritage Open Days (September). Other times by arrangement with the Secretary, the King's School (the cathedral school): tel 01227 595 501; www.kings-school.co.uk

The Old *Mikveh* (DP047120)

Rural last outposts in Kent of the 19th-century Anglo-Jewish 'aristocracy' before they ceased to be Jewish. Neither house was built by its one-time Jewish residents but in both cases private family burial plots were established on the estate, which is why they are included in the present guide.

Former David Salomons' Estate

Salomons Conference Centre, Broomhill Road, Southborough, TN3 0TG

The country seat of the eccentric scientist David Lionel Goldsmid Stern Salomons, the second Baronet (1851–1925), nephew of Sir David Salomons (1797–1873), the first Jewish Lord Mayor of London and a prominent campaigner for Jewish political emancipation in England (1858). Sir David acquired Broom Hill Cottage in 1829 and engaged *Decimus Burton* to convert the property into a substantial country house in the 'Italian style'. His nephew, David Lionel, added the **stables** (*William Barnsley Hughes*, 1894, Grade II★), the **water tower** (with well beneath, 1876, Grade II) and the **science theatre** (1894–6), both of which he designed himself. Broomhill also lays claim to being the first house in the country to use electricity for cooking. The theatre is a wonderland of gadgets, state-of-the-art in their day, including a photographic studio and dark rooms, electric blinds, which still work, and a self-playing Welte 'echo' organ (restored

with the help of a Heritage Lottery Fund grant in 1998). Little else of the original interior survives besides the two **memento rooms**, a small museum of Salomons' family effects.

The first interment in the small **burial ground** on the estate was that of SYBIL GWENDOLEN, d 18 December 1899, second daughter of the second baronet. It is uncertain whether or not the plot was ever consecrated for Jewish use, since, of the eight marked graves, three are those of Christians, all members of the BLUNT family. One even has a cross carved on the back. The Gothic sandstone chapel in front of the plot actually pre-dates it, having being built by the Abergavenney family (*c* 1853), and is therefore unconnected.

LOCATION: Railway to Tonbridge. By car: from Tunbridge Wells drive via Southborough in the direction of Speldhurst. Signposted. On the estate, the burial ground is located due south of the main house, on Broomhill Bank Road near the junction with Lower Green Road.

OPENING HOURS: Memento rooms open to the public on Monday, Wednesday and Friday 14.00 to 17.00. Visits to the house and burial ground by arrangement with the Salomons' Estate Manager: tel 01892 515 152; www.salomons-estate.com

Former Goldsmid Family Estate

The Schools at Somerhill, Tonbridge, TN11 0NJ

This house (Grade I) was described by Pevsner as 'an ambitious Jacobean mansion' comparable with Hardwick Hall in Derbyshire. Attributed to *John Thorpe* 1611–13 (note the dated lead hopper heads). The sandstone ashlar façade remains much as built, but the interior went through successive alterations, not least by Sir Julian Goldsmid (1838–96), who greatly enlarged it, particularly with the addition of the **stables** (*c* 1877–9) and a **clock tower**. It remained in the family until 1981. A gazebo in the grounds was designed by *Hugh Casson*.

The private family **burial ground** has an unusual boundary wall (Grade II), which has a curved gabled profile in a kind of 'Spanish Colonial' style, with decorative metal grille-work. Inside are eight Jewish graves: the earliest burial, ODETTE, five-year-old daughter of OSMOND and ALICE D'AVIGDOR GOLDSMID, d 27 May 1915, is adorned with the statue of a cherub. Two more burials of Gentile relatives are found close to the entrance, one marked by a Celtic stone cross.

ACCESS: Via school secretary: tel 01732 352 124; www.somerhill.org

The **Goldsmid Hall**, Tudeley Road, TN11 0NW, is the former Goldsmid estate **Workingmen's Institute**. The 'Arts and Crafts'-style house bears the Goldsmid family crest, of sandstone, featuring a lion and a hand; *inscription* JG 1895. Inside, a mural (1897) depicts estate workers in a suitably rustic scene. In 2000 the building became a community hall and a venue for weddings and conferences.

ACCESS: tel 01892 835 137; www.goldsmidhall.org

NB Not to be missed is the delightful **All Saints Tudeley Church** nearby. The Crucifixion windows are by *Marc Chagall* (1967), the only example of his stained glass in Britain. They were commissioned and installed by the D'Avigdor-Goldsmids, by then members of the parish church, in memory of their daughter Sarah who drowned in 1963.

LOCATION: Somerhill is 2.5km south-east of Tonbridge. The burial ground is situated between Somerhill and Tudeley, near a railway bridge on Hartlake Road (east side). Take Tudeley Lane eastbound and turn left (north) at the junction with Hartlake Road (ie in the opposite direction from Tudeley Church).

Canterbury Jews' Burial Ground

Whitstable Road, CT2 8DQ

1760

Outside the medieval town walls, predating the construction of the first **Canterbury Synagogue** (1762–3) in **St Dunstan's**. What was probably the northern wall of the Georgian synagogue, built of red brick, was unearthed in a dig at **21–4 St Dunstan's Street**, CT2 8BH in 2009.[9] The Whitstable Road cemetery served the whole of Kent. The Egyptian-style entrance gates were probably contemporary with the **Old Synagogue**. Restored in 1998 with the assistance of the Heritage Lottery Fund and Canterbury City Council. Sadly, much of the vegetation, including the old sycamore overhanging the gravestone of the synagogue's secretary, JACOB JACOBS, d 10 January 1873, at the back of the cemetery, had to be cut down because of structural damage to the site. His handwritten diary, now in Southampton University Archives, is the principal source on the history of the Canterbury community. Many tombstones are now illegible; partial records survive from 1831 to 1870 and a site survey was carried out in the 1970s. Trusteeship by the Board of Deputies in London was due to be formalised in 2014. *Plaque.*

LOCATION: Entrance between 26 and 28 Whitstable Road, just north of the junction with Forty Acres Road.

ACCESS: Heritage Open Days (September). Key c/o Canterbury Rock, 12 Whitstable Road, CT2 8DQ; tel 01227 458 393 (business hours only). Enquiries: heritage@ canterbury.gov.uk

DOVER

Dover Hebrew Cemetery

Old Charlton Road, Copt Hill, CT16 2QA

1868

On Old Charlton Road in an area to the north-east of the town where cemeteries cluster. The Jewish cemetery is situated on the south side of the road, above St Mary's Cemetery. Bounded by high flint walls, this is an exposed site, badly eroded as a result of an over-rigorous management regime by the Trustees, the United Synagogue in London. Most of the marked graves are at the top of the hill, all facing north-west.

A Jewish community existed in this important naval town (the closest part of the UK to France, 32km away over the English Channel), at least since the 1770s, although no records are extant prior to 1842. A purpose-built Greek-revival synagogue (*William E Williams*, 1862–3) in Northampton Street was irrevocably damaged during heavy bombing in the Second World War and was demolished in 1950. The street no longer exists. Most Jewish residents fled for fear of invasion.

A series of *plaques*, including the *foundation stone* of the synagogue, may be seen inside the cemetery, as well as a broken, partially legible, tablet to REVD RAPHAEL I COHEN, minister of the congregation and founder c 1848 of Sussex House, a Jewish boarding school in Dover. His wife, BLOOMA COHEN, is buried beneath the single chest tomb in the centre of the site. First interment: CATHERINE ISAACS, d 2 August 1868, but her grave is not visible among the earliest tombstones in the back row. Two war graves include one of a Dutchman killed in 1944. The *ohel* apparently burnt down. There are no burial records but a field survey compiled in 1996 is kept by the local undertakers, for the cemetery is in occasional use.

LOCATION: Postcode above is for St Mary's Cemetery Lodge.

ACCESS: Locked iron gate on Old Charlton Road. Keyholders: Hambrook & Johns, Funeral Directors and Monumental Masons, 1 Beaconsfield Avenue, Dover, Kent, CT16 2LS; tel 01304 202 498.

MARGATE

Margate Synagogue

Godwin Street, Cliftonville, CT9 2HA

Cecil J Eprile and Reeve & Reeve (Robert Dalby Reeve), 1928–9

Solid but unadventurous red-brick synagogue for a community founded in 1913, designed by the young United Synagogue architect *Eprile* working together with an experienced local man, a church-builder. The long (south) wall faces the street (Albion Road); the Ark is

in a polygonal copper-covered apse under a *Magen David*. Minister's house attached. *Foundation stone*.

INTERIOR: A shallow barrel-vault and plastered walls. A semi-circular arch separates the Ark apse; the semi-glazed dome is decorated with a gilded sun design, blue sky and clouds with a panelled surround. Steel columns support the gallery, which is on three sides, but with a single staircase from the vestibule. Downsized at the rear. The panelled gallery fronts match the central dark oak *bimah* and classical Ark, which has very traditional gilded *Luhot* set in a scrolled pediment. The standard Hebrew *inscription* 'Know before Whom you stand' is painted in gold on the cornice. The *duhan* is elevated on seven marble steps with a central oak pulpit. The current pews, arranged lengthways, came

from the former **Derby Synagogue**. The disused basement was formerly the schoolroom; no *mikveh*.

LOCATION: Junction of Albion Road and Godwin Road.

OPENING HOURS: *Shabbat* morning and festival services. No telephone line at synagogue. Email: secretary.mhc@hotmail.co.uk and other contacts under 'Margate' at www.jewishkent.org.uk

Chatham Memorial Synagogue

364–6 High Street, Rochester, ME1 1DJ

H H Collins, 1865–70, Grade II*

Built under the private patronage of wealthy Naval Agent Simon Magnus, who bought the freehold of the site of an earlier synagogue (c 1750) and dedicated the new building to the memory of his son.

ROCHESTER CATHEDRAL

Look out for the splendid 14th-century **Chapter Room doorway** that contains the only complete[10] example in stone of the allegorical figures of Synagoga and Ecclesia (Synagogue Vanquished and Church Triumphant) in Britain. Synagoga is represented as a young woman, blindfolded, with a broken staff, the 'Old Law' (that is, the Law of Moses, the *Torah*) falling from her grasp. The Law is represented by the *Luhot*, the pair of round-headed tablets, which was the badge that the Jews of medieval England were forced to wear. By the time the Chapter Room door was carved, in all its high-Gothic glory, the Jews, including the community in Rochester, had been gone from England for at least 50 years.

Chatham Memorial Synagogue Ark and *Bimah*

The present synagogue has an elevated north frontage faced with Kentish rag stone and Bath stone dressings, with columns and decoration both outside and in of red Mansfield stone, a Lombardic gabled roof, wheel window and 15m (50ft) Romanesque square tower, complete with spire and finials, perhaps taking its cue from Rochester Cathedral itself. Glazed link to 1972 communal hall. *Foundation stone* and memorial *inscription* on pediment. The Hebrew lintel inscription from Ecclesiastes 4:17 contains a chronogram.

INTERIOR: Romanesque, of unexpectedly high quality, mostly made by leading London firms. The colourful Minton tile floor extends into the vestibule; a timber-clad (deal) raised collar roof and red-and-white patterned brickwork. Note the intricate naturalistic carving of the clustered columns by *Caudy & Gibbs*, with flora found in the Land of Israel, including the vine, pomegranate, palm, lotus, olive, wheat, bulrush and lily. The Ark screen covers the south wall, with a prominent central pulpit. The *bimah* is immediately in front and much of the

Chatham Memorial Synagogue (GF9M0509)

seating faces it, prefiguring later Reform reordering. The *parohet* is hung inside the Ark, perhaps attesting to early Sephardi influence in this congregation. *Inscription* is the standard 'Know before Whom you stand …', plus Proverbs 3:16 in the soffits.

The gallery is at the rear only, with a metalwork grille that matches the balustrading of both *duhan* and *bimah*. The original gasoliers by *Defries* of London have not survived.

STAINED GLASS: Glazed *Luhot* over the Ark. Some original grisaille windows by *Smith & Miers* of London suffered war damage; modern glass by architect *Hilary Halpern*, a descendant of the Magnus family, who lived locally until his death in 2013. The interior was restored to the original colour scheme in 1997 with the help of English Heritage, and Halpern supervised external renovations in 2002. Striking sunburst Holocaust memorial window in the gallery by *Sherif Amin* (2003).

LOCATION: Street frontage on south side of High Street, opposite Ship Lane and Ship Inn public house.

Chatham Jews' Burial Ground

Behind synagogue

The only burial ground in Britain attached to a synagogue, like a churchyard. However, it is situated at a higher level than the synagogue, on a steep bank with a high wall adjoining St Bartholomew's Hospital to the rear, from which the land was acquired. The burial ground is early 1780s, pre-dating the present synagogue, but the burial records have not been traced. Many tombstones in the middle, probably the oldest section, seem to have disappeared.

Dominated by the granite obelisk to LAZARUS SIMON MAGNUS, d 7 January 1865 aged 39, which used to be visible from the High Street as specified by his bereaved father, SIMON MAGNUS, patron of the current synagogue. Magnus Senior is buried under another obelisk at the back of the cemetery (d 30 November 1878). The lengthy *inscription* tells us that Magnus junior was elected mayor of Queenborough (on the Isle of Sheppey) three times. He played a key role in bringing the railway to the Medway towns, but died prematurely in an accident, still a bachelor, hence his father's desire to perpetuate his memory. Site restored 2000.

OPENING HOURS: *Shabbat* and festival services. Heritage Open Days (September). Other times and groups by appointment: tel 01634 847 665; www. chathamshul.org.uk

Memorial to Lazarus Simon Magnus at Chatham's Jewish cemetery (GF9M0519)

SHEERNESS

Sheerness Old Jews' Burial Ground

Between 2 and 4 Hope Street, ME12 1QH

1804

Documented from 1806. Jews had been resident in the town since the 1790s. A Gothic-style synagogue with 'Grecian' Ark was built in 1811 in Sheppey Street, Blue Town. It was dismantled in 1887, by which time the community had dwindled almost to extinction. The burial ground is now a neglected backyard behind the High Street. Only 11 stones were extant in 1973, and the site was entirely overgrown in 2002. Cecil Roth, back in 1950, managed to read the earliest stone as dated 1804, the latest 1855; neither is still legible. Now under the trusteeship of the Board of Deputies in London.

ACCESS: Locked. Key c/o Sheppey Estates, 6 Hope Street, ME12 1QH; tel 01795 666 297.

Isle of Sheppey Cemetery, Jewish Section

Halfway Road, Minster on Sea, ME12 3BS

1859

This must be the smallest Jewish cemetery in England. Enclosed within a privet hedge, immaculately kept by Swale Borough Council, funded by the Board of Deputies, as Trustees. They inherited responsibility from the private Isle of Sheppey General Cemetery Company; the records are lost. However, the tiny plot contains only 11

headstones, in two rows, facing west, all belonging to members of two families, Jacobs and Levy. The earliest interment in the corner (south-east) is that of CATHERINE, RELICT OF ISAAC JACOBS d 7 May 5619 [=1859], aged 84; the last burial ESTHER wife of HENRY JACOBS, d 20 June 1899, aged 78.

LOCATION: Also known as Halfway or Queenborough/ Queenboro Cemetery. Near the north-east corner of the municipal cemetery with boundary on to Halfway Road (A250).

ACCESS: During general cemetery hours, via main entrance.

GUILDFORD

Possible Medieval Synagogue

Beneath 50 Guildford High Street, GU1 3ES

A rescue dig by Guildford Museum in November 1995 revealed a small blind-arcaded chamber under this shop. It had Norman stone arches and a stone ledge for seating around the walls, with vestiges of painted decoration. It was tentatively identified as a synagogue c 1180,

possibly the undercroft or rear extension of a stone 'Jew's House' as at **Norwich** or **Lincoln** (*see* below). Isaac of Southwark and Winchester had a house in Guildford that was ransacked in 1274. Guildford's medieval Jewry was centred on the wool trade, until expulsion by Queen Eleanor, wife of Henry III and mother of Edward I, in 1275. Fabric analysis showed that our site had indeed been demolished and filled in, and much of the stone was plundered for secondary use in the latter part of the 13th century. A silver penny from the reign of Henry II, minted 1251–72, was found, plus pottery dated c 1280. A niche in the east wall may have been for the Ark, scorch marks may mark the location of the *Ner Tamid*, while two diagonally placed holes on the door lintel may have once held a *mezuzah*. Plans to create a glass-covered floor display under the then Burton's clothing store (now Monsoon), beneath which the site was located, were stalled in 1997 because of lack of funds. However, at least the site has been preserved.

ACCESS: Not currently accessible to the public.

Possible Medieval Synagogue, Guildford
(Photograph reproduced with kind permission of Guildford Borough Council)

ELSTREE

Liberal Synagogue, Elstree

Hertfordshire, WD6 3EY

Grade II

This synagogue is housed in a former Church of England school (1882–83) close to the Old Parish Church of St Nicholas, built in a rustic Arts and Crafts style. The building was rescued from redundancy in 1976 by the Hertsmere Progressive Synagogue, which had begun in 1969 as the Stanmore Liberal Jewish Congregation. In 2004 the name was changed to the Liberal Synagogue, Elstree. The conversion created light, flexible spaces for worship, social and educational purposes, with a new entrance foyer (1998) linking the two wings of the old building. However, the Ark faces west. *Stained glass* by *Roman Halter*.

ACCESS: *Shabbat* and festival services. Other times and groups by appointment: tel 020 8953 8889; www.tlse.org.uk

HERTFORD

Hertford Cemetery, Jewish Section

Bramfield Road, SG14 2HZ

A triangular plot reserved for the Faudel-Phillips family. George Faudel-Phillips was Lord Mayor of London in 1896–7. He was the younger son of Sir Benjamin Samuel Faudel-Phillips, the first baronet, also Lord Mayor in 1865–6.

The family lived nearby at **Balls Park** (off Mangrove Road), SG13 8QE/8FJ, a fine house of *c* 1638–42 (Grade I), redeveloped in 2010–12 as upmarket apartments with new-build houses on the estate (P & G Grade II), the listings notwithstanding.

The first burial in Hertford Cemetery was the wife of the second baronet, HELEN NEE LEVY, the fourth daughter of JOSEPH M [LEVY] LAWSON, editor of the *Daily Telegraph* (buried at the **West London Reform Cemetery** in Islington), and sister of Lord Burnham. Her burial and the consecration of the plot by the Revd Isidore Harris, minister of the **West London Synagogue**, took place on 9 August 1916. On his death in 1922 Sir George was buried under the same flat stone bearing the family crest; two other matching memorials over the graves of three of their children, and the Gentile spouse of the third baronet.

LOCATION: On Bramfield Road (north) side of the cemetery, close to the boundary and main gate.

ACCESS: During general cemetery hours.

The Ark, Reading Synagogue (DP085890)

READING

Reading Synagogue

Goldsmid Road, RG1 7YB

William G Lewton, 1900, Grade II

Reading's Jewish community started in 1886 as an overspill from London and prospered. The well-appointed 'Edwardian' red-brick synagogue with Bath stone dressings is by *William G Lewton*. It was built in 1900 in Junction Road – afterwards renamed Goldsmid Road in honour of Reading's Jewish MP, Sir Francis Goldsmid.

Despite the Moorish horseshoe arch over the main entrance, at the end (west) of the long street (north) wall, and the arcaded windows, the building is thoroughly English with its slate pitched roof, chimney and timber lantern (flèche) capped by an onion-shaped copper dome. This latter was a feature of town halls and fire stations of the period. Hebrew date 5661 (=1900) in the glazed fanlight. Hebrew *inscription* simply says 'Reading Synagogue'. *Foundation stones.*

INTERIOR: A single flight of concrete stairs leads to the landing and U-shaped gallery. The synagogue has a semi-open roof with exposed beams and

East window, Reading Synagogue
(DP085892)

ornate ceiling vents. Only two iron columns with cushion caps support the gallery wrapping around three sides, perhaps suggesting early use of concrete.

Moorish elements are incorporated into the Ark: a crenellated parapet, miniature square towers and marble *Luhot* set within a horseshoed gateway. An ample central *bimah*.

STAINED GLASS: Original coloured and leaded glass lights in attractive foliate patterns, plus roundels at either end.

Vestiges of a *mikveh* that was never put into use survive in the basement under the vestibule. Hall by *R J Sneller* of Reading (1956). Curiously, there is no burial ground at Reading, interments being performed in London.

OPENING HOURS: *Shabbat* and festival services. Other times by appointment: tel 01189 571 018; www.rhc.org.uk

Lantern, Reading Synagogue
(DP085886)

B RIGHTON'S JEWISH HERITAGE is among the richest and most visually varied in the country. Brighton's Jewish community dates back to at least 1789 when a synagogue was opened in Jew Street. In the early 19th century fashionable neighbourhoods were laid out under the commercial patronage of the Goldsmid family, and today **Brighton and Hove** can probably boast more streets named after wealthy Jewish notables

than any other town in Britain. Look out for Goldsmid Road, Davidgor Road, Julian Road, Lyon Close, Montefiore Road and Osmond Road. Several 'Palmeiras' in Brighton recall the Portuguese title bestowed on Sir Isaac Goldsmid by the King of Portugal in 1846, while 'Somerhill' was the family estate in Kent. Surprisingly, there is no 'Sassoon Street', given the fact that members of this Baghdadi-Indian Jewish clan also resided in the town and socialised with the Prince of Wales, the future Edward VII, who made Brighton as fashionable a resort as it had been in the days of the Prince Regent. Today, after a period of recession in the 1990s, Brighton is buzzing once again.

Middle Street Synagogue, opened in 1875, is one the finest high Victorian synagogues in England. It forms the centrepiece of a heritage that includes an earlier Regency-style synagogue at Devonshire Place, remodelled by

City of Brighton & Hove
DAVID MOCATTA
1806–1882
Anglo-Jewish Architect
Remodelled this building as the City's first purpose built Synagogue in 1838

David Mocatta, the first Anglo-Jewish architect and designer of Brighton's railway station; an old cemetery at Florence Place (1826); and two of the quirkiest architectural curiosities possessed by British Jewry: the private 'penthouse' synagogue-cum-temple built facing the sea on Brunswick Terrace by Philip Salomon, brother of the first Jewish Lord Mayor of London, and the Sassoon Mausoleum, intended as the last resting place for one of the Jewish 'merchant princes' of India, Sir Albert Sassoon. With its prominent trumpet-shaped dome, the Sassoon Mausoleum rivals the Royal Pavilion itself in exoticism.

Follow the Brighton Jewish Heritage Trail (*see* below) to discover a little-known but fascinating part of the Millennium City of Brighton's Regency and Victorian architectural heritage.

The Gallery, Middle Street Synagogue (J020167)

Middle Street Synagogue

66 Middle Street, Brighton, BN1 1AL / Thomas Lainson, 1874–5, Grade II★

Opulent jewel in the crown of the South Coast's most elegant Regency resort

Middle Street Synagogue's architect, *Thomas Lainson*, was known to the Jewish community through his work for Sir Francis Goldsmid (1808–78) as Surveyor to the Wick Estate in Hove, laid out from 1830. Sir Francis was the son of Sir Isaac Lyon Goldsmid (1778–1859), who played a leading role in the struggle for Jewish emancipation in England.

The synagogue hides behind a low-key Italian Romanesque façade on a narrow street built on a bed of shingle – a source of concern ever since. Close examination of the front elevation reveals the use of expensive stone: polished Aberdeen granite for the main columns with Portland stone bases. The window shafts are of red Mansfield stone with Bath stone caps and bases. The wheel window in the gable with stone tracery is set off against the white brickwork of the front, with a jolly note of colour injected by the red-and-blue glazed brick dressings over the windows and along the cornice.

Jewish symbolism on the façade is also low-key. Over the entrance is carved a Hebrew *inscription*: 'How full of awe is this place! This is none other than the House of God, and this is the gate of heaven' (Genesis 28:17), a favourite quotation often found in British synagogues. Here it contains a chronogram for the equivalent Hebrew year when the building was opened: 1875. A stone tablet in the shape of an open *Torah* scroll bears more Biblical references, this time in Latin script; above in the gable the *Luhot* contain an abbreviated form of the Ten Commandments. These *Luhot* are amongst the earliest examples in Britain of this symbol appearing on the front of a synagogue, where on a church one would expect to find the cross.

INTERIOR: Nothing prepares the visitor for the sumptuousness of Middle Street's interior. It is basilican in plan and a riot of marble, brass, mosaic, stencilling, gilding and stained glass, much of it donated by the Sassoon family, the synagogue's chief patrons. The richly decorated capitals of the iron columns that support the gallery are individually fashioned from hammered iron and copper; each sports a different representation of flora from the Land of Israel. The whole composition is dramatically set off against the black and white chequered floor of Italian marble.

The original windows were of 'rough plate-tinted cathedral' glass, leaded in geometrical designs, some of which survives on the west front. The *stained-glass* panels were introduced between 1887 and 1912. Two windows in the gallery are dedicated to the memory of the young Hannah Rothschild, Lady Rosebery, who died in 1890 and was buried in an imposing tomb in **Willesden Cemetery** in London. The glazed *Luhot* above the Ark are by *Westlake* (1887) as is the window opposite in the west gallery. Poorly lit because of its internal position, this window is perhaps unique in Britain. Its symbolism, which relates the signs of the zodiac to the Jewish months of the year, has a long history in Jewish art.

The Ark is set within a canted apse and is top-lit through a glass semi-dome (*Westlake*, 1887)[1] unlike that in any other synagogue in England (although **Glasgow's Garnethill** also has a glazed dome over the Ark). The east wall is covered with gilded Lincrusta wallpaper, embossed and gilded, with mosaic work, featuring a sunburst motif.

The magnificent brass pulpit decorated with openwork arabesques was donated by Sir Albert Sassoon (builder of the **Sassoon Mausoleum** – *see* below) in 1887.

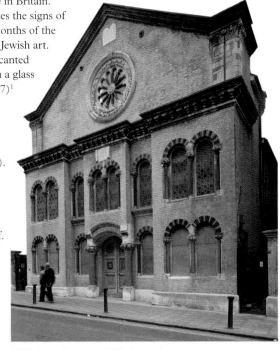

Middle Street Synagogue (E020047)

View to the rear (J020166)

The elegant *bimah* is accessed from the rear, an unusual design found elsewhere in this period only in **Liverpool** at **Princes Road**. The wrought-iron balustrade was later enriched with brass scrolls and acorn finials. Such decorative embellishments were gradually introduced, helpfully labelled with dated donors' *plaques*, some of which line the walls of the vestibule. Read these carefully and you learn, for example, that the brass grille over the Ark replaced the original wooden doors in 1915, while the old grille was reused over the main entrance at the rear of the prayer hall.

The Ark (J020165)

The synagogue has splendid light fittings, electroliers rather than gasoliers. It is reputed to be the first synagogue in Britain to have installed electricity, in 1892.

The brass *hanukiah* on an Italian black marble pedestal, dated 5605 (=1845), was brought from the **Regency Synagogue** at **Devonshire Place** (*see* below).

OPENING HOURS: Occasional services and opening to the public some Sundays, including Brighton Festival (May) and Heritage Open Days (September). Other times and group bookings by appointment through Brighton and Hove Hebrew Congregation (West Hove Synagogue), 31 New Church Road, Hove, BN3 4AD: tel 01273 888 855; www.bhhc-shul.org/middlestreet.html

Discover Brighton's Jewish Heritage

Numbers refer to Jewish sites on the Heritage Trail maps. Letters refer to general landmarks. Extant Jewish sites are indicated in bold in the text.

Distance: 6.25km (3.9 miles) on foot.

Map 1: Central Brighton, 2km (1.2 miles) from Middle Street to Devonshire Place and the terminus of Volk's Electric Railway.

Map 2: Kemp Town, 1km (0.6 miles) from the terminus east to the Sassoon Mausoleum (plus 1.25km back to Palace Pier).

Map 3: from Kemp Town to Hove, 2km (1.2 miles) from the terminus west to Brunswick Terrace.

○ *Start from* **Middle Street Synagogue** ❶*.*

Walk up (north) to the end of **Middle Street,** *away from the sea. You are now in the heart of* **The Lanes***. Follow the road bearing right into* **Duke Street** *to the junction with* **Ship Street,** *and from there turn right into* **North Street***. Cross at the lights into* **Bond Street***.* **Jew Street** *is an (at present) unmarked narrow alleyway, between shops at* **14 and 15 Bond Street,** *to your left (west). Jew Street forms an L-shape coming out on* **Church Street** *where the street sign is located.*

Former **Jew Street Synagogue** ❷

Jew Street, BN1 1UT

This brick alleyway is the site of Brighton's first synagogue, from 1789 to *c* 1800. Although not officially recorded, its existence had given rise to the street name as early as 1799. All that remains of what is thought to have

been the synagogue building are a bricked-up window opening and arch in a fragment of wall, built in courses of local rubble flint, on the left as you enter from Bond Street.

○ *Follow* **Jew Street** *to its end, and turn right into* **Church Street** *as far as the* **Royal Pavilion (A)***. Detour through the rear of the* **Pavilion Gardens** *(by* **The Dome (B)** *and* **Brighton Art Gallery & Museum (C)***) to admire John Nash's exotic Indian domes (1815–22, but sadly in parts reproduction fibreglass). Exit through the* **Main Entrance,** *with its Hindu-style canopy, onto* **Pavilion Buildings***. Turn left at* **Castle Square** *and make for the busy dual carriageway intersection (A23) at* **Old Steine***. Cross over through the green with its fountain and war memorial to* **St James's Street** *immediately opposite. Keep going until you reach* **Devonshire Place** *on your left. Turn away from the sea up Devonshire Place. The synagogue is on the right-hand (east) side.*

Former **Regency Synagogue** ❸

38 Devonshire Place, BN2 1QB

Benjamin Bennett, 1823–4, remodelled by David Mocatta, 1836–8, Grade II

This was Brighton's first purpose-built synagogue, initially erected by local builder *Benjamin Bennett*. It was afterwards remodelled by architect *David Mocatta*, whose other surviving synagogue, commissioned by Sir Moses Montefiore at **Ramsgate**, is still in use. Mocatta's chief contribution to Brighton was its railway station

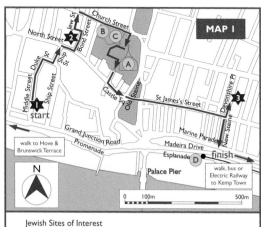

Jewish Sites of Interest

1 Middle Street Synagogue
2 *site of former Jew Street Synagogue*
3 *former Devonshire Place Synagogue*

Other Sites of Interest

A The Royal Pavilion
B The Dome
C Art Gallery & Museum
D Volk's Electric Railway terminus

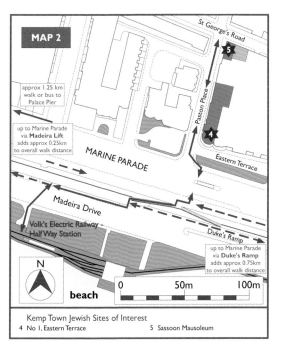

St George's Road

5

approx 1.25 km
walk or bus to
Palace Pier

up to Marine Parade
via **Madeira Lift**
adds approx 0.25km
to overall walk distance

MARINE PARADE

Paston Place

Eastern Terrace

4

Madeira Drive

Volk's Electric Railway –
Half Way Station

Duke's Ramp

up to Marine Parade
via **Duke's Ramp**
adds approx 0.75km
to overall walk distance

N

beach

0   50m   100m

Kemp Town Jewish Sites of Interest
4 No 1, Eastern Terrace   5 Sassoon Mausoleum

**The former Regency Synagogue
at Devonshire Place** (DP052739)

City of Brighton & Hove
DAVID MOCATTA
1806–1882
Anglo-Jewish Architect
Remodelled this building as
the City's first purpose built
Synagogue in 1838

Blue plaque (DP052741)

Inside the building the
ceiling lantern survives,
a feature typical of the
Regency period.
The adjoining house,
37 Devonshire Place
(Grade II), was the rabbi's
house. *Private*.

○ *Turn back and make for the
seafront. During the summer season,
walk down the other end of
Devonshire Place via the elegant
early-Victorian **New Steine** to the
Promenade. Take **Volk's Electric
Railway (D)**, 'Great Britain's First
and Oldest Electric Railway …
Operating since 1883', to the **Half
Way Station** (runs daily every 15
minutes 10.15 or 11.15 to 17.00 or
18.00, **Easter to end September**,
including Heritage Open Days
'subject to weather conditions';
tel: 01273 292 718 or www.
volkselectricrailway.co.uk and links
there to Brighton and Hove City
Council website's 'Transport' pages
for variations and group bookings).*

*The restored (2013) **Madeira
Lift**, 1890, Grade II (accessed
through the venue 'Concorde II', runs
daily 9.30 to 19.30 Easter to last
Sunday in September, tel 01273
673 311) takes you up to **Marine
Parade** where you will see a little
further on to your right (east) the
elegant curved corner of **Eastern
Terrace**. The alternative routes, via
the **steep stairs** (six flights) or up
Duke's Ramp (0.75km; 0.5 mile),
are best reserved for the most fit
and those desiring a work-out!*

*Off-season, the energetic may
walk or cycle along the front.
Unfortunately, there is no bus that
runs all the way along the
Promenade between Kemp Town
and Hove. Buses run from the city
centre. Brighton & Hove Bus
Information, tel: 01273 886 200.*

*NB Look out for **buses** in
Brighton named after notable Jews
with connections to the city. Among
them are Baron Goldsmid, and
architects David Mocatta and
George Basevi (whose family left the
Jewish community). 'Thomas Lainson'
is also one of the fleet. (See
www.buses.co.uk for the full list.)*

(1841) and he is associated
with other stations on the
London to Brighton line,
including the magnificent
viaduct at Haywards
Heath. The stucco façade
of Devonshire Place
Synagogue is somewhat
altered, especially on the
ground floor, but retains its
symmetrical appearance
with central doorway and
Tuscan pilasters under a
plain pediment. The
inscription under the
pediment reading JEWS'
SYNAGOGUE 5598 (=1838)

was reinstated as
a planning condition for
the conversion of the
building into nine flats in
2007. This was thanks to
the intervention of Jewish
Heritage, while the English
Heritage *Blue Plaque* for
David Mocatta was the
result of local initiative.
(A City of Brighton
and Hove blue *plaque*
commemorating the
architect was also affixed at
Brighton Station in August
2014). Note the reinstated
inscription D. MOCATTA
ARCH.T on the edge of the
band over the fanlight.

Eastern Terrace ❹

Kemp Town, BN2 1DJ

Grade II

This palatial stucco-fronted Regency building now subdivided into faded flats with the address **2 Court Royal Mansions**, with elegant curved corner bay, was the holiday home of Sir Albert Sassoon (1818–96), son of the Jewish 'merchant prince' of India, Sir David Sassoon, and a 'buddy' of the Prince of Wales, afterwards King Edward VII. Sir Albert was buried around the corner in the family mausoleum that he had built in 1892 in **Paston Place**. The two sites are apparently connected by an underground tunnel.

❍ *Walk up **Paston Place** to the corner with **St George's Road** where the very distinctive mausoleum stands.*

The Sassoon Mausoleum (F030076)

Sassoon Mausoleum ❺

83 St Georges Road, Kemp Town, BN2 1EF

1892, Grade II

The flamboyant trumpet-shaped dome of the square single-storey mausoleum cannot be missed. The copper dome was once covered in gold leaf. The glazed drum was restored in the 2000s as part of the Kemp Town Regeneration Scheme. The lotus-leaf crenellations to the parapet add to the exotic appearance, as do the lobed arches over the doorways. The remains[2] were removed in 1933 and the Sassoon Mausoleum was for many years part of a pub, the Hanbury Arms. In 2012 it became the venue for the burlesque club 'Proud Cabaret Brighton'. Don't be misled by the recently uncovered 'Bollywood'-style murals that decorate the ceiling inside the revamped 'Bombay Ballroom'. These post-date the Sassoons. However, Pevsner did comment that the Sassoon Mausoleum did not look out of place in a town that boasted the Royal Pavilion. Albert Sassoon's connections with India were more genuine than those of the Prince Regent.

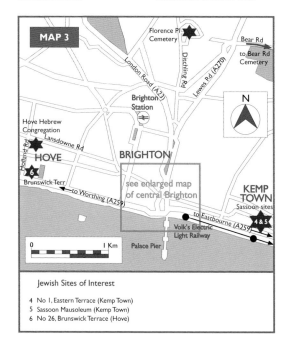

MAP 3

Florence Pl Cemetery

Bear Rd
to Bear Rd Cemetery

London Road (A23)

Ditchling Rd

Lewes Rd (A270)

Brighton Station

N

Hove Hebrew Congregation

Lansdowne Rd

Holland Rd

HOVE

BRIGHTON

Brunswick Terr

see enlarged map of central Brighton

to Worthing (A259)

KEMP TOWN
Sassoon sites

to Eastbourne (A259)

4&5

Volk's Electric Light Railway

0   1 Km   Palace Pier

Jewish Sites of Interest

4 No 1, Eastern Terrace (Kemp Town)
5 Sassoon Mausoleum (Kemp Town)
6 No 26, Brunswick Terrace (Hove)

➊ *Return by **Volk's Electric Railway** to the **terminus**. From here, **Brunswick Terrace** is a pleasant **2km (1.2 mile or 20–30 minute) walk** along the **Promenade** in the other direction (west) towards Hove. You could instead take a bus along the Promenade and alight at **Brunswick Terrace**. (NB More buses run from Brighton city centre) or bring your bike and make use of the **bicycle lane** along the Promenade.*

Former **Roof-top Synagogue** ➏

26 Brunswick Terrace, BN3 1HJ

Grade I

Stand on the Promenade and look up on the roof of this elegant Regency block (west side), laid out by *Amon Henry Wilds* with *C A Busby* in 1824–8. Make out a miniature classical temple surmounted by a 'pepper pot' octagonal dome on a drum. This was the private synagogue of Philip Salomons (1796–1867), brother of Sir David, first Jewish Lord Mayor of London, who lived at no. 26. There was a serious fire in the building in 1852 and it is thought that the little 'temple' was built sometime between then and Salomons' death in 1867. Architecturally it conforms nicely to visions of the Jerusalem Temple drawn by European artists since the Renaissance. Inside, the dome now functions as a kind of summerhouse. It has seating around the walls and a fine view overlooking the seafront. Slender iron supports in the room behind are perhaps vestiges of a gallery. *Now a private flat.*

End of walk.

The 'Penthouse' synagogue on the roof of Brunswick Place (DP052730)

OTHER JEWISH SITES IN BRIGHTON AND HOVE

Hove Hebrew Congregation

79 Holland Road, Hove, BN3 1JN

A conversion of the 1883 Holland Road Gymnasium carried out in 1929–30 by Newcastle architect *Marcus Kenneth Glass*. The pretty plasterwork Ark inside is identical to those that were at **Sunderland Synagogue** and **Clapton Synagogue** in London, both by Glass. The former has been badly damaged (*see* below) and the latter

destroyed, making his last intact Ark in Brighton all the more valuable.

OPENING HOURS: *Shabbat* and festival services: tel 01273 732 035; www. hollandroadshul.com

Brighton Progressive Synagogue

6 Lansdowne Road, Hove, BN3 1FF

It is impossible to guess from the 1938 modernist minimalist makeover by local architect *Edward Lewis* that this synagogue had started life as a brick Victorian gymnasium. If you stand well back, the pitch of the roof is visible. Brighton Liberal Synagogue (as it was originally called) is one of a tiny number of Liberal congregations that were established before the Second World War, in 1935. No doubt purely by coincidence, *Edward Lewis* was of Sephardi Jewish extraction, being a great-great nephew of Sir George Lewis, solicitor to King Edward VII.[3] For an anticipated congregation

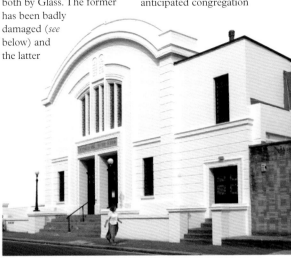

Hove Hebrew Congregation (DP052742)

of 300, Lewis gave it a geometric, cream-washed cement stucco façade. This is punctuated by an asymmetrical horizontal strip window at the right, counterbalanced by the rectangular entrance, with a reddish-brown brick dressed surround, ranged to the left. Symbolism was restrained, confined to a small blue-painted steel *Magen David* over the front entrance.

INTERIOR: Also originally very restrained; a star-shaped *ner tamid* hanging from the ceiling and a hexagram window pierced through the corner by the Ark wall. The original floor-to-ceiling Ark, 6.1m (20ft) in height, and concealed lighting behind the gallery, were among the notable innovative features of this building, which earned a write-up in the architectural press.[4] Pity that this adventurous Ark was replaced *c* 1949 by the current conventional classical one. The interior has also been compromised by the addition of more stained glass. In the 1950s the congregation expanded their premises into the house next door.

OPENING HOURS: *Shabbat* and festival services: tel 01273 737 223; www.bhps-online.org

NB Worth a detour is the nearby **Brighton and Hove Reform** (formerly **New**) **Synagogue** (*Derek Sharp Associates*, 1966–8), Palmeira Avenue, BN3 3GE. An unusually distinctive 1960s building, it has important *stained glass* by *John Petts*.

ACCESS: tel 01273 735 343; www.bh-rs.org

BURIAL GROUNDS

Florence Place Old Jewish Burial Ground

Florence Place, off Ditchling Road, Brighton, BN1 7GU

1826, Grade II

Brighton's first Jewish cemetery, opened in 1826. The original *ohel* by *David Mocatta* (1837) was replaced by the current octagonal red-brick structure with red stone dressings by *Lainson & Son* in 1891–3. Look out for the colourful inscription on the tombstone of HENRY SOLOMON: 15 YEARS CHIEF OFFICER OF POLICE OF THE TOWN OF BRIGHTON, WHO WAS BRUTALLY MURDERED WHILE IN THE PUBLIC DISCHARGE OF THE DUTIES OF HIS OFFICE ON THE 14TH DAY OF MARCH 1844. IN THE FIFTIETH YEAR OF HIS AGE. He now (since 2014) has a dedicated blue plaque affixed to Brighton Town Hall.

The late Victorian wrought-iron gates with their piers, the front wall and even an original ironwork lamp post immediately outside are all listed (Grade II).

LOCATION: On the east side of Florence Place, just beyond the school and

Florence Place Cemetery (F030084)

before the bend in the road (that ends in a cul-de-sac).

ACCESS: Locked. By appointment through West Hove Synagogue, 31 New Church Road, Hove, BN3 4AD; tel 01273 888 855.

Bear Road Cemetery

Meadowview Road, off Bevendean Road, BN2 4DE

1920

Also known as Meadow-view after the housing estate built on the old part of the municipal cemetery next door. Opened in 1920 and the current burial ground for Brighton's Jewish community. The *ohel* features First World War memorial glass. The extensive site was further enlarged in 1978 on council land from the Hove Cemetery, known as 'Bear Road', next door. The Holocaust memorial (2000) in the form of a 6ft (1.8m) high, uncut slab of Cornish granite with cast bronze decoration is by *Gerald Zebrak*.

LOCATION: Signposted from Bear Road. Take Bevendean Road. Reached via the more recent Meadowview Road, which serves the housing estate.

ACCESS: On-site caretaker. By appointment through West Hove Synagogue, 31 New Church Road, Hove, BN3 4AD; tel 01273 888 855.

NB Reform and Progressive burials take place at **Hove Cemetery**, Old Shoreham Road, BN3 7EF (1882). Three plots – sections 19, 21 (from 1957, with *ohel*) and 23 – are all located on the far west side of the extension, north side of Old Shoreham Road.

EASTBOURNE

Eastbourne Synagogue

22–23 Susan Road, BN21 3TJ

Housed in a converted stuccoed Victorian building, probably previously shops, since 1920. The community in this seaside town was established in 1918 and has never exceeded 50 members, its current size. The first floor was fitted out as a synagogue, with a simple, slightly Gothic-style wooden Ark, which today is preserved in the former gallery, now a meeting room, on the second floor. The present Ark (1972) is placed against the chimney breast, incorrectly, on the north-west wall. Modernised. Eastbourne functions independently of any of the synagogue groupings, services being conducted along slightly Reform lines.

OPENING HOURS: *Shabbat* and festival services: tel 01323 484 135; see Jewish Small Communities Network entry on Eastbourne Hebrew Congregation www.jscn.org.uk

Eastbourne Cemetery, Jewish Section

Hide Hollow, Langney, BN23 8AE

1922

A neat municipal plot surrounded by low privets. The gravestones are arranged in lines either side of the central path. Earliest headstone, slightly damaged, of ISAAC PINCUS d 19 May 1922.

LOCATION: Signposted from the main Hide Hollow roundabout (Junction B2104/B2191).

The Jewish plot is on the southern boundary of the cemetery at the end of the main entrance drive (sections C and D).

NB Eastbourne Liberal Jewish Community (founded 2001) also has a plot at Langney.

ACCESS: Open during general cemetery hours: tel 01323 766 536.

BOURNEMOUTH

Bournemouth Hebrew Congregation

Wootton Gardens, BH1 1PW

Lawson & Reynolds, 1910–11

Last gasp of red-brick seaside orientalism for British Jewry's favourite holiday town. Bournemouth Hebrew Congregation was formed in 1905. *George Joseph Lawson* was a successful local builder and developer, former mayor of Bournemouth, Liberal, committed Congregationalist and active temperance campaigner. The long east wall closes the street. The curvy roofline punctuating the buttressed bays is quite art nouveau, while the pair of roof lanterns are typical of public buildings of the early 20th century. Note the attractive interlocking mullioned window arcade under the squat little tower with its square leaded dome, which marked the original entrance, at the far (north) end. Gilded

Hebrew *inscription: Bet HaKnesset* ['the synagogue']. Cleverly enlarged in 1957–62 (*A E Green & M G Cross*) by the addition of three matching bays at the Ark end (south): you can hardly see the join. The new entrance at the other end (north) is an unwelcome intrusion. *Foundation stones.* Later additions including Murray Muscat Centre by *Geoffrey Anders* of *Peter Greed, Luck, Anders and Partners* (1970–2) and *Mikveh* (1976).

INTERIOR: A barrel-vaulted prayer hall with ribbed ceiling. In 1957–62 the long west wall was pushed back creating a slightly lopsided appearance; the gallery was built off cantilevered beams but remains unaltered only on the east side (left-hand side when facing the Ark). The 1960s Ark wall features the columns *Yahin* and *Boaz* – the pair of porch columns in Solomon's Temple – in a mosaic surround made by Florentine craftsmen. It is reminiscent of the contemporary (rebuilt) **Central Synagogue** in London, Great Portland Street. Gilded Hebrew *inscription*: 'Know before Whom you Stand'. Modern central *bimah.*

STAINED GLASS: The attractive green-hued *Magen David* windows and those in the tower are original; the rest date from the 1960s. Unusually turned down for listing by the DCMS in 2010

against the expert advice of English Heritage.

OPENING HOURS: *Shabbat* and weekday services. Visitors and groups by appointment: tel 01202 557 433; www.bhcshul.co.uk

Bournemouth East Cemetery, Jewish Section

Gloucester Road, Boscombe, BH7 6JB

1906

Earliest tombstone 1908. The *ohel* is constructed of ashlar limestone with tapered buttress turrets at the four corners decorated with curly scroll copings. It is reminiscent of art nouveau designs found on the continent,[5] but extremely rare in Britain.

Detail of the tower, Bournemouth Synagogue (AA046079)

Bournemouth East Cemetery Ohel (BB for SJBH)

The Hebrew *inscription* in the tympanum is from Psalm 23:4; the *ohel* is dated '5682 1922' on both gable ends. Of interest are the First World War graves, including those of German and Austrian Jewish prisoners-of-war captured in France and Belgium in 1915. Reserved plots only are available at Boscombe.

בית הכנסת

ACCESS: During general cemetery hours.

NB Post-war Jewish plots were opened at **Kinson Cemetery**, South Kinson Drive, BH11 8AA, in 1948 (Reform) and 1953 (Orthodox); and at **Throop** (1996) Broadway Lane, Throop, BH8 0AE, 1996 (Orthodox).

ALDERSHOT

Aldershot Hebrew Cemetery

Redan Road, GU11 4ST

1865

A Jewish community was formed in this garrison town in 1864 and, in the same year, applied to the Aldershot Burial Board for a separate section of the civilian cemetery at Redan Road cemetery.[6] The triangular plot at the north-eastern tip of the cemetery was purchased outright for £50 and was consecrated in 1865. The stone boundary walls and entrance were constructed by local builder *Joseph Stoodley*. It seems unlikely that there was ever an *ohel* since services are recorded as having taken place in the open air. The broken-down structure inside the cemetery, which has walls with a curved profile, has latterly[7] been identified as the grave of Harriet Cohen, d 1880, and four of her children who died in infancy.

The 1886 Queen's Regulations recognised Judaism as a separate 'denomination' for the purpose of chaplaincy in the Armed Forces. In 1892, Harriett's son, Revd Francis Lyon Cohen, who was a native of Aldershot (his father was Woolf H Cohen), became the first officially appointed Jewish army chaplain anywhere in the world. He and his successors took services at the local synagogue, which was not purpose-built and has long ceased to function.

The Jewish cemetery, which has an unkempt air, is now the responsibility of the United Synagogue in London. The burial register is apparently lost but field surveys have been carried out. There are lengthy but eroded *foundation stones* in Hebrew and English on the gate posts; also an interesting memorial to PTE DAVID COTT SCOTT, 2ND DRAGOON GUARDS (QUEENS BAYS) KILLED WHILE PREVENTING A COMRADE FROM COMMITTING SUICIDE SEPT 6TH 1900 AGED 20 YEARS.

ACCESS: Locked gate on Redan Road, but accessible from inside the main cemetery on account of the low internal boundary walls. Key c/o United Synagogue Burial Society (based at Bushey Cemetery): tel 020 8950 7767; www.theus.org.uk

PORTSMOUTH

Portsmouth and Southsea Synagogue

The Thicket, Elm Grove, Southsea, PO5 2AA

This comfortable red-brick and stucco villa (*c* 1910?), with its original leaded lights, fireplaces and panelled walls, contains unexpected Judaica treasures. The synagogue was added to the rear in 1936 (builder *R J Winnicott*) and contains the original Ark from the Georgian (1780) synagogue in White's Row, Portsea, wrongly placed on the north wall. It was fortunate that the community abandoned the docks for the suburbs: White's Row was bombed during the Second World War. The fine classical two-tiered Ark, of mahogany and gilded, with urn finials and crown, was badly restored in 1983.

Georgian tombstones at the old Jewish cemetery in Southsea (AA027893)

The *duhan* and other furnishings are mainly 1930s.

INSCRIPTIONS:
Standard *Ma Tovu* in archway to apse and gilded 'Know before Whom you stand before the Holy One Blessed be He' (abbreviated) on the Ark frieze. The medallion on the scroll beneath the Ark's *Luhot* bears a Hebrew text adapted from I Kings 8:9: 'Nothing remained of the Ark except the Tablets of the Law', which may

כִּי עַתָּה הִרְהִיב ה' לָנוּ וּפָּרִינוּ בָאָרֶץ
גָדוֹל יִהְיֶה כְּבוֹד הַבַּיִת הַזֶּה הָאַחֲרוֹן
מִן הָרִאשׁוֹן לִפְרָט
בָּנֹה בָנִיתִי בֵּית זְבֻל לָךְ מָכוֹן
לְשִׁבְתְּךָ עוֹלָמִים 5 5 4 0

Portsmouth and Southsea Synagogue foundation stone
(BB for SJBH)

be an enigmatic reference to a past rebuilding of the Ark. Look out also for *foundation stones* preserved from White's Row. In the glazed *succah* just before

you enter the main prayer hall is preserved a heavily incised and crudely blue-painted Hebrew lintel stone containing the date 5540 (=1780) buried in a chronogram.

On a dark (north-west) stairwell behind the Ark are stone fragments laid by leaders of the congregation: Benjamin Levi, Abraham Woolfe and Gershom ben Benjamin on *Lag b'Omer* (18 Iyar) 5540, corresponding to 23 May

The Georgian Ark at Portsmouth and Southsea Synagogue (AA027868)

1780. Another more official ceremony was obviously held several weeks later because two further stones are dated 10 Sivan 5540 (=13 June 1780) and bear the names of both David Tevele Schiff, Rabbi of the Ashkenazi Great Synagogue in London, and of the Sephardi *Haham* Moses Cohen D'Azevedo of **Bevis Marks**. Look out too for the synagogue clock, decorated with the Royal Coat of Arms of George III, probably installed as a token of patriotism during the Napoleonic Wars. Unique too are the pair of large round-headed windows flanking the Ark, which contain the full text of the Ten Commandments in both Hebrew and English. These outsize *Luhot* date from 1843. The *Mikveh* (1936) is now a broom cupboard.

OPENING HOURS: *Shabbat* and festival services. Visitors and groups by appointment: tel 02392 821 494; www.jackwhite.net/portsmouth-synagogue

Portsmouth Old Jews Burial Ground

Jews' Lane, Fawcett Road, Southsea, PO4 0LG

1749

Documentary proof exists for the purchase of this attractive burial ground, once known as 'Lazy Lane', by 'the Jews' Synagogue' in 1749, making it the oldest in the English provinces. By 1812 Portsmouth was probably the most influential Jewry outside London and was the fourth largest as late as 1851.

A synagogue existed in White's Row from 1742. As in other ports such as Plymouth, Southampton, Chatham and Sheerness, Portsmouth Jews acted as naval agents during the Napoleonic Wars. The red brick *ohel* is dated 5641 (=1881), the third on site as attested by the lengthy Hebrew *inscriptions* preserved inside: the scrolled tablet contains the date *Erev Rosh Hodesh* (eve of the New Moon) of Ellul 5541 (= 21 August 1781) when the *ohel* and walls were 'finished', and contains too an earlier date, probably 1768, with reference to the wardens of the synagogue, who are named. Another inscription below records the construction of a second *ohel*, FIFTY ONE YEARS LATER, on *Rosh Hodesh* Ellul 5592, corresponding to 27 August 1832, built when the cemetery was extended to the west, the first of several enlargements.

The oldest tombstones by the path near the *ohel* include some carved reliefs using traditional Jewish symbolism rare in England, during the Georgian period, for example raised hands denoting a *Cohen*, and pouring pitcher denoting a *Levi*. An unusual practice at Portsmouth was the use of bilingual inscriptions on the tombstones, Hebrew on the front with English on the back. Burial records survive from 1835.

LOCATION: Street frontage between junctions with Darlington Road and Graham Road. The postcode given above is based on the row of houses adjacent including nos. 270–4.

ACCESS: Key c/o Portsmouth and Southsea Synagogue: tel 02392 821 494.

Kingston Cemetery, Jewish Section

New Road, Copnor Bridge, Portsmouth, PO2 7RA

1902

The earliest burial, ABRAHAM EDWARD COYNE, otherwise EDDY COHEN, d 9 April and buried 11 April 1902, aged 27, is located at the corner of the plot (north-east) near the boundary on New Road, which is separated from the general cemetery (*Charles Smith* (landscaping) and *George Rake* (buildings), 1856, P & G Grade II) by a privet hedge. The northern extensions of this cemetery, including the Jewish section, lie outside the designated area. The Jewish community was allotted their plot in 1893 and the *ohel* was built in 1900. It is in red-brick Queen Anne-revival style, an unusual choice for a cemetery building. However, the side windows are in triplets, with almost Gothic triangular heads.

A new Jewish section was opened at the **Lawn Cemetery, Catherington Lane**, Horndean, Waterlooville, PO8 0TH, in 1988.

LOCATION: Via the north gate on New Road (not the main entrance on St Mary's Road which is for vehicular traffic). The postcode given above is that of the florist shop immediately opposite the gates in New Road.

ACCESS: During general cemetery hours.

The Emanuel Memorial Fountain on the seafront at Southsea, erected in 1888 in memory of the first Jewish mayor of Portsmouth (AA028976)

Emanuel Memorial Fountain

Canoe Lake Gardens,
The Esplanade, Southsea, PO4 0RR

1888, Grade II

Memorial fountain to Emanuel Emanuel, Bavarian-born first Jewish mayor of Portsmouth 1866–7, erected by his children *Barrow Emanuel* (1841–1904), of architects *Davis & Emanuel*, and Katie Emanuel, Lady Magnus (1844–1924). Emanuel Emanuel was the first Jew to be elected to the Portsmouth Council in 1841, steadfastly refusing to take the oath to serve 'on the true faith of a Christian', according to the Test Acts, which were then still in force. He was theoretically liable for a fine of £500 for every vote he participated in, but was never challenged. Indeed, both the borough council and Portsmouth's MPs were active in the cause of Jewish political emancipation, which was effectively achieved in 1858.

A rather un-Jewish choice of winged angel under an ironwork canopy overlooks the park and Esplanade, one of Emanuel's main contributions to the development of the town. The green and gold paintwork is peeling and rusting; sadly the granite fountain no longer works.

LOCATION: Opposite Southsea Pier. The postcode given above is that of the block of flats called St Helens Court on St Helens Parade, situated just behind.

SOUTHAMPTON

Southampton Old (Common) Cemetery, Jewish Section

Cemetery Road, SO15 7NN

P & G Grade II* and *ohel* Grade II

Delightfully verdant, this was the first Jewish plot included in the scheme for a municipal cemetery in England. It was originally located on the boundary but is now right inside thanks to later extensions. Southampton Common Cemetery was itself one of the earliest landscaped cemeteries in the country, opened in May 1846 on land taken from Southampton's ancient common. It was initially laid out by *John Claudius Loudon* (1783–1843), but on his death the council held a competition, won by *William Henry Rogers*. Rogers' landscaping scheme was implemented with modifications by *W B Page*, a local nurseryman. Another competition (1844) was held for the main buildings: the brief specified the use of Elizabethan, Norman and Gothic styles. London architect *Frederick John Francis* (1818–96) was the winner. He chose English Norman style for the Church of England, Early English Gothic for the Nonconformists and Elizabethan for the lodge (1848, all Grade II). It seems that the Jewish 'chapel' was a slightly later addition, designed in Tudor style in keeping with the lodge, on the northern side of the cemetery.

The rubble-stone *ohel* has a Tudor doorway and fireplace, but ogee window-heads on the long walls – perhaps an injection of something slightly more exotic. The *bet taharah* was added much later.

The first Jewish burial appears to have taken place in 1854, but there was no separate Jewish burial register at this date. The grave of ABIGAIL MOSELY, aged 3, d 8 or 9 March and buried 10 March 1854, may be found in the southernmost corner, close to the *ohel*. The Jewish section was apparently enlarged in 1884.

An organised Jewish community was established in Southampton in 1833; an Italianate synagogue was erected in Albion Street by *H H Collins* (1864–5; demolished 1964). The current **Southampton Synagogue** is a modest converted Methodist chapel at **Mordaunt Road**, Inner Avenue, SO14 6FW, consecrated 1964 (tel 02380 220 129; www.sotonhebrew.org.uk). A new burial plot was opened at **Hollybrook Cemetery**, Tremona Road, SO16 6HW in 1971.

LOCATION: Take Cemetery Road off The Avenue (A33). The entrance to the Jewish section is just before and to the right of the main lodge and entrance gates.

ACCESS: During general cemetery hours.

FURTHER INFORMATION: See The Friends of Southampton Old Cemetery (formed 2003), website: www.fosoc.org

It is likely that there was a Jewish presence in the Channel Islands in the Middle Ages, given their geographical proximity to Normandy. The French influence is still very strong here, not only in the street names but also in the political and legal system based on the *Etats Jersiaises*. The Channel Islands are not formally part of the United Kingdom, but are classified as a 'Crown Dependency'.

The history of the Jews in the Channel Islands is also very different from that on mainland Britain. During the Second World War, a mere 20 miles of English Channel saved Anglo-Jewry from the Holocaust. But the Nazis did get as far as the Channel Islands. A *plaque* in the **Jersey Jewish Cemetery** at Tower Road,[8] **St Helier**, commemorates three JEWISH RESIDENTS OF GUERNSEY DURING THE GERMAN OCCUPATION. DEPORTED ON 21 APRIL 1942 TO THEIR DEATHS AT AUSCHWITZ-BIRKENAU. One had been born in Katowice, Poland, and the other two in Vienna. Another *plaque* (2001) marks the actual place of their deportation at **St Peter Port, Guernsey**. In front of the **Westmount Crematorium, St Helier** (Westmount Road, JE2 3LP) is a multi-lingual memorial to the slave labourers of many nationalities, including Jews, who perished in the Channel Islands between 1941 and 1944. Another Holocaust memorial *plaque* (1969), in Hebrew, is to be found as part of the **Hammond Memorial**, near Longis Common, on **Alderney**.

In fact, most of the Jews resident in the Channel Islands on the outbreak of war were evacuated ahead of the invasion. Individual Jews had been present in the Channel Islands in the 1760s, on Guernsey, although no organised community was ever established either there or on the smaller islands of Alderney, Sark and Herm. The community in **Jersey** dates from the 1830s. In 1843 a synagogue was built in the yard of a house at 21 Grove Place, afterwards 47, then **100 Halkett Place** (demolished 2000). This synagogue was in use intermittently until *c* 1870 while doubling as a Masonic hall. Ironically, the site is now occupied by an almost identical mock-Georgian house. There was, until recently, no system of statutory protection of historic buildings in the Channel Islands. Ironic too that the two Jewish cemeteries on Jersey were left untouched by the Nazis. No Jewish community records have survived from before the war.

A new Jersey Jewish Congregation was constituted in 1961. *Shabbat* services are held at the small **Jersey Synagogue**, Petite Route des Mielles, St Brelade, JE3 8FY (corner Route des Genets); tel 01534 744 946. It was designed by *Norman Green*, 1972, using a former Wesleyan Methodist schoolroom. There were about 85 members of the congregation in 2010.

Westmount Jewish Cemetery

Westmount Road, St Helier, JE2 3LQ

1836

Next door to the now destroyed 'Strangers' Cemetery', and close to the Westmount Quarry, the Jewish plot was acquired in 1834 and the first burial was in 1836, although many of the oldest tombstones in the rear portion of the long, narrow site are no longer legible (earliest legible 1849). Enlarged towards the gate in 1873; the first burial in the new section 1888. A single row of graves on each side face each other across a wide central gravelled path. The cemetery is enclosed within high coursed rubble stone walls.

In 2014 the site of the old quarry was being prepared for residential development. In 2010 the Jewish community had observed Jewish law and refused an offer by the Parish of St Helier to relocate the oldest Jewish

Multi-lingual memorial to slave labourers during the Second World War (BB for SJBH)

burial ground in Jersey (it still has reserved graves). Instead, developers Dandara agreed to repair the wall and create an appropriate garden in front of the entrance.[9]

LOCATION: Near to the beginning of Westmount Road, before it loops and bends northwards away from the sea; north-east side, inside car park. Postcode above is for the existing Westmount Park flats.

ACCESS: Locked gate in wall. Key c/o Regal Construction: tel 01534 865 333, email admin@regal-con. co.uk

Almorah Cemetery, Jewish Section

Richmond Road, St Helier, JE2 3GY

1877

Founded in the 1860s by a dissenting faction in the quarrelsome congregation. The Almorah Cemetery itself was opened in 1854 by the Nonconformist St Helier General Cemetery Association, which was modelled on the English cemetery companies. Laid out by *C B Saunders*, the cemetery was divided into four sections: Roman Catholics at the north-west, Baptists and Congregationalists at the

Gravestone in Almorah Cemetery (BB for SJBH)

north-east, Methodists at the south-east and 'Others' at the south-west, where the tiny railed-off Jewish plot is located.

The first burial was that of LEWIS LEOPOLD, a prime mover in the acquisition of the site, d 3 July 1877, aged 61. The latest of the nine extant stones is dated 1916, plus an extra gravestone dated 1920 just outside the Jewish plot. There is an unsubstantiated story that during the Second World War the tombstones were laid flat to prevent discovery and desecration by the Nazi occupiers. Certainly, the tombstones are not now *in situ* and there are more burials than grave markers; one gravestone has a Gothic motif that could almost be mistaken for a cross. Another story current is that some of the tombstones were removed by Protestant descendants of Jews in an effort to hide their origins during the Occupation.

Rescued from neglect in the 1980s and now looked after by the Cemeteries Department in cooperation with the Jersey Jewish Burial Trust.

ACCESS: The railed Jewish plot is situated to the left (south-west) of the main path leading from the castellated main gates on Richmond Road/ Le Clos de Debénaire to the chapel. During general cemetery hours.

THE WEST COUNTRY

THE WEST COUNTRY is one of the richest parts of England in terms of historic Jewish sites. Remote from London and much of England, from the late 17th century the region developed strong naval and mercantile connections with Portugal, Gibraltar, the Cape and the West Indies. The oldest synagogues in the country (after London's Bevis Marks) are to be found in Devon, in the naval dockyard of **Plymouth** and the cathedral town of **Exeter**. Opened in the 1760s, both are still in use, and their small and friendly communities especially welcome holidaymakers who can help out with the *minyan*. An informal community of Jews scattered around Cornwall has reconstituted itself as Kehillat Kernow (Cornish for Cornwall) and holds Reform-style *Shabbat* and festival services (see www.kehillatkernow.com). Former synagogue buildings dating from the Regency period still exist in the charming Cornish fishing ports of **Penzance** and **Falmouth**.

Old Cornish place names such as 'Market Jew Street' and 'Marazion' long gave rise to romantic legends about early Jewish arrivals by sea in medieval and even Roman times, and their association with the tin mining industry which flourished in the area. Hard evidence, unfortunately, is lacking. From the 1720s onwards Jews, such as the enterprising Leman Hart, founder of Leman Hart Rum, set up business in the West Country. Well-preserved Georgian Jewish cemeteries await discovery in both Devon and Cornwall and elsewhere in the south-west: in the bustling port city of **Bristol**, where Jews were resident from

the 1740s, and the fashionable Georgian spa towns of **Bath** and **Cheltenham**. Some of the furnishings of both Cheltenham's elegant Regency synagogue and Bristol's solid Victorian stone synagogue pre-date their buildings.

Further Reading

For more information on the Jews of the West Country the following are available locally:

- Friedlander, E *et al* 2000 *The Jews of Devon and Cornwall: Essays and Exhibition Catalogue*. Bristol: Redcliffe
- Pearce, K and Fry, H[1] (eds) 2000 *The Lost Jews of Cornwall*. Bristol, Redcliffe
- Pearce, K 2014 *The Jews of Cornwall: A History, Tradition and Settlement to 1913*. Somerset: Halsgrove
- Samuel, J 1997 *Jews in Bristol*. Bristol: Redcliffe
- Susser, B 1993 *The Jews of South West England*. Exeter University Press
- Torode, B 2011 *The Hebrew Community of Cheltenham, Gloucester and Stroud*, 3rd edition. Cheltenham: privately printed
- For information on the Susser Archive, see www.jewishgen.org/ JCR-UK/Susser

The Georgian Ark at Plymouth Synagogue (AA036062)

Plymouth Synagogue

Catherine Street, PL1 2AD / 1761–2, Grade II★

Built over 250 years ago, the oldest Ashkenazi synagogue in the English-speaking world

Built in the days when riots against 'Dissenters' from the Church of England were still a real possibility, Plymouth's historic synagogue is tucked away on a side street. It is correctly aligned but with the front door, at west, effectively 'around the back'. The pair of large round-headed windows in the street-facing east wall suggest that the unremarkable stone-and-brick, rendered and whitewashed building, roofed in Cornish slate, was just another Nonconformist meeting house.

The congregation still possesses the original lease, which was held in trust by a friendly Christian, because in those days Jews were not permitted to own property. The architect of the Plymouth synagogue, like that of Exeter's (*see* below), is unknown. In all probability, he was a local master-builder, and the plain pine seating, timber floor and other interior woodwork was constructed by dockyard carpenters.

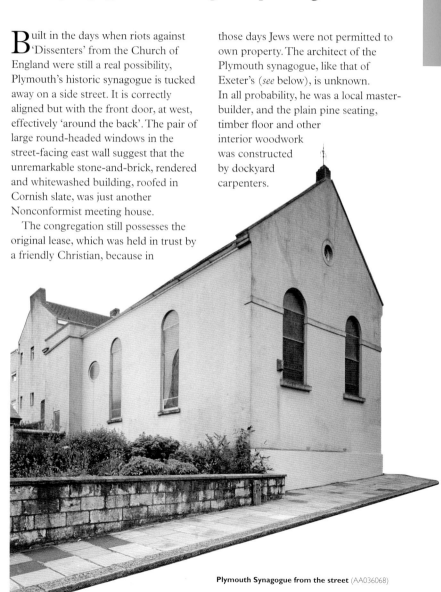

Plymouth Synagogue from the street (AA036068)

The stuccoed entrance front, with prominent cornices, scrolled brackets and segmental-headed openings, dates from a hundred years after the building of the synagogue: it is thought to have been added in 1863–4. The lintel stone over the entrance is probably not original. A verse from Psalm 95:6 contains a chronogram of the Hebrew year 5522 (=1761–2). The three-storey Victorian vestry house opposite was built, as its keystone declares in Latin characters, in AM 5634, corresponding to 1874. Inside, the tiled *mikveh* can be seen. For many years (until the mid 2000s) it lay hidden beneath the floorboards. This rainwater *mikveh* probably dates from the opening of the vestry house. It replaced a *mayan* or spring water *mikveh* that was fed by a well that is known to have been used in the 18th century until 1834 when it was compulsorily acquired by the corporation and subsequently disappeared under the Guildhall (also opened in 1874) situated just to the north-west of the synagogue.[2]

INTERIOR: The Minton terracotta floor in the vestibule is typically Victorian and the present staircases were created at the same time. Notice the Royal Family prayer board hanging in the vestibule. The names of King George V and Queen Mary are deceptive: the canvas has been overpainted and in fact dates from 1762.

Two steps up access the small prayer hall. The thickness of the wall suggests that this was once the outside wall. The pair of cast-iron columns on plinths flanking as you enter emphasise the alignment of entrance, *bimah* and Ark. It is not certain when these columns were added; perhaps they symbolise *Yahin* and *Boaz*, the pair of porch columns in Solomon's Temple. The prayer hall is simple, with a flat coved ceiling, and plastered and whitewashed walls. Much of the space is occupied by the generous *bimah*, its rounded corners topped by tall brass lamp standards, eight in all. An unusual feature is the integral curved bench seating arranged

Plymouth Synagogue (AA036065)

The interior (AA036067)

round the outside of the *bimah*. The sole remaining brass ball chandelier (originally there would have been three hanging from the ceiling rose vents) is reproduction.

Originally, there was only a west gallery facing the Ark; the extensions along the sides, also carried on slender columns, were later additions. Much care was taken to match the new gallery fronts with the original section, high panelled and painted, and topped with a token metal, lattice-work *mehitzah*.

All attention is focused on the lavish decoration of the gilded Ark. The Ark remained a free-standing piece of furniture in the Georgian period. With its broken pediment, fluted Corinthian pilasters, carved finials and urns, and oversized blue and gold *Luhot*, the Plymouth example, perhaps made in Holland or the German Lands, has been

likened to the baroque Arks of the synagogues of Venice. The *inscription* on the cornice separating the two tiers of the Ark is from Psalm 5:8 and contains the date Hebrew 5522, corresponding to 1761–2. Unfortunately, the Ark was badly restored in 2002, losing its gentle golden patina.

STAINED GLASS: 20th century, replacing the original clear Georgian glazing.

OPENING HOURS: *Shabbat* and festival services. Heritage Open Days (September). Other times and groups by appointment: tel 01752 263 162; email phccaretaker@yahoo.co.uk; or via contact details on website: www.plymouthsynagogue.co.uk. Schools, student and educational groups: please book through Plymouth Centre for Faiths and Cultural Diversity: tel 01752 254 438; www.pcfcd.co.uk

Exeter Synagogue

Synagogue Place, Mary Arches Street, EX4 3BA

1763–4, Grade II*

Exeter's tiny synagogue, opened a year after Plymouth's, on 10 August 1764, originally had an even meaner setting than Plymouth's. It opens directly onto the street to which it managed to give its name: 'Synagogue Place'. Such Jewish street names are rare in England. The present Greek-revival porch, flanked by fluted Doric columns, was added in 1835–6. At the same time, the façade was stuccoed and the ground floor rusticated. A second storey was later added, lost in bomb damage during the Second World War, exaggerating the present squat character of the building. Originally, the synagogue apparently had no windows at all, being lit only from above by a lantern (replaced in 1997–9 by *Stephen Emanuel*).

Exeter Synagogue was constructed only 10 years after an Exeter MP had lost his seat for supporting Henry Pelham's deeply unpopular Jewish Naturalisation Act[3] – the so-called 'Jew Bill' of 1753 that caused rioting in the streets. It was soon repealed.

INTERIOR: The Hebrew *inscription* painted on a *mizrakh* plaque over the inner entrance to the prayer hall quotes three Biblical verses that make

The Ark at Exeter Synagogue (AA046084)

to yield the date 5524, corresponding to 1763–4.

Exeter's delicate metalwork ovoid *bimah* is most elegant and stylistically unique in the country. The interlocking curved metalwork of the balustrade matches that of both *duhan* and *mehitzah*. Look out for the box pews with unusual book rests that are hinged and tilting for use when standing. Most uncomfortable for worshippers!

During replacement of the roof lantern in 1997 an original oak timber, perhaps from a man-of-war, was found. It was turned into a carved sculpture by *Marcus Vergette* and is now on display in the synagogue office.

OPENING HOURS: Some *Shabbat* and festival services (traditional and progressive). Heritage Open Days (September). Other times and groups by appointment: tel 01392 251 529; www.exetersynagogue. org.uk

mention of Jerusalem.[4] Moreover, the Hebrew date is hidden in a chronogram based on the word 'Jerusalem', and a fourth verse from the *Shulchan Aruch* (*Orakh Haim*, 94) specifically states 'Pray according to the Law towards Jerusalem.' The orientation of the Ark was corrected from north to south-east in the alterations of 1836, when this plaque was made.

The prayer hall itself is tiny and mainly top-lit through the reconstructed lantern. The ceiling is plain plastered, with a deep cove, plain plastered walls above dado height and a timber-boarded floor. Four brass single-tier chandeliers hang from the ceiling.

As at **Plymouth**, the three-sided gallery is of later date than the building itself, inserted at the same time as the remodeling in 1835–6. The gallery is supported by slender cast-iron columns, painted and stencilled.

Exeter's Ark is much simpler than Plymouth's and has been carefully restored, with the help of English Heritage and the Heritage Lottery Fund, to what is thought to have been the original gilded and marbleised effect. During the restoration work (by *Eddie Sinclair*, 1997–9) no fewer than 29 different paint layers were uncovered. Exactly the same *inscription* is painted on the cornice between the two tiers as is found at Plymouth (from Psalm 5:8), here also functioning as a chronogram. A different selection of Hebrew letters is made,

PLYMOUTH

Plymouth Hoe Old Jews' Burial Ground

Lambhay Hill, PL1 2NW

A pine-filled haven enclosed by a high stone wall. Apparently an extension of Sarah Sherrenbeck's back garden, which was in existence from at least 1726, and probably first used for burials in 1744. The site, near Plymouth Hoe, is documented with certainty from 1758. It was purchased by three London Jewish merchants, who no doubt also put up the money: £40. The acquisition of the cemetery thus pre-dated the formal establishment of the Plymouth Hebrew Congregation. Extended in 1811 by locally resident Jews, plus one Christian 'John Saunders of Plymouth, gentleman', presumably just in case the legal entitlement of Jews to own land was queried. No burial register survives, but the second of two surveys in the 20th century was carried out by Rabbi Dr Bernard Susser, then minister of the congregation, in 1972. In the interim more of the inscriptions had disappeared. The earliest he identified, along the north wall but only partially legible, bore the date 5522 (=1761–2). The middle portion of the cemetery is sunken, reached by a stone staircase, with possibly the remains of an *ohel* immediately behind the gate.

ACCESS: Locked wooden gate at the rear of HM Customs and Excise car park (at postcode above) on Lambhay Hill. By appointment Plymouth Synagogue: tel 01752 263 162 or via contact details on website: www. plymouthsynagogue.co.uk

Gifford Place Jewish Cemetery

Rear of no. 49 (caretaker's lodge), Gifford Place, Mutley, PL3 4JA

1868

Acquired in 1868[5] and still in use by Plymouth's Jews. A neat, lawned site next door to the Old Plymouth Cemetery, Ford Park. The registers are incomplete; the earliest stone on site dates from 1873. *Ohel* rebuilt 1958.

ACCESS: This cemetery is on an incline and can be viewed from above from the alleyway at the rear of Gifford Place. Locked gateway next to the caretaker's lodge on the corner of Gifford Place. Entry Code. By appointment Plymouth Synagogue: tel 01752 263 162 or via contact details on website: www. plymouthsynagogue.co.uk

EXETER

Bull Meadow Jews' Burial Ground

Magdalen Street, Bull Meadow, EX2 4HS

1757, Grade II (boundary wall)

The original lease for this site, adjoining the Old Dissenters' burial ground in Bull ('Bury') Meadow, is preserved at the Devon Archives and Local Studies Service, and is dated 18 May 1757. It was acquired from 'the brothers and sisters of the house or hospital of lepers of Saint Mary Magdalen without the Southgate of the City of Exeter', who made the erection of the substantial boundary walls a condition of the sale. These are of red brick, and well buttressed. The cemetery was extended in all directions, beginning in 1807, then in 1827 and 1851, the latest extensions doubling the size of the original plot.

Consequently, the oldest tombstones are today to be found in the centre. The earliest partially legible stone is: NANCY, wife of MOSES LAZARUS, dated in Hebrew 5570 (=1810). By the 1970s the whole site was threatened by plans for the building of an inner bypass road. A new Jewish section had been opened in the **Exwick Cemetery** (Exwick Road, Exeter, EX4 2BT) after the Second World War and the lease for Bull Meadow had expired without anyone noticing; Exeter Hebrew Congregation had never acquired title. This oversight was rectified in 1977 for £750, and the cemetery underwent restoration in the 1980s.

Behind the modern *ohel* an archway, with keystone and imposts, survives in a porch, probably a vestige of the original late 18th- or early 19th-century *ohel* on the same site. It is known from the synagogue minutes that in the 19th century members of the congregation were deputed to spend three nights in the *ohel* after a new burial in order to guard against body snatchers. No early original burial records survive, but this cemetery was the subject of a number of site surveys in the 20th century.

LOCATION: On Magdalen Street, next door to Parkside Court and overlooked by Magdalen Bridge Court, both with postcode EX2 4HS. Bounded on the west by Bull Meadow Road.

ACCESS: Locked. Key c/o Exeter Synagogue: tel 01392 251 529.

PENZANCE

Former **Penzance Synagogue**

Rear of The Star Inn, 119 Market Jew Street, TR18 2LD

1807

Now shabby backroom premises for The Star Inn (Grade II),[6] whose picturesque façade is on Market Jew Street. From around the back (car park on **Jennings Street**) the round-headed windows and hipped slate roof, with shingles reaching down over the rendered walls, clearly indicate a plain Nonconformist-style meeting house. Typically for the Georgian period,

The Star Inn, off Market Jew Street, Penzance, to the rear of the Old Synagogue (AA037193)

The remains of the old synagogue in Penzance, seen from Jennings Street (AA037194)

the synagogue was discreetly tucked away from (potentially hostile) public gaze.[7] Built in 1807,[8] on the back yard of an 18th-century house once owned by the Branwell family (of Brontë fame) at no. 1 **New Street**, it replaced an earlier synagogue of 1768 probably on the same site. In 1837 the synagogue acquired this house and a neighbouring cottage (nos. 1 and 2 New Street) and incorporated them into the congregational premises.[9] In 1906 the defunct synagogue was sold and used as a chapel, initially for the Plymouth Brethren and, remarkably, the gallery[10] and interior fittings survived almost intact until the 1980s. The crudely painted *Luhot* were rescued and are now in the **Jewish**

Tombstone of Jacob James Hart, a nephew of Leman Hart, 1846 (AA029487)

Museum in London.[11] A painted Hebrew *inscription* over the Ark is still in Penzance, in a private collection.[12] A chronogram embedded in the verse 'He opens for us the gates of mercy' gives the Hebrew year 5580, corresponding to 1820.

LOCATION: The Star Inn is on the corner with no. 1 New Street, TR18 2LZ. However, the synagogue behind is best seen from round the back, from the car park on Jennings Street.

Penzance Jews' Burial Ground

Lestinnick Terrace, TR18 2HB

Grade II

One of the best-preserved Georgian Jewish burial grounds in Britain, with almost 50 tombstones, many of Cornish slate. Completely hidden behind high stone walls, probably completed in 1844–5, soon after the freehold was purchased for £50 (1843).[13] By this time the surrounding area was undergoing rapid development, but the packhorse track at the side (east) down to the harbour, survives. The earliest extant lease dates from

1810 and the freehold seems to have been acquired in 1844. A partial Hebrew *inscription* on the oldest, broken but legible, tombstone (in the third row from the back) yields the date 25 Shevat 5551 (= 30 January 1791). There is an interesting coffin-shaped slab stone for JACOB JAMES HART ESQ: LATE HER BRITANNIC MAJESTY'S CONSUL FOR THE KINGDOM OF SAXONY AND A NATIVE OF THIS TOWN WHO DEPARTED THIS LIFE IN LONDON ON 19TH FEBRUARY AM 5606 [=1846] AGED 62 YEARS. These two and a number of other tombstones, together with the boundary walls and the remains of the *bet taharah* by the entrance, are listed Grade II. In October 1941 bombing destroyed part of the front wall and several headstones, which were subsequently replaced with English-only memorials. The latest burial took place in 1999. Now under the trusteeship of the Board of Deputies; a Friends of Penzance Jewish Cemetery was established in January 2014 and a year later a grant of £13,000 was received from the Heritage Lottery Fund.

ACCESS: Locked gate set back between 19 and 20 Lestinnick Terrace. By advance appointment only, key c/o The Director, Penlee Museum, Morrab Road, Penzance, TR18 4HE: tel 01736 363 625; restrictions on photography.

CONTACT: www. penleehouse.org.uk

FALMOUTH

The Old Synagogue, Falmouth

Summerhill Studio, 1 Gyllyng Street, Smithick Hill, TR11 3EH

1808, Grade II

On a prominent elevated site overlooking Falmouth harbour, reputedly so that the merchant-worshippers could keep an eye on the packet boats entering the bay. Jews had been in business in the town since at least 1766. A simple Regency red-brick 'chapel' building, partially rendered with granite dressings, hipped slate roof and large round-headed windows. The Ark was located on the east wall (under the roundel) facing the sea and access was formerly from the rear. The present doorway in the east wall post-dates 1879 when the building ceased to function as a synagogue; it was sold in 1892. The *mikveh* disappeared. Nothing is left inside save two painted red wood Tuscan columns from the gallery, but even these are probably no longer *in situ*. The painted wooden *Luhot* are now in the **Jewish Museum** in London. The building is much restored and has been converted into a flat and studio. *Plaque*, 2000.

Falmouth Jews' Burial Ground

Old Falmouth Road, Ponsharden, TR10 8AB

Scheduled Ancient Monument; two memorials Grade II

A secluded grassy site, overhung with trees and with a rubble stone boundary wall, broken in places. Vestiges of an *ohel* can be seen behind the gate. Jews were settled in Falmouth from the 1720s. Contiguous plots at Ponsharden were presented to the Jews and to the Congregationalists by Sir Francis Basset, Lord de Dunstanville (1757–1835) *c* 1780. One of the earliest burials was that of ESTHER, wife of BARNET LEVY, in 1780, but the earliest legible tombstone in

The Old Synagogue, Falmouth: the east wall (AA046090)

The Old Synagogue overlooking Falmouth Harbour (AA046093)

The Old Jewish Cemetery, Falmouth, general view (AA046096)

Hebrew is now that for ISAAC son of BENJAMIN, died on Monday 17 Heshvan and buried Tuesday (18 Heshvan) 5551 (= 25 October 1790) (Grade II). Also buried along the back wall is ALEXANDER MOSES, known as ZENDER FALMOUTH, the founder of the community, d 24 Nisan 5551 (=28 April 1791) (Grade II). Both these stones are made of Cornish slate. The last consecutive burial recorded on the surviving stones was in 1868, with another in 1913. The *bet taharah* has disappeared. No records survive, but the site has been well documented in a number of field surveys in the 20th century comprehensively (along with **Penzance**) collated by Keith Pearce,[14] who concluded that there were a total of 53 known burials and 33 graves with headstones. All face north.

Under the formal trusteeship of the Board of Deputies of British Jews since 1962, the site was cared for by the town council, but its poor condition has lately been cause for concern. Together with the Congregationalist Cemetery next door, the Jewish Cemetery was declared a Scheduled Ancient Monument in 2002 to protect it from neighbouring development. Long-standing plans for the building of a Sainsbury's supermarket nearby finally came to fruition in 2014. These included agreement to erect a temporary protective fence around both of the cemeteries, with a secure gate. The Friends of Ponsharden Cemeteries was formed in December 2013.

LOCATION: Easily missed! The locked wooden gate is almost concealed by ivy. It is close to the roundabout at the intersection of the Falmouth Road (A39 Penryn bypass) and the Old Falmouth Road (B3292), at Ponsharden, to the north-west of Falmouth. The postcode given above is that of the nearby Lidl store.

ACCESS: The broken boundary walls meant that unofficial access was possible until the temporary security fence was erected in June 2014. However, look out for the newly formed Friends of Ponsharden Cemeteries online for further details.

TRURO

Possible vestiges of Truro Jews' Burial Ground

St Clements Hill, TR1 1PY

A blocked-up archway in a rubble and sandstone wall is all that remains of this lost site, probably Georgian and gone out of use by 1840. Some obscure references to a 'Jews Burying Ground' and 'Gue Burying' have been unearthed in the local tithes records *c* 1834–6.[15]

LOCATION: North side by the police station (postcode TR1 1PY), almost opposite Trennick Lane.

Headstone in Falmouth of Giteleh Benjamin, wife of Isaac Menassah, 1794 (AA046100)

BRISTOL

Bristol Synagogue

9 Park Row, BS1 5LP

Hyman Henry Collins with
Samuel Charles Fripp, 1870–1,
Grade II

A necessarily unusual plan
of a synagogue on an
awkward elevated site,
a former quarry, by the
senior London-based
Jewish architect of
Victorian England, with
the assistance of the
city surveyor. *Collins'*
synagogues have had a
poor survival rate, Bristol
and **Chatham** being the
only extant examples
outside London. Here,
built in dressed local rubble
stone in Collins' favourite
Italianate style, with
a roomy arched porch
with seats inside. The
ornamental gates are dated
1921; a Hebrew *inscription*
from Isaiah 2:5 is found in
the stone band under the
parapet. The roof is clay-
tiled and hipped. The
substantial three-storey
minister's house projects
forward to the side, with
20th-century accretions
behind, now derelict.
The location of *mikvaot* in
Bristol remains elusive,
but it is unlikely that one
existed at the synagogue.

INTERIOR: The main
prayer hall itself, very
unusually, runs at right
angles behind the front
porch, which forms a
screen, in order to preserve
the correct orientation of
the Ark on this difficult site.
(They didn't quite succeed;
the Ark is oriented to the
north-east rather than the
south-east.) The result was

**Bristol Synagogue, Park Row
exterior** (AA042268)

Detail of gate (AA042267)

an L-shape on plan. Much
altered internally, largely
because of bomb damage
during the Second World
War when the elaborately
decorated ceiling was lost.
The gallery is carried on
slender iron columns;
the rear gallery was badly
extended in the 1970s
to provide classroom
accommodation. The
Italianate Ark is typical of
Collins, whitewashed in
keeping with the rest of the
room, with gilding and
fish-scale decoration to the
canopy. Standard Hebrew

inscription in archway:
'Know before Whom you
stand.' The roomy *bimah*
has a curved integrated
choir stall behind and a
warden's box in front, open
metalwork balustrading and
plush crimson velvet
upholstery.

FURNISHINGS: Of much
interest are the fixtures and
fittings brought from other
buildings, although the
provenance of some of
these items has not been
fully established. Several
incarnations of a synagogue
existed in Temple Street

since before 1756, consecrated 1786, rebuilt in Regency-cum-Grecian style 1842, only to succumb to railway development for Temple Meads Station in 1868. The four brass lamp standards on the *bimah* came from Temple Street. The curved mahogany Ark doors are reminiscent of those at *John Davies'* **London New Synagogue** of 1838 – or may well have been directly inspired by *Spiller's* **London Great Synagogue** of 1790. The elaborate wrought ironwork surrounding the glass *Luhot* (possibly *Jacobs* Bristol Blue glass) seems to have come from the 1842 building (originally being the window above the Ark) as did the glass lantern *ner tamid*. Note the historic Royal Family prayer board from **Ramsgate Synagogue** (1833) and the large brass *hanukiah*, part

17th-century Dutch and part 18th-century English, probably put together in Bristol for the Temple Street Synagogue in its Georgian phase.

OPENING HOURS: *Shabbat* and festival services. Heritage Open Days (September). Other times and groups by appointment, through mobile number on website: www. bristoljewishcommunity. org, or email: bristolhebrew congregation@btinternet. com

Jacob's Well

33 Jacob's Well Road, Constitution Hill, BS8 1QD

Scheduled Ancient Monument

Controversy still rages over the identity of the underground spring beneath the building on the corner. Finally designated an Ancient Monument in 2002, described as a

medieval *bet taharah*, but originally (1986) claimed to be a *mikveh* dated by the stonework from *c* 1140. More correctly, a *mayan* or natural spring (*mayim hayim*) used for purification purposes. This claim was based largely on the grounds of the existence of a flight of steps down into the pool and a hardly legible *inscription* on the limestone lintel deciphered to read *zokhlin*,[16] Hebrew for 'flowing' [waters], a term found in the *Mishnah*. Reinterpretation as a *bet taharah* by archaeologists is based purely on the circumstantial fact of its proximity to the known location of the burial ground of Bristol's lost medieval Jewry on **Brandon Hill**. However, this was situated further up the hill on the other side of the road. Jewish

Interior view to Ark (AA042101)

Entrance to Jacob's Well (AA052490)

connections unproven, but unquestionably an important site, forming part of Bristol's medieval watercourse.

NB The latest owners, like some of their predecessors, have colourful ambitions to market Jacob's Well water.

ACCESS: Currently no public access.

St Philip's Jewish Cemetery

Barton Road, BS2 0LF

1759, Grade II (boundary walls)

The Bristol Jewish Burial Society claims to have been founded in 1744,

and this burial ground is documented from 1759. It sustained damage by fire in 1901; the *ohel* and caretaker's house have long disappeared, and the site has an unkempt air. The rubble Pennant stone walls have been topped with an unsightly concrete coping and there is now no sign of the 'Doorway with segmental head and plaque over' in the official list description. No records survive, but two field surveys were carried out in the 1990s, the second by Alan Tobias and the Jewish Genealogical Society of Great Britain. According to

this, the earliest legible stone of some 160 identified was that of a DAUGHTER OF JACOB, WIFE OF LEKKISH, d 18 October 1762, in the neglected north-west corner, but it has not been possible to verify the Hebrew date. The last burial was in 1944.

LOCATION: On corner with Les Brown Court, BS2 0NA.

ACCESS: Locked metal gate on Barton Road. Key c/o Bristol Hebrew Congregation Burial Society, through mobile number on website: www.bristoljewishcommunity.org, or email: bristolhebrewcongregation@btinternet.com

Ridgeway Jewish Cemetery

Oakdene Avenue, Fishponds, Eastville, BS5 6QQ

1898

Known simply as 'Fishponds', this cemetery was opened in 1898 and extended in the late 1920s. The earliest tombstone on site is that of SOLOMON DIAMOND d 28 February 1898, aged 29, along the street (north) wall near the whitewashed *ohel* (1933), which is immediately behind the entrance. *Foundation stones.* Steps behind lead gently down the sloping site. An ivy-covered plot to your left (east) contains interments from an earlier burial ground in the private garden of Bristol glassmaker Lazarus Jacobs, at Great Gardens, **Rose Street** (known as Brook Court Cemetery in the 1900s), opened 1811, acquired by the congregation in 1830, only to be compulsorily purchased by the Great Western Railway in 1913. In September 1924 27 graves were transferred to Fishponds. According to Tobias (1999) only 12 of these tombstones can be identified today. The earliest is that of 18-month-old JULIA ALMAN, d 14? Shevat 5571[17] (=8 February 1811). The latest burial, according to Tobias, was that of JOSEPH ABRAHAM d 30 January 1867.

LOCATION: Near corner with Elmhurst Avenue.

ACCESS: Locked entrance on Oakdene Avenue. Key c/o Bristol Hebrew Congregation Burial Society, through mobile number on website: www. bristoljewishcommunity. org, or email: bristolhebrewcongregation @btinternet.com

BATH

Bath Jewish Burial Ground

Greendown Place, BA2 5DD

1812, Grade II

Opened in 1812 – the original deed has been rediscovered in the Bath Record Office. No other records survive, but site surveys conducted by Judith Samuel and Bernard Susser in the 1980s and 1990s found 38 tombstones, the oldest being towards the left (north) wall: SARAH MOSES d [?] Kislev 5573 [=? November 1812]. All face west, not east. A secluded and tranquil garden cemetery surrounded by high

Pennant stone walls. The Bath stone *ohel* is located on the end of a terrace of early 19th-century cottages. Long derelict, the *ohel* was restored with a new roof in 2010 by the Friends of Bath Jewish Cemetery (2005) who regularly garden. The older tombstones are of Pennant stone and there are two fairly crude chest tombs; one to the left of the entrance bears the civil date 23 October 1823, and the other the name JOSEPH SIGMOND, a well-known Jewish dentist in Bath from the 1790s.

A synagogue existed in fashionable Bath Spa during the Regency *c* 1821 in the former New Theatre at 19 Kingsmead Street, replaced 1841–2 by a purpose-built house of worship in **Corn Street** by *H E Goodridge*, a major name in the West Country, closed 1901 and demolished 1938. There was no *mikveh*, the Jewish community having recourse to the city's baths. The cemetery was taken into Trusteeship of the Board of Deputies of British Jews in 1915, and the last burial took place in 1942.[18]

LOCATION: On the corner between listed early 19th-century houses, the end of terrace no. 2 Greendown Place, BA2 5DD and the detached 174 Bradford Road (1806).

ACCESS: Occasional Open Days. Volunteers welcome. Contact the Friends of Bath Jewish Cemetery: www.bathjewishburial ground.org

GLOUCESTER

Coney Hill Cemetery, Jewish Section

Coney Hill Road, GL4 4PA

A small hedged plot in the north-west corner contains remains from the *c* 1780 Jewish burial ground, adjoining St Michael's Parish burial ground, in **Organ's Passage**, or Organ's Alley, also known as Gardner's Lane off Barton Street, cleared in 1938 for a children's playground with the sanction of the Trustees, the Board of Deputies of British Jews, but contrary to Jewish law. Several incomplete field surveys exist; about 27 tombstones survive, many badly weathered or fallen, grouped in five rows. The oldest legible inscription is: ELIZ[A?] WIFE OF MR ISAIAH ABRAHAM d 13 August 5567 (=1807), aged 50, and the latest is dated 1886.

The cathedral town of Gloucester had a Jewish community in the medieval period, larger than Bristol's, Hereford's or Exeter's, located in the area of Eastgate, called Jewry Street in the 14th century. Jews returned probably in the 1760s; a synagogue is recorded from 1792, but the community had disappeared by 1850. *Plaque*.

LOCATION: Via main entrance at south-west corner of cemetery. Take Coney Hill Road on the east side of the A38 (Eastern Avenue).

ACCESS: During general cemetery hours.

Cheltenham Synagogue

Synagogue Lane, off St James's Square, GL50 3PU

William Henry Knight, 1837–9, Grade II*

The street name 'Synagogue Lane' was reinstated in the 2000s, but in fact cannot be documented with certainty before 1946. The synagogue itself is devoid of identifying sign or symbolism. It has an understated white stucco 'chapel' front with Roman Doric pilasters forming a fake portico, most appropriate for this elegant Georgian spa town. Apparently *Knight*'s first major commission; he afterwards laid out Cheltenham Cemetery and designed the Cheltenham Public Library, which, saved from demolition, is now the town's Art Gallery and Museum (1887).

The glass and lead lantern lighting the coffered saucer dome inside (very Regency) was made by *Nicholas Adam* for a cost of £15, restored in 1999.

INTERIOR: A bright top-lit space, plastered and painted with gilding to the beading of the dome and to the ceiling roses. The rear gallery with high latticework *mehitzah* is reminiscent of **Ramsgate**. Fixtures and fittings of exceptional interest, because they pre-date the building. The Ark and *bimah* were recycled from the 1761 **London New Synagogue**, Bishopsgate, which was replaced by *John Davies*' splendid new edifice in Great St Helen's in 1838. The Cheltenham congregation spent £86 on a wagon to transport the furnishings from London. The classical, light timber Georgian Ark and *duhan* feature a typically

The Royal Family prayer board, which actually dates from the reign of George II (AA029080)

Georgian spindle metalwork balustrade, with *bimah* to match. The *bimah* and pews retain extremely rare original rattan upholstery. Paint analysis in 1998 of the Royal Family prayer board, one of a pair, revealed the overpainted name of George II (1727–60), making it the earliest example in the country. The makers were *Cole & King* of London, who went out of business in 1730.

STAINED GLASS: 1950s leaded lights. Originally the large round-headed 'chapel' windows flanking the Ark would have been filled with clear glazing. Strangely, the present panels do not quite match.

OPENING HOURS: *Shabbat* Friday night and occasional Saturday morning and some festival services. Heritage Open Days (September). Other times and groups by appointment

Cheltenham Synagogue (AA029083)

The congregation apparently did not keep burial records before 1893. The earliest partially legible tombstone is at the north-west corner: ANNIE DAUGHTER OF ISRAEL AND MARIA MOSES OF THIS TOWN, d ? 5601 (= 1841). Burials from Stroud, Ross, Hereford and Gloucester took place in Cheltenham until 1872. War memorial on rear wall.

LOCATION: Corner with Malvern Street.

ACCESS: Locked door to *ohel* on Elm Street. Key c/o Cheltenham Synagogue, via website: www. cheltenhamsynagogue.org. uk or Cheltenham Tourist Information Centre (The Wilson): tel 01242 237 431.

The interior of Cheltenham Synagogue (AA029077)

Cheltenham's Ark (AA029073)

via website: www. cheltenhamsynagogue.org. uk or Cheltenham Tourist Information Centre (The Wilson): tel 01242 237 431.

Cheltenham Jewish Burial Ground

Elm Street, GL51 9DE

1824

Originally acquired 1824, with later extensions 1835, 1860 and perhaps again in 1892–3. The high red-brick and buttressed walling is mainly Victorian. Enter through the modern red-brick *ohel*. Another gate and small garden area lie beyond. The site is neatly kept, with short grass underfoot.

STROUD

Former **Stroud Synagogue**

29 Lansdown, GL5 1BG

J P Lofthouse, 1888–9

With its whitewashed gable end on the street, stuccoed front and ground floor rustication, there is nothing to indicate this building's former identity as a synagogue built in 1888–9. The short-lived Stroud community was formed *c* 1878. Sold 1907 and in 1908 converted into a dwelling house, then subdivided into two semis. In 1989 part of the Hebrew inscription over the Ark 'I will set the Lord always before me' (*Shiviti*), was still visible in an upstairs bedroom. Now estate agent's office. There was never a cemetery in Stroud: burials took place at Gloucester and later in Cheltenham.

LINCOLN AND EAST ANGLIA

THE EASTERN COUNTIES of England that face the continent of Europe are the location of some of the most antique relics of Anglo-Jewry. Medieval stone houses with Jewish associations survive in the cathedral cities of **Lincoln** and **Norwich**, as reminders of an earlier Jewish presence in England, predating the Cromwellian Resettlement by 360 years.

A small Jewish community had arrived in the 11th century from Rouen, following the conquest by William of Normandy in 1066. While

formal ghettos were never instituted in England as they were on the continent, the Jews in England did tend to be clustered in distinct quarters or streets often near the commercial centre of town. The 'Jewry' was also sometimes situated close to the seat of power, either the royal castle or the cathedral, in the hope that this might bestow protection on the Jews whose unpopular role was usually as debt collector on behalf of the crown, clergy or gentry. Because of restrictions imposed by the Roman Catholic Church, Christians were forbidden to lend money on interest and left this occupation to the Jews – who were permitted to do little else. Medieval stone rather than timber houses have traditionally been associated with Jews because these afforded greater security to the elite Jewish moneylenders for their gold and financial records – or so it was thought.

Lincoln was the scene of a notorious blood libel in 1255, when, at Easter, the Jews were accused of the ritual murder of a Christian child. The claim was that the Jews used the blood in the red wine and *matzah* (unleavened bread) used in the Passover rite, effectively in a re-enactment of the Passion of Jesus. This was a calumny that struck terror into Jewish communities all over the continent during the medieval period and later. It is salutary to recall that the

earliest recorded instance of the blood libel was in England, in the city of Norwich in 1144. Shrines were erected to 'St William of Norwich' and 'Little St Hugh of Lincoln' in both Norwich and Lincoln cathedrals. The remains of the shrine in **Lincoln Cathedral**, broken down during the Cromwellian period, can still be seen in the south choir aisle, attached to the choir screen.

Georgian Jewish cemeteries remain in smaller East Anglian towns such as **King's Lynn**, **Ipswich** and **Great Yarmouth**, places where Jewish communities have long ceased to exist. To find Jewish life in this part of England today you will need to make for the university town of **Cambridge**. Even in Cambridge (the term-time influx of students notwithstanding) and Norwich the communities remain small, but make up in enthusiasm for what they lack in numbers.

The Jews' House, Lincoln (AA053588)

Jews' House and Jews' Court

15 The Strait, LN2 1JD (Jews' House Restaurant)
and 2–3 Steep Hill, LN2 1LS (Jews' Court), Grade I

Explore the world of Anglo-Jewry's medieval heritage in the cathedral city of Lincoln

Built between 1150 and 1180, these Norman stone houses are probably the site of the only standing medieval synagogue in Britain,[1] rivalling the famous Rashi Synagogue at Worms in Germany (which was in any case rebuilt in the 1960s). They stand on a picturesque cobbled street (west side) that, as the address suggests, rises steeply up towards **Lincoln Cathedral**.

The actual synagogue itself is thought to have been located on the first floor of **Jews' Court** (the building on the right hand side; *see* p 130) where there is a niche in the east wall that may be the vestiges of the Ark. Pevsner, however, dismissed this niche as a fireplace, and other authorities contest the originality of the wall. Access to the synagogue was thought to have been through the decorated Romanesque doorway of the neighbouring **Jews' House** (the building on the left hand side). However, other opinion considers that access from the rear via a lost back stair would have been more likely.

Documentary evidence indicates that before the Expulsion in 1290 this house was owned by a wealthy Jewess, Belaset, daughter of Solomon of Wallingford. She was hanged in 1290 for coin clipping, a frequent accusation made against Jews in medieval England, and her property forfeited to the king. Early 20th-century tourist literature capitalised on the baseless claim that the body of Little

St Hugh was thrown by the Jews into a well inside the front room or basement of Jews' Court.

The fabric of both Jews' House and Jews' Court has been considerably altered over time. The fine stonework (of coursed rubble stone with limestone dressings) of the Jews' House, with its typically Norman round-headed window openings on the upper floor (the double-headed window on the left is the best preserved) and delicately carved hooded arch over the main door, has been periodically restored, most recently (1990s) by *Nimbus Conservation Ltd* of Somerset, under the direction of architect *Colin Holland* of Lincoln City Council. The original 12th-century doorway is placed off centre, part of the building's charm, and it has a truncated medieval chimney breast above. The end chimney stacks are 18th century. Pevsner judged that the coursed rubble stone of the facade of Jews' Court was 17th century. Both buildings are built on an incline; Jews' Court has an extra, third, floor. In both cases the openings have been altered, with the addition of extra doors and windows, including attic dormers in the roof. The pitched roofs have been replaced, red tile for Jews' House and blue tile for Jews' Court.

INTERIOR: Here too, changes have been made, and the precise arrangement and number of the original rooms in both buildings is the subject of some dispute.

The Jews' House and Jews' Court, Lincoln (AA053588)

To meet building regulations the heights of the ground-floor rooms of Jews' Court, and hence the floors of those above, were raised in the early 1930s. The attic floor of the 'synagogue' was removed, making the height of this room much greater than before. The rooms to the rear were probably 18th-century add-ons.

Jews' Court was rescued from threatened demolition in 1928 by the local archaeological society, which carried out the restoration. Now called the Society for Lincolnshire History and Archaeology, today it occupies the building, which is cared for in an arrangement with Jews' Court Trust, established in 1966.

Occasional religious services are once again held in the 'synagogue' by the Liberal Jewish community that was formed in Lincoln in 1993. A new metalwork entrance gate to The Strait, featuring a Star of David, was installed in 2015.

OPENING HOURS: Society for Lincolnshire History and Archaeology at Jews' Court and Jews' Court Bookshop: access to ground floor only during business hours. Heritage Open Days (September). Tel 01522 521 337; www.slha.org.uk. There is currently a restaurant on the ground floor of Jews' House. The upper rooms are not open to the public.

AARON OF LINCOLN

The identity of a third Grade I listed Norman stone house further up at **47 Steep Hill**, LN2 1LU, corner Christ's Hospital Terrace, has latterly been contested to the extent that the *plaque* on the wall now reads: THE NORMAN HOUSE FORMERLY KNOWN AS AARON THE JEW'S HOUSE. 'Aaron of Lincoln' (1190–1268) was the most successful Jewish moneylender in England. He provided financial services to King Henry III. A cartoon caricature in the margins of the Colchester (Essex) forest roll of 1277 in the National Archives is labelled in Latin 'Aaron son of the Devil'. In it he is shown wearing the 'Jewish badge' that Jews in many parts of medieval Europe were obliged to wear in order to distinguish them from Christians. In England, the Jewish badge took the form of the *Tabulae*, Latin for the 'Tablets of the Law'. Even if it wasn't his actual home, this stone building undoubtedly shares features in common with the Jews' House on The Strait.[2] *Private business premises.*

BURY ST EDMUNDS

Moyse's Hall Museum

Cornhill, IP33 1DX

Grade I and Scheduled Ancient Monument

The oldest parts of Moyse's Hall have been dated by experts[3] to *c* 1180. In 1181 a blood libel, the case of 'St Robert of Bury St Edmunds', is recorded. On Palm Sunday 1190 Crusaders killed 57 Jews, and Jewish settlement ended in the town of 'St Edmundsbury'. The Jewish connection to Moyse's Hall is a local tradition that goes back at least to 1771. It rests largely on the name itself: 'Moyses', the pronunciation perhaps derived from the Hebrew name Moshé.

The Norman undercroft at Moyse's Hall in Bury St Edmunds (BB for SJBH)

However, Moys, Mose and Moyse are also common surnames in Suffolk. The Jewish association remains entirely unproven.

Stylistic analogy can certainly be drawn between the vaulted undercroft of Moyse's Hall with that of the Rashi synagogue at Worms. The undercroft would have been used for business purposes, for storage of goods, while the two rooms upstairs would have been the hall and bedchamber of the residents.

The building has been much restored. Original medieval stonework is mainly confined to the south-facing front on Cornhill, especially the Perpendicular-style double-light window over the main entrance. The stone on this façade, of flint and ashlar dressings, is the same kind as that found on the west front of the **Abbey of Bury St Edmunds** itself.

The wall of the right-hand (east) range collapsed (1805) and was rebuilt early in the 19th century; the whole building was heavily restored by *George Gilbert Scott* in 1858. He replaced a clock tower of 1791 with the one we see today. The L-shaped range to the rear, **41 Cornhill**, dates from the 16th century, and was integrated into the museum in 1972. Since 1899 Moyse's Hall has been the home of the museum of local history.

INTERIOR: The impressive undercroft, now part of the exhibition area, is typically Norman. It has massive stone vaults, early Gothic in the main space, Romanesque to the rear. The vaults spring from two substantial cylindrical piers with square capitals. The aisles are divided into three bays each. *At left* is a medieval doorway with the remains of a medieval stone spiral staircase built into the wall. The mock fireplace, with 12th-century stone columns and a 16th-century oak beam, came from a house in **Hatter Street**, demolished in the 19th century and described in the museum literature as 'formerly the Jewish Quarter'.

Whatever the truth of its Jewish associations, Moyse's Hall is probably the oldest domestic building in East Anglia and is a rare example of Norman domestic architecture dating from the second half of the 12th century. The museum was reopened in 2002 after refurbishment funded by the Heritage Lottery Fund.

OPENING HOURS: Daily except public holidays. Tel 01284 706 183; www.weststow.org

NORWICH

Jurnet the Jew's House

167–9 King Street, NR1 1QW

Grade I

Supposedly the oldest dwelling house in Norwich, also known as the 'Music House' and 'Wensum Lodge', this building shelters a 12th-century stone-vaulted undercroft. This undercroft represents the extent of the original house occupied by Isaac, son of Jurnet the Jew, in the 13th century. It is beneath the original part of the house that runs back east to west with its gable on King Street. The walls of the house are constructed of flint rubble with stone dressings, and it has a pantile roof. The L-shaped extension running north to south was built slightly later. The fabric of this portion of the house, which runs parallel with the street, is mostly 17th century.

The Jurnet family came from Normandy. Mercantile links with Norwich were then developing. Isaac Jurnet (d 1235) was a merchant and moneylender and perhaps one of the richest men in Norwich, if not in the land. A 13th-century anti-Semitic cartoon preserved at the National Archives depicts 'Isaac de Norvic' as a king with three faces, surrounded by horned devils. In about 1225 Isaac purchased the house from John, son of Herbert Curry, but it remained in his family for barely 40 years. After his

Undercroft of Jurnet's House (BB039763, BB039762)

death in 1235, the inheritance was fragmented between Isaac's male descendants: one of his grandsons Hake (another Isaac) was imprisoned in the Tower of London and forcibly baptised, and by 1266, a quarter of a century before the Expulsion, the entire estate was no longer in Jewish hands.

From the 16th century

the building was known as 'Paston House', after the family who owned it during that period and who undertook alterations and additions, and from the 17th century as 'Isaac's Hall' or the 'Music House'. The latter name stuck well into the 20th century.[4] Acquired by the local authorities in 1959–61, the building is now an adult education centre, known

Jurnet's House (DP002957)

Look out for…

IN NORWICH CATHEDRAL

In 1997 a chapel of reconciliation, called the **Chapel of the Holy Innocents**, was dedicated on the site where the body of the 'martyred' child St William was laid out in the cathedral, beneath the present organ case.

IN THE TOWN CENTRE

A *plaque* on **Henry's Bar and Café,** the site of the historic **Lamb Inn** in the **Haymarket**, NR1 1QD, marks the **site of the Medieval Jewry** 'between the castle and the Market Place', in the quarter known in the Norman period as Mancroft. The synagogue seems to have occupied an unusually central location in the town and was architecturally distinctive. It is traditionally believed that the Jewry was burned down at the Expulsion in 1290.

Three synagogues are recorded as predecessors of the present one in **Earlham Road**, NR2 3RA (*Wearing, Hastings & Rossi*, 1968). 'The Jews New Synagogue and Schools' is clearly marked as 'No. 71' on Francis Blomefield's 1746 map of Norwich.[5] It was situated to the south-west of **Norwich Castle** on an unmarked lane running between Hog Hill and the Cheese and **Hay Market** – a spot, coincidentally almost identical with the assumed location of the medieval Jewry of Norwich. The so-called 'Regency Synagogue' was opened in a house, dating in part back to the 17th-century, in **Tombland Alley** close to **Norwich Cathedral** in 1828. The Ark niche could still be identified in the 1960s, and in 1997 a service of

Restored Regency houses in Tombland Alley, near the cathedral. No. 2 is thought to have contained the Regency Synagogue
(Courtesy Maureen Leveton)

since 1966 as 'Wensum Lodge'. In 1982 the historic undercroft was turned into an atmospheric wine bar named after Jurnet the Jew.

ACCESS: Accessible to visitors to the Centre for Adult & Continuing Education and to patrons of Jurnet's Bar in the basement (the undercroft).

Norwich Jewry, sometimes referred to as Mariners Lane *c* 1750; closed 1826. However, the exact location of the cemetery, behind the car park of the 'cash and carry' at 60–70 Ber Street, cannot now be established with certainty. No records are extant and it is not marked on early maps of the city.

POST-RESETTLEMENT SITES IN EAST ANGLIA

NORWICH

Vestiges of **Norwich Old Jews' Burial Ground**

Horns Lane, *cr* Ber Street, NR1 3EW

A section of old boundary wall with several keystones incised GAW 1820 is possibly all that marks the earliest burial ground of the post-Resettlement

commemoration was held in the restored building at **2 Tombland Alley**, NR3 1HL (Grade II), thought to have housed the synagogue, although the precise location is disputed. In 1849 this synagogue was replaced by a new one in St Faith's Lane, with a classical portico by *John Bunn* 1848–9.[6] It stood on the corner of newly created 'Synagogue Street', a rare accolade in post-Resettlement England, all bombed in 1942.

Quakers Lane Jews' Burial Ground

St Crispin's Road,
cr Talbot Square, NR3 3AN

1813

Also known as Gildencroft Jewish Cemetery, this was acquired in 1813 in the vicinity of St Martin at Oak Church and the Friends' Burial Ground. Closed by the Burial Act in 1854. No records have survived but several field surveys have been carried out since 1872, when the site was already becoming neglected. Today it consists of a small gravelled area, no more than 10m by 15m, enclosed by high walls much rebuilt, with scarcely a dozen headstones, none of which is legible.

NB The *plaque* on the wall outside the burial ground should be ignored: the Hebrew date written in Hebrew block reads 5640, which corresponds to 1880 and not 1840 as given in the English. In any case, neither date is historically accurate!

LOCATION: Steps up from St Crispin's Road (north side), now part of the

A147, Norwich's inner ring road, on the corner of the junction with Talbot Square. Bounded on the other side by Quaker's Lane.

ACCESS: Locked gate. Norwich Hebrew Congregation: tel 01603 623948; www. norwichsynagogue.org.uk

Norwich City Cemetery, Jewish Section

Bowthorpe Road, NR2 3TN

1856, P & G Grade II

This is one of the earliest Jewish plots in a corporation cemetery in England, dating back to the opening of the Bowthorpe Road cemetery in 1856. The city of Norwich, in fact, had boasted the first public cemetery in Britain at the Rosary (1819), and was one of the first local authorities to establish a burial board after 1853. The Jewish plot has its own grilled gate (locked) under a tall brick-built Gothic arch on Bowthorpe Road. An *inscription* overgrown with ivy reads: JEWISH CEMETERY/*BET HAYIM* (in

Norwich City Cemetery, Ohel
(BB for SJBH)

Hebrew), decorated with a *Magen David*. Inside, the Jewish plot retains its simple Gothic-style *ohel* (1856) by *E E Benest*, surveyor to the city's new burial board, who laid out the whole cemetery; most of his other buildings on site have been demolished. The Norwich Burial Board granted £100 for the erection of the *ohel*. Of red-and-yellow brick, with stone dressings and tile roof, it still stands in the middle of this verdant spot overhung with mature trees.

The oldest graves are concentrated in the north-east section and face west. That of JUDAH MOSES KISCH d 18th July 1856, aged 46, opposite the *ohel*, has a fine carved scrolled headstone. This section also contains First World War graves, including a double headstone for two brothers: CYRIL ISAAC LEVINE and MYER JOSEPH LEVINE, FLIGHT LIEUT. R.A.F KILLED IN AEROPLANE COLLISION MAY 8TH 1918 AGED 18.

It is surprising to find a row of cremation memorial plaques in a cemetery that serves a nominally Orthodox community. In March 2013 medieval remains of 17 persons, identified by archaeologists as murdered Jews, were reburied in Bowthorpe Road's Jewish section. The bones had been excavated close to the Jewry during city centre redevelopment for Chapelfield Shopping Centre in 2004. The discovery became subject of a BBC *History Cold Case* documentary entitled *The Bodies in the Well*. However, the evidence (including DNA testing) remains tantalising circumstantial. New *plaque*.

LOCATION: Situated to the left (north-west) of the crematorium from the main gate for Earlham Crematorium, 193 Earlham Road, NR2 3RG.

ACCESS: Through hedge from main cemetery during general cemetery hours. At other times contact Norwich Hebrew Congregation: tel 01603 623948; www.norwichsynagogue. org.uk

KING'S LYNN

Millfleet Jews' Burial Ground

Stonegate Street, PE30 5EG

Grade II

This is the only vestige of a long defunct community, in existence in 1787 and perhaps dating back to as early as the 1740s. In the 18th century King's Lynn was a thriving trading port situated on the mouth of the River Ouse, with links to north European ports across the North Sea.

Tombstone in Millfleet
(BB for SJBH)

It is now a rather sleepy Norfolk town with some handsome Georgian buildings. A synagogue existed in Tower Street but was already demolished in 1812. A second synagogue existed in a small building in a yard to the rear of 9 High Street between 1826 and 1846, but seems to have ceased functioning in the latter year; nothing is known of the appearance of either building.

The burial ground is documented from 1830 but burials go back at least to 1811. No records survive, but several field surveys have been conducted. To the south of the town,

the entrance originally faced the Boal Fleet, later called the Mill Fleet, a stream that was subsequently culverted and built over to become one of the town's principal roads. Since 1915 the cemetery has effectively[7] been under the care of the Board of Deputies in London, who persuaded the town council to restore it when the area was redeveloped in the 1960s. Today, the small, neat plot is enclosed within a wall that Pevsner claimed contains some 16th-century brickwork.[8] There are no more than 18 headstones, not all *in situ*, on a gravel floor, and the Hebrew inscriptions are no longer legible. Passers-by can view the interior through the grille in the gate. *Plaque*.

LOCATION: South side of the Millfleet, in front of a blocks of flats called Millfleet House, and just before you reach Tower Place, PE30 5DF (north side).

ACCESS: Locked. Key held at King's Lynn Tourist Information Centre, The Custom House, Purfleet Quay, PE30 1HP: tel 01553 763044; www.visitnorfolk.co.uk

GREAT YARMOUTH

The Old Jews' Burial Ground

Alma Road, NR30 3HA

1801

Also known as Tower Road or Blackfriars Road, this cemetery lies just outside and abutting the knapped-flint medieval town walls of Great Yarmouth, which

Millfleet Jews' Burial Ground (BB for SJBH)

Unusual decorative tombstone at Alma Road (BB for SJBH)

were completed in 1396. It is situated just north of the south-east tower known as **Blackfriars Tower** and is close to the former Garden Gate. Before the reinvention of Great Yarmouth in the 19th century as a holiday destination (it is still popular with caravanners) the town looked inland to its port on the River Yare (famous for its herring), turning its back on the sea and protected by the remains of the medieval town walls. Yarmouth is perhaps the best post-medieval illustration in Britain of the ancient Jewish practice of burying the dead outside the city limits. London's **Cripplegate** and **Jewbury** in York are the prime medieval examples. Jerusalem, of course, is the model.

The burial ground was acquired by a lease (now lost) in 1801 and became freehold in 1838. It was 'disused' by 1885, and the first of several field surveys the following year recorded the earliest tombstone inscription as 1802 and the latest as 1853. Our survey (1999) agreed with

previous findings that the earliest legible *inscription* (in Hebrew) is that of SIMON SON OF NAPHTALI DIED ON FRIDAY NIGHT AND BURIED SUNDAY 7 SHEVAT 5563 [=30 January 1803]. He was identified by Cecil Roth as Simon Hart, a silversmith who was one of the signatories to the original lease. Only 11 headstones now remain, semi-legible, in two rows, including three all dated 1846 at the front. Now effectively[9] under the trusteeship of the Board of Deputies and restored as part of a local regeneration scheme *c* 2002.

LOCATION: Just outside (east) of the town walls, on the south side of Alma Road. Look out for Blackfriars Tower. The postcode given above is that of Great Yarmouth Pottery, next door; their address is 18–19 Trinity Place, which lies on the other side of the wall behind the cemetery.

ACCESS: Locked but visible through the grille in the new red-brick wall. Key c/o GYB Services Ltd (maintenance contractors on behalf of Great Yarmouth Borough Council):
tel 01493 742200;
gybs.group@ncsgrp.co.uk

Great Yarmouth Old Cemetery, Jewish Section

Kitchener Road, NR30 4HU

1858

In the early 19th century Yarmouth devised its own unique street numbering system, consisting of east-west passageways called Rows, nos. 1–145, running between the three main north-south thoroughfares. Two synagogues are recorded: first at Row 108 and afterwards at Row 42, the latter also known locally as 'Jews' or 'Synagogue Row' (although these designations never appeared on any map), which was situated off Market Place. The second synagogue, opened in 1847, was very modest but purpose-built apparently to the designs of a member of the congregation, *Michael Mitchell*.

Portions of the new public cemetery were reserved for 'non-conformists' and 'Jews' on its opening in 1855, the year before **Bowthorpe Road**, Norwich. The Jewish plot is very private, enclosed by high flint walls. The earliest burial in the Jewish section was that of DAVID LEYSER COHEN, buried 5 August 1858. His stone is now partially legible, located by the sycamore in the south-east corner. In 1999, 24 tombstones were counted; 41 burials are recorded in the registers, the last on 29 January 1936.

LOCATION: North-west corner of Yarmouth Old Cemetery.

ACCESS: Only accessible via the locked gate on Kitchener Road. Key c/o GYB Services Ltd (maintenance contractors on behalf of Great Yarmouth Borough Council):
tel 01493 742200;
gybs.group@ncsgrp.co.uk

FURTHER INFORMATION: Friends of Great Yarmouth

Cemeteries via website of Great Yarmouth Preservation Trust: www.greatyarmouth preservationtrust.org

Caister Cemetery, Jewish Section

Ormesby Road, Caister-on-Sea, NR30 5NL

1906

The earliest burial in the large L-shaped Jewish section of Caister Cemetery (1906) was in 1929: SOPHIA, wife of HENRY JACOBS, d 29 June, buried 1st July 1929, aged 74. Only a handful of plots have been used out of the 150 reserved for the Jewish community. Ten headstones were counted by our survey in 1999, but since then at least one more has appeared, for the late Victor Bishop, a native of Great Yarmouth, who was our guide that day. They all face west, and five are matching in design. The burial registers are kept at the Town Hall. A list of interments provided by the council shows 12 names, including one cremation and one name of doubtful Jewish descent. After a period of neglect from *c* 1888 the synagogue was revived and rededicated in 1899 for use mainly by holidaymakers, but did not survive the First World War. It is strange that a town with so few Jews has had no fewer than three Jewish cemeteries.

LOCATION: This is the public cemetery on Ormesby Road (not the church cemetery at the corner of Ormesby and Norwich Road). The

Jewish plot (plot H) is located in the north-east corner of the old (southern) section, behind a privet hedge.

ACCESS: During general cemetery hours.

IPSWICH

Salthouse Lane Jews' Burial Ground

off Star Lane, Ipswich, IP4 1BP

1796, Grade II

This charming Georgian cemetery is located in an area under redevelopment as student housing for University Campus Suffolk (2014). The old street name 'Salthouse Lane' has disappeared from maps of the town, going the way of older alternatives: Salthouse Street, St Clement's, Green Man Lane and Roger's Court – the latter being the name by which the site was known in 1796. Completely enclosed by listed high red-brick boundary walls (*c* 1764, partially rebuilt) that actually pre-date the cemetery. Look carefully to spot two stone Georgian

parish boundary markers, one outside to the right of the gate, the second in the corner of the north wall within.

The plot contains about 35 headstones (plus some fragments) arranged in seven rows, chronologically. Closed in 1854 under the Burial Act and afterwards badly neglected: by 1893, the dilapidated *ohel* had been appropriated by a neighbour. No records are extant, but several site surveys have been carried out over the years, the earliest back in 1883. The oldest legible stone recorded by our survey (1999), in Hebrew, was that of SAMUEL SON OF MESHULLAM DIED TUESDAY AND BURIED WEDNESDAY 13 TEVET 5564 [=28 December 1803], in the middle of the back row.

Ipswich Jewry, which may date back to the 1740s, had a purpose-built synagogue (1792–3) in the 'Upper Rope-ground in St. Helens', afterwards numbered 73–5 Rope Walk. The builder was *John Gooding*, the landowner, whose brother, *George Gooding*, may well have

Salthouse Lane (BB for SJBH)

been the architect. *George Gooding* was responsible for the Ipswich Corn Exchange (1812). From both surviving descriptions and, remarkably, an illustration,[10] we know that the Ipswich Synagogue was built in Regency 'Gothik' style, a unique example in England. It had fallen out of use by 1867 and was demolished about ten years later. In 1915 the graveyard was taken under the care of the Board of Deputies in London.[11]

ACCESS: Keyholder via Ipswich Borough Council Conservation and Urban Design department: tel 01473 432934/5. Email conservation@ ipswich.gov.uk

Ipswich Old Cemetery, Jewish Section

Cemetery Lane, IP4 2TQ

1855, P & G Grade II*

Like **Bowthorpe Road**, Norwich and **Kitchener Road**, Great Yarmouth, this Jewish plot was one of the earliest acquired in a public cemetery, in 1855 when burials began. This suggests that Jews were still dying in Ipswich, even if organised Jewish life in the town had ceased by this date.

The situation of the Jewish plot on the western extremity of the Old Cemetery, at Cemetery Road, suggests that it may have lain outside the original boundaries of the architect-designed scheme (landscaping by *Robert Davidson*, architects *Cooper & Peck*, 1854–5), but we cannot be sure. The whole cemetery was afterwards

(1921–8) extended beyond Belvedere Road, to create the Ipswich New Cemetery. The Jewish plot certainly lies well secluded behind a succession of two ornamental wrought-iron gateways. It is a long narrow piece of land situated in a grassy hollow, very rural.

According to the council's records there are a total of 30 burials, but only 15 headstones and four unmarked mounds can now be seen arranged in a single line at the far (north) end of the plot. These include the graves of RABBI SOLOMON SCHILLER-SZINESSY (1820–1890) and of his wife, SARAH, d 21 April 1901 aged 70. Hungarian born, he had a colourful career as a rabbi in Hull and Manchester where he defected to the newly emerging Reform movement. He afterwards turned to academia and became reader in rabbinics at Cambridge University. In 1999, the most recent burial was in 1985.

LOCATION: At the western end of Ipswich Old Cemetery, on the south side of Belvedere Road. Behind a locked gate to the left (west) of Cemetery Road just before you come to the gate to the main cemetery at the end of the street.

ACCESS: The key can be obtained from the cemetery office next door (10 Cemetery Road): tel 01473 433580.

NB It has not been possible to verify a claim (2012) that a disused Jewish plot existed outside the walls of the cemetery at

the former **St Audry's Hospital**, St Audry's Park Road, Melton, IP12 1SY. Now redeveloped as flats (after 1993), this site, which dates back to 1765–7 (Grade II), began as a Union Workhouse and in the 19th century became the Suffolk County Asylum.[12]

CAMBRIDGE

Cambridge Traditional Jewish Congregation

3 Thompson's Lane, CB5 8AQ

Cecil J Eprile and R J Hersh, 1937

The congregation met in a series of rented rooms until the construction in 1937 of the current purpose-built synagogue. Located in the historic city centre, the synagogue is discreetly set back with a forecourt, in a side street, although the red brick jars with the predominant yellow hues of the ancient university town. By United Synagogue architect *Cecil J Eprile* together with *R J Hersh*, a former student of Gonville and Caius College. The dominating new porch and hipped roof were added in 1990; Eprile's roof was probably flat.

INTERIOR: In the old top-lit vestibule the *foundation stone* boasts scholarly credentials with the Latin name for Cambridge, 'Cantabrigia', written in Hebrew letters! The prayer hall is an odd shape: an irregular hexagon, reputedly built around the elegant semi-elliptical Ark, which is claimed to be

Italian. It is classical in style with early rococo detailing to the doors. As the enamelled *inscription* tells us, this Ark was presented in 1915 to the previous synagogue in Ellis Court off Sidney Street (*c* 1910). Original panelling and parquet flooring; otherwise the utilitarian synagogue (there is no other fixed furniture) was noteworthy only for the lack of space for female worshippers who were long relegated to an alcove, a reflection perhaps of the few women students at the university in the 1930s. By 2013 this situation had been rectified.[13] Sliding doors link to the communal hall at the rear.

Today, there are 870 identifying Jews in Cambridge (2011 Census) and, after protracted debate and planning obstacles, in 2011 a *mikveh* was finally opened. However, it is under the auspices of the local Habad-Lubavitch Hasidim and is located in **St Peter's Street**, CB3 0BD (opposite Lawson Gallery picture framers), rather than on the Thompson's Lane site.

A successful application for immunity from listing in 2015 suggested that the site may be redeveloped in the future.

NB With the influx of refugees during the Second World War a Jewish cemetery was opened at the **Cambridge City Cemetery**, Newmarket Road, CB5 8PE, in 1941; a separate Reform section followed in 1984. Both communities now use plots (since 2004) at the site of **Cambridge**

City Crematorium, Huntingdon Road, CB3 0JJ (known as 'Dry Drayton'). American Jewish servicemen were buried at the **American War Cemetery**, Madingley Road, Coton, CB23 7PH (the A1303), in the outskirts of Cambridge.

OPENING HOURS: *Shabbat* and festival services. A lively community centre during term time. Visitors by appointment via the website: www.ctjc.org.uk

Cambridge Synagogue Ark
(BB for SJBH)

ROUND CHURCH

A tradition has it that the Norman Church of the Holy Sepulchre, known as the Round Church, on the corner of **Bridge Street**, was the site of the medieval synagogue. The Jews were expelled from Cambridge in 1275. A community seems to have been re-established in 1774 but had died out by 1847, when a congregation was formed in a private house at 7 Hobson Street (formerly Hobson's Lane). This too fizzled out until 1888 when Chief Rabbi Hermann Adler visited the town to establish an organised community. By this time religious tests had been abolished at Oxbridge, enabling Jews to graduate and receive higher degrees and fellowships (1871).

(Courtesy of Corpus of Romanesque Sculpture)

THE MIDLANDS

Jews have made their home in Birmingham, Britain's second city, since the early days of the Industrial Revolution. Lord George Gordon was converted to Judaism in **Birmingham** in 1787. Birmingham Jewry has never been a big community, today numbering about 2,200 people (2011 census), down from a peak of 6,600 in 1918. Their surviving heritage is largely Victorian.

Birmingham boasts the oldest active 'cathedral synagogue' in Britain. Only ten years ago, the magnificent Grade II★ Listed Singers Hill Synagogue (1855-6) was written off by many as having no future. Back in the Millennium year 2000, barely 20 visitors showed up at Singers Hill on the very first European Jewish Heritage Day that took place in the UK. Over the years, Jewish Heritage UK campaigned hard to prevent closure and encouraged the stalwarts who cared about their building to undertake essential repairs. Today, the immediate vicinity, conveniently situated close to New Street Station, has been transformed, thanks largely to the nearby Mail Box development, the 1960s Royal Mail sorting office, now painted bright red and converted into an attractive complex of shops and restaurants. In the winter of 2014-15 the synagogue's interior was repaired and completely redecorated and

the building was officially rededicated by the Chief Rabbi in March 2015, just as this guidebook was going to press. Thus, Singers Hill Synagogue has regained its position as the flagship of Birmingham's tiny Jewish community, an example to be emulated elsewhere.

Smaller Jewish communities developed elsewhere in the Midlands during the Victorian era. Jewish entrepreneurs – manufacturers, wholesalers and retailers, as well as small tradesmen and travelling salesmen – found business opportunities in growing towns. In some cases, these towns were dominated by a particular industry. For example, the Five Towns of Staffordshire, 'The Potteries', were so called because of the concentration of factories in that area producing ceramics, from tableware to tiles. **Coventry** in the 19th century was a centre for clock- and watch-making (a typical Jewish occupation); in the 20th century it was better known for cars. Over in the East Midlands, **Nottingham** was famous for its lace, and **Northampton** for its leather boots and shoes.

View from the gallery at **Singers Hill** (AA035656)

Singers Hill Synagogue

Blucher Street, B1 1HL

Henry R Yeoville Thomason, 1855–6, Grade II★

The oldest still-functioning 'cathedral synagogue' of England, now over 150 years old

Opened in 1856, Singers Hill Synagogue was designed by leading Birmingham architect *Henry Yeoville Thomason* (1826–1901), who was also responsible for Birmingham's **Council House and Art Gallery** – both well worth a visit (*see* Heritage Trail, p 146). The banqueting hall in the Council House in particular has a grand Italianate interior which, with its barrel-vaulted ceiling and superimposed order of gilded Corinthian columns, is very reminiscent of Singers Hill Synagogue.

Memorial lamp in the vestibule
(AA035648)

Singers Hill is built of red brick with stone dressings. The complex includes two houses for the resident ministers, the whole forming three sides of a quadrangle around a courtyard. There is no *mikveh*. In the central range the generous vestibule lined with donors' plaques is set back behind an arcaded porch with an enormous wheel window above.

INTERIOR: The main prayer hall is built on a basilican plan, with the 'nave' separated from the side aisles by arcades. This was a plan that was to become a hallmark of the 'cathedral' synagogue type in the second half of the 19th century. The gallery is supported on three sides on a superimposed order

Front elevation (AA031194)

of columns, of Bath stone, in a manner that has been characterised as 'Gibbesian'. The columns are set base-to-capital, with Corinthian capitals above and foliated cushion capitals below, all richly gilded. The gallery has box-fronts but has lost its low ornamental wrought-iron *mehitzah*, which was removed in the 1930s.

The mahogany Ark is set in an apse in the east wall and is backlit from above by three round-headed windows separated by Corinthian pilasters, in a composition probably inspired by *John Davies'* **London New Synagogue**, opened in 1838. The ark surround was afterwards altered, but the original semi-circular marble *duhan*, decorated with blue, yellow and gold mosaic, was revealed during renovation in 2014-15 when the later timber platform constructed over it was removed.

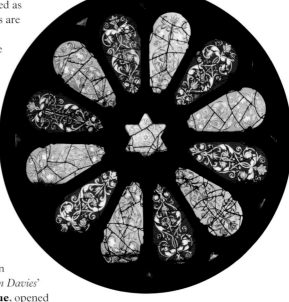

The west window (AA035665)

The Bimah (AA035654)

The Victorian *ner tamid* was taken down and replaced by the current 'Aladdin's lamp' in the 1960s.

The present *bimah* is also not original. Under the influence of Reform thinking (Singers Hill always had the reputation of being the *Englischer Shul* of Birmingham Jewry), the *bimah* was dismantled in 1937 in favour of a combined Ark-*bimah*-pulpit arrangement at the east end, with a choir gallery above, a move that accentuated the cathedral-like axis of the building. At this point too the Victorian stained deal pews were replaced by plush upholstered seating, and the overall seating capacity was increased to accommodate 1,000 people. The patron was synagogue president Oscar Deutsch, of the Odeon Cinema chain, and he used his own cinema architect, *Harry W Weedon*. Fashions change: a central *bimah* was reinstalled in the 1980s and the choir moved to the rear (it had begun life on the *bimah*). The present *bimah* is thought to have come from the bombed **Osborne Street Synagogue** in **Hull**, dating from 1903.

The interior has been redecorated a number of times, most recently in the winter of 2014–15. Thomason's original plans for the design of Singers Hill, including rare colour-wash decorative schemes for the Ark, survive in Birmingham City Archives, of particular value for modern restoration work.

Singers Hill retains its original and most splendid ornamental gas chandeliers. In the 1870s a fire broke out in the building, apparently caused by overheating, owing to the presence of 336 gas lighting jets. Temperatures regularly reached 31°C (88°F) in the gallery, no doubt causing some of the ladies to faint on *Yom Kippur*. Ventilators were installed, and in 1904 the gasoliers were converted to electricity.

STAINED GLASS: The three stained-glass windows behind the Ark date from the opening of Singers Hill in 1856. These are worked in a rich diaper pattern with the *Luhot* featured in the central window. The fine red and blue glass in the west wheel window also survives, but the figurative stained glass on the long walls is a more recent addition, replacing simple leaded lights. The new windows were executed by *P A Feeny* and *D B Taunton* of *Hardman Studios* of Birmingham (1956–63) and are unusual in that they depict the human form – rare but not unknown in Jewish art. The subject matter ranges from the traditional (Bible stories and holidays) to contemporary themes such as the

'Israel Reborn'; 1960s stained glass by Hardman Studios (AA035663)

'Emancipation of the Jews', 'World Aid to Israel' and the 'Emergence of Israel', the latter based on a prize-winning design by *Fay Pomerance*, neé *Levy*, a member of the congregation. Delightfully bold panels can also be seen in the adjoining **Children's Synagogue**, created in 1957–9 by *Cotton, Ballard & Blow.*

Upstairs, see the Victorian Library and the Council Room, fitted out in 1937 with a splendid semicircular table and lined with portraits of Jewish worthies. Charity was dispensed to the local Jewish needy through a hatch made in the panelled doorway to a small office behind the library.

OPENING HOURS: *Shabbat* and some weekday services. Heritage Open Days (September). Other times and groups by appointment: tel 0121 643 0884; www.birminghamsynagogue.com

Original gas lamp, now converted to electricity (AA035646)

Discover Birmingham's Jewish Quarter

Numbers refer to Jewish sites on the Heritage Trail map. Extant Jewish sites are in bold. Letters refer to general landmarks.

Distance: 0.5km

Time: 1/2 hour, but allow 2 to 3 hours for visiting Inge Court and Singers Hill Synagogue.

● *From the front of* **New Street Station**, *cross over in front of Debenham's department store. Follow the signs for the* **Hippodrome Theatre,** *which is next door to* **Inge Court**, *the starting-point for the walk.*

The Birmingham Back-to-Backs, Inge Court ❶

55–63 Hurst Street and 50–54 Inge Street, B5 4TE, Grade II

One of the last remaining back-to-backs of early 19th-century Birmingham. Inge Court represents a housing type that was once prevalent in English industrial cities, originally run up by speculative builders to house 'respectable' working families on modest incomes, but which gradually descended into slums. Restored in 2004 by the Birmingham Conservation Trust (architects *S T Walker & Duckham*) and opened to the public. Now in the care of the National Trust.

The earliest of the series of four reconstructed interiors dates from the 1840s when the house at **50 Inge Street** (built 1809 and converted into a back-to-back pair *c* 1821) was occupied by a Jewish family called Levi. Inge Court lies in the heart of Birmingham's former Jewish Quarter.

In **Hurst Street** was one of the earliest Jewish schools in the country, dating from 1843. No doubt the Levi family sent their children there. No trace of the school remains.

OPENING HOURS: Generally Tuesdays to Sundays; open on some public holidays. Admission charge. Admission by timed ticket and guided tour only. Telephone to check times and to book. Shop. Tel 0121 666 7671 (booking line) or 0121 622 2442; www.nationaltrust. org.uk/birmingham-back-to-backs/

LITERATURE: Upton, C 2005 *Living Back to Back*. Chichester: Phillimore.

● *Cross* **Hurst Street** *and turn right into* **Ladywell Walk**. *Next left is* **Wrottesley Street**. *The next site is on the corner.*

Former **Wrottesley Street Synagogue** ❷

Chung Ying Chinese Restaurant, 16–18 Wrottesley Street, B5 4RT

The site of the **Wrottesley Street Synagogue**, a short-lived breakaway from the Birmingham Hebrew Congregation in the 1850s. Today the building

identified by local historians as the former synagogue is in the heart of Birmingham's China Town. However, the red-brick and terracotta building is late Victorian, clearly not the purpose-built Greek-revival synagogue by *Norton* (probably *Thomas Norton*) of Birmingham, opened in 1853 near the Ladywell Baths. A later incarnation of the Wrottesley Street congregation, the Birmingham Beth HaMedrash and Talmud Torah used this building for worship between 1901 and 1928. It was the precursor of the present-day **Birmingham Central Synagogue**, which acquired its own purpose-built home at 133 Pershore Road, Edgbaston, B5 7PA (*Hurley, Robinson & Son* 1959–61). In 2013 the congregation sold the synagogue for redevelopment, and downsized to the remodelled communal hall. Only a few of the important series of 44 frosted and etched glass windows designed by *R L Rothschild* and made by *Coventry Glass*[1] could be reused. The rest were being dispersed.[2]

● *Return to* **Hurst Street**. *Turn right (north) away from Inge Court. Cross busy* **Smallbrook Queensway** *and continue up* **Hill Street** *all the way to* **Navigation Street**. *Turn left and walk under the fly-over to the* **Mailbox**, *the former Royal Mail sorting office, redeveloped as flats, shops and offices. Signposted, but you can't*

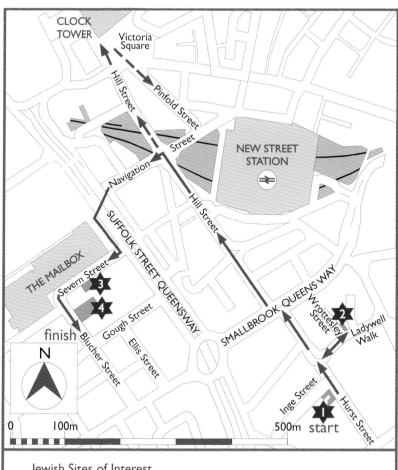

Jewish Sites of Interest

1 Birmingham Back to Backs
2 *former* Wrottesley Street Synagogue
3 *former* Severn Street Synagogue
4 Singers Hill Synagogue

miss it because the façade is painted bright red! Bear left around the Mailbox into **Severn Street**. The next site is on your left.

Former **Severn Street Synagogue** ❸

The Athol Masonic Hall,
60 Severn Street, B1 1QC

Richard Tutin, 1825–7, Grade II

Vestiges of Birmingham's Regency synagogue survive, deceptively hidden behind the late Victorian make-over of the façade by

Essex & Nicol (1891) for the Freemasons. Severn Street Synagogue was opened in 1809 but, along with several churches in the vicinity, was attacked and looted during the Dissenter Riots of 1813 and was rebuilt in 1825–7 by *Richard Tutin*. After the erection of Singers Hill in

The Ark at the former Severn Street Synagogue (Courtesy of Birmingham City Council X713554/15)

1856, Severn Street was sold to the Athol Lodge and became the Masonic Hall. The Birmingham Jewish 'Lodge of Israel' was established in 1874 and henceforth shared use of the building, thus enabling the link with the Jewish community to continue.

INTERIOR: If you are lucky enough to gain access (lately being marketed as a banqueting suite), you will see that, despite heavy alteration and major additions to the building, the main hall still preserves the Grecian character of the former synagogue, especially in the Ark surround, with fluted Doric columns, which now forms the backdrop to the master's chair. Originally, the room itself was severely classical in style, with plastered walls, moulded cornices, corner pilasters and panelled dado. The gilded star-spangled ceiling dates from a later period. The windows are now blocked so that today the space is entirely lit by artificial light. A story that the Jewish-born composer Felix Mendelssohn practised his oratorio *Elijah* on the organ that stands in the corner during his concert tour of Britain cannot be true. Mendelssohn visited Birmingham in 1846, while the organ is dated in Roman numerals 1851. The banqueting hall beyond, with Stars of David decorating the brackets, was added by *Henry Naden* in 1871–4.

❍ Continue up Severn Street and turn left into **Blucher Street**, passing **Scholar's Gate, 80 Severn Street**.

This is the building of the former **Severn Street School**, the first Nonconformist Christian School in Birmingham. This school was started in 1809, the same year as the Severn Street Synagogue. The building largely dates from the early 1850s, with a western extension added by *Thomason* in 1869–70. For a long time a neglected 'Building at Risk', the school was converted into smart apartments in 2012. The whole neighbourhood is undergoing radical regeneration.

Singers Hill Synagogue ❹

(see above, p 142–5)
Blucher Street, B1 1HL

Former **Birmingham Hebrew Schools**

Ellis Street, B1 1QL

❍ *Now the side of the synagogue, best viewed from the car park.*

Successor to the Birmingham Hebrew Schools in Hurst Street. Also by *Thomason*, 1862. The shell of the school, with its tall round-headed windows, lives on, much altered (1884 and 1933–4 by *Essex & Goodman*), as the communal hall. An infants' school was later built on the corner of **Blucher Street** and **Gough Street**, by *C Whitwell & Son* 1901, now completely disappeared.

❍ *Return to the **Mailbox**. Stop for a drink at a canal-side café.*

*Optional extension: Retrace your steps under the fly-over and along **Navigation Street**. Turn left up steep **Hill Street** making for the*

Clock Tower (locally nicknamed 'Big Brum') of **Birmingham City Art Gallery** (1881–5) and **Council House** (1874–9), both designed by Henry Yeoville Thomason in florid Italianate style. Tours of the Council House, including the **Banqueting Hall**, by appointment only: tel 0121 303 2438.

*Return to **New Street Station** via **Pinfold Street**. NB The most direct route to Singers Hill Synagogue from the station is via signs to the Mailbox.*

OTHER JEWISH SITES IN BIRMINGHAM

Former **Birmingham Hebrew Schools**

Highgate Centre,
157–61 St Luke's Road, B5 7DA

Functional red-brick school by *Essex & Goodman* 1931–2 added to a Victorian building at no.157 St Luke's Road. The latter was built as a boys' school for the Children's Emigration Homes in 1877, founded five years earlier (1872) by John Throgmorton Middlemore to promote the resettlement of destitute children and orphans in Canada. This institution expanded to occupy nos. 157–61 in order to include girls on the same site, but moved to Selly Oak in 1928. St Luke's Road was then acquired by the Birmingham Hebrew Schools and *Essex & Goodman* were engaged to redevelop the site, leaving the original building at no. 157 intact. The new Jewish school was successor to Ellis Street and precursor to the present-day King David Jewish Primary School in Moseley, opened 1966.

The St Luke's site received a direct hit during an air raid in 1940. No one was injured and the school reopened in 1952. By that time, however, the Jewish community had largely moved away from a neighbourhood that had become notorious as a red-light district. The buildings were subsequently used by Birmingham Social Services, and were slated for demolition in summer 2015.[3]

Betholom Row Burial Ground

Between Bath Row and Islington Row, Edgbaston, B15 1NE

1823

This cemetery, known by a corruption of one of the Hebrew terms for 'cemetery', *Bet Olam*, meaning 'House of Eternity', was the third burial ground of the Birmingham Jewish community. The two predecessors of Betholom Row fell victim to railway development. The original cemetery had been located in the Froggery in the garden of Birmingham's second known synagogue. **New Street Station** now stands on the site. Its successor was at **Granville Street** *c* 1766, in use until about 1825. Some remains were removed to **Witton Old Cemetery** (*see* below) in 1876. Betholom Row narrowly escaped a similar fate, the case against the Midland Railway Company being successfully fought in 1881 right up to the House of Lords. Ironically, today, the badly neglected Betholom Row is a site seriously at risk.

Unfortunately, few tombstones remain, the records are lost, and the site is overgrown and inaccessible to the casual visitor.

LOCATION: Opposite Five Ways Station. A locked gate in the whitewashed wall by the side of the main road. Metal steps descend behind into the undergrowth! The postcode given above is that of the closest building, the new-build red-brick Bath Court at 166 Bath Row.

Witton's Jewish Cemeteries

Since the mid-Victorian period the last resting place of most of Birmingham's Jews. Comprises two sections, located to the north and south of College Road. The old section is contiguous with the main municipal cemetery, which

Tombstone, 1871 (AA044807)

was opened in 1863, but separate from it, the Jewish cemeteries being privately owned.

Witton Old Jewish Cemetery

The Ridgeway, College Road, Erdington, B23 7TD

1868–71, P & G Grade II

In 1868 two and a half acres at the north-east corner of the corporation cemetery was sold to the Jewish community and its own gateway, with stone piers topped by little pyramid caps, was created on The Ridgeway. However, the most interesting feature in the Jewish section was shockingly demolished *c* 2005 when it should have been listed: a rare octagonal rubble-stone *ohel* in Gothic style by London Jewish synagogue architect *Hyman Henry Collins* (1871). The prototype plan was copied in increasingly simplified form, in both of the subsequent burial grounds of Birmingham Jewry, at **Witton New** and **Brandwood End**. A granite obelisk (1876, Grade II) commemorating the re-interment of the remains from **Granville Street** is situated to the south within a railed-off area. No tombstones were preserved. Along the wall behind are some 30 fragments of tombstones from **Betholom Row**. Burial registers extant from 1872.

ACCESS: Separate entrance from The Ridgeway. Open. On-site caretaker.

Witton New Jewish Cemetery

Warren Road, B44 8QH

1937, *Ohel* Grade II

Red-brick octagonal *ohel* by *Goodman* of *Essex & Goodman* (1937) features unusual figurative stained glass. In 1936 Singers Hill agreed to allow the newly formed **Birmingham Liberal Synagogue** to share cemetery space at Witton New in return for contributions towards its upkeep; the minister of the Liberal synagogue participated in the consecration that took place on 4 July 1937. The earliest Liberal burials are behind the hedge to the left of the *ohel*. The shared arrangement between Orthodox and Progressives continues in the extension (1994, *plaque*).

ACCESS: Across from the Old section with entrance gates on Warren Road. Open. On-site caretaker. Tel 0121 382 9900.

Brandwood End Cemetery, Jewish Section

Woodthorpe Road, Kings Norton, Stirchley, B14 6EQ

1918

In 1918 the Birmingham New Synagogue acquired a section of this municipal cemetery at Brandwood End (1895–9). Plain red-brick octagonal *ohel* probably post-Second World War. Copy registers extant.

ACCESS: Separate entrance on Broad Lane, B14 5BB, or via main gate on Woodthorpe Road during general cemetery hours.

OTHER SITES IN THE WEST MIDLANDS

WARWICKSHIRE

COVENTRY

Coventry Synagogue

Barras Lane, CV1 3AF

Thomas Naden, 1870, Grade II

A good, and now rather rare, example of a Victorian provincial synagogue, built in 1870 on a modest scale according to a limited budget, by Birmingham architect *Thomas Naden*. Of red brick in a simple Romanesque style, with Bath stone dressings.

INTERIOR: Open-timber pitched roof, very church-like, with exposed trefoil arched braces and high collar beams, carried on carved stone columns. It has only a rear gallery. The doors of the classical timber Ark feature pretty gilded panels, and the *bimah* is immediately in front.

STAINED GLASS: A colourful *Luhot* roundel over the Ark. On the north wall are modern panels on traditional themes, featuring figurative art by *Hardman Studios* of Birmingham (*cf* **Singers Hill Synagogue**). Two panels of older glass signed *HSJ* on the south wall have been removed to **Solihull Synagogue** (3 Monastery Drive, B91 1DW; tel 0121 706 8736; www.solihullshul.org). Curiously, when still *in situ* at Coventry, these had faced the wrong way, into the adjoining hall rather than into the synagogue. In the basement of the hall was a *mikveh*, constructed as part of the design, but long since disused and boarded over. Its entrance was from **Gloucester Street**; the blocked up street door is still visible.

Coventry Synagogue has had something of a chequered history, narrowly escaping demolition on grounds of public safety in 1920, and the congregation could not keep its rabbis (17 between 1870 and 1970). But it survived the heavy

View from the gallery of Coventry Synagogue (AA024826)

PRESENTED BY THE
COVENTRY HEBREW CONGREGATION
IN MEMORY OF BENJAMIN FISHER,
WHO DIED 6TH AV 5707–
23RD JULY 1947, AGED 79,
FOR DEVOTED SERVICES RENDERED
TO THE COMMUNITY

Menorah in modern stained glass by Hardman Studios of Birmingham, at Coventry Synagogue (AA024840)

eastern corner of the cemetery, adjoining the London & North Western railway line, which marked the extremity of the cemetery at the time. The plot was enclosed by a stone wall, now only partly extant. The earliest extant tombstone is dated 1866, prior to which burials had been sent to **Betholom Row** in Birmingham. There is a disused modern red-brick *ohel* with flat roof and two Reform burials by the entrance.

ACCESS: Via the main entrance on London Road during general cemetery hours.

bombing during the Second World War – in which Coventry Cathedral took a direct hit. Post-war alterations to the gallery and reconstruction of the porch and vestibule by *G N Jackson* (1964). In 2013 the building was sold to a private developer who is apparently living on site.

London Road Cemetery, Jewish Section

London Road, Whitley, CV1 2JQ
1864, P & G Grade II*

A steep grassed site on the edge of the city cemetery that was laid out in 1845–7 by the famous landscape architect and designer *Joseph Paxton* (1803–65), best known for the Crystal Palace built for the Great Exhibition in 1851. In 1864 the Jewish community purchased 500 square yards from the corporation at the south-

WOLVERHAMPTON

Former **Wolverhampton Synagogue**

St Silas Church, 49 Long Street, cr Fryer Street, WV1 1HU

Frederick Thomas Beck, 1903–4

The second purpose-built synagogue on the same site for a community that claimed to have begun in the 1830s. First opened in 1858, apparently destroyed by fire in 1903, and almost entirely rebuilt by a locally based church architect *Frederick Thomas Beck* in 1903–4. A modest but pleasing building, of pressed red brick with York stone dressings.

INTERIOR: The narrow galleried interior with its

The former Wolverhampton Synagogue (AA058418)

Luhot, **Wolverhampton Synagogue**

two-tier wooden Ark featuring outsize gilded *Luhot* was typical of first-generation immigrants from eastern Europe, but is now very rare. The attractive painted glass *Luhot* are signed C. GREENSTONE – DECORATOR. The Greenstone family were prominent members of the congregation.

The space was preserved largely intact until closure in 1999, but the building narrowly escaped demolition largely thanks to the Wolverhampton Civic Society. The building was purchased in 2000 by the Church of England (Continuing), a traditionalist branch of the Established Church that has retained the *Book of Common Prayer* and rejects women priests. The new congregation have

renovated the Ark, some pieces of the oak furniture and railing, light-fittings and the galleries (with their Lincrusta panelling). They dispensed with the slightly Gothic *bimah* and the box pews.[4] Look up and you will see the *Magen David* in the centre of the barrel-vaulted timber ceiling. The choice of blue and white décor came from the synagogue, but was not the more subtle cream and white colour scheme, with green columns, picked out with gold, when the building first opened.[5] A period iron fireplace with ceramic surround survives in an upstairs room. The disused *mikveh* that, unusually for Britain, was fed by a natural spring (*mayan*), was still extant in the basement in 2007. There are only three or four Jewish families left in Wolverhampton.

Wolverhampton Old Jewish Burial Ground

Thompson Avenue, *cr*
Cockshutt(s) Lane, WV2 3NP

1851, Grade II

As two *plaques* attest, this site was presented by the Duke of Sutherland to the Jewish community in 1851 – but they had to provide the substantial red-brick walls, completed in 1884 together with the adjoining red-brick and terracotta *ohel* and *bet taharah*. The *ohel* retains its original tiled fireplace along with four large marble prayer tablets, leaded (by local monumental masons *Hopcraft*, 1906) in meticulous Hebrew, the text comprising almost the whole of the funeral service. A complete liturgical text displayed on panels, tablets or painted directly onto the walls is rare in Britain, but was more widespread in Jewish communities in the eastern Europe, especially in the synagogue, where printed prayer books were in short supply.

The oldest tombstones (around 140, undocumented) are at the rear. The last burial was in 2000 by which time a second plot had been opened (1965) in the Victorian **Merridale Cemetery**, Jeffcock Road, WV3 7AE. Some remedial work has been carried out and basic maintenance instituted locally with the support of Wolverhampton City Council, aided by a reluctant contribution from the dissolved congregation. In 2010–11 the title was transferred to the Board of Deputies Heritage Ltd in

London, opening the way for an initial Heritage Lottery Parks grant of £9,800 in 2014.

LOCATION: Rear of Napier Road, WV2 3DX.

ACCESS: c/o Wolverhampton City Council, Historic Environment Section: tel 01902 555622

STOKE-ON-TRENT

Former **Stoke-on-Trent Synagogue**

Birch Terrace, Hanley, ST1 3JN

William Campbell, 1922–3

The organised Jewish community in 'The Potteries' dates back to 1873 but Birch Terrace was the first purpose-built synagogue. The little-known local architect *William Campbell* utilised local materials: red brick and Hollington sandstone dressings and Staffordshire Blue clay roof tiles. In 2006 the tiny congregation moved out, pending slated wholesale city centre redevelopment that has failed as yet to materialise. In the interim, the synagogue was leased out for a time as a dance studio. In 2015 it was still standing, empty, and looking increasingly forlorn.

The congregation took away key fixtures and fittings when they left. These included the leaded lights and the Minton tile *Magen David* on the square brick main entrance, the building's most recognisable feature. Situated at the end (west) of the long street-facing (north) wall, this entrance is flanked by two brick pilasters that taper and

break through the roof parapet, alluding to the Solomonic columns *Yahin* and *Boaz* that were, by the 1920s, a hangover from an earlier era. Located on the other side of the vestibule was the old schoolroom, now derelict. There was never a *mikveh* at Birch Terrace. From oral testimony, it is known that one had existed at the former Hanover Street Welsh Methodist chapel, previously used as the synagogue.

INTERIOR: There is a shallow barrel-vaulted ceiling and only a rear gallery facing the Ark. The building had good-quality joinery, which used a variety of timbers: oak for the classical Ark, pitch pine for the central *bimah*, pews and gallery fronts, and deal for the doorways (*see* next entry).

London Road Jewish Cemetery

Stoke-on-Trent and North Staffordshire Hebrew Congregation

London Road, Newcastle-under-Lyme, ST5 1LZ

1886

A quiet spot off a busy main road (A34), at the edge of the city cemetery, but entirely separate. It was purchased from local landowner the Duke of Sutherland for the nominal sum of £1 for the acre. The Duke even provided the bricks. The first burial: SAMPSON LIVINGSTONE, 7 FEBRUARY 1886 – is in the upper (eastern) half of the sloping site, close to the privet hedge that divides it in two. From oral testimony

(2000) we know that the cemetery used to have a hexagonal or octagonal red-brick *ohel* fronting London Road, which was bulldozed by a rogue builder in the 1970s. It must have been similar to the *ohalim* at **Birmingham**, **Witton Old** and **New**, the prototype there designed by *H H Collins* of London.

The replacement red-brick *ohel*, designed by *Hulme Upright & Partners* (1971), was remodelled in 2006 and converted into a synagogue to serve the much reduced congregation. With the help of a £43,700 Heritage Lottery Fund grant, fixtures and fittings were rescued from **Birch Terrace** and reused. These included the classical oak Ark, designed by the architect *William Campbell* himself. He visited **Blackpool Synagogue** to get some ideas, and the two Arks are not dissimilar; also the white 'Rose of York' fanlight from the gallery and the leaded lights, featuring traditional motifs, on a simple cathedral glass ground. Notably salvaged was the Minton tile *Magen David* that had decorated the main entrance, most appropriate in a region of the country famous for its ceramics. This has been affixed to the street elevation of the new synagogue.

LOCATION: West side of London Road (A34), opposite The Avenue and adjacent to London Road Bowling Club Ltd, where parking is available.

ACCESS: Via the Jewish Small Communities Network website: www.jscn.org.uk

OXFORD

Former **Carmel College Synagogue**

Mongewell Park, Wallingford OX10 8BT

Thomas Hancock, 1963–4, Grade II

MEDIEVAL JEWRY

There had been a medieval Jewry in England's most venerable university town, but no definite physical traces remain. A possible *mikveh* was uncovered on the site of the St John the Baptist Hospital, but the evidence, published in 1991, is inconclusive.[6] A medieval Jewish cemetery is believed to have been located within the **Botanic Gardens** (near the Rose Garden), and is marked by *plaques* (1931 and 2012). For more information visit the **Museum of Oxford** (Town Hall, St Aldates, OX1 1BX; tel 01865 252351; www.oxford.gov.uk/museumofoxford), where new panels were installed in the permanent 'Explore Oxford' display in 2013. This was on the initiative of the Oxford Jewish Heritage Committee (2006). See www.oxfordjewishheritage.co.uk and also www.jtrails.org.uk/trails/oxford for self-guided and guide-led walking tours of the city.

CURRENT JEWISH COMMUNITY

Oxford's Jewish community claims to have been founded in 1842. **Oxford Jewish Congregation** is at 21 Richmond Road, Jericho, OX1 2JL; tel 01865 514356; www.ojc-online.org. The synagogue was designed by *David Stern* 1971–3. His prayer hall remains, but the rest of the site was redeveloped by *Simone Bloom* and *Herbert & Partners* in 2005–6, with a very distinctive 'wavy' roofline.

There is also a Habad-Lubavitch House at 75–75A Cowley Road, OX4 1HR, behind which has been built a *mikveh (Thom Fehler Architects*, 2008).

WOLVERCOTE CEMETERY

Banbury Road, OX2 8EE

1894

The Jewish section of Wolvercote Cemetery is immaculately kept by the city council. Many central European refugees are buried here, the cream of the Oxford intelligentsia. Riga-born SIR

ISAIAH BERLIN (1909–97) has a simply carved buff-coloured stone. On an adjoining plot, separated by a large redwood tree, are the graves of three non-Jewish spouses of Oxford Jews.

LOCATION: Situated close to The Lodge at 441 Banbury Road.

ACCESS: During general cemetery hours. Main gate automated. On-site caretaker.

The grave of the philosopher Sir Isaiah Berlin at the Oxford Jewish Cemetery
(AP for SJBH)

A radical new use is planned for the important modern synagogue at Britain's only Jewish public school.

Hancock's dramatic wedge-shaped concrete block building was the first 1960s synagogue to be listed for its architectural significance. Forming a sculptural group with *Sir Basil Spence*'s **Amphitheatre** (1965, Grade II), it became the centrepiece of the Carmel College campus. The boarding school was founded by unconventional rabbi Kopel Rosen and lasted from 1953 to 1997. In 2006 the tranquil, rural site, through which the Thames flows, was finally sold out of the Jewish community for some £10 million. Bespoke developers Comer Homes intend to convert the synagogue into a swimming pool and café for the housing estate planned for the site (2014–15). This means that the expanses of stained glass by Israeli designer *Nehemiah Azaz* on the curved end walls will remain on display. Note his signature jagged Hebrew lettering on the concave west wall (the shortest side) and his floor-to-ceiling Creation cycle on the convex former Ark wall. This sequence reads vertically and from right to left, following the

Carmel College Synagogue and amphitheatre (AA958277)

Hebrew text from Genesis chapter 1. It culminates in the daring ruby-red abstract figures of Adam and Eve on the bottom left-hand side.

NB Don't miss the Grade II★ listed former **Julius Gottlieb Gallery** and pyramid-shaped **Boathouse** down by the river, also by *Spence* (1968–70).[7]

THE EAST MIDLANDS

NORTHAMPTON

Towcester Road Cemetery, Jewish Section

Hardingstone, Northampton, NN4 8LS

1902

Used by the modern community that organised in 1885 in the Newland home of George Leopold Michel, a German-born leather merchant, attracted by the boot and shoe trade for which Northampton was famous. The current **Northampton Synagogue** (95–7 Overstone Road, NN1 3JW; tel 01604 633345 (voicemail); www. northantshc.org) was rebuilt by *R* (probably

Robert) *Gill* in 1966 on the site of the Swedenborgian New Jerusalem iron church that the Jews had acquired for worship in 1890. The church was converted into a synagogue by local architect *H H Dyer*, with *Lewis Solomon* acting as consultant from London.

The first adult burial in the whole Towcester Cemetery was that of the Jew MORRIS KUYASKI, known as MORRIS MORRIS, aged 49, on 16 April 1902. The grave has an iron coping. Yellow-brick *ohel* by *Robert Gill* (1958–60) in the extension (1960). The

Northampton community expanded as a result of the influx of central European refugees in the 1930s, wartime evacuees and service personnel (look out for three headstones to Czech airmen killed in action during 1944) and peaked in the 1960s at about 300. The community now numbers under 150.

LOCATION: South-east corner of the cemetery at the corner of Mereway and Towcester Road.

ACCESS: Locked gate on road, but can be reached through the hedges from main cemetery during general cemetery hours.

LEICESTER

Jewry Wall

St Nicholas Walk, LE1 4LB

In 1250 Simon de Montfort issued a charter to expel the Jews from the city of Leicester. The so-called 'Jewry Wall', the fabric of which is essentially Roman rubble brick and Derbyshire stone, marked the western boundary of the medieval

---

NORTHAMPTON'S MEDIEVAL JEWRY

Northampton Jewry has a recorded medieval pre-history as an important economic centre but little material evidence. However, in 1992 a forgotten Jewish tombstone, first unearthed in the 1840s, was rediscovered in the collection of the **Northampton Museum**. To date, this is England's only example of a medieval Jewish tombstone and bears a strong resemblance to those found in the Rhineland, the heartland of medieval Ashkenaz. Later the same year, the collapse of a culvert led to the discovery of several skeletons at the junction of **Maple Street** and **Temple Bar**, off the **Barrack Road**, a location that corresponds with the supposed site of the medieval Jewish cemetery.

FURTHER INFORMATION: Northampton Museum and Art Gallery, 4–6 Guildhall Road, Northampton, NN1 1DP; tel 01604 838111; www.northampton.gov.uk/museums and www.jtrails.org.uk/trails/northampton

Jewish quarter. The site actually contains the foundations of a Roman bathhouse, dating from *c* 150 CE, excavated by Kathleen Kenyon in 1936–9, during the first major archaeological dig in Leicester. (Kenyon is well known for her work in British Mandate Palestine.) According to current scholarship, the name 'Jewry Wall' possibly derives from the word 'Jurat' meaning a medieval town councillor. No mention is made of the unhappy history of the Jews in Leicester in the Middle Ages, of which it indirectly serves as a reminder.

ACCESS: Forecourt of Jewry Wall Museum, 156–60 St Nicholas Circle, Leicester, LE1 4LB. Open access. Interpretation materials available via the museum: tel 0116 225 4971 and via www. leicester.gov.uk/

Leicester Synagogue

Highfield Street, LE2 1AD

Arthur Wakerley, 1897–8, Grade II

On a prime corner site, for a Jewish community that had been formed *c* 1866. The architect and Wesleyan Methodist temperance activist *Arthur Wakerley* (1862–1931) was elected mayor of Leicester in the Liberal interest in 1897. As built, the synagogue was much less ambitious than his original design, despite rapid approval by the relevant council committee of which he happened to be chairman. Essentially

The tower of Leicester Synagogue
(DP047008)

red-brick Romanesque, with a large recessed central doorway, flanked by pairs of round-headed windows. The prominent central tower, topped by an onion-shaped dome and octagonal lantern, all copper covered, injects a slightly exotic note. The gilded Hebrew *inscription*, the standard *Ma Tovu*, 'How goodly are thy tents, O Jacob …', over the entrance, is decorated with carved corbel heads representing the *hoshen* (breastplate) of the *Cohen Gadol* (High Priest) with its chains and 12 precious stones denoting the Twelve Tribes of Israel. *Foundation stones.*

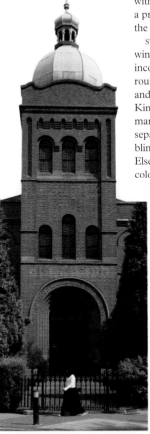

INTERIOR: An intimate panelled vestibule with fine chequerboard mosaic Star of David floor. The prayer hall is almost square on plan but with canted corners to the east wall. It has a flat ceiling and only a rear gallery, supported by two slender cast-iron columns with slightly Egyptian-inspired capitals. The classical Ark, of Spanish mahogany, is in a semi-octagonal apse under a round arch, decorated with attractive stencilling and the verse *Ma Nora*, 'How awesome is this place …' (Genesis 28:17), in gilded Hebrew block in the soffit. The *bimah* is immediately in front with brass lamps and a prominent pulpit to the side.

STAINED GLASS: Just one window over the Ark incorporating in a pair of roundels the *Sifrei Torah* and *Luhot* and the harp of King David, flanked by marble *Luhot* tablets, separately placed in blind window recesses. Elsewhere, original coloured and leaded lights. The original mint green colour scheme was retained during redecoration *c* 1989.

A basement at the eastern end of the site contains the *Mikveh* (1900, renovated 1984 by Rabbi *Meir Posen*). The two-storey school wing, also by *Wakerley* (1901), has original panelling. The 1950s communal hall, built on a vacant bombsite across the road, was sold in 2013, a move that, combined with an English Heritage and

Ark, Leicester Synagogue (DP047001)

Heritage Lottery Fund Repair Grant in 2012, should serve to secure the future of this unusual synagogue.

LOCATION: Junction of Highfield Street and Upper Tichborne Street.

OPENING HOURS: *Shabbat*, some weekday and festival services. Heritage Open Days (September). Other times and groups by appointment. Tel 0116 254 0477; www.jewish-leicester.co.uk

NB Postal address: POB 6836, Leicester, LE2 1W2.

Gilroes Cemetery, Jewish Section

Groby Road, LE3 9QG
1902

In the newly opened Gilroes Cemetery. The consecration coincided with the first interment, that of NINA ROSINA, the 14-year-old oldest daughter of FRANK L and LIZZIE BERGER on 18 July 1902, in the south-west corner (row S1). A series of extensions after the Second World War. Two prominent red granite memorials include that of JACKSON CEMMILL, d 15 May 1936, aged 57, with a large *Magen David* in the place where a cross would otherwise appear. The red granite tradition in the Cemmill family continues in the newer sections. Red-brick *ohel* (1928) in the old section, was extended and reordered in 1981. *Plaques.*

LOCATION: Via main entrance off Groby Road (A50). Jewish sections (S, SX, SN) are in the south-east corner.

ACCESS: During general cemetery hours.

FURTHER INFORMATION: Heritage Lottery Fund Project 2013–14 at www.gilroes.org.uk

NOTTINGHAM

Nottingham Hebrew Congregation

Shakespeare Villas, NG1 4FQ, Grade II

This former galleried Wesleyan Methodist chapel by *Simpson* (1854) was converted for use as the Orthodox synagogue in 1954. It has a Classical-revival stuccoed façade, painted blue and white, with giant fluted Corinthian pilasters. English *inscription* on the entablature. A hall was added to the rear in 1977.

INTERIOR: The panelled pews and elegant oval gallery with ornamental fronts and clock are all original, but the restored building also houses the red, grey and cream granite and marble baroque Ark screen from the lost Moorish-style Chaucer Street Synagogue (*William Henry Radford*, 1889–90, demolished 1991), but here it is on the north wall. Pulpit by *Frank Broadbent* (1937). Clear chapel-style glazing.

German Jewish textile merchants in Nottingham had a peripatetic synagogue from at least 1827. The modern community had no relationship with its medieval predecessor, whose synagogue, known from documentary sources, existed from 1257.

LOCATION: Corner of Shakespeare Street and Shakespeare Villas.

OPENING HOURS: *Shabbat*, festival and some weekday services: tel 0115 947 2004; via www.jscn.org.uk

Former **Nottingham Mikveh**

Victoria Leisure Centre, Gedling Street, Sneinton, NG1 1DB

In 1897 Jacob Weinberg endowed two *mikvaot* at public bathhouses. The one at the Radford Baths has long since disappeared, while vestiges of the second at the Victoria Baths (1896) were extant inside a locked storeroom in 2002. Thanks to a popular campaign aided by the Victorian Society, the historic building, with landmark clock tower, was reprieved from demolition in 2008 and incorporated into a £9-million resurrection as the Victoria Leisure Centre, opened in 2012. It is believed that the storeroom still survives.

LOCATION: Corner of Bath Street.

North Sherwood Street Jews' Burial Ground

North Sherwood Street, NG1 4EN

1823

On land originally belonging to the Nottingham Corporation

but purchased outright in 1946. Almost a courtyard hidden behind a high stone wall. In use till 1869; the *ohel* has disappeared. Burial records have also been lost so the true number of burials is not known; only about 15 standing stones can be seen in the long grass, although the ground is large enough to take more. At the back, German inscriptions on the surviving slate *plaques* on a low sandstone obelisk, commemorate BERTHA NATHAN METZ, d 2 May 5677 (=1917). She was born in Westphalia on 24 June 5581 (=1821). The *inscription* over the entrance is not original.

LOCATION: Next door to 274 North Sherwood Street, NG1 4EN, on east side of street, about 30m from junction with Forest Road East.

ACCESS: Locked. Nottingham Hebrew Congregation: tel 0115 947 2004.

Hardy Street Jewish Cemetery

Radford, NG7 4AX

1869

Larger successor to **North Sherwood Street**. The land was purchased and sold to the congregation by Jacob Weinberg for five shillings. Enclosed by high stone walls, and an internal stone wall running parallel to Hardy Street divides the grassy site in two. Buildings on site have disappeared. With the exception of one suicide (1941) isolated near the west wall, the

The Ark at Nottingham Hebrew Congregation (BB for SJBH)

NOTTINGHAM CASTLE MUSEUM AND ART GALLERY

Lenton Road, NG1 6EL

Has on permanent loan a collection of 18th-century ritual Judaica thought to have come from Germany when the Nottingham Jewish community was established.

OPENING HOURS: Daily (March to October), Wednesday to Sunday (November to February). Groups by appointment. Admission charge. Tel 0115 876 1400 or Nottingham Castle pages reached through www.nottinghamcity.gov.uk

BETH SHALOM HOLOCAUST CENTRE

Acre Edge Road, Laxton, Newark, NG22 0PA

Purpose-built (1995) in the grounds of a 19th-century farmhouse, as Britain's only dedicated Holocaust Memorial and Education Centre. Museum, memorial gardens, cinema, bookshop and educational programmes.

OPENING HOURS: Monday to Friday and some Sundays. Groups by appointment. Admission charge. Tel 01623 836627; www.bethshalom.com

tombstones all face west, not east. Closed in 1947 except for reserved plots.

LOCATION: Locked gate under pediment next door to the Hardy Street car park of Spring Court, 83–5 Waterloo Crescent, NG7 4AX.

ACCESS: Locked. Nottingham Hebrew Congregation: tel 0115 947 2004.

Wilford Hill Jewish Cemetery

Loughborough Road, NG2 7FE
1937–40

In use. One and a quarter acres was purchased from the corporation in 1936 and laid out as a cemetery with a large *ohel* and *bet taharah* by *Frank Broadbent*, with modernist vertical strip windows and a skylight. Consecrated by the Chief Rabbi in 1937, but the first burial was of ROSA FONSECA (BENJAMIN), d 4 March 1940, in the north-west corner.

LOCATION: From the A52 (Nottingham ring road), make for Nottingham Southern Cemetery (Wilford Hill Cemetery) at postcode given above. The Jewish cemetery lies on its eastern boundary. Drive past the main cemetery

Wilford Hill Ohel, interior
(BB for SJBH)

until the end of the railings and turn immediately right (south) down an unmarked bridle path ('Old Road' on Google maps). The *ohel* is to your right, the car park to your left.

ACCESS: Locked. Nottingham Hebrew Congregation: tel 0115 947 2004.

NB Nottingham Progressive Synagogue has a plot within Nottingham Southern Cemetery.

DERBY

Nottingham Road Cemetery, Jewish Section

Nottingham Road, DE21 6FN
1902

Extended 1944 for a Jewish community founded in 1899. They worshipped in a synagogue in a former Victorian villa, 270–2 Burton Road, from *c* 1922 until 1986 (partially demolished). At its peak the community numbered about 200 people, enhanced by evacuees and refugees during the Second World War.

A neat plot, separated from the rest of the cemetery by a tall privet hedge. Earliest burial: JOHN TRAPP, d 19 September 1906, aged 42, identified by a simple undated grave marker in the south-east corner. Modern red-brick *ohel*.

LOCATION: In extension to north of Nottingham Road. Locked gate on Cumberland Avenue, so enter via internal gate from main cemetery.

ACCESS: Key at main cemetery office: tel 01332 672761.

F acing out west towards the New World, the Port of **Liverpool** on the Mersey Estuary was, from the Georgian period, a magnet for migrants both from Ireland, and to the West Indies and America. Discovery of an old indenture in 1996[1] proves that Jews were resident in the city as early as 1742. Liverpool Jewry's first purpose-built synagogue in Seel Street, not far from the docks (*plaque on wall*), was designed in fashionable Greek-revival style in 1807–9 by *John Harrison*, nephew of the well-known classicist *Thomas Harrison* of Chester. Until the second half of the 19th

century, Liverpool was home to the second largest Jewish community outside London, numbering about 3,000 people in 1860. From the 1880s newer immigrants congregated around Brownlow Hill, Crown Street and Pembroke Place, where the green-tiled shopfront (probably Edwardian) to **P. Galkoff's Kosher Butcher Shop** has been preserved.[2] By this period Liverpool's Jewish community was fast becoming outstripped by **Manchester**'s.

Historically, the two cities were keen rivals during the Industrial Revolution. Liverpool's Jewish population dropped from about 7,500 in 1971 to 2,160 in 2011 (Census). However, the world-class **Princes Road Synagogue** still stands as eloquent testimony to the contribution of Liverpool's Jews to the life of the city.

The Hebrew inscription on the oldest surviving tombstone in the Jewish burial ground at Pendleton (Brindle Heath) in Salford, Greater Manchester, yields the civil year 1795. The burial ground was purchased the previous year. Attracted by economic opportunities thrown up by the Industrial Revolution, Manchester in the later 19th century became a magnet for

Jewish refugees from Russian Poland. Jewish entrepreneurs played a key role in the development of textile manufacturing, which was the basis of the wealth of 'Cottonopolis'. Today, while the industry has all but disappeared, Manchester Jewry still numbers over 25,000 (2011 Census) people, the second largest Jewish community in Britain, after London. In fact, Manchester is home to the only UK Jewish community that is still experiencing overall[3] population growth.

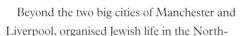

Beyond the two big cities of Manchester and Liverpool, organised Jewish life in the North-West is nowadays sparse. Small communities developed in the Victorian period in the satellite Lancashire mill towns, but few had purpose-built synagogues, while **Blackpool**, **Southport** and St Anne's on the coast were once popular holiday destinations. Today, St Anne's-on-Sea is the most active Jewish community on the Fylde coast, founded 1927. The current synagogue building at Orchard Road, FY8 1PJ (tel 01253 721831; website via www.jscn. org.uk), dates from 1959–64 (by *Maxwell Caplan*).

Newer suburban communities have developed in the south Manchester hinterland of Cheshire but do not compare in strength with the Jewish population of the North Manchester suburbs of Broughton Park and Prestwich. A small colony existed in 18th-century Whitehaven, on the coast of Cumbria, but Jews never penetrated as far north as Lancaster and Carlisle, nor into the Lake District beauty spots (other than on vacation).

Princes Road Synagogue (AA028040)

Princes Road Synagogue

Liverpool Old Hebrew Congregation, Toxteth, L8 1TG
W & G Audsley 1872–4, Grade I

The most lavish High Victorian 'orientalist' synagogue in England

Older sister to London's **New West End Synagogue**, Princes Road was designed by the Scottish-born Audsley brothers, who were based in Liverpool from the 1860s. In the 1890s they emigrated to America, where *George Audsley* (1838–1925) was an organ builder and prolific writer on applied ornament, influenced by his contemporary *Owen Jones*. Princes Road itself was, from the 1840s, a fashionable tree-lined boulevard in the up-and-coming Toxteth district. The western end named Princes Road and the eastern end Princes Avenue, by the end of the century the street was lined with a series of palatial places of worship built for the prosperous new middle classes.

View from the street (AA028033)

The west window (AA028037)

The Audsleys' won a limited competition for the synagogue, having just completed the **Welsh Presbyterian Church** (1865–8, Grade II), with its soaring spire, on the other side of the street, now a Building at Risk. The contrast between the style of the two buildings is marked. The Audsleys justified their eclectic choice of style for Princes Road because it 'Blended together ... enough of the Eastern feeling to render it suggestive, and enough of the Western severity to make it appropriate for a street building in an English town'[4] 'Suggestive' probably of the Jews' supposedly 'Eastern' origins, while not so alien as to make it – or the Liverpool Hebrew

Front entrance (AA028035)

Congregation – out of place.

The 'Western' element was largely in the façade, now more 'early 13th century' (as Pevsner deemed it)[5] than ever, shorn of its six octagonal turrets, declared unsafe in 1960. However, the deep arched portal is in shape more horseshoe than Gothic or Romanesque, and the overall design, tripartite red-brick and stone front elevation with corner turrets, the wheel window set within a horseshoe arch and the cusped horseshoe-shaped portal dominating the façade, was later repeated at **St Petersburgh Place**. Here, at Princes Road, the *Luhot* are placed high up at the apex of the gable, which is stepped and crested in outline. In the tympanum over the doorway is a gilded *Magen David*. The communal hall behind was added in 1898.

INTERIOR: Note the discreet brass plate *foundation stone* on the inside of the massive oak door (base of central column) as you enter the vestibule. Also the First World War memorial in the form of a marble scroll. Look down at the decorative tiled floor, which features both the *Magen David* and the English rose. The Hebrew greeting in the floor in front of the doors to the prayer hall is from Deuteronomy 28:6.

Inside, the parallels with the New West End continue: the barrel-vaulted basilican prayer hall with clerestory, the arcaded aisles in five bays carried on octagonal columns, the turreted gilded Assyrian Ark (restored after fire damage in 1978) set within a large horseshoe arch, here cusped, the arch being repeated at the other end of the space. The enormous round windows at either end are filled with *stained glass* by *R B Edmundson & Son* of Manchester. The gilded Hebrew *inscription* painted around the deep blue cupola of the Ark is from Isaiah 2:5. Behind, the choir loft is disguised by an arcaded balustrade. On the floor of the synagogue, the original pitch-pine pews run the length of the side aisles, the space around the lavish marble *bimah* being kept clear. As in London, the *bimah* is slightly displaced to the west, but here is accessed from the rear rather than from either side. It was presented in 1875 by David Lewis, the founder of Lewis's landmark department store, which traded in Liverpool city centre until the first decade of the 21st century. The Ark, *bimah* and pulpit were all carved by stonemasons *Alfred Norbury* of Liverpool. The original brass gaslight fittings by *Hart Son Peard & Co.* (London) survive, hung by chains from wall brackets affixed along the side galleries. Unusually, there are no central chandeliers.

Princes Road and St Petersburgh Place each possess a delightful wall clock with a Hebrew face, here under the west gallery and by top clockmakers *J Sewill*, the shape of which is modelled on the Ark. The mint green colour scheme, with red stencilling and gilding, has been restored to the Audsleys' design. Narrowly escaping redundancy and closure in the early 1990s, today this magnificent synagogue, restored with the help of the World Monuments Fund,

The Ark (AA028045)

English Heritage and the Heritage Lottery Fund, is a Grade I listed building.

LOCATION: Princes Road is the B5175. The synagogue is at the corner with Selborne Street.

OPENING HOURS: *Shabbat* and festival services. Heritage Open Days (September). Shop. Other times and group bookings by appointment: tel 0151 709 3431; www.princesroad.org

The Ark and *Bimah* (AA028042)

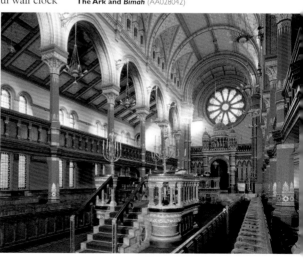

Former **Liverpool New Hebrew Congregation**

Unity Theatre, 1 Hope Place,
L1 9BG

Thomas Wylie, 1856–7

Heavily altered yellow-brick Italianate façade, originally with a triple-arcaded open porch and side wings, not unlike Birmingham's **Singers Hill** – its exact contemporary. However, Hope Place was built with small side turrets and a dome that, in its original form, was a structural disaster and pronounced unsafe. It was replaced in 1863 by a less ostentatious shallow faceted and hipped saucer dome by prominent Liverpool architect *Sir James A Picton*, while the builder *Dixon*, who worked with the nonentity of an architect *Wylie*, successfully sued the congregation for damages. Picton's dome, too, has now gone, needlessly removed in 1997–8 on the conversion of the unlisted former synagogue (closed 1935) into the Unity Theatre (*Mills, Beaumont, Leavey & Channon* of Manchester) – a project ironically funded by the National Lottery. *Plaque.*

INTERIOR: Vestiges of the arcades of the original porch can be seen in the upstairs theatre cafe,

The former Liverpool Hebrew Schools, Hope Place, built in 1852
(AA045464)

which was created by the insertion of a new floor and by bringing forward the front of the building.

Former **Liverpool Hebrew Schools**

Joe H Makin Drama Centre of
Liverpool John Moores
University, 1 Hope Place, L1 9BG

JW & J Hay, 1852

The Liverpool Hebrew Schools were founded in July 1841, making them one of the earliest institutions of their kind outside London. The substantial purpose-built brick schoolhouse pre-dated the synagogue by five years. It has stone quoins and decorated Gothic windows on the ground

floor and side. Originally, the building was two stories high, with a basement, and extra classroom space in the deeply pitched roof, lit through skylights.[6] The upper floors and roofline have been substantially altered and the decorative buttresses now continue all the way up the walls. Recently looking rather neglected. The original brass *plaque* from the opening of the school in 1852 is one of the items on display (2014) at the new (2011) Liverpool King David High School, Childwall Road, L15 6WU.

LOCATION: Next door (left side) to the Unity Theatre, and sharing the same address. On the corner with Pilgrim Street.

Ceramic sign over the former P Galkoff's kosher butcher's shop in Pembroke Place (AA030651)

Greenbank Drive Synagogue, front elevation (AA031180)

Liverpool New Hebrew Congregation

Greenbank Drive, Sefton Park, L17 1AN

Alfred Ernest Shennan, 1936–7, Grade II*

One of the best modernist synagogues in the country, designed by a local worthy for the Liverpool New Hebrew Congregation, decamped from **Hope Place**. *Alfred Shennan*

(1887–1959) became leader of the Conservative Party on Liverpool City Council and was a staunch Anglican who designed many churches on Merseyside. However,

The interior seen from the gallery (AA030489)

he also excelled in pubs and cinemas and was later knighted for his efforts towards the construction of the Mersey Tunnel. His only synagogue was faced in 'golden brown' bricks laid in intricate patterns, reminiscent of Dutch and Scandinavian modernism of the era. Structurally, it made extensive use of reinforced concrete and steel. The (by this period) 'traditional' tripartite façade was given an original treatment through the use of tall vertical windows and countervailing curves in the quoins, arches and window surrounds, plus a series of stepped and gabled buttresses on the long walls. *Foundation stones.*

INTERIOR: Light and airy thanks to the generous glazing. The cantilevered gallery wraps itself around the three sides, with a graceful segmental curve mirrored in the curve of the oak pews facing the Ark. The barrel-vaulted ceiling has an unusual clerestory arcade carried on continuous concrete girders. The building was twice damaged by fire, in 1959 and 1965, and the current Ark is not original, although its art deco style is in keeping with the building. Despite publicly funded repair work in 1981, the congregation continued to lose members and gave up by 2008. It is to be hoped that a sympathetic new user will eventually be found for this fine building, whose qualities have been praised by the Twentieth Century Society.

LOCATION: Close to junction with Ullet Road and Smithdown Road. Currently closed (2015).

Childwall Synagogue

Dunbabin Road, L15 6XL

Kenmore Kinna, 1937–8

Safely suburban to blend in with the surrounding 1930s housing. Both materials and overall design have much in common with its contemporary **Greenbank Drive** but its execution is not nearly so stylish. Side bays, a bit Romanesque, sit uneasily with the single-storey Dutch gables over the ancillary spaces. These gables may owe something to the famous medieval

Gilded Star of David ceiling vent, Childwall Synagogue
(AP for SJBH)

Gothic Altneuschul in Prague. *Foundation stones.*

INTERIOR: The first Orthodox synagogue in Liverpool to place the *bimah* towards the Ark

(although still separate from it). Not commented on at the time was the fact that the building itself actually faces the wrong way: north – the generous site notwithstanding! Extensions to the rear by *W M & M W Shennan* of Birkenhead (1947–8). *Mikveh* by Rabbi *Meir Posen* 1976.

LOCATION: Corner with Queens Drive (A5058).

OPENING HOURS: *Shabbat* and weekday services: tel 0151 722 2079. Website via www.jscn.org.uk

JEWISH BURIAL GROUNDS IN LIVERPOOL

Listed here in roughly clockwise order, driving east and then north from the city centre, rather than in strict chronological order.

Deane Road Cemetery

Deane Road, Kensington, L7 0ET

1836–7, Grade II (screen wall and front railings)

Badly neglected at the time of our original survey in 1999, but fully restored in 2011–12 with the aid of a half-million-pound Heritage Lottery Fund grant. This is Liverpool's most historic Jewish cemetery, with a fine Greek-revival screen, now back in pristine creamy condition. The stucco and stone-faced wall is actually built of red brick, as is evident from inside the cemetery.

The gateway at Deane Road cemetery, before renovation (left: AA041075) **and after renovation** (right: Linda Baldock)

Inscription on the architrave in Hebrew and English HERE THE WEARY ARE LAID AT REST. The oldest legible tombstone (the records are incomplete) on the back wall is for REBECCA LYON, 27 May 1838. There are some imposing monuments to the great and good of Liverpool Jewry, including retail giant DAVID LEWIS (1823–85). The domed Romanesque canopy for Baroness MIRIAM DE MENASCE (1851–90) stands out here, but is a type that was widely used in Central Europe (such as in Berlin's massive Weissensee Jewish Cemetery). She was a Liverpool-born girl who married a Sephardi merchant banker from Alexandria, created a Baron by Emperor Franz Joseph of Austria.

Superseded by **Broadgreen** in 1904, although the last reserved plot was used in 1929.

The visitor centre (2011–12) with 'green' roof was designed by environmental architects *Cass Associates* and executed by *Owen Ellis Partnership*, both of Liverpool.

LOCATION: North end of Deane Road, just off Kensington Street (A57).

ACCESS: Locked. Open Days usually third Sunday of every month; Gardening Days first Sunday (volunteers welcome); Heritage Open Days (September). Other times and groups by appointment. Princes Road Synagogue: tel 0151 709 3431; www.deaneroad cemetery.com

Broadgreen Jewish Cemetery

1 Thomas Drive, L14 3DL

1904

Successor to **Deane Road**. In use. Brick Gothic style *ohel* with stone dressings and slate pitched roof and red-brick caretaker's house. The oldest tombstone on the neatly gated and mown site is that of ISAAC BENJAMIN – WHO ACTED AS SEXTON TO THE LIVERPOOL OLD HEBREW CONGREGATION FOR 30 YEARS, d 1 July 1904, aged 77 – to left (south) of the central pathway. Contains remains from two earlier Liverpool burial grounds, both now disappeared. First: badly weathered stones laid flat are from the back garden burial ground at **133 Upper Frederick Street** (1789–1902), transferred in 1923. *Plaque*. Two old photographs of that cemetery can be seen in the *ohel* at Broadgreen. Second: in unmarked graves are the reinterred remains of 127 burials from the **Oakes Street Jewish Cemetery** (1802–37), which was situated off Boundary Place, London Road, L3.

ACCESS: Locked. Princes Road Synagogue: tel 0151 709 3431. Further information via www. princesroad.org

Green Lane Jewish Cemetery

Green Lane, Tue Brook, Stoneycroft, L13 7DT

1839

A complete contrast to **Deane Road**, the cemetery of Liverpool's Old Hebrew Congregation. Green Lane – the cemetery founded by the breakaway New Hebrew Congregation, afterwards **Hope Place** and subsequently **Greenbank Drive** – languishes on the Jewish Heritage UK Sites at Risk list. It has been completely abandoned, is overgrown and the gate has been sealed up. Responsibility lies with Greenbank Drive Ltd, a company formed on the closure of the synagogue. The earliest tombstone,[7] that of LYON MARKS, d 9 September 1842, aged 61, was still in good condition when the site was passable in 2001. A partial field survey was made in the 1970s; the burial registers were destroyed in a fire. The substantial caretaker's house and *bet taharah*, built against the *c* 1860 stone and brick wall on Green Lane, are both demolished. Closed in 1921 when **Long Lane** was opened.

LOCATION: At the northern end of Green Lane (B5189), east side, near junction with Derby Road, next door to St Cecilia's Roman Catholic Church, whose postcode is used above.

ACCESS: Not currently possible. The key used to be c/o Greenbank Drive Synagogue.

Rice Lane Jewish Cemetery

Hazeldale Road, Walton, L9 2BA

1896

For the Liverpool Independent Jewish Burial Society. A bleak urban

Rice Lane Jewish Cemetery
(AP for SJBH)

cemetery permeated by an air of neglect. The first burial, which took place on 4 July 1896, of SOLOMON HESSELBERG, aged 72, is amongst the oldest graves situated towards the rear.[8] Here too are two small *ohalim* for prominent rabbis. Main *ohel* demolished. Closed 1991.

LOCATION: At end of Hazeldale Road, off Stalmine Road, off Rice Lane (A59) going north.

ACCESS: Local caretaker via Merseyside Jewish Representative Council: tel 0151 733 2292.

Long Lane Jewish Cemetery

Long Lane, Fazakerley, L9 9AG

1921

Successor to **Green Lane** for the Liverpool New Hebrew Congregation, and now in the ownership of **Greenbank Drive** Ltd. Disused red-brick *ohel* but otherwise neatly kept, although the early burial registers have been lost. The oldest extant tombstone is along the back wall: JACOB SIMPSON d 25 October 1921.

LOCATION: North side of Long Lane (B5187), travelling south, just before the junction with Stopgate Lane. On the boundary of Everton Cemetery, the postcode of which is given above.

ACCESS: Locked. Keyholder via Merseyside Jewish Representative Council: tel 0151 733 2292.

West Derby Cemetery, Jewish Section

Lower House Lane, L11 2SF

1927

For the Liverpool Federated Jewish Burial Society. Now closed except for reserved plots. Rusty iron gates, tidy inside but rather bare. Oldest *inscription* just to the right (east) of the main path that divides the site: ESTHER WIFE OF HARRY BLACK, d 23 September 1927. No *ohel*. Cared for by Liverpool City Council. No separate Jewish burial register was kept.

LOCATION: At southern tip of the West Derby Cemetery (1884), at the corner of Lower House Lane (east side) and Storrington Avenue. Go past the main cemetery lodge on Lower House Lane, the postcode of which is given above.

ACCESS: Locked. Key by advanced appointment by email: cemeteries-and-crematoria@liverpool.gov.uk

Allerton Cemetery, Jewish Section (Reform)

192 Woolton Road, L19 5NF

1929–30

A Liberal Jewish congregation was formed in Liverpool in February 1927, making it among the earliest in the country. At their first Annual General Meeting in 1929, it was announced that a burial ground 'had been allocated' by Liverpool City Council

at Allerton Cemetery (1909) and that it had been consecrated.[9] In 1935 the Liberals purchased **Hope Place Synagogue** when the latter moved to **Greenbank**. For 50 years (1927–77) the congregation was styled 'Liverpool Progressive Synagogue', but is today affiliated with Reform Judaism (Liverpool Reform Synagogue, 28 Church Road North, L15 6TF: tel 0151 733 5871; www.lrshul.org).

The neatly lawned plot is informally bounded by a mixture of privet and holly hedges, with gaps. Mature trees adorn the corners. There are about five rows of tombstones placed back to back, oriented to both north and south in a configuration common elsewhere in this cemetery. Unlike the separate Orthodox cemetery, known as **Springwood** (*see* below) located on its far north-eastern edge, the Reform plot inside Allerton Cemetery is not officially designated as 'Jewish', although it is full of tombstones bearing Hebrew lettering and Jewish symbols. The Reform section is referred to on official maps merely as plot 'Gen[eral] 1c' and is known by cemetery staff to include the graves of non-Jewish spouses. The Reform also make use of Allerton

Allerton Cemetery Reform Section (SK for SJBH)

Crematorium across Springwood Avenue.

Reform burials are entered into the general registers kept by the council; back volumes (1909–2000) have been lodged at Liverpool Record Office. The earliest tombstone on site is that of HENRY SOLOMON d 30 June 1930 'in his 84th year'.[10] The next, dated 1931, is a partially buried flat stone just in front.

Beyond the hedge on the north side of the plot are a further three tombstones. One of these commemorates DAVID IAN CONWAY, aged 50, bizarrely without a date. Perhaps he was not buried beneath, but elsewhere. There is also a custom among Jews to bury suicides at the edge or just outside the cemetery.

LOCATION: Section General 1c of the main Allerton Cemetery on Woolton Road. Follow the path behind the former cemetery lodge, bearing to the left.

ACCESS: Via the main entrance on Woolton Road during general cemetery hours.

NB **Springwood** Jewish Cemetery (Orthodox) and *ohel* was consecrated by **Childwall Synagogue** in 1951. It is located in a triangular plot at the north-eastern tip of the Allerton Cemetery extension that lies north of Springwood Avenue, before the junction with Hillfoot Road. Springwood can be reached in a pleasant six- or seven-minute walk through the main cemetery and across Springwood Avenue (L25 7UN). Gate usually left open.

View from the gallery (DP002937)

Manchester Jewish Museum

190 Cheetham Hill Road, M8 8LW
Edward Salomons, 1873–4 Grade II*

Housed in the delightful Moorish-style former
Spanish and Portuguese Synagogue in Cheetham,
once the hub of Manchester Jewish life

The façade of the former synagogue is pleasingly symmetrical, modest in scale, built of Manchester red brick with a central projecting gable and a slate roof. The entrance is framed within a horseshoe arch, Andalusian in inspiration; this shape is repeated in the window heads of the five-light arcade above. The lower floor windows are more ogee in form and other Islamic-inspired decoration occurs in the inlaid blue 'vitrified' marble bosses over the doorway and in the gable, arabesque decoration in the tympanum of the door arch and the use of slender columns. The windows were originally all filled with Islamic-inspired geometric coloured glass, now surviving only in the street façade and at gallery level. There is a gilded Hebrew *inscription* over the doorway from Psalm 93:5.

The choice of Moorish style was consciously appropriate for a Sephardi congregation, since it harked back to its roots in the Iberian peninsular. The opening up of rail and shipping routes between Britain and the Mediterranean basin during the 1850s and 1860s brought Sephardi Jewish textile merchants from Gibraltar, Morocco, Tunisia, Greece, Corfu, Turkey and Aleppo (Syria) to Manchester in increasing numbers. The prime mover in the construction of a purpose-built synagogue in the Spanish and Portuguese tradition in Ashkenazi-

dominated Manchester Jewry was Isaac David Belisha, grandfather of the Cabinet minister Leslie Hore-Belisha. However, there is no evidence that the German-Jewish-born architect *Edward Salomons* was inspired by the Spanish synagogues of Toledo and Cordoba, which were little known in his day. Rather, he explicitly acknowledged the influence of the Alhambra in Granada. *Owen Jones'* celebrated study started a fashion for 'Orientalism' in Victorian England.[11]

INTERIOR: The *Ehal* is classical in style, of marble, pink granite and alabaster, but framed within a bold and cusped horseshoe arch. *Inscription*: Psalm 145:18 (*Ashrei* prayer). The decoration of the walls, especially of the Ark wall and open timber ceiling, was originally much more elaborate than it appears today, being covered in large part with a diaper pattern. Gold stencilling was applied to the window mouldings, gallery fronts and iron columns. Look carefully, and you will see that one of the columns was regilded to its original state during the restoration of the building in the early 1980s. The *tevah* is displaced to the west end of the space in accordance with Sephardi tradition; indeed it is physically attached to the west wall, making it the only example in Britain of the bi-polar arrangement characteristic of Italian synagogues. It has an openwork metallic balustrade, painted gold, the design inspired by *mashrabiya* work as encountered in Egyptian mosques. Similar patterning occurs in the half-glazed front entrance doors.

STAINED GLASS: The original rose window over the Ark was replaced by the present *Shiviti* window sometime between 1913 and 1923. *Shiviti* is the first word of Psalm 16:8,

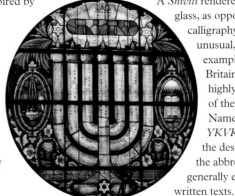

which begins 'I have set the Lord always before me', and is favoured for devotional prayer boards and pictures hung in the synagogue, especially in the Sephardi and Oriental Jewish traditions. The accompanying text is usually drawn from Psalm 67 and is set out in the form of the *menorah* or seven-branched candelabrum, an interpretation based on 14th-century Cabbalistic writings.

A *Shiviti* rendered in stained glass, as opposed to calligraphy, is highly unusual, and this example is unique in Britain. Note too the highly unusual use of the full Hebrew Name of God, *YKVK*, at the top of the design, rather than the abbreviation generally employed in written texts.

The cycle of high-quality stained glass panels on biblical themes in the downstairs windows was put in at the same time, as was the pair of rather art nouveau windows depicting the 'Pillar of Fire' and 'Pillar of Cloud' upstairs in the gallery, flanking the Ark. A typed catalogue giving detailed explanations of each of the windows and the source texts of other Hebrew *inscriptions* in the building is included in the museum display. Find it on the brass lectern. Behind the Ark

The *Shiviti* east window (DP020936)

Façade of the former Manchester Spanish and Portuguese Synagogue, now the Manchester Jewish Museum (AA012583)

The Tevah (DP020938)

don't miss the *foundation stone* that was discreetly set in the outside back wall, now inside the extension.

The Spanish and Portuguese Synagogue escaped the fate of its Ashkenazi equivalent down the street, the Manchester Great Synagogue, which was demolished in 1986, despite its

Stained glass (above: DP020928, above right: DP020930)

Grade II listing. The Spanish and Portuguese Synagogue was rescued through the determined efforts of a local group of enthusiasts led by Welsh Catholic-born historian Bill Williams. It opened as the Manchester Jewish Museum in 1984, conceptually England's only equivalent of the much bigger Jewish museums of continental Europe, which are housed in historic synagogues (think of Amsterdam, Venice or Prague).

OPENING HOURS: Sunday to Thursday 10.00 to 16.00; Friday 10.00 to 13.00. Closed Saturday, Jewish and bank holidays. Admission charge. Shop. Guidebook. Events. The museum offers guided Manchester Jewish Heritage Trails on Sundays once a month during the summer. Telephone for details and group bookings: tel 0161 834 9879, www.manchesterjewishmuseum.com

Discover Jewish Cheetham

Numbers refer to Jewish sites on the Heritage Trail map. Letters refer to general landmarks. Extant Jewish sites are indicated in bold in the text.

Distance: 2km on foot.

Manchester Jewish Museum ❶

➲ *Our starting point for this walk. From the **Museum** walk south along Cheetham Hill Road towards Manchester city centre, the skyline of which you can see in the distance. Bus numbers 89 and 135 from the city centre stop outside the museum. Parking is available at Manchester Fort shopping centre which is almost next door. Alternatively, it's a walk of 10–15 minutes from **Victoria Station** (Manchester Metrolink and Mainline). Turn left out of the station and walk uphill over the railway bridge and north (away from the city centre) up Cheetham Hill Road. Cross at lights. The Museum is on the east (right-hand) side. If you come by train, take in the sites along Cheetham Hill Road first and then continue the tour along Derby Street.*

Cheetham Hill Road

Cheetham Hill Road is still a busy thoroughfare, one of the principal routes out of the city to the north, eventually becoming Bury Old Road. The bottom of Cheetham Hill (formerly called York Street) was the point of arrival for the

Detail of terracotta and foundation stone of the former Manchester Talmud Torah, Bent Street, Cheetham, saved from almost total demolition in 2005 (DP020959)

majority of Manchester's Jews who came as refugees from eastern Europe in the 1880s, 1890s and 1900s. Immigrants arrived at **Victoria Station** via the Transpennine Railway and found lodgings in the immediate vicinity in the slums of Red Bank. This area, and much of Cheetham, was badly bombed during the Second World War, and is currently undergoing massive redevelopment – a mixture of high-density flats and retail sheds. Ironically, during the 2000s the slums of Red Bank were

transformed into the so-called 'Green Quarter'. Beyond the museum, the decaying landmarks of Manchester's Jewish heritage are all buildings at risk.

Pass the redeveloped site of the demolished Ashkenazi **Manchester Great Synagogue** (*Thomas Bird*, 1857–8, Grade II listed), at no. 140, on the corner of **Knowsley Street**. Happily Bird's **Cheetham Town Hall (A)** (*Thomas Bird*, 1853–6, Grade II) still stands directly facing on the other side of the road (no. 107),

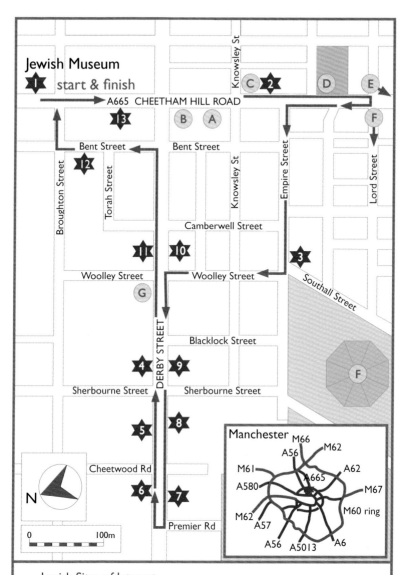

Jewish Sites of Interest

1 Jewish Museum
2 *former* New Synagogue
3 *former* Jewish Soup Kitchen
4 Cohen & Wilks
5 Imperial Waterproof Co
6 Levy & Weisgard
7 Victoria House

8 Derby House
9 Anchor *or* Empire Cap Works
10 Jacob Cohen warehouse
11 Marks & Spencer warehouse
12 *former* Talmud Torah School
13 Michael Marks' house

Other Sites of Interest

A *former* Cheetham Town Hall
B *former* Cheetham Assembly Rooms
C *former* Manchester Free Library
D St Chad's Church

E *former* Independent Chapel
F Strangeways Prison
G *former* Ice Palace

Manchester Jewish Soup Kitchen (DP020950)

Italianate, like his lost synagogue, with a fine ironwork canopy, now restored, but for a long time on the Heritage at Risk Register. Next door (no. 109), the more fussy **Cheetham Assembly Rooms (B)**, built as the Poor Law Union Offices in 1861–2, (architect unknown, Grade II), were used for many Jewish weddings.

➲ *Cross Knowsley Street.*

Immediately beyond is the yellow brick and stone of the **Manchester Free Library (C)** (*Barker & Ellis*, 1876, Grade II), and right next to it (at no.122) is the former **Manchester New Synagogue ❷** (*Ogden & Charlton*, 1889), designed by the somewhat eccentric Mancunian *William Sharp Ogden* (1844–1926), whose office was in Cheetham. Ogden's obsession with 'movement' in architecture prefigured art nouveau, but is hardly reflected in the conventional red-brick Romanesque of his New Synagogue, nor indeed in his design for the Talmud Torah School across the road in Bent Street (*see* below). The New Synagogue has been badly knocked about; it has lost its parapet, balustrade and pair of little turrets on the roof,[12] and there is nothing left of the interior, which, like many other sites on our route, is now used as a

warehouse. Nevertheless, the bold *Magen David* design in the tracery of the round window on the façade betrays its original function.

Pass the yellow-stone Perpendicular **St Chad's Roman Catholic Church (D)** (*Weightman & Hadfield*, 1846–7, Grade II) with its garden, the sole piece of greenery in this very urban setting. Before you cross Cheetham Hill Road at the lights, take in the former **Independent Chapel (E)** (*c* 1840, Grade II) at the very bottom of Cheetham Hill Road, at no. 19, on the other (west) side of the street. Until recently a furniture store, this building was once home to the **Manchester Central Synagogue**. Just before it, on the corner of Park Place, stood the **Manchester Reform Synagogue** (*Edward Salomons* 1857–8) until it was bombed in 1941. As you cross take in the excellent view of **Strangeways Prison (F)** (*Alfred Waterhouse*, 1866–8, Grade II) to the west down **Lord Street**.

➲ *Turn back (north) and take the second left (west) into* **Empire Street**.

To your left, at the junction with **Southall Street**, is the former **Philanthropic Hall** or **Jewish Soup Kitchen ❸** (*Thomas J Bushell*, 1905–6), facing the

blank wall of Strangeways. The prison, with its octagonal roof and north Italian-style chimney-cum-watchtower, is a looming presence that dominates this area. The Soup Kitchen is all Edwardian red brick and terracotta, with its function proudly displayed beneath the scrolled pediment over the main entrance, not unlike the **Soup Kitchen for the Jewish Poor** in the East End of London that opened several years earlier (*see* above). Badly restored as studios for an Asian radio station in 2006. Unfortunately the *foundation stones* have been removed.

➲ *Cross over* **Empire Street** *and walk up* **Woolley Street** *which takes you into* **Derby Street**.

Wide Derby Street was the commercial street of Cheetham and today is still lined with factories and warehouses, now gently decaying. Many of these were built for Jewish entrepreneurs.

➲ *Turn left (west) into Derby Street and walk down its south (city) side as far as* **Premier Road**, *viewing the buildings on the* **other (north)** *side first. Cross over and walk back towards Cheetham Hill Road viewing the buildings on the* **south** *side of Derby Street.*

Derby Street north side

Immediately opposite is the bright red brick and yellow terracotta former **Ice Palace (G)** (*W E Leeson* 1910–11), built as a skating rink, which was frequented by many Manchester Jews.

A series of **factories and warehouses** follows, all built in the early years of the 20th century employing new concrete technology combined with grandiose classical vocabulary. Many of these were designed for Jewish textile firms by the young *Joseph Sunlight* (1889–1978), who made his fortune from commercial building in Cheetham and speculative housing in Broughton Park and Prestwich (*see* **South Manchester Synagogue** below). **Cohen & Wilks** ➍ (*Joseph Sunlight*, 1915–16) to the right (east) of **Sherbourne Street** sports a pair of Tuscan columns. An enormous urn-shaped finial decorates the roof of the premises that occupy the plot at **58 Derby Street** between **Sherbourne Street** and **Cheetwood Road**, for the **Imperial Waterproof Company** ➎ (*Joseph Sunlight*, 1918–21). Next to it, on the other corner of Cheetwood Road, look out for a lion gargoyle in the keystone over the main entrance to the premises of waterproof-raincoat manufacturers **Levy & Weisgard** ➏ (*Joseph Sunlight*, 1915–18). Beyond, the overblown aedicule – a four-sided open structure – erected on the roof of the building closest to the bottom of the street (at Waterloo Road) cannot be positively identified with *Sunlight* but is certainly his style.

➲ *Cross the road.*

Derby Street south side

More factories: **Premier House**, now called **Victoria House** ➐, a garment factory, with giant

fluted Ionic columns with drooping volutes (obscured by hoardings) was also designed by *Joseph Sunlight* in 1920–2, as was **Derby House** ➑ (1919–20), with classical pediment, for waterproof-garment manufacturers Messrs M Fidler.

At **55 Derby Street**, on the corner with **Blacklock Street**, stands the **Anchor** or **Empire Cap Works** ➒ (*Charles Swain*, 1915), first erected for Russian-born Nathan Hope, who founded the company in 1853. Jewish immigrants dominated cap-making and waterproof-garment-making in Manchester in the late 19th and early 20th centuries. Just inside the fine terracotta corner entrance can still be seen the original green and white glazed tiling on the stairway and the later name 'Empire Works' in the black and white mosaic floor. To the side on Blacklock Street was the staff entrance, still clearly marked 'Workpeople'.

Beyond **Woolley Street**, at **39 Derby Street**,

is another red-brick warehouse with a hexagonal corner turret. This warehouse was built, as indicated by the *inscription* J.COHEN in the terracotta band along the side,[13] for **Jacob Cohen** ➓ (*T A Fitton*, 1902–3), a 'smallware' manufacturer.

The long-neglected **Manchester Jews' School** (*Edward Salomons*, 1868–9) occupied the large site beyond **Camberwell Street** until it was finally demolished for redevelopment in 2013. Built in a vaguely Italianate style, this was only the second purpose-built Jewish school in Manchester, and lasted until the early 1940s. In its day it claimed to be the largest primary school in Greater Manchester, with 2,000 on the roll. A famous old boy was playwright Jack Rosenthal, who wrote *The Evacuees* and was married to the actress Maureen Lipman.

Over the road, at **46 Derby Street**, almost opposite, is the original **Marks & Spencer**

The former Anchor Cap Works, no. 55 Derby Street (DP020955)

Anchor Cap Works, entrance (BB for SJBH)

Warehouse ⓫ (*Alfred H Mills*, 1900–1). Michael Marks moved from Leeds, where he had started his 'Penny Bazaars', and the firm was founded in Manchester in 1894. Marks built this warehouse around the corner from his home, **Michael Marks' House, 135 Cheetham Hill Road ⓭**, in one of the few Victorian terraces left in the street. Marks was living in that house in 1894, the year in which he signed the contract with Tom Spencer. The triple-gabled red-brick warehouse was the first building project undertaken by the company. An extension with cantilevered roof was added behind in 1921, but in 1924 Marks & Spencer moved their registered offices to London. From 1928 until after the Second World War the former Manchester headquarters of M&S was occupied by the *News Chronicle*. The building is now partially used as a mosque and Muslim school.

➲ *Cross over Derby Street again (to the north side). Walk past Marks & Spencer's warehouse and turn left down **Bent Street** until you reach **Torah Street**.*

(DP020962)

Torah Street got its name upon the opening of the **Manchester Talmud Torah School ⓬** (*Ogden & Charlton*, 1894–5). The building was somewhat less ambitious than Ogden had originally envisaged. Only the single-storey central range was constructed initially. The two-storey wings that had formed part of the original scheme were added only later, to the north in 1902 and to the south in 1930–1, by the successor firm of *(W R) Sharp & Cowburn*. Saved from almost complete demolition in 2005 and reroofed, but the *foundation stones* have been obliterated.

➲ *Continue along Bent Street and turn right into **Broughton Street**. You will see the **Manchester Jewish Museum** almost opposite back on **Cheetham Hill Road**.*

End of walk.

OTHER SITES IN GREATER MANCHESTER

NORTH MANCHESTER

CITY OF MANCHESTER

Former **Manchester Central Synagogue**

Heywood Street, Cheetham, M8 0PP

John Knight, 1926–8

A somewhat ostentatious red-brick façade, with Roman porch and Grecian detailing, masking reinforced concrete engineering by *Lambourne & Co Ltd*. The design perhaps a little 'retro' for the period. Closed in 1979 on amalgamation with the Broyder Shul[14] in Bury New Road, which had purchased (1959) a disused red-brick Gothic Methodist chapel on Leicester Road, Salford 7; the combined congregation was renamed the Central and North Manchester Synagogue. The lifespan of the purpose-built Heywood Street synagogue was a mere 50 years – which must constitute something of a record – while the chapel conversion on Leicester Road that succeeded it lasted barely 30 (closed 2008 and demolished). The neglected old Central Synagogue is a monument to the Jewish communal edifice complex of the twentieth century. In 2012 it was a Pakistani Shia mosque.

LOCATION: On the corner with Bellott Street. The postcode given above is that of the entrance to the Hussania Mosque, situated at the side of the building at 54 Bellott Street.

Collyhurst Jews' Burial Ground

Knightley Walk, M40 8LF

1844

Established by the first breakaway Manchester New Synagogue. After reunification in 1851 the cemetery was used mainly for infant burials, apparently until 1872. Extreme neglect by the Manchester Great Synagogue and fascist vandalism in the 1930s led almost to the complete destruction of the site. Today, no memorials survive in what has become an unkempt green, maintained by Manchester City Council, in the middle of a post-war housing estate. Inaccurate *plaque* belatedly erected by the Jewish community in 1986. Was slated to undergo landscaping as part of waterworks upgrading in 2013–15.

LOCATION: Knightley Walk is situated within a housing development on the west side of Queen's Road (A6010) almost opposite Monsall Street.

ACCESS: Gates may be locked but the site is visible through the railings. Manchester Beth Din: tel 0161 740 9711.

Crumpsall Jewish Cemetery

Crescent Road, M8 5UR

1884

For the Manchester Great Synagogue. A simplified Gothic *ohel* (by *George Oswald Smith*) of character dominates this quite large and exposed hilltop site, originally next to the Union Workhouse, now the North Manchester General Hospital. The *ohel*, of red brick with a slate roof, has unusual triangular-headed windows and is dated 1888 in its gable (north, car park, side). Sadly neglected, a stained-glass fanlight over the entrance by *R B Edmundson & Son* has disappeared. Victorian survivals inside include substantial panelled doors, decorative ceiling vents and an iron charity box built into the wall like a safe. *Foundation stones.*

The oldest surviving tombstones (from 1885) are located close to the central pathway that slopes down from the *ohel*. The grave of NATHAN LASKI (1863–1941), a prominent community figure in Manchester Jewry, is in the front row to the right (west) of the *ohel*. MICHAEL MARKS, d 31 December 1907 aged 44, the founder of Marks & Spencer, is buried further

Crumpsall Jewish Cemetery date stone (SK for SJBH)

View from the gates of Crumpsall Jewish Cemetery Ohel (SK for SJBH)

back in the same section under a tall grey granite obelisk, topped by a draped urn. The lettering has been re-gilded. Spot it two rows behind the prominent white columned and canopied monument to JULIUS SAMTER, d 20 February 1910.

LOCATION: The postcode given above is that of Clarkesville Farm at the bottom of a steep pathway on the north side of Crescent Road close to the junction with Chataway Road (opposite side).

ACCESS: Currently vehicular access remains up this steep path. The gate

Michael Marks' tombstone (SK for SJBH)

at the bottom is usually open and there is an on-site caretaker's house just inside. However, the sale in 2013 of unused land on site for housing development was likely to lead to changes. Contact North Manchester Jewish Cemeteries Trust for up-to-date information: tel 0161 795 0735; www.nmjct.org

Blackley Jewish Cemetery

1106 Rochdale Road, M9 6FQ

1897

For the Manchester Central Synagogue, afterwards shared with the North Manchester Synagogue with which it merged in 1978. The present nondescript *ohel* is post-war (*A Roland Walsingham*, 1946). It replaced an earlier *ohel* (possibly in Egyptian style by *Joseph Sunlight*, 1914) that was destroyed by fire – along with the burial registers left inside. A large scrubby site, the tombstones in many places being well spread out suggests that there are many unmarked graves. Clusters of stones date from the flu epidemic of 1919, in addition to several First World War graves. Undergoing renovation (2015).

LOCATION: Rochdale Road (A664) east side just before junction with Victoria Avenue (A6104). Sharp turn into gates.

ACCESS: Keypad affixed to pedestrian gate. Contact North Manchester Jewish Cemeteries Trust for code and for vehicular access: tel 0161 795 0735, www.nmjct.org

Philips Park Cemetery, Jewish Section

Riverpark Road, Eastlands, M40 2XP

1875, P & G Grade II

In 1875 the South Manchester Synagogue purchased part of the Dissenters' section of the first municipal cemetery in Manchester (*Paull & Ayliffe*, landscaping by *William Gay*, 1866–7). This vast Victorian cemetery lies in north-east Manchester not far from the Manchester City football stadium (built for the Manchester Commonwealth Games in 2002), in an area that has undergone extensive redevelopment. The immediate area is now referred to as Eastlands rather than Miles Platting or Bradford as formerly.

The Jewish section was laid out by *Isaac Holden*, architect of the conversion of the building in All Saints that served as their first synagogue from 1872. No sign today of his *ohel* but notice the stone gateposts marking the private path that led to it, which have been incorporated into the outside boundary wall. Last burial 1949 and closed 1953. The sole First World War military grave to LT LEONARD FLEET of the ROYAL FLYING CORPS, the first Jewish airman killed in the Great War (dated 27 October 1917) was amongst those vandalised in 2000. The Jewish section was restored and rededicated in May 2013, thanks to the efforts of

Bernard Stonefield of South Manchester Synagogue, Prestwich builder Harry Johnston and the Friends of Philips Park Cemetery. Poignantly, new grave markers have been placed on unmarked graves, including those of many babies buried together with unrelated people. New *plaque*.

LOCATION: Make for the 'Roman Catholic' entrance on Riverpark Road, which forms the northern boundary of the cemetery. The Jewish plot lies directly opposite, inside the northern entrance to the 'Dissenter's' section, across Bank Street.

ACCESS: Open during general cemetery hours. Friends of Philips Park Cemetery www.foppc.com

CITY OF SALFORD

Higher Crumpsall Synagogue

Bury Old Road, M7 4PX

Pendleton & Dickinson, 1928–9, Grade II

Dubbed the 'White Synagogue' when opened on account of its 'glistening' polished artificial stone-clad façade, Higher Crumpsall was designed in so-called 'free classical' style by Cheetham architects *Basil Pendleton* and *Charles Dickinson*, neither of whom was Jewish. They had previously designed the **Sha'are Sedek Synagogue**, while the builders, *William Thorpe & Son* of Cornbrook, had recently completed **Withington Synagogue**, both for the Sephardim

of South Manchester (*see* below).

In plan, Higher Crumpsall Synagogue could be said to be 'back-to-front' owing to the need to orientate the Ark correctly towards Jerusalem. Thus it offers its elevated Ark end to the street, in a blind, classical semi-circular apse. Look carefully to see the lion-head gargoyles decorating the cornice above, a typically classical motif but surprising in a synagogue. Three-dimensional representational art in the synagogue is extremely rare and this façade detail is not encountered anywhere else in British synagogue architecture. The principal entrance is at the side (south-west corner) and has a hooded door-case and Hebrew *inscription* Psalm 100:4) on the lintel.

INTERIOR: A side lobby, lined with wooden founders' *plaques*, leads into a generous vestibule across the rear of the building. In the vestibule look out for the scale model by *Stanley Shaw* (2005). Behind the classical exterior, the synagogue was state-of-the-art steel-framed construction, utilising large-span girders and truss-work in the ceiling and cantilevered galleries. The steel was manufactured by *Robinson & Kershaw* at the Temple Ironworks in Manchester, who claimed to have erected the first steel-frame building in the city in 1905.

Inside, Higher Crumpsall has a well-designed worship space, acoustically sound – well adapted for the choral

Art deco 'Jerusalem Rebuilt' east window at Higher Crumpsall Synagogue (AA040180)

services for which it was known – and high quality fixtures and fittings of marble, brass and oak. Most of the fittings were made by local firm *J & H Patteson* and remain largely the same as on the day the building was opened. They include the Ark, *duhan* and *bimah*; the marble front of the reading desk is six inches thick and weighs nearly a ton. A feature of the classical Ark is the pair of jewel-like coloured mosaics symbolising the *hoshen* or breastplate worn by the Biblical High Priest to represent the Twelve Tribes of Israel. The curved sliding doors (also by *Patteson*) are made of solid oak. The numbered oak pews, upstairs and down, provide seating for 900. Spot the many Stars of David dotted around the space, especially in the half-glazed doorways, and original bronze light-

fittings, all quite deco, as are the lotus-leaf grilles fronting the choir galleries. There are two of these, in a highly unusual arrangement, one on either side of the Ark. The massive 'carriage' lantern

Lion gargoyle on the Ark apse at Higher Crumpsall Synagogue (AA040183)

hanging from the middle of the ceiling arrived in the 1950s, reputed to have been destined for the Leicester Square Odeon in London's West End.

Higher Crumpsall spawned a look-a-like 'Down Under': Caulfield Hebrew Congregation (1960–61), 572 Inkerman Street, Melbourne, designed by Manchester-trained architect *Anthony Hayden* who emigrated to Australia in 1949. Born Abraham Isaac Hershman, Tony Hayden was the son of Crumpsall's long-serving cantor, Solomon Hershman.[15]

STAINED GLASS: The pair of windows depicting *Jerusalem Rebuilt* (east window) and a *Vision of the Temple* (west window) render traditional symbolism in modernist style. The 'Temple' is cubic in treatment, with vertical ribbon openings and central dome, reminiscent of the architecture of *Patrick Geddes* and *Austin Harrison* in British Mandate Palestine. The sunray radiating out from behind is typically art deco. The pair of vertical windows flanking the Ark depict, at left, the *Luhot* and altar, and at right, open *Sefer Torah* and *hanukiah*, both panels with *Magen David* and the symbols set inside wreaths. Crumpsall's stained glass is contemporary with the building, having been made by *Humphries, Jackson & Ambler Ltd* of Cornbrook.[16] The possibility remains that they were working to designs by *A Seward & Co.* of Lancaster, given the similarity of the windows flanking the Ark to stained glass at **Southport Synagogue** (*see* below).

Essential conservation work was carried out in 2004–7, at a cost of *c* £300,000, thanks largely to public funding, for what remains one of the best 1920s synagogues in the country. It deserves a new lease of life, fortunately being situated in the midst of one of the fastest-growing Jewish communities in Europe.

LOCATION: On Bury Old Road (A665) at Cheetham Village, west side, near 'Half Way House' junction with Leicester Road. Bus no. 135 from city centre and Manchester Jewish Museum.

OPENING HOURS: *Shabbat* and weekday services. Heritage Open Days (September). Other times by appointment: tel 0161 740 1210.

North Salford (Roumanian) Synagogue

2 Vine Street, M7 3PG

Housed in a substantial Manchester red-brick former merchant's house, this is the successor to the original purpose-built synagogue in **Ramsgate Street**, M8, by cinema architect *Peter Cummings* (born Caminesky) in 1915–24. Traces of that building have almost been obliterated – and even the street pattern has been completely altered – save fragments of a red-brick wall on the north side of **Willerby Road**, M8 9YG, containing one barely legible sandstone corner stone out of four originally set. But the interior fittings were reinstalled at Vine Street in 1953. In 1941 the name of this congregation, founded in 1914, was changed to the North Salford Synagogue. This was out of fear of attack given that its members were designated 'enemy aliens' because Roumania had entered the Second World War on the side of the Axis Powers.

OPENING HOURS: *Shabbat* and weekday services. Tel 0161 792 3278.

Brindle Heath Jews' Burial Ground

Brindle Heath Road, Pendleton, M6 7EE

1794

All that remains of the oldest Jewish burial ground in Manchester. Originally the site extended to the south-east, almost as far as Ford Lane and, presumably, burials remain beneath. The small enclosed grassy plot was landscaped in 2004 by Manchester Groundwork, and is now maintained by Manchester City Council. It contains five tombstones, no longer *in situ*. A finely carved and exceptionally legible inscription commemorates RABBI ISAAC THE SON OF YEKUTIEL WHO DIED ON SATURDAY NIGHT AND WAS BURIED ON SUNDAY 25 TISHREI 5556 [= 9 OCTOBER 1795] on the earliest extant Jewish tombstone in Manchester.

LOCATION: Brindle Heath Road, east side. Almost opposite a new housing estate on Maurice Drive, the postcode of which has been cited above.

ACCESS: Can be viewed through the railings if the gate is locked. Manchester Beth Din: tel 0161 740 9711.

The oldest surviving Jewish tombstone in Manchester at Brindle Heath, Pendleton
(BB for SJBH)

Holy Law Synagogue

Bury Old Road, Prestwich,
M25 0EX

Theodore Herzl Birks, 1934–5

By a little-known young
Jewish architect who
probably landed the
commission because he
was known to Israel
Sunlight, president of the
synagogue, as chief
draughtsman in the office
of his son, architect *Joseph
Sunlight*; a window inside is
dedicated to the Sunlight
family. Compared at the
time with *Cecil Eprile*'s
Hendon Synagogue in
London, an exact
contemporary.

Pleasing elevated
International Style
tripartite façade, here in
pink-grey brick. The façade
of Holy Law was influential
locally, being reproduced
after the Second World War
in red brick at the new
city centre **Manchester
Reform Synagogue**,
Jackson's Row, M2 5NH
(*Levy & Cummings*
1952–3), **Prestwich
Hebrew Congregation**
(The 'Shrubberies'), Bury
New Road, M25 9NW
(*Eric Levy*, 1961–2), and
nearer to Holy Law, at
Heaton Park Synagogue,
Middleton Road, M8 4JX
(*Eric Levy & Partner*
[*Michael Cummings*],
1965–7).

INTERIOR: Conventional,
made more so by the
reordering of the *bimah*
from the east back to the
centre by *Howard &
Seddon* (1961–2), who also
extended the gallery. Note
the shiny jet-black columns
topped by seated heraldic
lions that flank the Ark;

quite Masonic in
appearance. Accretions of
ancillary spaces based
around the original
Victorian house, now too
large for the congregation.

OPENING HOURS: *Shabbat*
and weekday services:
tel 0161 740 1634.

Prestwich Village
Jews' Burial Ground

Bury New Road, M25 1AF

1841

In use from 1841 to 1884,
the successor ground to
Brindle Heath was
shared by the Manchester
Great Synagogue and
(second) **Manchester
New Synagogue** (1889).
It is still legally the
responsibility of the Jewish
community. Completely
overgrown since 2004 and
declared a 'Site at Risk' by
Jewish Heritage UK. The
Gothic style *ohel* was
demolished by the Borough
of Prestwich in 1951 to
make way for a 'Peace
Garden' in front of the site,
to mark the Festival of
Britain. Inside – assuming
that the site has been
rendered passable! – the
Hebrew *inscription* on a
half-size tombstone tucked
against the north-west
(right hand) wall (visible
back in 2000) declares its
status as THE FIRST IN THIS
PLACE. It commemorates
REB MEIR SON OF BENJAMIN
ZE'EV HALEVI, known from
documentary sources by
his English name Meyer
Woolf, who was buried on
Sunday 13 Nissan 5601
[= 4 April 1841]. Another
interesting *inscription* is
located towards the back,
close to the central
pathway, on an unusual

slate stone, badly
renovated. The stone itself
was made by D. MCSHEE of
Bath Row, Birmingham.
Decorated with an
open *Sefer Torah*, it
commemorates JOSEPH
WOOLY, d 28 October 1884,
aged 88, WHO DIED IN THE
SYNAGOGUE WITH THE
SIYFRES TOWRA [*Sefer Torah*]
IN HIS HANDS. Some
imposing Gothic
headstones, plus flat stones
of the (North) Manchester
Spanish and Portuguese
community who shared
this cemetery from 1874.
Last burial 1914. Rusting
ornamental iron gates
donated by the Behrens
family are propped against
the wall, the Hebrew date
5611 [=1851] still legible
on them.

LOCATION: Near corner
with Sharp Street. The
postcode given above is
that of the business next
door at 425 Bury New
Road.

ACCESS: Locked entrance
on Bury New Road.
Contact Stenecourt
Synagogue for the key:
tel 0161 792 8399.

Manchester Reform
Cemetery (Old)

Higher Lane, Whitefield,
M45 7BY

1858

The earliest Reform Jewish
cemetery outside London.
A neat, compact site
surrounded by a high red-
brick wall, but passers-by
can peer in through
the gate railings at the
Victorian yellow-brick *ohel*
with its pitched slate roof.
The *ohel* has a large round
window in the gable at both
front and rear; one retains

its original leaded light, in the form of an eight-petal flower design. The floor of the *ohel*, which contains a columbarium of much later date, is of patterned terracotta. The tombstones mostly face west rather than east, and include some Gothic-style memorials with pointed heads. The oldest stones are located along the back wall.

LOCATION: Opposite McDonald's (M45 7BY) car park at junction of Bury Old Road (A665) and Bury New Road (A56).

ACCESS: Locked. Manchester Reform Synagogue: tel 0161 834 0415, www.mcr-reform. org.uk

Rainsough Jewish Cemetery

Butterstile Lane, Prestwich, M25 9UL

1923

A high red-brick curved boundary wall fronts this tightly packed, extensive cemetery laid out on a hilly site with steep gradients to all sides. Acquired by the **Manchester Central Synagogue** as a communal burial ground. Higher Broughton Synagogue (*Delissa Joseph*, 1906–7, demolished) had purchased its own plot outright in 1920 and in 1923 contributed to the erection of the first of two red-brick *ohalim*. Today the site is shared by ten congregations and burial boards including **Higher Crumpsall Synagogue** and the **Roumanian Synagogue**. The second *ohel* was demolished in a

Interior of the *Ohel* at Manchester's historic Reform Jewish cemetery in Whitefield (AA040085)

programme of renovation by the Rainsough Charitable Trust in 2005. The site was badly vandalised in 2000 and again in 2005, thanks to the lack of provision of an adequate rear boundary wall, belatedly rectified, and the recent landscaping is to be welcomed.

A memorial to remains removed in 1998 from the supposed medieval Jewish burial ground at **Winchester** is located at the bottom of the slope to the south. *Foundation stones.*

ACCESS: Usually open Sunday to Thursday, Friday morning. North Manchester Jewish Cemeteries Trust: tel 0161 795 0735, www.nmjct.org

Whitefield Jewish Cemetery

Old Hall Lane, M45 7TN

1931

Opened by the Manchester United Synagogue. Enter through the red-brick *ohel* with its low-slung pitched roof (1931). Burial rights were subsequently acquired

by Higher Prestwich Hebrew Congregation (from 1957) and Whitefield Hebrew Congregation (from 1974). The strictly Orthodox Adath Yisroel community, composed initially largely of refugees from central Europe who came to Manchester on the eve of the Second World War, joined them *c* 1939, followed by the Machzikei Hadass communities, mainly Hasidic groups, from 1955. The strictly Orthodox have a separate section of the burial ground, to the right of the *ohel*. Burials tend to be haphazard, according to sex or family groups rather than in consistent rows. A new *ohel* was constructed over the grave of the Manchester Rosh Yeshivah, RABBI YEHUDAH ZE'EV SEGAL d 22 Shevat 5753 [=13 February 1993], and many candles are lit inside by Hasidim. To the rear (with its own entrance on the right-hand side of the lane before you reach the old entrance) is the separate Whitefield Hebrew

Congregation cemetery, opened 2000. It has a lavish yellow-brick *ohel* (2000)[17] with an attractive series of stained glass windows by *Prestwich Glass*.

LOCATION: Old Hall Lane is off Phillips Park Road West. Next door to Worsley Hill Farm, the postcode of which is given above.

ACCESS: Usually open Sunday to Thursday, Friday morning. Further information from Manchester United Synagogue (Meade Hill Road Synagogue): tel 0161 740 9586, www.meadehillshul.co.uk and/or Machzikei Hadass: tel 0161 792 1313 (synagogue). The Whitefield section is generally locked; Whitefield Synagogue: tel 0161 766 3732, www.thewhc.co.uk

SOUTH MANCHESTER

CITY OF MANCHESTER

Former **South Manchester Synagogue**

Wilbraham Road, Fallowfield, M14 6JS

Joseph Sunlight, 1912–13, Grade II

Built for the prosperous Ashkenazim who had moved south and in 1872 formed a breakaway in All Saints from the Ashkenazi Great Synagogue in Cheetham. Russian-Jewish immigrant *Joe (Joseph) Sunlight* (born Schimschlavitch, 1889–1978), at the age of 24 was winner of a limited competition, in which six architects participated, for what was his only known commission for a religious building. Wilbraham Road was built in the style of a Turkish mosque with dome and minaret, in a bold, almost cubist, treatment, clad in buff glazed terracotta. Sunlight professed to have used St Sophia of Constantinople as his model, with a much scaled-down tower derived from Westminster Cathedral. In the estimation of *British Architect*, the whole gave 'a very satisfactory effect of an Eastern place of worship'.[18] 'Byzantine' synagogues were becoming fashionable on the continent in this period and the ambitious young architect likewise employed innovative building technology: reinforced concrete for the 10.7m (35ft) span of the dome and for the lattice girders carrying the gallery, thus dispensing with the need for column supports beneath – the earliest application of this technology in a fully realised manner to synagogue architecture in Britain.

In 2003 a new South Manchester Synagogue by *Michael R Ashworth* of *Buttress Fuller Alsop Williams* was opened in Bowdon, Cheshire. The threat of closure was averted by a scheme to convert Wilbraham Road into a student centre, the synagogue being conveniently situated close to the university campuses. Controversially, the scheme, by *Provan & Makin*, involved the insertion of a floor at gallery level. This compromised the technical achievement of Sunlight's original design but was the price paid for successfully keeping the synagogue in Jewish use.

OPENING HOURS: *Shabbat* and weekday services during term time. Other times by appointment: tel 0161 928 7171.

The former South Manchester Synagogue (AA028507)

Withington Congregation of Spanish and Portuguese Jews

8 Queenston Road,
West Didsbury, M20 2WZ

Delissa Joseph, 1925–7, Joseph
Sunlight 'supervising architect',
Grade II

Delissa Joseph (1858–1927) died shortly before his last synagogue was opened, but the well-preserved set of drawings in Manchester City Architects Department contradicts *Joe Sunlight*'s claim to any input into the design scheme. Whereas the Ashkenazim of **Wilbraham Road** had opted for 'an Eastern style of architecture' in 1913 as interpreted by Sunlight, the taste of the Withington Sephardim was severely European neoclassical. A monumental interior, three storeys high, the scale is a surprise behind the low-key massed red-brick and Portland stone façade.

INTERIOR: Lavish in its use of white marble, which contrasts dramatically with the rich red Wilton carpet and the bronze drop electroliers, all original by *General Electric Co Ltd* of Manchester. The imposing Ark is raised on seven steps, the *tevah* displaced to the rear with the oak pews facing it, the traditional Sephardi layout. The giant order of Ionic columns at Withington must surely ultimately derive from the 17th-century Portuguese Great Synagogue of Amsterdam, the 'mother' congregation of the Spanish and Portuguese communities in England. Single stained-glass window behind the *Ehal* was brought from the earlier synagogue (conversion) in **Mauldeth**

Road (1904). *Foundation stones*, plus memorial tablet on the exterior wall behind the Ark apse.

In 2010 the breakaway **Sha'are Sedek Synagogue** (*Pendleton & Dickinson*, 1924–5), around the corner in Old Lansdowne Road,[19] was closed, sold to developers, demolished and housing was built on the extensive site. The breakaway congregation made up of Jews from the *Edot Mizrakh*, mainly Persia, Iraq, Aden (Yemen) and Egypt, often French- or Arabic-speaking, remerged with the Withington Spanish and Portuguese. The combined congregation, now styled the Sha'are Hayim Sephardi Synagogue of South Manchester, had shared services between the two sites from 1996. Meanwhile, like the South Manchester Ashkenazim, the Sephardim planned to construct a brand new synagogue further out, in Hale Barnes – to be named Sha'are Sedek (Architects: *Ashworth, Jackson & Walker*).

OPENING HOURS: *Shabbat* and weekday services: tel 0161 445 1943.

Southern Cemetery, Jewish Section

Barlow Moor Road, M21 7GL

1892, P & G Grade II

A section of the Southern Cemetery in Chorlton-cum-Hardy (opened 1879) was begun in 1892 by Reform Jews and was later shared with both Ashkenazi (**South Manchester** from 1924) and Sephardi congregations (**Sha'are**

The Ark, Withington Spanish and Portuguese Synagogue (AA040146)

Southern Cemetery: the Gothic-style entrance gates and *Ohel* (AA040131)

Sedek from 1934, **Withington**, 1957) south of the city centre. A well-preserved Gothic *ohel* of sandstone and slate with black and white chequered floor. It is similar in both style and materials to the Anglican, Catholic and Nonconformist chapels elsewhere in this cemetery, all designed by *H J Paull*, but was probably erected later. Close by is an unusually ornate canopied memorial, featuring elaborate carvings of griffins and other mythic beasts, to ABDULLAH ELLIAS, d 30 May 1911. A window was dedicated to him in the (North Manchester) Spanish and Portuguese Synagogue in Cheetham Hill Road (**Manchester Jewish Museum**). Simple gravestone of architect *Joseph Sunlight*, d 15 April 1978, to the right of the main path.

NB The imposing Romanesque Manchester Crematorium next door was designed by Jewish-born synagogue architect *Edward Salomons* in 1892 – one of the earliest such facilities to be built in the entire country. Indeed, Salomons, a Reform Jew, from a German background, was himself cremated at the Southern Cemetery when he died in 1906.

LOCATION: At far western end of the cemetery on Barlow Moor Road. The Southern Cemetery Lodge and Office is located at 212 Barlow Moor Road, M21 7GL.

ACCESS: Separate gate on Barlow Moor Road is usually locked, so use the small gate into the general

Tomb of Abdullah Ellias, 1911 (AA040134)

cemetery situated about 200m to the right. Once inside go through the metal security gate (remember to close the sliding bolt behind you) that leads into the Muslim section. Walk around the side into the Jewish section. Southern Cemetery Lodge and Office: tel 0161 227 3205; South Manchester Synagogue, Bowdon: tel 0161 928 2050.

OLDHAM

Failsworth Jewish Cemetery

Cemetery Road, M35 0SN

1919

Next door to the Failsworth general cemetery but separate from it. For what was then known as the **Holy Law** Beth Aaron Synagogue, nicknamed the 'Claff Shul' or 'Red Bank

Shul', which had started life as perhaps the oldest of Manchester's immigrant *hevrot* in 1864. The conventional red-brick *ohel* was consecrated on 22 June 1919 before the first burials in July 1919. *Foundation stone* outside and consecration *plaque* inside. This extensive cemetery has been tidied up and the borders have been planted with shrubs.

ACCESS: Usually open, Sunday to Thursday, Friday morning. Holy Law Synagogue: 0161 740 1634.

TRAFFORD

Urmston Jewish Cemetery

Chapel Grove, M41 9BB

The earliest burial at Urmston appears to have been in 1878 (although records are incomplete),

the land having been acquired by the (North) **Manchester Spanish and Portuguese**. From 1891 they shared the site with the **Manchester New Synagogue**, whose architect *William Sharp Ogden (Ogden & Charlton,* 1894) built the first of two brick and terracotta *ohalim,* closing Albert Avenue. It was demolished *c* 2007. The surviving *ohel* at Chapel Grove (1900) was built for the Manchester Burial Society of Polish Jews or *Polisher Hevrah Kadisha,* latterly styled the Manchester Jewish Burial Society.

A separate entrance for the Sephardim with rusting gate and almost illegible *foundation stone* inscription (there is a chronogram in there somewhere) on Chapel Grove. Lacks an *ohel,* but in this section

'Taj Mahal' monument to Haym Mordecai Levy at Urmston Jewish Cemetery
(AA040119)

are some of the finest memorials in a Jewish cemetery in England, including a highly unusual carved granite 'Taj Mahal' for HAYM MORDECAI LEVY, d 17 November 1923. Whitefield Synagogue section from 1959.

ACCESS: Usually open, Sunday to Thursday, Friday morning. North Manchester Jewish Cemeteries Trust: tel 0161 795 0735, www.nmjct.org

THE REST OF THE NORTH WEST

CHESHIRE

Former **Delamere Forest School**

Blakemere Lane, nr Frodsham, WA6 6NP

J W Beaumont & Sons, 1919–20

Latterly a residential special needs school, Delamere was built as 'The Jewish Fresh Air Home and School', a euphemism for a sanatorium for child sufferers from TB, a disease once prevalent in the slums of Manchester's Red Bank and Strangeways. The architects of the original red-brick buildings with Westmoreland slate roofs were a Manchester firm better known for the Whitworth Art Gallery (1894–1908). The original hinged casement windows that opened wide so that the patients could be wheeled outside into the fresh air were removed sometime after 2002. Extensions (1927–8) including the assembly hall also by a Manchester firm, *Pendleton & Dickinson*, who designed two synagogues in the city (*see* above).

Assorted post-war additions included a swimming pool. The gardens and internal courtyards gave a cosy cottage feel to the place. Closed and sold to renewable energy company Community Windpower Ltd of Frodsham in 2011. Unfortunately, the empty buildings were ransacked by metal thieves over the Easter bank holiday in 2012. *Foundation stones.*

LOCATION: Take the A556 old Chester Road. Turn onto the B5152 towards Delamere Forest and Frodsham.

LANCASHIRE

BLACKBURN

Blackburn Old Cemetery, Jewish Section

Whalley New Road, BB1 9SR

1900

An L-shaped enclosed plot on an exposed hilly site situated within a vast municipal cemetery that dates back to 1857.

Blackburn's Jewish community began in the 1880s; a synagogue was opened in the Old Technical Schools, Paradise Lane in 1893 and a *mikveh* in 1896, probably reopened 1904, in the Turkish Baths, Richmond Terrace. The synagogue moved to 19 Clayton Street in 1919; closed 1970s.

Initial opposition (1896) from the Council to 'sectarian' burials was overcome and the earliest interment, of an infant, LEOPOLD GORDON, 7 months, took place on 17 September 1900.

The earliest marked grave is to be found in the far corner against the back (south) wall: MAUDE, wife of SOLOMON JACOBSON, d 29 August 1906 aged 24. After years of neglect, the site was restored in 1997 and is in occasional use.

LOCATION: Follow the signs to Whalley. Cemetery gates are on the east side of Whalley New Road before Agate Street, facing Talbot Funeral Services. The Jewish plot is at the top right-hand corner of the hill (south-east) from the main entrance on Whalley New Road. Park by the office at the main gates and take the steep walk up.

ACCESS: Walled but not locked. Open during general cemetery hours. Blackburn with Darwen Council Cemeteries Department: tel 01254 202021.

PRESTON

Preston Old Cemetery, Jewish Section

New Hall Lane, PR1 4SY

1913, P & G Grade II

Lies within the City Cemetery, itself opened in 1855. The Preston Jewish community claimed to have been founded in 1882. They used temporary and converted premises, including the Temperance Hall (1899), Edman Street (1903–4) and a large red-brick terraced house in Avenham Street (PR1 3BN) 1905 and 1932–1985. (A prominent relief, in the style of *Benno Elkan's Knesset Menorah* in Jerusalem (1956), adorned the lower wall of the house.[20]) The oldest legible tombstone in the neat Jewish plot, which is separated from the general cemetery by railings, is: SARAH LEFKOVITCH d 6 May 1913, aged 34, situated closest to the redundant modern red-brick *ohel*, although according to the council's records the first burial took place on 3 January 1913.

LOCATION: The Jewish section lies at the south-eastern corner of the cemetery behind New Hall Lane but its street gate is kept locked. Enter via the main cemetery gates at the other end, that is, by the roundabout at New Hall Lane (A59) and Blackpool Road (A5085), opposite the Hesketh Arms public house, and follow the New Hall boundary to the far end.

ACCESS: The internal gate is usually open during general cemetery hours. Preston Cemetery Office, New Hall Lane, PR1 4SY: tel 01772 794585.

BLACKPOOL

Blackpool Synagogue

Leamington Road, FY1 4HD

R B Mather, 1914–16, Grade II

A jolly seaside synagogue built in 'Edwardian orientalist'[21] style not ten minutes' walk from Blackpool's North Pier. In the 1900s this was the smart end of town where the Jewish community, founded in the 1890s, clustered in the new, solidly middle-class Raikes Hall[22] development, which included Blackpool's Old Grammar

School (*Rotts Son & Hennings*, 1904–5, Grade II) next door, now used by the Salvation Army. The town's Jewish community was always small but was augmented during the summer by holidaymakers from Liverpool and Manchester. The synagogue's architect was *Robert Butcher Mather* (1852–1933), a staunch Catholic and Conservative former mayor of Blackpool (1897–8), a circumstance which may well have helped ease the planning process (although, unfortunately, his drawings can no longer be traced). Unclear if he designed any churches; his practice thrived principally on speculative residential developments and hotels.

Blackpool Synagogue is built of red Accrington

**The cupola,
Blackpool Synagogue**
(AA040387)

Interior, Blackpool Synagogue (AA040164)

Luhot in the form of an engraved and polished silver *plaque*, now at **St Anne's Synagogue**. During the 1960s redevelopment, the *bimah* was replaced and extra seating was installed. The present *bimah* and the non-matching pews at the back of the prayer hall are thought to have come from the old Finchley Synagogue (*Cecil J Eprile*, 1935) in London.[23]

STAINED GLASS: Generous and of good quality, installed from 1921, but unfortunately partially obscured by the gallery. On traditional themes, the colours add to the warmth of the space.

Closed and sold in 2012, the future of Blackpool's handsome synagogue remains uncertain (2015).

FURTHER INFORMATION: Legacy website http://blackpoolunited hebrewcongregation.org

brick, stone and terracotta, with a hexagonal lead-covered cupola and quite art nouveau curves to the roofline on the exposed long (west) wall. Named and dated in the street-facing south gable (housing the Ark) plus a record eleven *foundation stones* (on the west wall, now badly eroded). Not flattered by the later extensions attached.

Originally, the vestibule had, somewhat unusually, been situated at the back of the building (dictated by the orientation of the Ark). Above, the space behind the upstairs gallery had folding doors, doubling up as classrooms cum committee room. The synagogue was extended in phases after the Second World War: to the rear of the prayer hall (1955–7), and gallery over (1962–3); then to the side, on the site of the house next door, where the new front entrance was created (1965–6). The defunct *mikveh* in the basement was part of the original scheme.

INTERIOR: The shallow barrel-vaulted prayer hall was once top-lit by a coloured glass laylight, now blocked. The gallery, with its attractive open timber front, wraps around the walls of the intimate space. The polished mahogany Ark, in classical style on the south wall, had unusual

Layton Jewish Cemetery

Talbot Road, FY3 7HG

1901

Established 1898, but the first burial was of an infant, LIONEL MORRIS, three months, 16 January 1901. The oldest tombstone on site is in the right-hand (south-east) corner behind the front boundary: JULIA GORDON COWEN d 14 June 1904. A hedge at the back obscures a Reform section, dating from 1948; the congregation was set up in the previous year (1947). *Ohel* (1926–7) of brown brick with hipped roof. It is now derelict; the roof lantern is open to the sky and the doors and windows are blocked up so that the surviving coloured glass and diamond leaded lights can no longer be seen from outside.[24] *Foundation stones* and datestone '1927' in tympanum. Closed except for reserved plots.

The Jewish cemetery is separate from the general **Layton Cemetery**, FY3 7BB, next door (opened 1871). Pop in there to see the family tomb of *Robert B Mather* (1852–1933), the architect of **Blackpool Synagogue**. Along with his two wives and several of his children, Mather is buried under a tall granite obelisk, topped by a very Catholic praying angel, which is found a little way along the main path, just to the right. The tall obelisk can be spotted through the railings from the street outside. The immediate neighbourhood boasts **Mather Street** named after him.

NB A new Jewish section [section P] was opened at the far south-east corner of the **Carleton Cemetery, Stocks Lane, Poulton-Le-Fylde FY6 7QS**, in 1967, serving both Orthodox and Reform separated by a pathway. Modern red-brick *ohel*.

LOCATION: Coming from the coast, at the end of Talbot Road where it becomes Westcliffe Drive. The Jewish cemetery is on the left (north) side, just past the general Layton Cemetery, and right next door to the Layton Institute, the postcode of which is given above.

ACCESS: Usually open, or contact Carleton Cemetery Office: tel 01253 882541.

Southport Synagogue

3 Arnside Road, PR9 0QX

Packer & Crampton, 1922–6

Rather fussy Italianate frontage of artificial stone with stucco decoration and red brick side bays, built for a community founded in 1893. The semi-circular porch is similar to that at **Wilson Road, Sheffield** (*see* below), a slightly later building. *Inscription:* The Hebrew text of Genesis 28:17 is painted on the frieze under the dome. Designed by the local partnership of *Goodwin Simpson Packer* and *Alfred Crampton* after a limited competition, and built entirely by local labour. Packer was active in church and civic affairs (an officer of the Southport Temperance Lodge of Freemasons and a Conservative councillor), and the practice undertook a number of local church-related commissions: alterations, church schools, communal halls and vicarages etc. *Foundation stones.*

INTERIOR: Central plan; a shallow quadripartite dome over the main space with cantilevered galleries around three sides, utilising steel and concrete. The curvy baroque Ark screen of brown veined marble dominates the south-east wall. Marble *Luhot* are affixed to the frieze fronting the choir. The marble *duhan* incorporates a central pulpit on an alabaster pedestal, with original oxidised silver railings cast by art metalworkers

Southport Synagogue (DP166640)

C J Thursfield & Co of Birmingham, who also made the pair of *menorot* and lamp standards for the matching marble *bimah*. The building opened with generous stained glass by *A Seward & Co.* of

Lancaster, most notably the triple panels over the choir. Some of the ancillary spaces were part of the original scheme, but not the *Mikveh* in the basement, *c* 1942, and in use. The dwindling congregation continues to defy the odds and has carried out some repairs and redecoration, including a concrete tile roof

OPENING HOURS: *Shabbat* and festival services. Other times by appointment: tel 01704 532964; website via www.jscn.org.uk

Southport Cemetery, Jewish Section

Cemetery Road, PR8 6RH

1894

Two Jewish plots are located in the Southport Cemetery (known as Duke Street Cemetery, opened 1866). This cemetery was laid out by *W P Goodwin*

Packer, the father of *Goodwin Simpson Packer*, architect of **Southport Synagogue**. Packer Senior was borough surveyor of Southport. According to the synagogue's records, the first burial in the small Jewish **Old Section**, tucked into the north-east corner on **Cemetery Road**, was that of JOSEPH HOMPES, aged 78, on 9 May 1894, but the earliest tombstone on site is SARAH SAQUI d 14 July 1894. Closed 1938. The much larger, L-shaped, **New Section** (1924) is on **Duke Street**, PR8 5EL, on the west side of the cemetery, and is still in use. Here, find a small red-brick simple Gothic *ohel* (1940) and *bet taharah* (1964). *Foundation stones.*

ACCESS: Enter via the gates on Cemetery Road and Duke Street (opposite Duke Avenue) respectively, usually open during general cemetery hours. Southport Synagogue: tel 01704 532964.

During both the First and Second World Wars so-called 'enemy aliens' were interned on the Isle of Man. Amongst these were German and Austrian Jewish refugees, who, ironically, formed the majority of the 14,000 inmates at the string of camps on the island between 1940 and 1945. The cream of the central European refugee intelligentsia wound up on the island and enjoyed a rich cultural life within its confines. They included Dadaist painter *Kurt Schwitters*, sculptor *Benno Elkan*, glassmaker *Erwin Bossanyi* and the founder of the Amadeus Quartet. *Nikolaus Pevsner* was very briefly sent to Huyton Camp on Merseyside.

Today there is no official Jewish community on the island, but informal get-togethers are occasionally organised by individuals in private houses or hotels. There are thought to be as many as 200 Jews living on the Isle of Man, many intermarried, in addition to a number of unaffiliated Israelis working there.[25] In common with the Channel Islands, the Isle of Man enjoys the status of an off-shore tax haven operating outside the jurisdiction of the UK.

Kirk Patrick Churchyard

Holy Trinity Church, Patrick Road, Patrick Village, IM5 3AW

In the early 18th-century churchyard of Holy Trinity are two simple military-style Jewish gravestones: of HERMAN JESCHKE dated 31 March 1916 and HEINRICH

ABRAHAM, 21 July 1917. According to copy parish registers, 'Henry' Abraham, aged 31, was buried on 24 July 1917; and Jeschke, the only deceased identified as 'A Jew', aged 48, was not buried until 2 June 1916. In 1927 there were apparently six extant Jewish graves. Railed off

in a neat plot nearby is a row of graves of Turkish Muslims who were also among the over 200 prisoners who died at the **Knockaloe Camp** situated opposite the churchyard. In 1962 the German War Grave Commission was given permission to exhume their dead for reburial at the German cemetery at Cannock Chase in the West Midlands. It is now hard to imagine that the green farmland on the other side of the lane was the overcrowded home of OVER 20,000 GERMAN CIVILIANS INTERNED DURING THE PERIOD OF THE GREAT WAR 1914–18. *Plaque.*

LOCATION: Take the A27 towards Peel. Junction with Patrick Road (to the east). Postcode above is for Patrick Vicarage.

ACCESS: Open access.

Knockaloe Farm (BB for SJBH)

Douglas Borough Cemetery, Jewish Section

Glencrutchery Road, Douglas, IM2 6DB

1940

Burials in the Jewish plot in the main municipal cemetery (1899) date from 1940. The stones face in different directions; none to the east. The earliest burial was of a baby EVA HERMANN, 11 November 1940, the day-old child of inmates at the Port Erin Camp. The earliest Jewish tombstone, with a Gothic profile, is that of ADOLF STRAUSS, d 30 December 1940, aged 63. Most of the other tombstones of internees are plain military-style stone markers decorated with a *Magen David*. However, a cluster of four such gravestones placed back to back, in a separate corner of the plot, together with the slate stone of artist *Arthur Paunzen*, lack the star. According to the records, his was the earliest burial in the entire plot: d 8 and buried on 10 August 1940. Perhaps their Jewish status was doubtful. During the Second World War a makeshift synagogue was set up in a Nissen hut at Onchan Camp. Memorial *plaque* in the form of a tombstone in the opposite corner under a tree.

LOCATION: On the main A2, north side, between Mountain View and Greenfield Road.

ACCESS: Open during general cemetery hours. On-site cemetery office: tel 01624 696329.

Salomon Gruber gravestone (BB for SJBH)

The Manx Museum

Kingswood Grove, Douglas, IM1 3LY

Houses the island's archives and has a permanent display relating to the story of wartime internment.

OPENING HOURS: Usually Monday to Saturday 10.00–17.00. Free admission, shop, café. Tel for group bookings: 01624 648017, www. manxnationalheritage.im

YORKSHIRE AND HUMBERSIDE

THE HISTORIC CATHEDRAL CITY OF **York** was home to one of England's most important medieval Jewries. Clifford's Tower stands as a potent reminder of the martyrdom of 1190 commemorated in the *kinah* (elegy) written by Rabbi Yomtov of Joigny, which is recited on *Tishah B'Av* (the Fast of the 9th of Av) to this day by Ashkenazi Jews all over the world. Only in 1990 did the *Herem* (ban) placed on York by the medieval rabbinical authority Rabbenu Gershom officially expire. In fact, a Jewish community was organised in the city in the 1890s, but still remains very small.

The port of **Hull**, on the north mouth of the River Humber, facing out to the North Sea, was in the 1880s second only to the Port of London as a point of arrival for Jewish refugees from eastern Europe. While many were transmigrants, travelling onwards across the newly built Transpennine Railway to Liverpool and thence to  America, a few wound up in Hull or in the fishing port of **Grimsby** on the opposite (south) bank of the Humber. Today these communities, never large, have almost dwindled away. But Grimsby's little synagogue with its terrific lion and unicorn stained-glass roundel, presented in 1906 by Mrs Szapira of Boston, Lincolnshire, still survives.

The 'Steel City' of **Sheffield** and the textile towns of Yorkshire attracted Jewish entrepreneurs during the Industrial Revolution. German Jewish woollen merchants, most prominent among them Jacob Moser, settled in **Bradford**; Moser later became mayor. Formerly Jewish-owned shops and warehouses can still be seen in Bradford's 'Little Germany' quarter, which is undergoing gentrification.

Bradford's Reform Synagogue is a delightful Islamic Revival gem, still open for business, now not inappropriately surrounded by the mosques of Manningham.

Montague Burton founded his multi-million-pound clothing business, which evolved into the chain of Burton stores, in 1904. He produced menswear in the Leylands, the 'East End' of **Leeds**. Leeds Jewry is remarkable for its relentless suburbanisation – and its fractious congregational history (umpteen synagogues!) – from the slums of the Leylands, through Chapeltown and Moortown Corner to Alwoodley ('Allyidly') and beyond. Leeds' Jewry has more than halved in size since 1945, today numbering about 6,850 (2011 Census), putting it a long way behind Manchester, Britain's second Jewish city. Leeds' city-centre Victorian Great Synagogue at Belgrave Street, LS2 (*Perkin & Brookhouse*, 1861; rebuilt by *Stephen Ernest Smith*, 1877–8) was closed in 1983 and demolished. *Plaque*. Fortunately, the stained glass was rescued and can now be seen, somewhat incongruously, in the suburban post-war **Leeds United Hebrew Congregation**, known as UHC or Shadwell Lane (*Peter Langtry-Langton*, 1983–7). The pretty Ark from Belgrave Street is also at Shadwell Lane (in the *Bet HaMidrash*). LOCATION: 151 Shadwell Lane, LS17 8DW; tel 0113 269 6141; www.uhcleeds.com

Doorway, Bradford Synagogue (AA038925)

Bradford Synagogue

7A Bowland Street, BD1 3BW
T H & F Healey, 1880–1, Grade II★

A little-known 'orientalist' gem in the heart of Yorkshire

The 'woollen town' of Bradford is unique in that it boasted a Reform synagogue before it acquired an Orthodox one. In 1873 a Bradford 'Jewish Association' was founded by textile merchants from German-speaking central Europe, where Reform Judaism was flourishing. The architects of the Bowland Street synagogue were the *Healey Brothers*, *Thomas* and *Francis*, known chiefly for the design of numerous churches in West Yorkshire. None of their other buildings, however, was quite like the Bradford Synagogue, built in an eclectic Islamic-revival style, both outside and in. The desire of their clients to acculturate to English norms did not apparently dampen their taste for exotic architecture.

The Bowland Street synagogue is a small building built into the terrace and is not situated on a main thoroughfare. Nevertheless, its sole street façade (north) is very distinctive. It is constructed of local ashlar with stringcourses of red sienna and cream stone, a technique known as *ablaq* in Arabic, which is especially associated with Egyptian Mamluk architecture. Other elements are inspired by Moorish Spain and north Africa.

Of the two entrances at either end of the façade, the main west doorway is under a lobed horseshoe arch carried on twin red-granite columns, the capitals of which are decorated with Arabic-style

patterns and carved arabesques, while the doors have geometric panels. The Hebrew *inscription* above is from Isaiah 26:2, decorated with a Star of David, and over the entrance is a stone arcade. The secondary (east) doorway is under an ogee arch. Above is a decorative light in the shape of an eight-pointed star set within a multi-lobed rosette, the edges of which are decorated with geometric strap-work inside a square panel.

The street elevation (AA038923)

The façade has four large two-light plate tracery windows. The windows are masquerading as 'oriental' on account of their ogee-shaped hood moulds, but are at bottom Victorian Gothic. They are filled with geometric coloured and leaded lights, based on the eight-pointed star motif. Above, the roofline (the pitched roof itself is covered in slates) is crested – another Islamic-inspired feature. The Hebrew *inscription* in the

The Ark at Bradford Synagogue (AA038930)

stars. *Inscription*: first line of the *Shema* prayer (Deuteronomy 6:4).

The prayer hall is arranged according to the Reform plan, with combined Ark and *bimah*, plus pulpit, all facing the congregation at the east end. The pitch-pine pews face forward and there is no gallery for the women. Bradford was the first Reform synagogue in the country built without a gallery.[1] However, it would be wrong to deduce that this was on account of the egalitarian views of the congregation. At the time of the opening in 1881 the *Jewish Chronicle* reported that: 'There being no gallery, the ladies were seated on one side of the Synagogue and the gentlemen on the other.'[2] In fact, separate seating was maintained in Reform synagogues in England until the 1930s.

Like continental Reform synagogues, Bradford introduced an organ. The small choir 'loft' is over the entrance vestibule facing the Ark. It is framed under a cusped arch, mirroring that over the Ark, and has a wooden grille decorated with fretwork in the form of eight-pointed stars, a recurring motif in this building. At the opening, the non-Jewish Bradford Choral Society, a mixed male- and female-voice choir, provided the musical accompaniment.

The Ark is made of wood, painted white and gilded, on a marble base. Its tall angular form is unique, with a miniature hexagonal domed kiosk, the shape reminiscent of Mughal India. Once again, geometrics, arabesques and eight-pointed stars all feature in the carving, while the timber grille-work in the arch and door fronts is termed *mashrabiya* – a feature typical of Egyptian mosques. The marble *Luhot* are painted in black.

Of especial interest at Bradford is a collection of artefacts acquired from the Bezalel Academy of Art & Design in Jerusalem (founded by *Boris Schatz* in 1906) by the synagogue's patron Jacob Moser (1839–1922), who was an ardent Zionist. Moser visited Palestine in 1908

band beneath the central *Magen David* is the standard *Ma Nora* quotation from Genesis 28:17.

INTERIOR: Reached through a modest vestibule at west, the prayer hall is of much plainer construction than the outside would lead us to suppose. It is roofed by a timber and coffered barrel vault braced by two iron tie beams. The ceiling is painted a deep pinky-red (not the original colour scheme) and is divided into ornamental panels, the plasterwork being in an interlocking eight-pointed star design. An expansive cusped and lobed arch frames the Ark apse at the east. The spandrels are highly decorated with arabesques, and the semi-dome behind is painted blue and decorated with gold

Detail of the Ark surround (AA038927)

View towards the Ark (AA038929)

and 1910. A Bezalel carpet on the steps of the Ark depicts the now demolished Herzliya Gymnasium in Jaffa – the first Zionist school in the country – of which Moser was also a patron. Two matching rugs, bearing a *menorah* motif on a red background, have the names 'Bezalel' and 'Jerusalem' woven in Hebrew letters into their borders. The congregation also possesses some works by the foremost artist of early Zionism, *E M Lilien*, whose black-and-white illustrations were influenced by *Aubrey Beardsley* and the English art nouveau.

The *foundation stone* is unusually placed inside the prayer hall. The ancillary schoolroom, built as part of the original scheme, was extended in 1956. In 2013 the Bradford Council of Mosques and the local Muslim community raised over £2,000 to fund urgent repairs to the roof. The Heritage Lottery Fund then stepped in to help the tiny community conserve and keep its unique synagogue in use.

OPENING HOURS: *Shabbat* and festival services. Heritage Open Days (September). Other times and groups by appointment: tel 01274 728925 (voicemail, so please leave a message) or via http://bradfordjewish.org.uk; www.bradfordsynagogue.co.uk

Former **Bradford Hebrew Congregation (Orthodox)**

15–17 Spring Gardens, BD1 3EJ

B S Jacobs, 1906

Just around the corner from the rival Reform synagogue, the Orthodox synagogue was a latecomer to the Bradford Jewish scene. Designed by Hull's Jewish synagogue architect in coursed sandstone and ashlar, with an octagonal tower and lead-covered dome over the entrance at one end (west).

Closed 1970 when the congregation decamped to the suburbs of Shipley.[3] Well cast in its latest incarnation as an Islamic primary school in a neighbourhood now predominantly Muslim.

Scholemoor Cemetery, Jewish Sections

Necropolis Road, Scholemoor Road, Lidget Green, BD7 2PS

1877, P & G Grade II

A pleasant landscaped site with lots of planting by the corporation, from whom the plot was acquired in 1877 by the Reform synagogue, as the founding congregation in the town, and shared with the Orthodox synagogue from 1886. The cemetery itself was laid out 1857–60. The slightly Gothic sandstone *ohel* was erected before the first interment took place, on 19 May 1877 (JONAS

SALOMON KOPPEL, d 17 May 1877), east of the *ohel*. *Ohel inscriptions*: on north gable: Isaiah 57:2; south gable: Psalms 49:18. Post-war Reform extension, while a second Orthodox plot (1913) is to be found in the 20th-century northern extension of the cemetery at **Birks Fold**, with modern *ohel*.

NB Prior burials, from 1858, of some 20 Bradford Jews (including HERTZ, BIELEFELD and SCHLOESTEIN) took place in an unconsecrated section of the **Undercliffe Cemetery** without Jewish rites.

LOCATION: The old Jewish sections are on Necropolis Road at the southern boundary of the cemetery.

ACCESS: During general cemetery hours. Enter via main gates at Necropolis Road and turn immediately right (east), but be prepared to climb over the low railings!

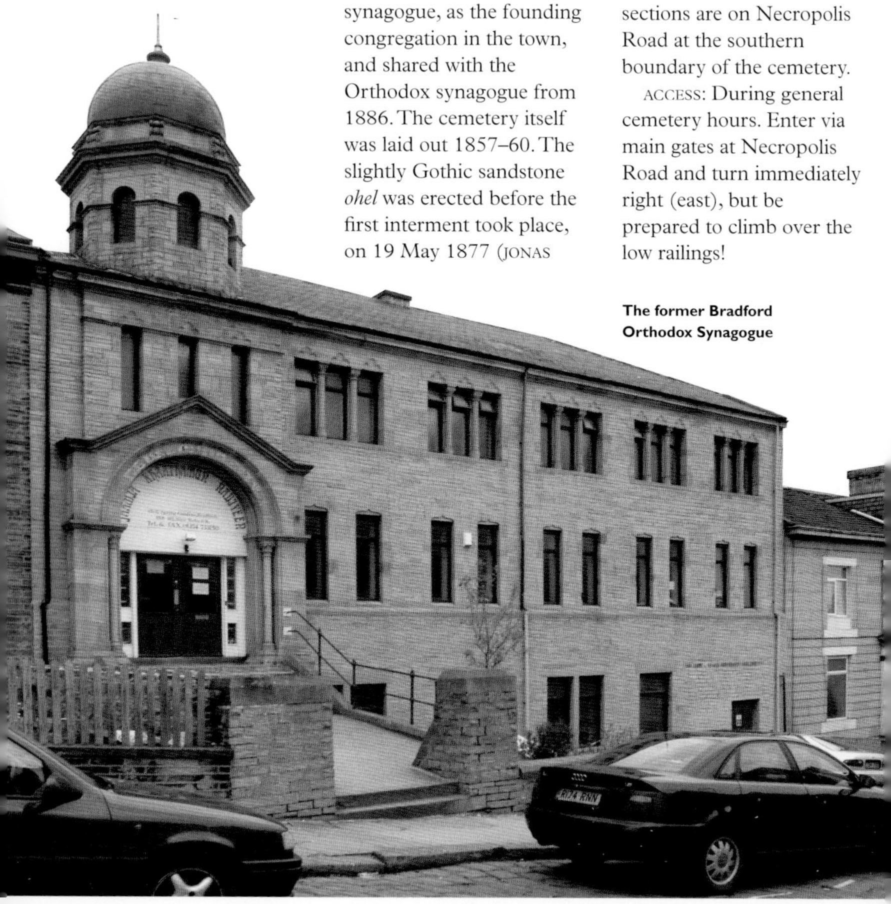

The former Bradford Orthodox Synagogue

Former **Leeds Hasidic Synagogue**

46–8 Spencer Place, Chapeltown, LS7 4BR

Kirk & Tomlinson, 1934–5

This unremarkable building, with a rendered and painted projecting entrance and porch, survives in the grounds of the new Leeds Islamic Centre and Central Jamia Mosque. A total of eight barely legible *foundation stones* on the front, which were the only clue[4] to its former identity, have now gone. Behind, the former prayer hall is of reddish brick with a pitched roof. The synagogue was designed by local architects for an Ashkenazi congregation founded in 1897 that worshipped according to the so-called 'Sephardish', that is, *Nusakh Ari*, liturgy. Closed early 1980s.

ACCESS: Just visible behind the new mosque from the main entrance (ornamental gateway inscribed 'Leeds Islamic Centre') on Francis Street.

Little remains of other Jewish places of worship that once proliferated in the Chapeltown area, which is now enjoying a mosque-building boom. The former **Hevras Tehillim (Psalms of David) Synagogue**, 38–40 Reginald Terrace, also by *Kirk & Tomlinson* (1938), closed 1973, was demolished in 2003. Its *foundation stones*, recorded by our survey, were rescued and taken to the **Etz Chaim Synagogue** (*Owen*

Diplock & Associates, 1979–81), 411 Harrogate Road, LS17 7BY (tel 0113 266 2214; www.etzchaim.co.uk), descendant of both of these congregations. Both Psalms of David and the building used from 1922 by the former **Chapeltown Hebrew Congregation**, at 58–60 Francis Street (corner with Hamilton Place and derelict in 2012), appear to have begun life as conversions. A Victorian house (*c* 1860) at **21 Leopold Street**, LS7 4DA has been designated 'House of Faith' and was marked with a Leeds Civic Trust *blue plaque* (2012). The text states that it was used as a synagogue in turn by the only Spanish and Portuguese congregation in Leeds (1924) and by the Reform (1952–60), and then became the first mosque in Leeds (1961–74).

Leeds' Jewish Tailors' Trade Union Building

25 Cross Stamford Street, Sheepscar, LS7 1BA

J J Wood, 1910

Solid Edwardian red-brick building with stone and/or faience dressings, heavily

The Leylands was at one time only second in importance to London's East End as a centre of the Jewish 'rag trade' (BB for SJBH)

over-painted in red and black, with a Welsh slate roof. Erected for the Leeds Amalgamated Jewish Tailors', Machinists' and Pressers' Trades Union, founded in 1893, making it the first independent Jewish trades union in the country. It was eventually absorbed into the National Union of Tailors and Garment Workers. Chiefly of interest for the *inscription* on the façade, now partially obliterated.

LOCATION: Now part of the A61 (Roseville Road) going north past the roundabout at the junction with Sheepscar Street South.

Former **Leeds New Synagogue**

98 Chapeltown Road, LS7 4BH

J Stanley Wright & Clay, 1929–32, Grade II

Now Northern School of Contemporary Dance. Perhaps the last flowering of the Islamic Revival as reinterpreted in the era of art deco. A huge 'Byzantine' synagogue, of reddish-brown brick, with concrete saucer dome and 'minaret' (actually a chimney) inspired by Turkish mosques, with what one commentator described as 'the portico of a neo-Egyptian picture palace grafted on to its front',[5] made of Portland stone. Architect *J Stanley Wright*, by this time Leeds-based, had served in Palestine and perhaps was inspired too by the work of modernist architects working under the British Mandate, such as *Austin Harrison* and *Patrick*

Geddes. The copper covering was added to the dome in 1938, before a belated official opening, to deal with structural problems caused by the reinforced concrete. Sold 1985 and sympathetically converted by Leeds City Council into a dance theatre and studios (*Allen Todd*, 1997–8) with help from the National Lottery. Leeds Civic Trust *blue plaque* (2012). *Foundation stones* in porch.

INTERIOR: Fine vaulted vestibule. Some original non-specifically Jewish features survive. With its sweeping gallery curving around three sides of the centrally planned space, it works well as an auditorium.

NB Some items from the Leeds New Synagogue, including the triple King George V Silver Jubilee windows by *David Hillman* (1937) (*see* cover and pp 58–61), can now be seen at **Leeds United Hebrew Congregation**, **Shadwell Lane**.

The former Leeds New Synagogue, now home to the Northern School of Contemporary Dance

Former **Leeds Jewish Institute and Jubilee Hall**

21 Savile Mount, LS7 3HZ

G Alan Burnett, 1934–6

A three-storey brick building with tall modernist metal-framed 'oriel' windows and a basement floor. Yellow-brick frontage, red brick to the rear.

The Institute had lacked a purpose-built home from its foundation in 1896. During the Second World War its popularity soared: sports, debating and dances were enjoyed by some 2,600 members. Closed in 1973 and, after a period as a trades union club, the building was converted (with help from the Lottery, regional and local funding) into the Leeds Media Centre by *Bauman Lyons Architects*, who also built the new extension in 2000–1. *Burnett*, a Catholic,[6] also designed the **Holy Rosary Church** (1936–7) next door to the former **New Synagogue**, as well as the **Beth HaMedrash**

HaGadol, 399 Street Lane, Moortown, LS17 6HQ (1969), reputedly the largest post-war synagogue outside London.

JEWISH BURIAL GROUNDS IN LEEDS

Gildersome Jewish Cemetery

251 Gelderd Road, LS12 6DJ

An extensive unremarkable cemetery visible from the motorway, it has three distinct sections, each of which originally had its own separate entrance in the high brick boundary wall, as well as its own *ohel*. The *ohel* in the oldest section (at the far west) was demolished, but the original ornamental red-brick gateway, with illegible *inscription* on the gable, survives. Here, legible tombstones (they mostly face north and west) date from the 1850s; complete surviving records start from 1853. However, it has been claimed that this cemetery was opened in 1840 before the formal establishment of a Jewish congregation in 1846, which became the **Leeds Great Synagogue, Belgrave Street**.

As you walk back (eastwards) notice the neat row of Second World War graves facing you by the path, parallel with the road. Enlarged in the 1940s (there is plenty of unoccupied green space) and currently shared by the two rival amalgamated congregations: the Beth HaMedrash HaGadol (now Street Lane) and the United Hebrew Congregation (now Shadwell Lane).

LOCATION: South side of the A62 south-west of Leeds city centre.

ACCESS: Open. Groundsmen usually on site. Leeds Beth HaMedrash HaGadol Synagogue (Street Lane): tel 0113 269 2181; www.bhhs.co.uk

Hill Top Jewish Cemetery

Gelderd Road, LS12 6DJ

1873

An isolated site but well worth the steep climb for the views across the city. Something of a nature haven too, uncommon among Jewish cemeteries, and affording a great contrast to **Gildersome** across the road. Purchased by the New Briggate congregation and historically shared by at least five defunct Leeds congregations. (New Briggate had a purpose-built synagogue in Merrion Street at the corner of St John's Place, designed by civic architect *W H Thorp*, 1890–4, demolished in 1926 for road widening in the city centre.) Remains of red-brick boundary walls that originally separated the various sections of the

cemetery are still standing, and two ruined *ohalim* are still visible. Headstones face in all directions. The oldest extant memorials (the earliest we identified were dated 1882) are clustered closest to the *ohalim*. Nearby a broken brick chest tomb for eminent and sometimes controversial rabbi ISRAEL CHAYIM DAICHES (1850–1937) of the Beth HaMedrash HaGadol.

The land was of poor quality, being located next to clay and limestone quarries, and in an area riddled with mine shafts. In 2006–7 engineers had to be called in when some graves on the lowest slopes collapsed. Records prior to 1917 are missing (apparently destroyed by fire); the last burial had taken place in the early 1990s.

LOCATION: Off the A62 northbound into Leeds. Not signposted but almost opposite **Gildersome** (same postcode cited), where parking is available.

ACCESS: Problems with subsidence led to closure to the general public in 2008, hence the large 'No Trespassers' notice! Barred to vehicular traffic but perfectly accessible on foot if you are prepared to tackle the steep, rough path. You will need your hiking boots and heavy clothing – and take care underfoot. You do enter at your own risk, however. Leeds Beth HaMedrash HaGadol Synagogue (Street Lane): tel 0113 269 2181; www.bhhs.co.uk. For documentation, including photographic survey, see: www.jewishgen.org/jcr-uk/

New Farnley Jewish Cemetery

717 Whitehall Road, LS12 6JL

1896

Acquired by the 'Polisher' congregation (Byron Street, 1891; later Wintoun Street, 1924; Louis Street, 1933–66) and the first burial took place on 30 June 1896. According to the long lintel *inscription* on the old red-brick *ohel* (1913) on Whitehall Road (in a not quite literate mixture of Hebrew, Yiddish and English), the main section of the burial ground was opened in 1901 by the *Anshei Poalim d'po Leedz*. The Leeds Jewish Workers' Burial & Trading Society had been founded in 1899, primarily to pay for funerals for its poor subscribers. At one time the largest burial society in Anglo-Jewry, in 1955 it was absorbed into the New Central Vilna Synagogue, now part of Etz Chaim. Behind the car park, at the south-east, is the cemetery (1935) of the Psalms of David Synagogue, which also amalgamated with the New Central Vilna. No fewer than four *ohalim* – material testament to the divisiveness of Leeds Jewry. The cemetery is still in use by both Etz Chaim (which holds most of the original records) and the Leeds United Hebrew Congregation.

LOCATION: Whitehall Road (A58), south side.

ACCESS: Open. Etz Chaim Synagogue: tel 0113 266 2214.

NB Records for all Leeds Jewish Cemeteries, including digital images of headstones, are becoming available online via www.jewishgen.org/jcr-uk/

DONCASTER

Rose Hill Cemetery, Jewish Section

Cantley Lane, DN4 6NE

1936

For the now defunct Doncaster Hebrew Congregation. Some *plaques* from the synagogue, housed in a room over shops at Thorne Road/Canterbury Road (1956–78), are preserved in the red-brick *ohel/bet taharah*. The *inscription* over the entrance mistakenly reads '3695' instead of 5695, corresponding to 1935. The ground is well kept, with neat rows of graves with short grass underfoot. The oldest headstone is that of RACHEL BERG, d 29 February 1936, in the second row to the right (north) of the *ohel*.

LOCATION: Separate gate off Ascot Avenue, south side, opposite Newmarket Road.

ACCESS: Locked. Key c/o Superintendent, Rose Hill Cemetery (postcode given above) during general cemetery hours: tel 01302 535191.

SHEFFIELD

Former **Sheffield Old Hebrew Congregation**

North Church Street, S1 2DH

John Brightmore Mitchell-Withers, Senior, 1872

The Hebrew *inscription* above the doorway (tympanum) identifies this building as a former synagogue rather than a church. The text is from 1 Kings 8:33 and contains a chronogram. This unassuming red-brick building, now in use as offices, is the only surviving synagogue in England built in Gothic (early English) style. The architect was a local church builder. There was a *mikveh* in the basement. Closed 1930.

The Sheffield community had started life at Figtree Lane *c* 1848, and acquired the epithet 'Old' thanks to the appearance of a breakaway immigrant 'New' Congregation at West Bar, *c* 1860. The quarrelsome congregations remained at loggerheads despite the intervention of the Chief Rabbi. At the **Sheffield Jewish Congregation and Centre**, 3 Brincliffe Crescent (Psalter Lane), S11 9AW (tel: 0114 255 2296; www.jewishsheffield. org.uk) can be seen all that remains of the New congregation's purpose-built synagogue (1914) at Lee Croft, off Campo Lane, which was bombed in 1940: a round-arched doorway with red-granite columns. The *foundation stone* is preserved in the *ohel* at **Ecclesfield** (*see* below).

LOCATION: East side, junction with St Peters Close.

The Gothic arch at the former North Church Street Synagogue in Sheffield (BB for SJBH)

Former **Sheffield United Hebrew Congregation**

Wilson Road, Ecclesall, S11 8RN

Rawcliffe & Ogden, 1929–30, Grade II

A substantial building for a suburbanising community, the locally based architects used all Sheffield-based contractors and craftsmen working to a high specification. The style was the brand of modern stripped classicism with art deco detailing fashionable in the period, of brick with artificial stone dressings. The projecting semi-circular entrance porch to the foyer is quite theatrical. Closed in 1997, and from 2000 the building became the 'City Church'. The Hebrew inscription (Genesis 28:17) around the porch frieze has been painted out, but the *Magen David* symbols are still visible on the roof pediment and gateposts. Most of the fittings have been removed from the light and spacious interior, including the Ark, *bimah* and some of the stained-glass windows. The pews downstairs by *J T Johnson & Sons* of Sheffield eventually went in 2007. *Foundation stones.* There was a *mikveh* with an unusual circular pool in the basement, taking advantage of the sloping site. The dwindling Jewish community transferred to the new-build **Kingfield Synagogue** (*Elden Minns & Co Ltd*, 2000) on the Sheffield Jewish community centre's site at Psalter Lane, S11 (*see* above).

Ecclesfield Jewish Cemetery

Colley Road, S5 9GU

Successor to and containing remains from the 1831–74 **Bowden Street** burial ground in the city centre, which was destroyed as a result of compulsory purchase in 1975. That site is now a car park. Ecclesfield is a large cemetery that straddles Colley Road, the older section, acquired by the Sheffield Old Hebrew Congregation in 1872 (but first burial apparently 1874; the registers have been lost) lying to the north, and the newer section, founded in 1931–2 by the Sheffield Central Synagogue (Campo Lane, 1914) to the south. The oldest gravestones (earliest legible 1877) are nearest to the fine modernist *ohel* by *Wynyard Dixon* (1931) that faces onto the street. Substantially built of yellow brick with a flat roof and unusual art deco shoulder-headed windows, this is perhaps the best 20th-century *ohel* in the country.

INTERIOR: Exposed yellow-brick walls; the floor is tiled with a *Magen David* design, repeated in the doors. The pews and the lectern with a brass *plaque* dated 5632 (=1872) came from the **North Church Street Synagogue**.

Internal doorway to the Ohel
(AA038914)

Foundation stones. Inscription over doorway from Isaiah 25: 8.

LOCATION: Postcode above takes you to the junction with Holgate Road on the south side of Colley Road. Entrances to both parts of the cemetery lie a few metres further along Colley Road to the east.

ACCESS: Locked. Contact Sheffield Jewish Congregation and Centre: tel 0114 255 2296; www.jewishsheffield.org.uk

The Ohel, Ecclesfield
(AA038909)

Walkley Jewish Cemetery

Waller Road, S10 5DP

A small and picturesque Victorian burial ground located on the steep slope of the Rivelin valley. Since the demolition of the *bet taharah* by the entrance there is nothing to indicate that a cemetery, rather than a patch of woodland, lies behind the stone boundary wall. It was acquired by the Sheffield Hebrew Benevolent Society (1873, an off-shoot of the breakaway Sheffield New Hebrew Congregation, West Bar *c* 1860), to help immigrants from eastern Europe. Documentary evidence indicates that the society purchased this plot of land located between the Church of England and Roman Catholic burial grounds at Walkley for Jewish use in 1884. However, at least two stones on site are dated 1880; and many others are overgrown with ivy and brambles.

LOCATION: Unmarked entrance on west side of Waller Road.

ACCESS: Contact Sheffield Jewish Congregation and Centre: tel 0114 255 2296; www.jewishsheffield.org.uk

---

THE BRIGHT FAMILY MAUSOLEA

ECCENTRIC MONUMENTS BUILT BY ECCENTRIC JEWS

The Bright family were of Sephardi origin, probably from North Africa, and they made good and married out of the faith into one of the leading steel-making families of Sheffield. They lived the life of country squires and had themselves buried in eccentric private mausolea on the edge of the moors just outside (west of) the city. Long abandoned, both sites were desecrated and badly vandalised in the 1980s. The empty shell of the large mausoleum built by Horatio Bright (1828–1906) in 1891 survives in a private garden at **Moscar**. (Its size would be worthy of an *ohel* in a conventional Jewish cemetery.) However, memorials remaining in the burial ground at **Rodmoor**, which had been acquired in 1831 (first burial 1848) by Horatio's father Selim Bright (d 1891), were deliberately demolished in December 2011 by a neighbouring landowner who had appropriated the site. These included two Gothic-revival monuments, of stone, which had very curious beehive-shaped domed roofs. Luckily, a few months earlier, a descendant of the Bright family had succeeded in gaining access (which our survey had never managed to do) and photographed these intriguing memorials for posterity.[7] *Not accessible to the public.*

Clifford's Tower

Tower Street, York Castle, YO1 9SA

Scheduled Ancient Monument

Dubbed the 'English Masada', this site is the most potent symbol of the martyrdom of medieval Jewry in England. In 1190, under the influence of their spiritual leader Rabbi Yomtov of Joigny, the Jews of York resolved to commit mass suicide on *Shabbat HaGadol* (the 'Great' Sabbath before Passover) rather than succumb to their persecutors. The proximity of the royal castle failed to protect the Jews, who had fled there seeking sanctuary from the mob, whipped up that Easter by religious hysteria while preparations for the Third Crusade were underway. King Richard I, the Lionheart, was abroad at the time.

The present clover-shaped (quatrefoil) limestone structure replaced the original wooden tower burnt down during the massacre. It dates from the 1245–72 rebuilding under Henry III and the projecting entrance gateway is largely 17th century. The name Clifford's Tower derives from Sir Roger Clifford, leader of the Lancastrians, who was hung from the tower by Edward II after the Battle of Bannockburn in 1314. Slate *plaque* at the bottom, and the site was landscaped to mark the

Clifford's Tower, York, in springtime (DP032727)

800th anniversary. Climb the steep steps for a splendid view over the City of York. The whole area (Coppergate) was threatened with inappropriate retail redevelopment – nicknamed by opponents 'Shoppergate' – until the secretary of state intervened and put a stop to it in 2004.

OPENING HOURS: Daily 10.00 to 18.00 (April to September), 10.00 to 17.00 (October), 10.00 to 16.00 (November to March). Admission charge. Guidebook available. Managed by English Heritage: tel 01904 646940; www.english-heritage.org.uk/visit/places/cliffords-tower.york

Probable **Medieval Jewish burial ground**

14 Jewbury, YO31 7PL

This site is identified by a barely visible red-granite *plaque* at the entrance to Sainsbury's supermarket (Fosse Bank) car park (right-hand side). It was partially excavated amid controversy by the York Archaeological Trust in the early 1980s.[8] The Hebrew *inscription* makes clear that the car park covers only 'a portion of the site.' The cemetery is known from documentary records to have post-dated 1177 and to have pre-dated 1230, when it was enlarged – demonstrating that the Jewish community remained active in the city 40 years after the 1190 massacre. The location of

the cemetery outside the medieval city walls is the best medieval example in England of conformity with ancient Jewish burial practice. But there is nothing to see here, nor has any other physical evidence of York's important medieval Jewry yet come to light. The synagogue is thought to have been located in the vicinity of 19 Coney Street (south) near the river in the city centre, while the historic street name **Jubbergate** may be derived from the medieval spelling of 'Jewe'.

LOCATION: On the opposite side of the main road that circles the city walls. Jewbury is a continuation of St Maurice's Road (A1036). The postcode above is that of the car park's office at 14 Jewbury.

YORK MINSTER'S 'JEWISH' ASSOCIATIONS

The 'Five Sisters' window in the north transept was reputedly paid for by a loan from the Jews of York. This five-light window is executed in abstract grisaille work without human representation, in accordance with the dominant tradition in Jewish art, but was more likely the result of Cistercian influence.

A fragment of 13th-century wall painting from the **Chapter House**, which depicts an allegorical 'Synagoga', is preserved at the Minster. It is not generally on view to the public, but a Victorian representation can be seen carved in stone over the portal (tympanum) of **St Wilfred's Roman Catholic Church**, Duncombe Place, YO1 7ED (*George Goldie*, 1862–4, Grade II) across from the Minster.

NB A self-guided Jewish heritage trail (leaflet, podcast and app) is available via www.historyofyork.org.uk. York Walk offers occasional walks led by a tour guide: tel 01904 622303; www.yorkwalk.co.uk

Fragment of York Chapter House's 'Synagoga'
(AA98/17619)

HUMBERSIDE

KINGSTON UPON HULL

Hull Old Hebrew Congregation

Osborne Street, HU1

1902–3, possibly by G Thorp of Hull

Successor to a series of synagogues perhaps dating back to as early as 1766. Nothing is known of the appearance of the first certainly purpose-built synagogue at 7 Robinson Row (1826–7), rebuilt in Grecian style by *W D Keyworth* in 1851–2.

Osborne Street, remodelled and extended in 1931–2 by *Allderidge & Clark* of Hull, was a casualty of heavy bombing of the port of Hull during the Second World War, but was rebuilt and reopened in 1955. Closed 1993. The present *bimah* at Birmingham's **Singers Hill Synagogue** is thought to have come from Osborne Street. Today, the blank walls of the rendered shell of the building betray no clue as to its former identity. The anonymous building is slated for demolition in the wholesale redevelopment

of this part of Hull, where immigrant Jews once clustered. A new Hull Hilton Hotel is likely to be built on the site.[9]

LOCATION: Around the back, on Anne Street. Next door to former Club Heaven and Hell, 16 Anne Street, HU1 2NP.

Former **Western Synagogue**

Linnaeus Street, HU3 2PD

B S Jacobs, 1902–3, Grade II

Built for the breakaway faction when Hull Hebrew Congregation split in two:

the foundation stones of both buildings were laid on the same day. A curious jumble of Romanesque (Lombardic cornice and round-headed windows), plus twin slate-covered turrets and some orientalising ogee window heads on the ground floor, but typically Edwardian in the use of red brick and yellow terracotta dressings. The architect *Benjamin Septimus Jacobs* became a leading light in the new synagogue. His name appears twice on the *foundation stone* as 'Honorary Architect' and as 'President' of the congregation. A terracotta *Magen David* in the gable and, over the doorway, unusual *Luhot* in the form of an open book. The synagogue is set back in a gated (*inscription* 1926) courtyard behind the Victorian buildings of the former Linden House, which, extended, served as the Hull Hebrew

Girls' School, with minister's house next door.

The synagogue was abandoned in 1992 when the dwindling Hull community merged and decamped to a converted engineering works in the suburbs at **30 Pryme Street**, Anlaby, HU10 6SH, taking the Ark from the Western with them. Ironically the old synagogue was rescued from dereliction by a missionary church calling itself the Judeo-Christian Study Centre, which has owned the building since 1999. Their enthusiasts even recovered some of the stained glass, stolen from what was at one time a Heritage at Risk building. Interior redeveloped. *Plaque.*

NB A Hull Jewish Heritage Trail walk and leaflet is available from Hull Hebrew Congregation. Further details are available via www.jscn.org.uk/small-communities/hull-hebrew-congregation

Hull 'New' Jewish Cemetery

69 Hessle Road, HU3 2AB

No bigger than a garden, at the side of the Alexandra Hotel public house and facing one of the busiest trunk roads in the city, this burial ground has a slightly dilapidated air. Not all of the fewer than a dozen surviving headstones remain *in situ*. Successor to the original Jewish burial

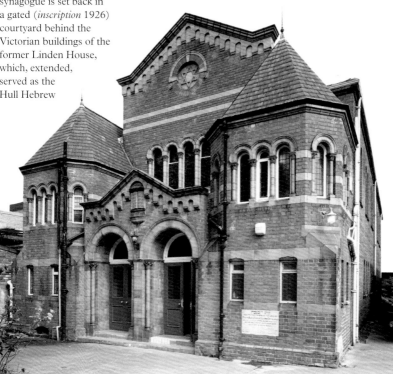

Former Western Synagogue, the front elevation (BB93/25442)

ground in Hull at Villa Place, Walker Street, also known as West Dock Terrace, was bombed during the Second World War and afterwards comprehensively redeveloped. Hessle Road apparently dates from 1804; a lease has been traced from 1812 but the registers are lost. The earliest clearly legible headstone in 1999 was that of SAMPSON ALEXANDER, d 11 June AM 5588 (=1828). Closed 1854 by the Burial Act.

There is an oral tradition in Hull that a first-floor room in the adjacent pub was used for services by itinerant Jews, although the Stars of David in the Edwardian window glazing are probably coincidental.

LOCATION: Hessle Road (A63), south side.

ACCESS: Key with the landlord of the Alexandra Hotel next door: tel 01482 327455.

Delhi Street Jewish Cemetery

Delhi Street, HU9 5QP

1858

Also known as Hedon Road, this ground is divided into two sections: to the south abutting Hedon Road is the 'Old' section established by **Hull Hebrew Congregation (Robinson Row)**, and the 'New', closer to Delhi Street to the north, for the **Hull Western Synagogue** from 1903. The 'Old' section was damaged by bombing in the Second World War and the registers have been lost; however, records of the Western's burials here and at **Ella**

Street (*see* below) have survived. In the 'New' section, the red-brick *ohel* (1921) by *B S Jacobs*, president of the Western Synagogue, has now been demolished.[10] His grandparents BETHEL and ESTHER JACOBS are buried under an obelisk near the gate in the 'Old' section. They were also the grandparents of OSMOND ELIM D'AVIGDOR GOLDSMID, who laid the *foundation stone* of the Western Synagogue. The cemetery was extended to the north after 1921.

In 2001 a controversial road-widening scheme for Hedon Road involved the construction of a bridge over the southern end of the cemetery. Some tombstones were laid flat or moved, but no bodies were disturbed, thanks to liaison between The Highways Agency and the London Beth Din.

LOCATION: Hedon Road (A1033), north side. The cemetery gate is on Delhi Street, next door to no. 45, whose postcode is cited above.

ACCESS: Locked. Key c/o Hull Hebrew Congregation, via www.jscn.org.uk/small-communities/hull-hebrew-congregation

Ella Street Jewish Cemetery

Ella Street, HU5 3DH

1889

This cemetery started life as the private ground of community patrons the FISCHOFF family, some of whose members are buried here under two prominent

obelisks. They were founder members of the Hull Central Synagogue (founded 1887 at School Street, off Waltham Street; moved to the Salem Chapel, Cogan Street, in 1914; bombed 1941). The burial ground was acquired by the **Hull Western Synagogue** when the Central and Western congregations amalgamated after the Second World War. The front of the site on Ella Street, occupied until the 1990s by the caretaker's house and *bet taharah* (*W A Gelder*, 1889), was sold and redeveloped as a private residence. However, the neat cemetery has been extended and a new *bet taharah* built in 2010.

LOCATION: Ella Street, west end, where it meets Sanderson Close.

ACCESS: Locked. Key c/o Hull Hebrew Congregation, via www.jscn.org.uk/small-communities/hull-hebrew-congregation

Marfleet Jewish Cemetery

Church Lane, HU9 5RL

A black basalt *foundation stone* propped up against the current 1973 *ohel* came from its predecessor, consecrated on 11 November 1923. However, the earliest dated headstone is that of REBECCA PEARLMAN, d 11 June 1935, in one of only two rows that appear to be pre-war. In use, but the records have not been traced.

LOCATION: Down a lane that also serves St Giles

Marfleet, which is signposted. (The postcode given above is for the vicarage.) Continue past the church until you reach the gate on the east side.

ACCESS: Locked. Key c/o Hull Hebrew Congregation, via www.jscn.org.uk/small-communities/hull-hebrew-congregation

GRIMSBY

Grimsby Synagogue

Holme Hill, Heneage Road, DN32 9DZ

B S Jacobs, 1885–8, Grade II

A small-scale provincial synagogue that has so far defied its fate and is still functioning. It is built of red brick in a simple Romanesque style with a Lombardic frieze, stone window hoods and Welsh slate roof, by Hull-based *B S Jacobs*.

A community had been formed in this fishing port *c* 1865 and struggled for years to raise the money for a purpose-built synagogue. Other significant local institutions were built close to the synagogue on Heneage Estate land (the philanthropic-minded Edward, Lord Heneage, was Liberal MP for Grimsby) during this period, including the former Holme Hill School (*Charles Bell*, 1876–8, Grade II) next door. The new synagogue was officially named the 'Sir Moses Montefiore Memorial Synagogue' after the grandee's death at the age of 101 in 1885. The gabled street-facing east wall is defaced by a shoddy and incongruous square Ark apse by builders *S Cartledge & Sons*, added at the same time (1933–5) as the unattractive hall extension to the side. *Foundation Stones. Luhot* in the form of an elongated open book in the pediment gable over the big round window. The entrance is down a side alley through a brick

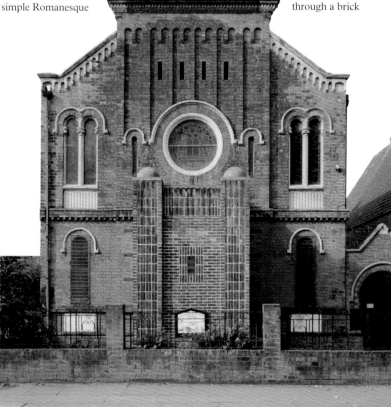

Grimsby Synagogue (AA038891)

The **east window of Grimsby Synagogue**,
presented in 1906 by Mrs Szapira of Boston, Lincolnshire (AA038881)

archway. This also leads to
the **Mikveh** at the rear.
A substantial but long-
derelict single-storey
red-brick building, it bears
the Hebrew *inscription*
MIKVEH 5676 (=1916) in
the gable.

INTERIOR: Inside the
synagogue is quite plain,
with a flat ceiling and
plastered walls. The
gallery runs around three
sides supported on slender
cast-iron columns with
gilded Corinthian capitals.
The Ark was altered and
the *bimah* replaced in
1933–5, but the pitch-pine
pews are mostly original.

The *Mikveh* at Grimsby
Synagogue (AA038888)

STAINED GLASS: The east
wall has a magnificent
roundel over the Ark,
featuring *Luhot* flanked
by the heraldic lion and
unicorn, derived from
the British royal coat of
arms, surmounted by
a crown and Star of David,
presented by Mrs L Szapira
of Boston, Lincolnshire in
1906. A witty symbiosis
of Jewish and English
symbolism. Other glass
dates from the 1930s and
later, by *James Clark &
Eaton* of London and *Simon
Kalson Ltd*, a Grimsby
Jewish firm established in
1879 (oral testimony).

LOCATION: Heneage Road, west side, between Wellington Street and Eleanor Street.

OPENING HOURS: *Shabbat* service, first Friday night of the month. Other times via Grimsby Library: tel 01472 323600.

Grimsby Jewish Cemetery

First Avenue, Nunsthorpe, DN33 1AA

1896

A deceptively quiet suburban cemetery that has been the victim of repeated vandalism. It was opened on ground acquired by the town council from the Yarborough Estate. Earlier burials had taken place in Hull, sometimes in Sheffield or Nottingham, and during the smallpox epidemic of 1871 in a plot, perhaps never consecrated, in the Grimsby Old Cemetery, Doughty Road. That site was bombed in 1943 and was subsequently cleared of memorials, though burials were left undisturbed. The first burial at Nunsthorpe was of an infant on 25 February 1896, but the earliest legible headstone on site dates from 1898. Nearby is a badly weathered stone commemorating five stowaways found dead in the hold of SS *Ashton* on its journey from Antwerp to Grimsby on 13 December 1908. A later extension contains two Second World War graves. Unremarkable *ohel*.

LOCATION: Path at junction with Cornwell Close, DN33 1DS.

ACCESS: Locked. Key via Grimsby Library: tel 01472 323600.

Interior view to the rear, Grimsby Synagogue (AA038885)

APTLY KNOWN AS BALLAST HILL, the long abandoned Ayres Quay cemetery in **Sunderland** dates from at least the 1780s. Today it remains a site at risk,[1] although no longer as isolated as it was in the 1990s. Back then, only the most intrepid of visitors would have been advised to tackle the steep slope situated in industrial wasteland between a slag heap and a factory close to the docks. The existence of this burial ground testifies to both the seniority and the decline of Sunderland Jewry, the oldest Jewish community in the north-east of England.

Tyneside, once a hive of shipbuilding activity, was on the shipping routes from the Baltic ports and from the 1880s received an influx of Jews escaping pogroms and poverty in the Russian Empire. Sunderland became home to *landsleit* who migrated *en masse* from the Lithuanian town of Krottingen (Kretinga), where the wooden houses were burnt down by a fire in 1889. Sunderland itself became a bastion of religious orthodoxy of the Mitnagdic variety; its Beth HaMedrash, *yeshivah* and *kollel* were highly respected.

Today, however, the mantle has passed to **Gateshead** whose unlikely name enjoys an international reputation throughout the

Orthodox Jewish world, synonymous with the 'Ivy League' *yeshivah* located in the town. The Gateshead Jewish community had started in the 1880s as an outgrowth of Newcastle's on the opposite, north, bank of the River Tyne, but its character was transformed by Jewish refugees from Lithuania and Germany, before and after the Second World War, who established the Gateshead *kehillah*, and one of the very last synagogues to open in Britain before the outbreak of war. Poignantly, Gateshead's parent communities on the continent were destroyed in the Holocaust. Gateshead's Jewish quarter is a thriving campus, a world apart. During term time, the approximately 300 resident Jewish families[2] are boosted by a student population of several

thousand. Gateshead alone bucks the trend of the seemingly interminable decline of the Jewish communities scattered throughout north-east England, most of which have already vanished or will do so very soon.

Sunderland Synagogue (DP003807)

Former **Sunderland Synagogue**

Ryhope Road, SR2 7EQ
Marcus Kenneth Glass, 1928, Grade II

In search of striking but threatened synagogues from the age of art deco

Rated by Pevsner as 'vigorous and decorative',[3] Sunderland's former synagogue has become a 'Heritage at Risk' building. It was one of a string of synagogues designed in similar distinctive style by little-known Newcastle-based Jewish architect *Marcus Kenneth Glass* (1887–1932).

Its immediate sister is the former **Jesmond Synagogue** in **Newcastle**, the earliest of the group, completed in 1915 and now used as a school (*see* below). In **London** his **Clapton Federation Synagogue** of 1931–2 was demolished in 2006. In the same year, Sunderland itself closed for worship.[4] Jewish life in this once thriving shipbuilding port has almost disappeared. Ryhope Road was the suburban successor to the Moor Street Synagogue by *J Tillman* of 1861–2, interior rebuilt and new *Mikveh* by *M & I R Milburn*, 1900 (demolished).

The architect himself described his new building as executed in 'a free Byzantine style … that it should be unmistakably a Synagogue'.[5] Certainly, Glass had a predilection for colourful façades. His three purpose-built synagogues all featured squat corner

East window, Sunderland (DP020515)

towers, a dominant curved gable which displayed the *Luhot* high above a starburst or sunray window; jolly red and yellow *ablaq* – alternating dark and light courses of brickwork, artificial stone dressings, arcaded porches with Byzantine basket capitals, tiling and mosaic. These common decorative 'oriental' features were interpreted in a striking cinematic art deco style. The details varied. For example, at Sunderland, the chosen Hebrew *inscription* in the gilded turquoise mosaic band with terracotta surround over the entrance is *Ma Tovu*, 'How goodly are thy tents, O Jacob' (Numbers 24:5). The same quotation occurs at Jesmond but was not used at Clapton.[6] Sunderland was the only one of the series that had a double-arched front entrance and two main doors. Clapton's entrance was very similar but reverted to a triple arch and three doors, as had originally been used at Jesmond, which has a proper arcaded porch. *Foundation stones.*

Sunderland Synagogue was the only one of Marcus Glass's synagogues that was built with a basement *mikveh* (with a back entrance from **Cedars Court**).

Detail of façade at Sunderland (DP003806)

A separate building for the **Sunderland Jewish School** was constructed next door in 1936, designed in matching style by *Cyril Gillis* of *S J Stephenson & Gillis* of Newcastle. Marcus Glass had died in 1932. The school has now been converted into flats.

INTERIOR: Internally as well as externally Glass's three purpose-built synagogues were similar in design. Ample vestibules were provided with concrete corner staircases to the gallery and half-glazed internal doors. The prayer hall was spanned by a deep barrel vault over the central aisle, which was originally painted to imitate a star-spangled sky. The gallery ran around three sides carried on slender iron columns – in the case of Sunderland with palmette capitals. The plasterwork Ark canopy was highly decorative, painted and gilded. It was classical in form but featured decoration of Islamic and Byzantine origin, especially the cushion capitals to the columns and the chevron patterns on the shafts. The best preserved of these delicate Arks is now no longer to be found in the North-East,

but down on the south coast at Glass's **Hove Hebrew Congregation**, a conversion (*see* above). The pulpits were also almost identical; Jesmond's can now be seen inside the *ohel* at Newcastle's **Hazlerigg Jewish Cemetery**. All these pieces must have been made by the same craftsmen, no doubt in Newcastle. At Sunderland, the other furnishings were reordered in 1968 in a return to tradition. Originally the Ark, *bimah* and

Stained glass at Sunderland (DP020511)   **Detail of pulpit** (DP020522)

The former Jesmond Synagogue, sister building to Sunderland's Ryhope Road and the demolished Clapton Federation Synagogue (AA028874)

pulpit were combined on a platform at the east with all of the stained oak pews facing forward.

STAINED GLASS: Large *Magen David* roundels in the semicircular mullioned windows at east and west. The richly coloured geometric panels in steel frames throughout the building were the best stained glass in any of Marcus Glass's synagogues. The designers and makers have not been identified.

Sunderland Synagogue was sold out of Jewish hands in 2009 and is still searching for a sympathetic new use. The fabric is slowly deteriorating. It is succumbing to the all-too familiar blights that plague empty buildings: fire and flood, vandalism and theft.

The architectural legacy of Marcus Glass in the north-east of England deserves better. He started life as Yekusiel Glaz, one of six children of a poor refugee family from Riga, Latvia, who arrived in Newcastle in the 1890s. His successful career as an architect – highly unusual for a first-generation Jewish immigrant – was cut short by his premature death at the age of 45. This must explain why this talented

architect has been largely forgotten and his legacy has gone unappreciated.

However, if you want to seek out other examples of Glass's work while you are in the North-East, then take the Metro into Newcastle to visit both **Jesmond** and **Ravensworth Terrace** (a conversion), and out to **South Shields**, where his imprint is discernible in the last synagogue that he designed, although it was completed by another architect. (*See* the relevant entries below.)

LOCATION: Ryhope Road (B1522), east side, corner with Cedars Court, SR2 7EN.

LEGACY WEBSITE: www.seligman.org.il/sunderland_jews.html

Detail of stained glass at Sunderland (DP020506)

Former **Sunderland Beth HaMedrash**

3 Villiers Street, SR1 1EP

This is a recent case of a building being rediscovered when, reputedly, it had been knocked down. Back in 1999, on our original field trip for the Survey of the Jewish Built Heritage, we went to check and found a possible candidate in Villiers Street *South*. However, it did not conform to various images – including some now available online – that claimed to be the building in question. On the 1919 Ordnance Survey map of Sunderland, the 'synagogue' is indeed marked on Villiers Street *South*, close to the junction with Pauls Road.

In the course of research for a conservation appraisal in 2009, Sunderland City Council identified this distinctive building further north on Villiers Street itself as the former Beth HaMedrash.[7] Built into the terrace, the three-storey red-brick street frontage is symmetrical, with simplified Dutch gables breaking through the pitched roofline over the former entrances at either end. Note the *Magen David* design on a stone medallion high up under each gable. The glazing is generous; the three pairs of round-headed windows in the central range are decorated with arched surrounds, little roundels and keystones. These details and all the other dressings are of sandstone.

The Villiers Street Beth HaMedrash was consecrated on 26 November 1899.[8] Villiers Street was then at the heart of Sunderland's East End, which was home to some 1,000 Jewish immigrants, many from the Lithuanian town of Krottingen (Kretinga). The institution, which included a *Heder*, became a bastion of strict *misnagdish* Orthodoxy, the northern equivalent of the **Mahzikei Hadas** in Spitalfields. There was a *mikveh* at the back of the premises. The Ark from Villiers Street migrated to the successor building at Mowbray Road (*see* next entry), thence to the schoolhouse on Ryhope Road, and it is now restored and in use at **Gateshead** Jewish Boarding School (Mechina), 10 Rydal Street, Gateshead, NE8 1HG.[9]

LOCATION: At the southern end of Villiers Street, west side. The postcode given above is that of the antiques business that currently owns this building and the one next door on the corner with Borough Road (12–14 Borough Road).

Former **Sunderland Mikveh**

2 The Oaks West, Hendon, SR2 8HZ

Originally an unprepossessing single-storey red-brick box, the remains of this little building with blocked up windows have been incorporated into the wall of the yards in a back alley. The *Mikveh* was built in 1936, correctly – according to Jewish law – preceding the opening of the successor Sunderland Beth

Former Beth HaMedrash, 3 Villiers Street
(Courtesy of Sunderland City Council)

HaMedrash around the corner in **Mowbray Road** (1938, demolished).[10]

LOCATION: Back alleyway on the south side of Mowbray Road. It runs parallel with Mowbray Close. The remains of the *mikveh* are near the top (north end), on the east side of the alley.

Ayres Quay Jewish Cemetery

Beach Street, SR4 6BU

Classed by Jewish Heritage UK as a 'Site at Risk', this long-abandoned burial ground is the oldest in the north-east of England, testifying to the seniority of Sunderland's Jewish community. Documented from 1801 but probably in use from the 1780s if not earlier, the cemetery, by then full, was closed in 1856. Today tombstones and the boundary wall are broken and overgrown. Even the obelisk commemorating DAVID JONASSOHN, the paternalistic owner of the Usworth Colliery (erected 1859; a space was reserved for such an important man), has collapsed. Jonassohn is chiefly remembered in Anglo-Jewish history as one of the four deputies who in 1853 unsuccessfully demanded Reform representation at the Board of Deputies in London.

The immediate neighbourhood has altered since our first visit back in 1998. Retail sheds have grown up around about and the city council's recycling tip is right next door. In 2010–11 a Friends' group began

restoration work, with the help of some funds raised from the city council and from the sale of Ryhope Road. This was a joint initiative of a Londoner with family roots in Sunderland and a Newcastle-based professional archaeologist. They secured the support of the Gateshead Hebrew Burial Society with a view to future maintenance of the cemetery locally. However, although some work was carried out inside the cemetery, it remains very well hidden in a clump of vegetation. The stone walls are just about discernible on Google Earth. At least trusteeship has now been vested in the Board of Deputies in London.

LOCATION: Make for Sunderland City Council's recycling facility on Beach Street, the postcode of which is given above. The burial ground is hidden behind trees on its north-east side. If you have difficulty locating the actual site, don't hesitate to ask the manager, who is pleased to assist. Ordnance Survey map reference: NZ 388 576.

ACCESS: Involves climbing into the opening in the boundary wall, about a metre above the ground. A small step ladder is useful!

Bishopwearmouth Cemetery, Jewish Sections

Hylton Road, SR4 7SJ

1856

This very large municipal cemetery was opened in 1856. Three non-contiguous Jewish sections were in use during the periods 1856–99, 1899–1926 and 1926 onwards. The earliest plot (no. 1) is located on the extreme north-east corner with Hylton Road; plot no. 2 is near the crematorium towards the west; and plot no. 3 is at the far north-west corner of the cemetery. This is the largest plot and is still in use, although the red brick *ohel* has been covered in graffiti. Hebrew *inscription*: BET MOED L'KOL HAI ('House of Meeting for all Living').

ACCESS Enter via the main gate on Hylton Road. Open during general cemetery hours.

Bishopwearmouth Cemetery (AP for SJBH)

Former **Leazes Park Synagogue**

Leazes Arcade, 12 Leazes Park Road, NE1 4PF

John Johnstone, 1879–80, Grade II

This imposing street façade, faced in typical Newcastle yellow sandstone, was once the 'cathedral synagogue' of Newcastle Jewry, and indeed of the entire North-East. It included classrooms, caretaker's house and a *mikveh* in the basement (unusually accessed from the front). Designed in eclectic Romanesque style with a 'Lombardy' frieze under the cornice by *John Johnstone* (1814–84), a Newcastle-based Scotsman who specialised in town halls. Leazes Park (originally called Albion Street) was the successor to Temple Street (1838), the first purpose-built synagogue in the city. It closed in 1978 and, after a spell as a downmarket shopping arcade, was gutted by fire until finally divided up for residential use.

The frontage is on a slope, not quite symmetrical, with a tripartite and gabled central range with entrance doors in the wings at either end featuring decorative lobed-arch surrounds. Square buttresses carry picturesque finials but the lobed roundel in the gable no longer contains any Jewish symbolism. However, Stars of David are espied in the upper-floor window heads.

The curved brick bay in the plain-brick rear wall (walk around the back into Percy Street) accommodated the Ark under a decorative fanlight (now gone).

The Romanesque façade of the former Leazes Park Synagogue, Newcastle upon Tyne (AA028875)

Former **Ravensworth Terrace Synagogue**

6–8 Ravensworth Terrace, NE4 6AU

Marcus Kenneth Glass, 1924–5

Marcus Kenneth Glass managed to impose his distinctive style on this Victorian terrace conversion, effectively almost an entire rebuild. The houses were left to the Newcastle United Hebrew Congregation formed out of two immigrant *shtiebl*-type congregations, the Beth HaMedrash (1891) and Corporation Street (1904). Cement rendered and cream painted with bands of red brick and artificial stone in a mock 'Byzantine' style. The six-bayed fenestrated façade has two tiers of tall round-headed windows and the doorway to one end (west). Closed 1969 and rescued and restored by a design studio in 1981. The *foundation stones* and *Luhot* outside have been painted out. However, the large *Magen David* window, situated over the main entrance, remains. It now dominates an upstairs room in the completely refurbished interior (1997).

Former Jesmond Synagogue, porch (DP058472)

Former **Jesmond Synagogue**

Eskdale Terrace, NE2 4DS

Marcus Kenneth Glass, 1914–15

The earliest of the cinematic series of synagogues by *Marcus Kenneth Glass*, of which only Sunderland's **Ryhope Road** is a listed building. This one has been converted internally into a school, but the exterior has been sympathetically restored. Retained is the sunburst stained glass, complete with Stars of David, that fills the expansive mullioned half-moon windows at either end. The style and plan of the building are almost a twin of Sunderland. Here, the porch has a triple arcade and the columns are embellished with lotus-bud capitals, but the turquoise and gold mosaic band contains the same Hebrew inscription, *Ma Tovu* (Numbers 24:5).

Thornton Street Jewish Cemetery

Charlton's Bonds Building, Waterloo Street, NE1 4DE

1835

Hidden away in a tiny enclosed courtyard, this was the first burial ground

One of the last remaining tombstones at the Old Jewish Cemetery, Thornton Street, Newcastle upon Tyne
(AP for SJBH)

of the Jews of Newcastle, acquired in 1835. A short distance outside the west walls of the old town, and known as Peel Street or Peel Lane, it was located not far from the site of the Temple Street Synagogue (1838 demolished), and the two sites were apparently at one time linked by a private passageway. Closed under the Burial Act in 1853, and the present tiny area of the cemetery is a fraction of the 250 square yards originally purchased. Only five weathered sandstone tombstones survive, not all *in situ* and the ground, restored in 1961, was covered in red gravel. No records.

LOCATION: Behind the former Waterloo Chambers, (a former Victorian bonded warehouse), which carries the inscription 'CHARLTON'S BONDS 1885', situated at the corner of Thornton Street and Peel Lane. Thornton Street is the north end of Waterloo Street before it intersects Westgate Road.

ACCESS: By permission of the occupants of the front premises. In 2015 the building was up for sale by owners Newcastle City Council, but it was established that access to the cemetery would continue as a condition of purchase.

St John's Cemetery, Jewish Section

Elswick Road, NE4 7XB

1857

Known simply as 'Elswick'. This is a real Victorian city cemetery with lots of atmosphere, overhanging trees, Gothic headstones, tall obelisks and urns. On an elevated site, there are good views south towards Gateshead, with *Anthony Gormley's* landmark *Angel of the North* sculpture in the distance. Puzzlingly, this Jewish plot, which is one of the earliest in the country, dating from the opening of a public cemetery (1857), lies outside the cemetery's Parks & Gardens designation. The entire cemetery was laid out by *John Johnstone* of *Johnstone & Knowles*, winners of a competition in 1855. Johnstone afterwards designed **Leazes Park Synagogue**. The plot, later extended, contains over 1,000 graves, all facing west. The oldest are located near to the gate on St John's Road. The *ohel* (1874) has disappeared along with the burial registers, but some field surveys have been undertaken.

ACCESS: Open during general cemetery hours. Enter from St John's Road, west side.

Hazlerigg Jewish Cemetery

Coach Lane, Gosforth, NE13

Also spelt Hazelrigg. Apparently acquired by the Corporation Street Synagogue (1904) in 1906. The oldest tombstones are along the back wall and the earliest legible dates from 1912. The red-brick *ohel* (1920), with a deeply pitched slate roof, fronts the street. Inside are displayed a series of colourful, mainly modern, windows from **Jesmond Synagogue** and the pulpit (1925). Modern *bet taharah* add-on and cemetery extension 1992. Shared with **Gateshead**, from at least 1908, whose newer sections are distinguished by separate rows designated for males and females.

LOCATION: Coach Lane, south side, almost opposite Elmwood Avenue.

ACCESS: Through locked *ohel* on Coach Lane. Key c/o Newcastle United Hebrew Congregation, The Synagogue (*Waring & Netts*, 1985–6), Graham Park Road, Gosforth, NE3 4BH: tel 0191 284 0959; www.uhc-newcastle.org

Byker and Heaton Cemetery, Jewish Section

Etherstone Avenue, NE7 7JX

1916

The plot consists of four very long rows of stones railed off from the rest of the cemetery (1890) which is also known as 'Benton Road'. The entrance is actually from Etherstone Road through the *ohel* (1922), which is a simple white-washed rectangular building with a pitched slate roof; the long wall is parallel with the street (north-south). The plot was acquired by **Jesmond Synagogue** on its opening. The earliest burial was of ETTA JACKSON, 3rd October 1916. Later extension and a modern *bet taharah* has been added to the rear.

ACCESS: Use the public entrance at the far north-eastern corner of Etherstone Avenue (postcode given above) rather than the main gate on Benton Road, during general cemetery hours. Closed Sundays, when the key to the *ohel* is available via Newcastle United Hebrew Congregation, Gosforth: tel 0191 284 0959; www.uhc-newcastle.org

View from the women's gallery at Gateshead Synagogue (AA028869)

Men's section at Gateshead Synagogue (SK for SJBH)

GATESHEAD

Gateshead Synagogue

180 Bewick Road, NE8 1UF

White & Pearson, 1938–9

An unpretentious but not displeasing red-brick synagogue by *R G Pearson* of *White & Pearson* (Newcastle), for the strictly Orthodox community that grew up around the Gateshead *yeshivah* established in 1927–9 by refugees from Europe. *Foundation stone* dated 25 Tammuz 5698 (=24 July 1938). The only decoration is a bold red and green coloured glass *Magen David* roundel over the Ark that bears the Hebrew year of opening in Hebrew letters (5699=1939). The clear-glazed double-height round-headed windows were a traditional feature of synagogues in central and eastern Europe from the baroque period, here transplanted to England.[11] The windows provide ample lighting to the interior – so important in a northern setting.

INTERIOR: The prayer hall is wider than it is deep, with the gallery along the back (west) wall hidden by a high fenestrated *mehitzah* made of little square lights set in a timber frame. The Ark is a plain timber cabinet placed against the east wall with a simple *shtender* immediately in front adorned with a painted *Shiviti*. The décor was modernised *c* 2009 in fashionable Israeli *yeshivah*-style; the forward-facing pews have made way for moveable seating and the dark drapes over the windows have been replaced by white blinds.[12] Designed with a *mikveh* attached, afterwards rebuilt (Rabbi *Meir Posen*, 1986). Other later extensions.

OPENING HOURS: All services, *Shabbat* and weekdays.

Exterior of Gateshead Synagogue (AA028867)

Preston Cemetery, Jewish Sections

Walton Avenue, NE29 9NJ

1856

The earliest gravestone is located on the far right (north-west) in the first row closest to the wall. It shows some discrepancies in the Hebrew text, compared with the entry in the general burial register kept in the cemetery office: SARAH ISAACS, aged 26, buried 6 July 1856. She was in fact from South Shields.

A synagogue is known to have existed in North Shields from 1870 at 20 Linskill Street, near the North Shields ferry landings. It is thought that burials go back much further to two lost plots dating from the early 19th century (Hawkies Lane and Chirton). The latter was apparently exhumed and reinterred at Preston in 1924 on the advice of the London Beth Din. The Gateshead community bury their *Shemos* in North Shields.

NB There is an entirely separate modern (1977) Reform cemetery with its own *ohel* elsewhere in this cemetery (Newcastle Reform Synagogue, The Croft, Kenton Road, NE3 4RF: www.newcastle reformsynagogue.co.uk)

LOCATION: Near the south-east corner of the cemetery.

ACCESS: Separate gate in wall on Walton Avenue locked, so use the main gates. During general cemetery hours. Cemetery office on site.

Former **South Shields Synagogue**

25 Beach Road, NE33 2QA

J A Page & Son, 1932–3

The only purpose-built synagogue for a community that dates back to the 1880s. It was built on the site of a house at 14 Ogle Terrace, acquired 1914 and demolished 1932. The architects *J A Page & Son* (1930–1) took over after the death in 1932 of the original architect, *Marcus Kenneth Glass* of Newcastle. This was the last of Glass's known synagogue designs and, for him, the least interesting, but superior to what actually got built. The long wall faces the street, of plain red brick with the entrance under a gable at one end (west). Rescued on closure in 1994 and converted into the South Tyneside Arts Studio by *Mario Minchella Architects*. The series of *foundation stones* are only partially legible; much of the original decorative glass has been removed except

Stained glass at South Shields
(AP for SJBH)

for the *Magen David* sunburst in the Ark wall; the *Luhot* remain on the gable. Vestiges of the iron column supports with palmette capitals can be seen inside the studios.

Harton Cemetery, Jewish Section

St Georges Avenue, Harton, South Shields, NE34 6EU

1899

The Harton Cemetery was opened in 1891 (gates, chapels and lodge by *Henry Grieves*, 1888–91, Grade II). According to the burial registers kept by South Tyneside Council, the first burial in the Jewish plot took place on 18 May 1899. The first tombstone inscription on site dates from 1900, among the earliest graves along the back, the whole plot being enclosed within a stone wall. In use.

LOCATION: To the south-east of South Shields just off the Shields-Sunderland Road (A1018).

ACCESS: The Jewish section is located in the north-east corner of the cemetery, accessible during general cemetery hours.

Former **Whitley Bay Synagogue**

2 Oxford Street, NG26 1AE

Whitley Bay was once a popular holiday town for the Jewish communities of the North-East. A resident congregation was established in 1922 and in 1937, swelled by German refugee families, acquired an end-of-terrace house at 2 Oxford Road. It is not entirely clear whether this was actually demolished or completely remodelled into the Whitley Bay Synagogue (1938) by Sunderland architect *Cyril Gillis* of *S J Stephenson & Gillis*. Remodelled again by *C Solomon* 1966. Closed in 1992 and some of the appurtenances were donated to the Jewish community of Tegucigalpa, Honduras. The neglected building was renovated in 2008 and became home to a dance studio. The *Magen David* and coloured glass in the rusting arched window-heads have been replaced by PVC. The greying cement-render and pebbledash has been painted powder blue and decorated with silhouettes of ballet dancers; this certainly brightens up the building!

LOCATION: Corner with Park Avenue.

NB There is a Jewish plot on the north side of **Whitley New Cemetery**, Blyth Road, NE26 4NH (near St Mary's

Lighthouse), dating from 1953. It has an *ohel* and separate gate on Blyth Road (A193). Accessible during general hours.

COUNTY DURHAM

DURHAM

Former **Durham Synagogue**

'The Chapel', Laburnum Avenue, DH1 4HA

John George Burrell, 1908–10

Purpose-built for a congregation formed in 1888 in this historic cathedral town. The architect was a local man. On a good-sized plot at the end of a cul-de-sac bounded by the North Eastern Railway, he utilised red brick, partially stuccoed and whitewashed, and hung the roof with slates. The synagogue went out of use in 1944 and soldiers were billeted in the building. It was sold in 1955 and alterations and later additions masked its former function. Quaintly

named 'The Old Chapel', the one-time comfortable residential private house and office has, since 1999, reverted to religious use – this time as Durham Presbyterian Church.[13]

DARLINGTON

Darlington West Cemetery, Jewish Sections

Carmel Road North, DL3 8RY

1926

In this neatly kept railed-off plot (section V), the earliest burial was that of BERTHA KLETZ, d 3 June 1926. The small community had been formed in 1884 and was peripatetic until the acquisition of Studley House, 9 Victoria Road, in 1930. In 1967 they moved to 13 Bloomfield Road, DL3 6RZ (www.darlington hebrewcongregation.org. uk), and are currently aligned with the Reform movement. A second plot was started in 1957 in the same section by the

The neat Jewish plot at Darlington's West Cemetery (AP for SJBH)

southern boundary with Salutation Road/Coniscliffe Road, surrounded by hedges. This part of the cemetery, a later extension, lies outside the area of this very verdant Victorian cemetery (*J P Pritchett*, 1856–8), which is included on the Parks & Gardens Register.

ACCESS: Via main gates during general cemetery hours.

HARTLEPOOL

Hartlepool Jewish Cemetery

Old Cemetery Road,
The Headland, TS24 0NA

Only half full, this cemetery is on an exposed site facing the sea. It is immediately next to the municipal Spion Kop Cemetery (1856) but is entirely separated from it by high red-brick walls. On the other side (west) the huge Steetley (later BritMag) works, that were our landmark back in 1999, have now been demolished. The Jewish cemetery was acquired in 1865 from the local landowner, the Duke of Cleveland, but the first burial appears not to have taken place until 1876.[14] The congregation had started in the 1850s and had a purpose-built synagogue in Whitby Street, West Hartlepool, designed in classical style by *William*

Harrison (1871–2, closed *c* 1968 and demolished).[15] The last trustee of the cemetery no longer lives in the town. *Ohel* demolished.

LOCATION: Western end of Old Cemetery Road.

ACCESS: Currently open.

FURTHER INFORMATION: Kehillat Middlesbrough: www.kmbro.weebly.com

NB **Bishop Auckland (Town) Cemetery**, South Church Road, DL14 7LB, has a tiny hedged Jewish plot dating from 1952. (Postcode is that of the Asda superstore nearby, on the east side of South Church Road (A689).)

TEESSIDE

MIDDLESBROUGH

Former **Middlesbrough Synagogue**

33 Park Road South, TS5 6LE

Archibald & Archibald, 1937–8

By local architects *Archibald & Archibald* working in association with *Jack Lazarus*, who happened to be brother of the president of the congregation. It seems that he was largely responsible for the austere modernist design, having spent some years practising in Palestine in the early 1930s. Certainly the cubist construction, which was complemented internally by

circular top-lights, concrete gallery and whitewashed concrete walls, was reminiscent of the work of the Central European International-Style architects such as *Richard Kaufman* and *Erich Mendelsohn* under the British Mandate. Fortunately, in Middlesbrough the architects opted to face the building in typically English red brick rather than harsh white concrete, which would not have been well suited to northern conditions. The synagogue became too large very quickly; by the 1930s Middlesbrough Jewry had already passed its peak. The community had been founded *c* 1865 and had a purpose-built synagogue in Brentnall Street in Romanesque style by *Edward Tidman* (1873–4, demolished). Some stained glass, notably the red-and-white *Luhot* window over the Ark, was transferred to Park Road South, and was extant in 1998 when the synagogue closed.[16] It is understood that this window is now in Gateshead, while others found their way to **North Western Reform Synagogue (Alyth)** in London.

The façade has been much altered for conversion into flats. Originally, the building had windows only on the ground floor; vertical metal-framed ribbon windows, in triples. Above, the wall was blank and unbuttressed. The *foundation stone* set low down on the plinth at the

Hartlepool Jewish Cemetery
(AP for SJBH)

extreme left-hand side (east) appears to have gone, as has the Hebrew inscription in the square door surround, but the big *Magen David* over the main entrance can still be seen from some distance. Hall attached (1956), which blocked access to the original *mikveh*. Flats, now called 'Lugs Lodge'.

LEGACY WEBSITE: Kehillat Middlesbrough: www.kmbro.weebly.com

Linthorpe Cemetery, Jewish Sections

Ayresome Green Lane, TS5 4DZ

1885

Linthorpe Cemetery, also known as Ayresome Green (opened 1869) is the oldest in Middlesbrough and is a local nature reserve. The first of two Jewish plots was consecrated by the Chief Rabbi in July 1885 and is located at the south-west corner at Nursery Lane and Burlam Road. The first burial, of DAVID ASHER BARNARD, took place on 18 September 1885, although the earliest legible tombstone at the time of our survey dated from 1887. The oldest row is closest to Nursery Lane. Here the graves face west, but are mostly correctly aligned in the successor plot, which was consecrated in June 1932. The first burial there was that of LEAH SIMON, d 6 October 1932, whose tombstone is on the back wall (this row faces west). The old plot's *ohel* has gone; the new plot's is situated along Ayresome Green Lane. For long disused and vandalised, it

was restored by *Hugh Massey Architects* as part of a major Heritage Lottery Fund project in 2004–7. The *ohel* is of red brick with a curved pediment containing a *date stone* (1932). Most of the large round-headed windows have been reinstated and the building is now in educational and communal use.

ACCESS: Separate entrances now blocked or locked, so use the main gate at Ayresome Green Lane/ Roman Road during general cemetery hours. Turn right (north) for the nearby new section; the old section is close to the public entrance on Nursery Lane, if it is open.

CONTACT: Friends of Linthorpe Cemetery: www.folc.org.uk

FURTHER INFORMATION: Kehillat Middlesbrough: www.kmbro.weebly.com

STOCKTON-ON-TEES

Former **Stockton** **Synagogue**

Hartington Road, TS18 1HD

T W T Richardson, 1905–6

Stockton's Jewish community started in the early 1870s as a spill-over from Middlesbrough,

Former Stockton Synagogue
(AP for SJBH)

6.5km (4 miles) away. In Accrington red brick with artificial stone dressings and a slate roof, this modest former synagogue was in keeping with the Edwardian terrace and could pass as a Nonconformist chapel. The local architect opted for so-called 'Renaissance' style with 'halo-arch' and not-quite Venetian window. Closed in 1972, today the building serves as the local Christian Science church. The Jewish symbolism has been removed, but the plain classical Ark surround is still extant inside under the original exposed timber roof with ties. Two houses immediately next door (left) have now been converted into the Stockton Central Mosque and Islamic Centre.

LOCATION: East side, near junction with top of Lawson Road.

Stockton Old Cemetery, Jewish Section

Oxbridge Lane, TS18 4HP

1885

The Stockton community separated from Middlesbrough in 1884, presumably through the acquisition of this burial plot in the town cemetery (opened 1871). The earliest burial was that of MIRIAM JACOBS, 15 July 1885, located at the north-west corner by the entrance.

ACCESS: East of the main chapel. Enter via main gates by South Lodge.

FURTHER INFORMATION: Kehillat Middlesbrough: www.kmbro.weebly.com

SCOTLAND

T HE HERITAGE OF SCOTTISH Jewry is concentrated in the 'two capitals' of **Edinburgh** and **Glasgow**. A community was organised in Edinburgh, the 'Athens of the North', from 1816. Individual Jews had earlier settled in Edinburgh, some attracted by the reputation of the university in

the medical sciences (especially as they did not operate a religious bar against 'dissenters', unlike in England at that time), such as the German-born Herman Lyon (also known as Heyman Lion), a successful 'corner operator' (Georgian English for a 'chiropodist') and dentist, who in 1795 was buried in a private vault on **Calton Hill**. Nothing remains of his 'tomb with a view', but the hill is well worth a visit for its eccentric structures, ranging from Regency 'Gothik' to Greek Revival, mostly erected during the Napoleonic Wars down to 1830.[1] Edinburgh Jewry has remained small, numbering about 100 in the 1820s, 2,000 at its peak in the 1920s and not quite half that today (*c* 990 people according to the 2011 Census).

Glasgow's Jewish community was founded in 1823 but was essentially a mid-19th-century product of the Industrial Revolution. The jewel in its crown is **Garnethill Synagogue**, opened in 1879, and situated just around the corner from Charles Rennie Mackintosh's famous

Glasgow School of Art (mainly 1907–8, shockingly gutted by fire in May 2014). By contrast, not a single Jewish building remains in the **Gorbals**, on the South Side of the River Clyde. Once the Glasgow equivalent of the Jewish East End of London, the Gorbals disappeared in wholesale post-war redevelopment: the tower blocks that dominated the area were a doubtful improvement on the Victorian slums – and are, in their turn, gradually being pulled down. Glasgow has more than its fair share of Jewish cemeteries, not a few of which are located in grim inner-city areas.

Visitors to Scotland seeking contemporary Jewish life (and kosher food) should first head for Glasgow whose Jewish community, although much diminished (*c* 3,400 in 2011 Census), remains the largest in the kingdom, accounting for just over half of the total. The Glasgow community has decamped to the outer suburbs on the South Side, mainly around Giffnock, East Renfrewshire. The Jewish population of Scotland as a whole has fallen below 6,000.

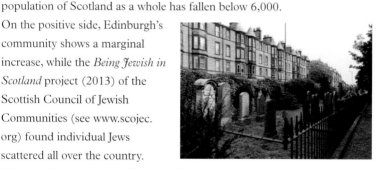

On the positive side, Edinburgh's community shows a marginal increase, while the *Being Jewish in Scotland* project (2013) of the Scottish Council of Jewish Communities (see www.scojec. org) found individual Jews scattered all over the country. A Jewish Network of Argyll and the Highlands has been set up. Nevertheless, tiny communities barely support a synagogue in **Aberdeen** and **Dundee**; about two dozen graves in the town cemetery in **Inverness** attest to the former existence of the most northerly Jewish community in Britain, while Jewish communities in Ayr, Dunfermline and Falkirk have left behind no material traces at all.

Garnethill Synagogue, Glasgow. View from the gallery (© Crown copyright RCAHMS 441365)

Garnethill Synagogue

129 Hill Street, G3 6UB

John McLeod in association with N S Joseph, 1877–9, Scottish A List

The 'cathedral synagogue' of Scotland

'Orientalist' elements can be detected in the yellow-stone predominantly Romanesque exterior, especially in the little turrets and the keyhole window above the door, but are much more apparent inside. As the address suggests, the synagogue is built on an elevated site, the awkwardness of which dictated a variant plan; Ark apse at east, the main entrance at north (Hill Street) with a grand entrance hall and a long vestibule that extends, at west, the width of the main prayer hall. The *inscription* over the entrance (Deuteronomy 32:12) contains a chronogram.

INTERIOR: The floors of the entrance hall and vestibule are laid with multi-coloured Minton tiles in a repeat diamond pattern containing six-pointed stars (restored with help from the Heritage Lottery Fund in 2008 by *Page/Park Architects*). The ceilings are of decorative stucco with an ornate and colourful cusped archway between, which is almost Indian in appearance. A grand staircase divides at the landing into two parallel flights, lit by glorious floral stained glass windows by *J B Bennett & Sons*.[2]

The basilican prayer hall has slender ironwork arcades (the columns with Byzantine cushion caps) that carry the women's gallery, which extends around three sides of the barrel-vaulted space. The gallery fronts are of gilded cast iron and are elegantly bellied. The deep rear west gallery contains the choir loft.

The pulpit (*c* 1896) is a dominating feature, placed in the centre of the Ark platform and projecting into the main space on a set of semi-circular marble steps. It is of rich inlaid marbles with horseshoe arches and *Magen David* designs. The floor of the *duhan* is chequer-work. The timber Ark is gilded, domed and turreted, not unlike that at the **New West End Synagogue** in London, a project on which *Nathan Joseph*, together with *George Audsley*,

Garnethill Synagogue, the main entrance
(© Crown copyright RCAHMS SC441364)

Garnethill's glazed apse (Courtesy of Garnethill Preservation Trust)

was engaged at the same time. In Glasgow, Joseph acted as consultant to another Scotsman, *John McLeod*, the son of a Dumbarton shipbuilder. He was an elder in the Scots Presbyterian Kirk who designed a number of churches.

At Garnethill the Ark is placed in an apse framed by a large horseshoe arch. The polygonal apse is filled with panels of black, yellow and frosted stained glass. A similar device had been employed at Brighton's **Middle Street Synagogue** a few years earlier, but skylights are a characteristic feature of Glasgow buildings.

Note especially the painted fanlight in the west gallery with Hebrew *inscription* from Psalm 113:3 (*Hallel* prayer) and the date in a roundel: AM 5619 (=1859). This was brought from the previous synagogue (a conversion) at George Street. *Mikveh* in the basement now gone.

The national importance of Garnethill was recognised by Historic Scotland when they underwrote major repair work in 1995–8, match-funded in part by the Wolfson Foundation, whose founder, Sir Isaac Wolfson (1897–1991), was born in the city of Glasgow.

OPENING HOURS: *Shabbat* morning and festival services. Heritage Open Days (September). Other times and groups by appointment: tel 0141 332 4151; www.garnethill.org.uk.

SCOTTISH JEWISH ARCHIVES

Since 1987 Garnethill has been home to the Scottish Jewish Archives Centre, which has rescued and stores a wealth of original material, including over 6,000 historic photographs. They maintain a database compiled from the incomplete burial records of Jewish cemeteries throughout Scotland, a magnet for genealogists. (It is not available online.) Thanks largely to the Heritage Lottery Fund (2008), a permanent exhibition has been installed (*Artan Sherifi* of *Arka Design Studio Ltd; Paula Murray* and *Alan Mackay*). The corridor approach displays a timeline of the history of the Jews in Scotland. Publications for sale.

OPENING TIMES: Open Sunday usually once a month. For other times and appointments: tel 0141 332 4911; www.sjac.org.uk

The *Bimah*, Garnethill Synagogue
(© Crown copyright RCAHMS SC924503)

Former **Queen's Park Synagogue**

60 Lochleven Road, G42 9JU

Ninian McWhannell (McWhannell & Smellie), 1924–7, Scottish B List

Behind a red-painted and rendered artificial stone façade that is basically Romanesque, this synagogue was a watered down version of Garnethill. It was closed in 2003 and sold for £410,000 to Arklet Housing Association Ltd, who converted it into five flats. Access to the building was reversed, with a front door punched into the semi-circular Ark apse on Lochleven Road, perhaps prompting the housing association's new name for the whole development

('The Ark'!). The impressive vaulted vestibule, situated on the Falloch Road[3] side, reminiscent of the **London New Synagogue**, was supposed to have been left intact. *Foundation stone* plus date stone in gable *Luhot*. The cycle of modern stained glass by *John K 'Jim' Clark* made to mark Glasgow City of Culture in 1989 was removed to **Giffnock Synagogue** (*see* below) (postal address 222 Fenwick Road, G46 6UE; tel 0141 577 8250; www.giffnockshul.co.uk) courtesy of a £40,000 grant from the Heritage Lottery Fund. Meanwhile, the Ark was transferred in 2004 to the new-build **Chodosh (Beis HaMedrash**

HaChodosh, 'The New') **Synagogue** (*R E Gonshaw*, interior *Joshua Benson*, 2004), 39 Northumberland Street, Salford, Greater Manchester, M7 4DQ.

Giffnock Old Synagogue

Maccabi and Youth Centre, 1 May Terrace, G46 6LD

1938

Look carefully at this site and you will see that at its kernel is the first suburban synagogue built in Glasgow just before the Second World War. The original Giffnock Synagogue has disappeared behind extensions on all sides. Walk around the back where the squarish Ark apse and some coloured glass in the windows above are visible. Inside, notice the gallery piers in the main hall and more coloured glass hidden away within the Ark apse. In the 1960s, the community outgrew May Terrace and moved to the present Giffnock Synagogue in Maryville Avenue (*Norman Bailey Samuels and Partners*, 1967–9[4]).

ACCESS: Tel 0141 638 6177.
LOCATION: Braidbar Road.

Langside Synagogue

125 Niddrie Road, G42 8QA

Jeffrey-Waddell & Young, 1926–7

Somewhat confusingly 'Queen's Park' Synagogue is really in Langside; 'Langside' synagogue is in Queen's Park. This unpromising, vaguely

The main entrance to the former Queen's Park Synagogue
(© Crown copyright RCAHMS SC924504)

The Ark, Langside Synagogue (© Crown copyright RCAHMS SC1096334)

modernist façade by *John Jeffrey-Waddell* hides a rare gem of an interior. The Ark and *bimah* and other decorative details, such as the clock on the gallery front, were lovingly carved by a member of the congregation, a Lithuanian-born cabinetmaker named *Harris Berkowitch* (c 1876–1956). The two-tier Ark, of timber with gilding, is in traditional eastern European folk-art style. The tall upper tier includes large gilded *Luhot*

with painted glass panels to either side, and the pediment contains a *Keter Torah* ('Crown of the Law') with gilded sunrays, both motifs long established in

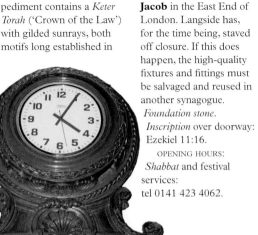

Clock at Langside Synagogue
(© Crown copyright RCAHMS SC1196961)

Jewish art. Compare with the **Congregation of Jacob** in the East End of London. Langside has, for the time being, staved off closure. If this does happen, the high-quality fixtures and fittings must be salvaged and reused in another synagogue.
Foundation stone.
Inscription over doorway: Ezekiel 11:16.
OPENING HOURS:
Shabbat and festival services:
tel 0141 423 4062.

Glasgow Necropolis, Jews' Enclosure

Cathedral Square, G4 0UZ

1832, Scottish A List

The Glasgow Necropolis was laid out in 1829–33 on the model of the prestigious Père la Chaise cemetery in Paris. The earliest burial in the entire cemetery was of one JOSEPH LEVI, aged 62, quill merchant, who was interred on 12 September 1832 in the tiny Jewish plot at the bottom. Levi had died of cholera, an epidemic raging in the city at the time. His coffin was filled with lime and water, either to prevent the spread of infection and/or as protection against grave robbers. The last burials took place in 1851, including one (of the two) still to be seen just outside the boundary wall, of a gentleman who had married outside the faith. The Jewish plot once had a *bet taharah* which was apparently demolished to make room for more burials.

The monumental column and iron gateway with stone scrolls was designed by *John Bryce* (1805–51) *c* 1835–6, who was also responsible for the contemporary Catacombs and Egyptian vaults elsewhere in the Necropolis. Bryce's column was supposedly modelled on Absalom's Pillar in Jerusalem but, being classical in form, actually looks nothing like it. It is topped by an urn finial rather than by a conical-shaped dome. Another urn, on the gate scrolls, has disappeared. The *inscriptions* are a combination of Biblical texts in Hebrew and English and a long quotation from Byron's *Hebrew Melodies*. Now gently crumbling away, this must rate as one of the most romantic Jewish sites in Britain.

LOCATION: At the very bottom of the hill. Enter from Cathedral Square and, once inside the Necropolis, take the left-hand path, parallel with Wishart Street, to the northern corner.

ACCESS: Open access.

FURTHER INFORMATION: Self-guided heritage trail of the Necropolis, ending at the Jewish section, available via www.glasgow.gov.uk

Glasgow Eastern Necropolis, Jewish Section

1264 Gallowgate, Parkhead, G31 4DR

1856, Scottish B List

Also known as 'Janefield' and 'Gallowgate'. An atmospheric early Victorian cemetery (1847) that lies peacefully in the looming shadow of Celtic football ground. The Glasgow Hebrew Congregation, then based at Howard Street, purchased the land from the Glasgow Eastern Necropolis Co in 1853; first burial 1856, extended 1891, closed 1914, last burial 1935.

LOCATION: At the back (south-west) of the Eastern Necropolis.

ACCESS: During general cemetery hours. Enter via main gate on Gallowgate, opposite the Forge Shopping Centre. Take the path to the right.

Craigton Cemetery, Jewish Section

Cemetery Road, Govan, G52 1SJ

1881

The Commerce Street Hevrah Torah, or New Hebrew Congregation, was founded in 1880 and in the same year acquired a plot in a privately owned commercial cemetery, which had opened in 1873. Commerce Street was the first *minyan* established by immigrants to the South Side of Glasgow (at 2 Commerce Street). First interment 1881, extended 1890–1 for use by **Garnethill** and closed in 1908.

In *c* 2006 Glasgow City Council took over control (and inherited the records) from the Craigton Cemetery Co and, as a result, the condition of the site has much improved. Unfortunately, most of the Jewish headstones had by this time already disappeared, along with the spiked iron railings. There were about 240 burials arranged in three rows in the easternmost corner, running parallel with the boundary wall on Crosslee Street. On our most recent visit (August 2014), we found in pieces the grey-granite urn on an obelisk for MARCUS COHEN, who was the last person to be buried in the plot, on 13 October 1908.[5] The rest of the plot was covered in brambles. A complaint to the council resulted in a complete clean-up and the monument was re-erected.

LOCATION: Make for the Cemetery Road entrance, just off Paisley Road West (A761), north side. Follow the path to the right around the eastern boundary wall (Crosslee Street side), against which the Jewish section is located. (The main entrance is from Berryknowes Road).

ACCESS: Gate open during general cemetery hours.

Western Necropolis, Jewish Section

Tresta Road, Maryhill, G23 5AA

1882, Scottish B List

Two half-illegible *foundation stones* on either side of the gates opening to the left-hand (west) side of this plot yield the Hebrew date 5643 (=1882/3). 1882 is the year in which the entire cemetery was opened, and the acquisition at the outset of a burial plot showed forward thinking on the part of the Gorbals' immigrant congregation, which was formally constituted as the Hevrah Kadisha Synagogue in 1889. It was later known as 'Buchan Street', after the old Baptist church at no. 33, which they used for worship from 1899 to 1972. Apparently the plot was early on repossessed by the Western Necropolis Co when the *hevrah* failed to complete the purchase. In 1895 **Garnethill** stepped in and extended the plot, partly as a philanthropic gesture and partly in a bid to fend off competition for

cheaper burials by immigrant congregations.

The site is divided into two by a central pathway with Hevrah Kadisha burials to the left side (west, behind railings) and Garnethill's to the right (east, behind hedge), which contains the disused red-brick and red sandstone *ohel* (B listed) built by the short-lived United Synagogue of Glasgow (1898–1906). Also shared with the Poalei Zedek (Tsedek, 'Workers of Righteousness') *hevrah* (11 Oxford Street) and, from 1929, with the Beth HaMedrash HaGadol, known from 1925 to 1956 as the New Central Synagogue, Rutherglen Road. Records lost.

LOCATION: On the southern side of the Western Necropolis, very near to the crematorium.

ACCESS: Usually open for pedestrians from Tresta Road. Key c/o Garnethill Synagogue: tel 0141 332 4151. Vehicles: use main gates. Then walk towards the southern wall of the crematorium.

Riddrie Jewish Cemetery

Cumbernauld Road, G33 2QS

1909

For the umbrella synagogue of the South Side, the Moorish-style South Portland Street (*James Chalmers*, 1898–1901, demolished 1974). Foundations of the *ohel* (1915) are visible a short distance behind the old gate and close to it may be found the earliest legible tombstone on site, JACOB

COHEN, d 3 March 1910, aged 50. Apparently shared with **Langside** until *c* 1980, but no burial registers seem to have survived. Today, situated in one of the grimmest parts of the city, this cemetery has suffered from vandalism. The city council has laid unstable stones flat. The boundary separating the Jewish cemetery from the general cemetery has disappeared.

LOCATION: Situated to the west of the main Riddrie Park Cemetery (1901) and contiguous with it. Blocked gate in the stone wall on Provenmill Road. There is a good view over the wall into the cemetery from this point (G33 1BQ).

ACCESS: Through the main gate on Cumbernauld Road. Glasgow Hebrew Burial Society: tel 0141 577 8226.

Sandymount Jewish Cemetery

Hallhill Road, Barlanark, G32 4RU

1905

Believed to have been opened in 1908[6] by the newly formed Glasgow Hebrew Burial Society, a mutual aid society funded by weekly subscriptions, on land contiguous with the municipal Sandymount Cemetery (1878). Back in 1999 the oldest tombstone was located in the south-east corner. However, since that time the Sandymount Regeneration Trust, set up in 2004, carried out extensive renovations and, in the process, conducted further research. Their research established that the first burial took place

on 25 September 1905, by the Poale Zedek *hevrah*, *ie* prior to the establishment of the burial board.[7] Not as densely packed as Glenduffhill, along the street (*see* next entry), but still containing some 2,200 graves. New signage and interpretation.

LOCATION: Postcode above is that of the caretaker's house at Glenduffhill further along Hallhill Road, travelling east. The closest entrance to the Jewish section is approximately opposite Croftspar Grove. Also accessible via Cemetery Road entrance, off Gartocher Road.

ACCESS: Sunday morning; Monday to Friday. Caretaker at Glenduffhill along the road. Sandymount Regeneration Project: www.sandymount.org.uk

FURTHER INFORMATION: *Sandymount Cemetery Heritage Trail* has a section on the Jewish cemetery, including brief biographies of some of the personalities buried there. Published by Glasgow City Council (2012).

Glenduffhill Jewish Cemetery

278 Hallhill Road, Barlanark, G33 4RU

1933

Overspill from Sandymount and contiguous with the general Glenduffhill Cemetery, which lies to its west. Acquired by the Glasgow Hebrew Burial Society in 1933. The bunker-like concrete two-storey *ohel*-cum-*bet taharah* (1933–4), with caretaker's house above, faces the street. A large cemetery containing at least 7,000 graves densely packed and in use. *Foundation stones.*

ACCESS: Sunday morning; Monday to Friday. On-site caretaker. Glasgow Hebrew Burial Society: tel 0141 577 8226.

Cathcart Jewish Cemetery

Netherlee Road, G44 3YZ

1927

Situated beyond the city boundaries in East Renfrewshire for **Queen's Park Synagogue**. *Ohel* (1931). *Foundation stone.*

Cathcart Jewish Cemetery (AP for SJBH)

Shared from inception with the former Pollockshields Congregation, which operated from a private villa at 161 Nithsdale Street, G41, between 1929 and 1984. Restored and landscaped in 1995 by *W S Atkins*. Holocaust memorial in the shape of a broken tombstone by *Lyn Wolfson* (2012).

ACCESS: Gate on street (corner Netherlee Road and Brenfield Road) locked, but accessible from the rear via the main Cathcart Cemetery, at whose far north-eastern corner it lies. Postcode above is that of the nearest houses on Netherlee Road. Main gate by the cemetery lodge at 160 Brenfield Road, G44 3JW.

NB Glasgow New Synagogue (Reform), founded in 1933, since 1952 has used a section of Cardonald Cemetery, 547 Mosspark Boulevard, G52 1SB.

Greenock Cemetery, Jewish Section

Bow Road, PA16 7JF

1911, Scottish B List

Greenock was an important point of arrival on Clydeside for Jewish immigrants from eastern Europe in the 1890s. A synagogue was opened in 1894 and a cemetery next door on Cathcart Street. For most, it was a transient stopover, on the steamship route from the Baltic to New York. The synagogue and cemetery were bombed during the Second World War, and post-war burials were sent to Glasgow. However, the historic town cemetery (*Charles Wilson*, 1846) contains a total of seven Jewish tombstones in a row, roughly facing east. The earliest is dated 1911 and the most recent 1945.

LOCATION: Enter via main entrance on Bow Road, almost opposite Iona Street. Take path to left and follow it parallel with the south-west boundary wall until it curves around towards a blocked gate in the wall, just where it bends away (northwards) from Bow Road. The row of tombstones is facing the path on your left-hand side.

ACCESS: During general cemetery hours. Enquires to Greenock Crematorium office at 1 South Street, PA16 8UG; tel 01475 715658.

Edinburgh Synagogue, west door
(AP for SJBH)

Edinburgh Synagogue

Salisbury Road, Newington, EH16 5AB

James Miller, 1929–32, Scottish B List

The first and only purpose-built synagogue in the Scottish capital since the foundation of the community in 1816. Put on the Scottish B List in 1996 and recipient of £300,000 of Heritage Lottery funding in 2003, it was judged an unusual red-brick building in the stone-built Scottish capital. Designed by a leading Glasgow architect, its cubist modernist massing, which disguises liberal use of reinforced concrete, is not dissimilar to buildings of the same period by *Cecil Eprile* for the United Synagogue in London, but possesses greater strength. The west elevation, with its central round-headed doorway, was intended to be the principal entrance, rather than the current approach from Salisbury Road from the north, but it is now obscured by an ugly extension of the premises next door, sadly detracting

from the impact of Miller's original scheme. *Foundation stone*; note the architect's signature. *Inscriptions*: north façade; Genesis 28:17; west façade: Psalm 118:20.

INTERIOR: The main roof of the prayer hall is a square with a shallow saucer dome and skylight, scarcely justifying the description 'Byzantine' that has been applied to this building. Traditional large round-headed windows and classical furnishings, including the French walnut Ark, contrast with the bald plastered walls and the technically advanced dome, suspended from the ceiling by steel hangers. The space was ingeniously downsized in 1981 by *Michael Henderson* of *Dick, Peddie & McKay* with the insertion of a floor at gallery level to accommodate the prayer hall upstairs and hall below.

STAINED GLASS: A variety of good-quality windows, all post-war. These include, in the foyer and Bet HaMidrash, six signed and dated windows by Edinburgh designer *William Wilson* (1957).[8] Two new windows by *Andrew D Johnston* were installed in the *bet midrash* when it was refurbished in 2012. *Mikveh* (1932, renovated 2004) and caretaker's house, both to the rear of the site, in a style contemporary with the synagogue. Stained-glass panel by *Valerie Simpson*.

OPENING HOURS: *Shabbat* and festival services. Heritage Open Days (September). Other times by appointment, tel 0131 667 3144; www.ehcong.com

representing the Angel of Death) carved in relief. *Plaque.*

ACCESS: Locked but visible through railings. Key c/o Edinburgh Synagogue; tel 0131 667 3144.

Braid Place Old Jews' Burial Ground

Sciennes House Place, off Causewayside, Newington, EH9 1NN

1820, Scottish B List

In use until 1867, making this the oldest Jewish burial ground in Scotland. A small gravelled plot that can be viewed from the street (south side) behind railings, rescued by the city council in the early 1990s. Hemmed in on three sides by the mellow grey sandstone walls of neighbouring buildings, it has been softly

Braid Place 'Angel of Death' tombstone (AP for SJBH)

landscaped with a few trees and shrubs, giving it the feel of a pleasant courtyard. Unfortunately, no burial registers have survived, having apparently been destroyed by a private developer. Earlier surveys identified a total of 29 inscriptions, and the oldest one currently legible (in Hebrew) dates from 1825. Several stones have ornate carved heads, one in particular with a scroll and featuring a lion head in profile and winged figure with sickle (probably

Newington Cemetery, Jewish Section

222 Dalkeith Road, EH16 5DT

1869, Scottish B List

Acquired 1867. Newington Cemetery, also known as Echo Bank, was itself opened in 1846 (architect: *David Cousin*) by a private cemetery company. Commercially run cemeteries were commonplace in 19th-century Britain, especially in Scotland, but tended to go out of business once all their clients had died! Rescued from dereliction

Jewish Section, Echo Bank (AP for SJBH)

by Edinburgh City Council and now immaculately kept.

Of special interest to literary buffs are a number of tombstones in memory of the SPARK and CAMBERG families, which have been restored by Robin Spark, son of the late novelist Muriel Spark. Much to the embarrassment of his Catholic-convert mother, he rediscovered his Jewish roots and became a member of the Edinburgh Hebrew Congregation.

LOCATION: On the street boundary, close to the lodge on Dalkeith Road, at address given above.

ACCESS: Open during general cemetery hours: tel 0131 664 4314.

Piershill Cemetery, Jewish Section

204 (The Lodge) Piersfield Terrace, Portobello, EH8 7BN

The youngest and largest of the Jewish cemeteries in Edinburgh, still privately owned by the Edinburgh Eastern Cemetery Co – so private that access to the burial records has not in the past been easy to achieve. The company holds general registers dating from the opening of the cemetery in 1883, but their Jewish records apparently go back only to 1938. This compares with registers from 1923 found in a cupboard by the Edinburgh Jewish Burial Society. This was the year in which the combined *ohel* and *bet taharah* was opened (February) in a new extension (April) to the north. The earliest Jewish tombstone on site dates from 1892 (MORRIS

LEVY, d 16 March 1892, aged 32). The stones face in all directions; some are placed back to back.

LOCATION: The Jewish sections lie towards the south-east from the main gate.

ACCESS: Open during general cemetery hours. Edinburgh Eastern Cemetery Co Ltd: tel 0131 620 7025; www.edinburghcemeteries.co.uk/piershill.htm

DUNDEE

Dundee Eastern Cemetery, Jewish Section

Arbroath Road, DD4 7JU

1889

Acquired 1988. First burial in a plot (Section R) at the north-eastern junction of the L-shaped Eastern Cemetery (1863). The narrow strip follows the boundary and consists of three rows of tombstones. Synagogues existed in a house in Ward Road (1878) and at 15 Meadow Street (a converted ware-house, now Meadow Lane) (1919, demolished 1972).

The current **Dundee Synagogue**, home to the restyled Tayside and Fife Jewish Community, is at 9 St Mary Place, DD1 5RB. (Make contact via the Scottish Council of Jewish Communities: tel 0141 638 6411; email: taysideandfife@scojec.org and www.scojec.org/communities/tfjc.) This building was erected by the council as compensation for compulsory purchase, although the Jewish community is tiny and

services sporadic.

An unusually interesting modern building by *Ian Imlach*, 1978–9, with steeply sloping walls, finished in whitewashed rough-cast concrete, and a twisted hyperbolic roof covered in grey Scots slate. Stylish use of natural materials in the minimalist interior, including wool, pebble stones and a blue-glazed tile *bimah*. This synagogue features a double Ark, the only one in Britain.[9]

LOCATION: Arbroath Road, north side, opposite Dalgleish Road.

ACCESS: Via main entrance to cemetery. Plot has a low stone boundary wall and iron railings. Its gate is left open during general cemetery hours.

ABERDEEN

Grove Cemetery, Jewish Section

Mugiemoss Road, Persley, Aberdeen, AB21 9NP

1911

Three rows on a gradient at the south-west corner of this formerly private cemetery, which was opened in 1898. The Jewish community in the 'Granite City' claims to date back to 1893, with a synagogue in Marischal Street opposite Trinity Quay, but no pre-Second World War records are kept by the present-day congregation. *Plaque* designating the JEWISH BURIAL GROUND on the stone wall behind, which separates the Jewish section from other burials higher up.

LOCATION: Enter via the main gates and bear to the right: tel 01224 697475.

ACCESS: Open during general cemetery hours.

NB The current **Aberdeen Synagogue** was opened in 1945 at 74 Dee Street, AB11 6DS. No. 74 is part of a B-listed Regency terrace, built in Aberdeen granite. www.aberdeenhebrew.org.uk

THE HIGHLANDS AND ISLANDS

INVERNESS

Tomnahurich New Cemetery, Jewish Section

118 Glenurquhart Road, IV3 5PB

The most northerly point of organised Jewish settlement in Britain. Of some 23 graves, the earliest inscription is in Hebrew, of a boy called HAIM TZVI, 6 Tevet 5666. This corresponds with the civil date 4 January 1906 given in the records kept by the Highlands Council at the Inverness Crematorium. The New Cemetery itself was opened in 1898. The Jewish plot, which is located along the southern boundary railings, has been in occasional use over the years, although there is today no Jewish community in the town.

LOCATION: South-west of Inverness on Glenurquhart Road (A82). Enter the main gates of the cemetery and turn right next to the car park.

ACCESS: Open during general cemetery hours. Enquiries to Inverness

Crematorium office, Kilvean Road, IV3 8JN: tel 01463 717849.

STORNOWAY, ISLE OF LEWIS, WESTERN ISLES

Sandwick Old Cemetery, Memorial to the shipwreck of the SS *Norge*

Lower Sandwick, HS1

A single pointed headstone bears the names of ten victims, Gentiles and Jews, who were among 635 passengers and crew who died following the sinking of the Danish vessel SS *Norge* off Rockall, to the west of Scotland, on 28 June 1904.[10] The ship was en route from Copenhagen to New York, carrying mostly Scandinavians and

(approximately) 240 Jews. This was the worst shipping accident to take place during the whole period of mass Jewish emigration from eastern Europe between 1881 and 1914. *Inscription*: Somewhat inappropriately accompanied by a verse from the New Testament Book of Revelations.

LOCATION: Plot no. 306 located by the sea wall, close to the Old West Gate. Enter by the sexton's house on Lower Sandwick and take the 'Carriage Drive' to the right, which leads to the Old West Gate. No full postcode available.

ACCESS: During general cemetery hours.

SS *Norge* memorial
(Courtesy of Stornaway Historical Society)

WALES

T HE VISITOR TO WALES will be struck by the quantity of Nonconformist chapels given place names such as *Zion, Bethel, Jerusalem, Salem* and *Carmel*. The chapel-going Christian Welsh were familiar with the 'Old Testament' and identified with the land of ancient Israel. In the Welsh language chapels were often referred to as *tabernaclau*. Prime Minister David Lloyd George's Welsh Nonconformist background has often been cited as a factor in the British Government's support for the cause of political Zionism through the Balfour Declaration in 1917.[1]

Overlooking the bay, **Swansea**'s Jewish burial ground dates from 1768, making it the earliest physical evidence of the presence of Jews in the principality. The exposed site on the old Townhill contains some fine Welsh-slate Georgian tombstones, inscribed in Hebrew block, sheltered from the wind by a high rubble stone wall.

Swansea apart, the surviving material heritage of Welsh Jewry is largely Victorian, and much of it has vanished. The Jewish community in the Welsh capital of **Cardiff** began in the 1840s. The total Jewish population of Wales has never exceeded about 4,300 (in 1967) of whom the vast majority (3,500) was to be found in Cardiff, the only Welsh community that has ever supported a choice of synagogues, 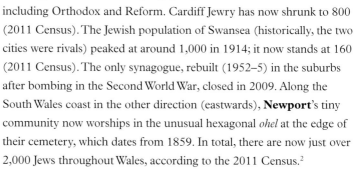 including Orthodox and Reform. Cardiff Jewry has now shrunk to 800 (2011 Census). The Jewish population of Swansea (historically, the two cities were rivals) peaked at around 1,000 in 1914; it now stands at 160 (2011 Census). The only synagogue, rebuilt (1952–5) in the suburbs after bombing in the Second World War, closed in 2009. Along the South Wales coast in the other direction (eastwards), **Newport**'s tiny community now worships in the unusual hexagonal *ohel* at the edge of their cemetery, which dates from 1859. In total, there are now just over 2,000 Jews throughout Wales, according to the 2011 Census.[2]

The settlement of small Jewish communities in the relatively isolated environment of the South Wales valleys was linked to the peculiar conditions of the mining economy of this region. Enterprising Jewish pedlars hawked their wares around the valleys, providing goods and services for the collieries, afterwards taking up residence, bringing their families and opening shops and businesses. The valley communities went into decline after the First World War, along with the coal mines that sustained them. Picturesque traces of small Jewish communities survive in several of the former mining towns of the South Wales valleys. Curiously, several Gothic-style former synagogues can still be found in South Wales (in contrast to England, where Gothic was almost exclusively Christian), at **Llanelli, Pontypridd** and **Merthyr Tydfil**. In fact, Merthyr's turreted 'Disneyland' synagogue is one of the most important, architecturally speaking, in the United Kingdom.

The Jewish populations of North and South Wales developed largely independently of each other. The development of small communities strung out along the North Wales coast in such seaside towns as Colwyn Bay, Llandudno and Bangor, was essentially an outgrowth of the industrial cities of north-west England, temporarily swollen by evacuees during the Second World War. There are no purpose-built Jewish buildings or sites in North Wales dating from before the Second World War. Llandudno Synagogue is a converted house, opened in 1945 and now used as a retreat by the Habad-Lubavitch movement. Only in 2010 was a Jewish plot (under Reform and Liberal auspices) established in the town's Llanrhos Lawn Cemetery.[3]

Former Merthyr Tydfil Synagogue (© Crown copyright RCAHMW, C526798)

Former **Merthyr Tydfil Synagogue**

Bryntirion Road, Thomastown CF47 0EE, 1876–7, Grade II

Disneyland in the Valleys

A unique 'Disneyland' double-turreted Gothic folly of a synagogue, complete with Welsh dragon perched on its gable. The frontage is of snecked rubble stone with ashlar dressings, and the steeply pitched roof is hung with Welsh slates. It perhaps owes something to the Romanticism of *William Burgess*, though the architect is unknown. On an elevated site closing the view up hilly Church Street, the synagogue dominates **Thomastown**. With its terraces of miners' cottages, now quite picturesque, Thomastown was once the Jewish quarter of Merthyr. The community was founded in 1848 and an earlier synagogue was built at John Street (1852–3), extant until the 1990s.

Closed in 1983, Merthyr's second purpose-built synagogue has been knocked about in its afterlife as a church and then as a gym. Currently standing empty and neglected; a scheme (2009) for redevelopment as flats was approved but has not materialised as yet (2015). Back in 1999 the original stone Ark surround, reminiscent of the door cases of Welsh churches, was still to be seen on the ground floor.[4] Badly eroded *inscriptions* over the front door arch contained a chronogram, not now legible. Fresh research has now dated the building with certainty. Inaccurate *plaques*.

Merthyr's eccentric synagogue is testimony to the importance of the Jewish community in this once prosperous Welsh mining town – although the hefty bill of £3,000 for its construction put them in debt well into the 20th century! The oldest surviving synagogue building in Wales, Merthyr's landmark synagogue (it is featured on the local town trail) surely rates as one of the most significant buildings in the history of synagogue architecture in the UK.

FURTHER INFORMATION: See Old Merthyr Tydfil website for unsourced photographs of the interior taken before closure: www.alangeorge.co.uk/synagogue.htm

View up Church Street
(AP for SJBH)

Merthyr Jews' Burial Ground

Brecon Road, Cefn Coed,
CF48 2PL

Sheep graze[5] in this picturesque cemetery on a steep site on the edge of the Brecon Beacons National Park. Dating from *c* 1865, extended 1935; the oldest tombstones are in the central section; the earliest one we spotted dated from 1874. The red-brick *ohel*, *c* 1898 (lintel *inscription*), now has a concrete roof. *Plaques* from **Merthyr Synagogue** inside. The last Jew of Merthyr, George Black, died in 1999, and responsibility for maintenance devolved upon the Board of Deputies in London in 2014. The burial registers were last heard of in private hands in Cardiff and can no longer be traced.

Merthyr's picturesque Jewish Cemetery (© Crown copyright RCAHMW, C526795)

LOCATION: Take the old Brecon Road (A4054) – not the A470 bypass road – north towards Brecon. On the hillside above the municipal cemetery, on the right-hand (east) side of the road.

ACCESS: The iron gates in the stone walls are usually open. Owing to the incline, it is not difficult to scale the walls with a small step ladder!

The Ohel (© Crown copyright RCAHMW, C526790)

A tombstone (© Crown copyright RCAHMW, C526792)

PONTYPRIDD

Former **Pontypridd Synagogue**

Cliff Terrace, Treforest, CF37 1RF

1895

A charming, simple Gothic stone building, with painted brick dressings, prominent finialled gables and steeply pitched Welsh slate roof that can be seen from some distance, being located on an elevated site above the Taff Vale Railway.

This synagogue could pass as just another chapel on the same street as the Calvary English Baptist Church. By a local architect named *Lloyd* of Wood Road (1895) for a community founded in 1867. Closed 1979. Basement *mikveh* now gone. Lintel *inscription* and illegible *foundation stones*. Divided into flats but the building is still called 'The Synagogue'.

LOCATION: Top of the street (north-west end) directly facing Wood Road, from where it can be seen.

Glyntaff Cemetery, Jewish Section

Cemetery Road, Glyntaff, Pontypridd, CF37 4BE

1894

The Jewish section (K) is at the far north-east corner of the municipal cemetery (1874–5). This is a tidy cemetery with short grass underfoot. Earliest burial 1894; oldest legible stone 1901. Prefabricated *ohel*.

ACCESS: During general cemetery hours. On-site cemetery office: tel 01443 402810.

Pontypridd Synagogue (© Crown copyright RCAHMW, C526800)

Former **Brynmawr** Synagogue

46 Bailey Street, NP23 4AH

W S Williams, 1900–1

A rediscovery of a former synagogue hitherto assumed to have been demolished.[6] It is certainly easy to overlook this well-appointed detached private house with lean-to garage set slightly back from the road. Now rendered and smartly painted in cream with a new pitch roof, nothing about the house gives away its former identity. No sign now of the 'rustic quoins and string courses'[7] it once possessed. The architect seems to have been a local chapel designer – but he did not double as the builder, as *Jenkins & Son* of Brynmawr were engaged. Bailey Street held only 86 people, with a single gallery at west. A *mikveh* was apparently housed in an attached shed, now gone. *Williams* is also known to have designed the lost synagogue in **Tredegar**, at Picton Street, 1875 (*see* below). The freehold of the Bailey Street synagogue was purchased in 1965, prior to its sale out of the Jewish community. Now included on the Brynmawr Heritage Trail.

LOCATION: On the north side of the section of Bailey Street that forms part of the B4248. Next to (west of) Brynmawr Fire Station, almost opposite the junction with Warwick Road.

Brynmawr Cemetery, Jewish Section

Harcourt Road, NP23 4TU

1919

For a community established in 1889. The cemetery itself had opened in 1854. An open, quite rural site; there is coal in the ground underfoot. The Jewish plot is a long strip with its northern edge on the north-western boundary of the cemetery (closest to Fitzroy Street). The vandalised *ohel* near this external boundary has been reconstructed like a bus shelter. The oldest legible tombstone is that of SIEGFRIEDT BALLIN d 20 December 1920, aged 86. An isolated grave of a suicide faces the wrong way (west), of a young woman whose husband apparently divorced her on account of being childless. The burial records are held by a Trustee in London.[8]

LOCATION: Postcode of Cemetery Lodge on Harcourt Road given above.

ACCESS: During general cemetery hours.

Former **Tredegar** Synagogue

14A Morgan Street, NP22 3ND

Appeals for funds to build a synagogue in Tredegar appeared in the *Jewish Chronicle* in September and October 1874 (the latter on the same page as an appeal for Merthyr). On application, a site in Picton Street was presented by the Tredegar Iron & Coal Company Ltd. The

'Synagogue' was clearly marked on the company's coloured town map of 1881.[9] Its construction appears to have been a struggle. In December 1875 another appeal had appeared in the press because the mortgage was in danger of being 'called in'. The Picton Street synagogue, designed by local chapel architect *W S Williams*, was finally consecrated by the 'Delegate Chief Rabbi' Herman Adler on Tuesday 29 March 1884. Williams was later responsible for the synagogue at **Brynmawr** (1901).

The plain two-storey building at no.14A Morgan Street has also been identified as the Tredegar Synagogue. Research has yet to establish when it superseded Picton Street. In any case, this building looks suspiciously like a converted house, the only distinguishing feature being the upstairs bay window.

Picton Street itself has completely disappeared in redevelopment: Gelli Close, NP22 3RE, is roughly the site where the Picton Street Synagogue once stood.

LOCATION: Morgan Street, west side. *Private house.*

NB Land for a Jewish cemetery at Tredegar was presented in the early 1870s by the Duke of Beaufort (who was also the local landowner in Brynmawr). Judging by the press appeals referred to above, funds were still required for the construction of the boundary walls. These did not materialise and the cemetery project foundered.

The façade of the former Cathedral Road Synagogue (© Crown copyright RCAHMW, C526804)

CARDIFF

Former **Cathedral Road Synagogue**

Cathedral Road, Riverside, CF11 9HA

Delissa Joseph, 1896–7, Grade II

Once the 'cathedral synagogue' of Wales, demolished behind the (east-facing) rubble stone vestibule in 1989 to make way for up-market chambers: 'The Executive Centre, Temple Court' (!) – despite having been listed. Exaggerated domes and turrets, here covered in lead, typical of *Joseph*'s fussy *fin-de-siècle* style. It was successor to the East Terrace Synagogue, 1858, enlarged 1874, demolished *c* 1949. Other earlier congregations were housed in converted premises. *Foundation stones.* Chronogram in *inscription* over archway (Isaiah 57:7).

Highfield Road Old Jewish Cemetery

Highfield Road, Roath Park, CF14 3RE

According to a restored wall *plaque*, land for this, the first Jewish cemetery in Cardiff, was donated by the Marquis of Bute in 1841, but this date cannot now be verified; earliest burials apparently 1845, but the earliest legible inscription (in Hebrew) is to a native of Wlodowa who died on 22 Tammuz 5612 (= 9 July 1852), to the west of the path. Look out for the Welsh dragon decorating a disused cast-iron water fountain (1893) in the Gothic rubble-stone *ohel* abutting the street. High stone walls surround this cemetery, which tapers to a southern point.

LOCATION: Highfield Road, south side, just beyond the railway bridge, travelling east in the direction of Roath Park Lake.

ACCESS: Locked. Key c/o Cardiff United Synagogue (rebuilt, *Stephen Rosenberg*, 2003), Cyncoed Gardens, CF23 5SL: tel 02920 473728; www.cardiffshul. org

NB There is a Reform Section (1949) in Cardiff Western Cemetery,

Highfield Road Old Jewish Cemetery entrance (© Crown copyright RCAHMW, C526808)

Cowbridge Road West, Ely, Cardiff, CF5 5TG; the successor Orthodox cemetery (1968), with *ohel*, is at Green Farm Road, on the north-eastern boundary of the same cemetery. Cardiff Reform Synagogue is housed in a former church in Moira Terrace, CF24 0EJ: tel 02920 491689; www. cardiffreformsyn.org.uk

NEWPORT

Former **Newport Synagogue**

3 Queen's Hill Crescent, NP20 5HH

Low-key red-brick school-cum-communal hall built in 1922 and remodelled as a synagogue by *James A Laurence* (1934). Closed 1997. Successor to the Romanesque-style Francis Street Synagogue, on the corner of Lewis Street (1869–71, demolished 1973). Wall tablet *inscription* survives. Now used as a private children's day nursery.

Newport Jewish Burial Ground

Risca Road, Stow Hill, NP20 4HY

1861

Acquired 1859. The unusual whitewashed hexagonal

Wall tablet on the front of the former synagogue at Newport
(© Crown copyright RCAHMW, C526391)

ohel on the corner of Risca Road (*inscription* 1928) has been used as a synagogue by the remnants of the community since the closure of **Queen's Hill Crescent**. The second plot adjacent (1946) has a modern *ohel*.

LOCATION: To south of Risca Road, contiguous with St Woolas Cemetery.

ACCESS: Both plots are locked. Keys c/o cemetery office, St Woolas Cemetery: tel 01633 263864. Occasional *Shabbat* morning services are held in the former *ohel*, now used as the synagogue.

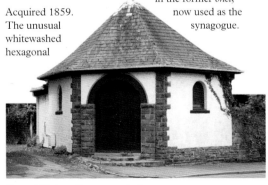

Newport *Ohel* cum Synagogue, exterior
(© Crown copyright RCAHMW, C526787)

SWANSEA

Swansea Old Jews' Burial Ground

High View, Mayhill, SA1 6US

1768

The original lease is in the City Archives. There was a series of later extensions. The oldest Jewish burial ground in Wales, this unexpectedly extensive site is located on a hill overlooking Swansea Bay. Some well-preserved Georgian headstones carved on Welsh slate, plus chest tombs, but no complete burial records from earlier than 1862.

The synagogue in Goat Street was bombed in 1941. New research has established that this synagogue was originally built in 1818, making it the first purpose-built synagogue in Wales.[10] In 1859 Goat Street was rebuilt on the same site, designed in Italianate style by *Henry J Baylis* (or

Newport *Ohel* cum Synagogue, interior (© Crown copyright RCAHMW, C526788)

Bayliss). A *mikveh* in a house in Wellington Road (1835) survived at least until 1903. After a fire in 1914, the Swansea community purchased Cornhill House, Christina Street, for conversion into school premises, a poultry yard and a basement *mikveh*. This site was in use from 1916 until after the Second World War, when it served as the main synagogue. The post-war (1952–5) purpose-built Swansea Synagogue, Ffynone Road, SA1 6BT, was the home of the community until 2009 when it was sold to the LifePoint Church. However, the Swansea Hebrew Congregation continues to hold services on Friday nights and *Shabbat* morning. The Mayhill cemetery closed in 1965 and a new plot was opened in the Oystermouth Cemetery, Newton Road, Mumbles, SA3 4SW.

LOCATION: Gate in wall at southern end of High View, before it meets Long Ridge.

ACCESS: High rubble stone walls. Locked. Key via www.jscn.org.uk/small-communities/swansea-hebrew-congregation

Former **Swansea Beth HaMedrash**

66–7 Prince of Wales Road, Greenhill, SA1 2EX

1906–7

Possibly purpose-built and now the three-storey building is converted into two flats. This was home to the 'Greeners' Shul', that is, Swansea's new immigrant Jewish congregation, which was formed in opposition to the *Englischer Shul* (if such a term can be used in Wales!) at Goat Street. From oral testimony,[11] we know that the Ark was on the east wall on the street side. Closed in 1955. The building was a rough-cast rendered and redundant shack when we visited it back in 1999.

LOCATION: North end of Prince of Wales Road, west side, beyond Thomas Row.

Former **Llanelli Synagogue**

Queen Victoria Road, SA15 2TH

Thomas Arnold, 1908–9

A pleasing, simple Gothic grey sandstone building with contrasting yellow-brick dressings and a slate roof by a local chapel builder, now appropriately in use as the Llanelli Free Evangelical Church. The church restored the derelict building in 1988–9.

The Jewish community was founded in 1902, the synagogue sold 1984. A famous son is the former Conservative Party leader Michael Howard. A memorial *plaque* to MATILDA RUBENSTEIN, dated 1947, has been retained inside as a reminder of the history of the building. Once had a *mikveh* in a separate outhouse at the back.

LOCATION: Corner Queen Victoria Road and Era Road.

The former Llanelli Synagogue (© Crown copyright RCAHMW, C839809)

IRELAND

DUBLIN, THE CAPITAL of the Irish Republic, boasts the oldest Jewish burial ground on either side of the Irish Sea, after the Resettlement cemeteries in the East End of London. It is thought that Jews arrived in **Dublin** as early as 1660–1, in parallel with the Cromwellian Resettlement in England. Portuguese Jews established a *minyan* in Crane Lane.

They included Manuel Lopes Pereira, Francisco Lopez Pereira and Jacome Faro, and close connections, undoubtedly based on familial ties, existed between them and the London community that became Bevis Marks. The Ballybough burial ground dates from 1718 and members of Bevis Marks were actually responsible for purchasing the freehold in 1748.

Ireland has, since the 17th century, attracted Jewish immigration in fits and starts. Between 1881 and 1914 some 2,000 Jews arrived from eastern Europe; however, few refugees from Nazism reached the Irish Republic, which remained neutral, during the Second World War. The Jewish population peaked at just under 4,000 after the war but, even at its height, Irish Jewry was never organised in more than a handful of towns: Dublin, Drogheda, **Cork**, **Limerick** and Waterford in the south and **Belfast**, Lurgan and Londonderry in the north. In Drogheda, Waterford, Lurgan and Londonderry the Jews left behind no material heritage in terms of purpose-built synagogues or burial grounds. The current Jewish population in the Irish Republic is estimated to be only 1,900[1] (2011 Census), about half of whom are affiliated with a synagogue.[2] A further 335 (2011 Census) reside in Northern Ireland, mainly in the capital Belfast, today the only functioning Jewish community[3] north of the border.

Like Jewish communities in Great Britain, organised Irish Jewry is not only shrinking but has become increasingly suburbanised. The post-Second World War flight to the suburbs has left historic synagogues in city centres marooned. This is a problem that besets city churches, but is not as acute for Christians as it is for Jews. Orthodox Judaism prohibits travelling on the Sabbath. The synagogue needs to be within walking distance of the community. While the challenge is at last being met to preserve in-use historic Victorian synagogues in Liverpool, Brighton and Birmingham, Dublin's fine **Adelaide Road Synagogue** (1892) became the victim of 'progress' in 1999. Historic building preservation and statutory protection is still in its infancy in Ireland, lagging a long way behind the UK. The speed with which Adelaide Road met its fate was shocking, reminiscent of the large-scale urban renewal demolitions experienced in Britain in the 1960s and 1970s before the conservation movement, headed by the Georgian Group and the Victorian Society, managed to fight back. Adelaide Road was willingly sacrificed to developers for an inflated sum, in an overheated property market, by a Jewish community that was in a serious state of decline.[4] Irish history is unpredictable, and so too is the history of the Jews in Ireland, but any future wave of immigration has irretrievably lost the potent connection with the Irish Jewish heritage that this flagship synagogue represented.

Belfast Hebrew Congregation, interior (Nigel Corrie)

Belfast Hebrew Congregation

49 Somerton Road, BT15 3LH

An influential 1960s circular synagogue with a star-shaped ceiling

This is perhaps one of the most important post-war synagogues in Britain.[5] It was designed by the Czech-born refugee *Eugene Rosenberg* of *Yorke, Rosenberg, Mardall* (1961–4), a practice better known for airport terminals. The leafy site does not advertise itself from the street and the originality of the principal building within it is revealed only from above. (Google Earth is recommended viewing!) The synagogue is completely circular in plan, encased within a concrete shell. Inside the circle,

the roof is in the shape of a hexagon, with cleverly positioned roof lights. The effect from above is kaleidoscopic. This synagogue introduced the *Magen David* motif from America into synagogue architecture in the UK. Circular synagogues are extremely rare.

INTERIOR: Unfortunately, this has been subdivided by the dwindling congregation. However, *Rosenberg*'s influential folded timber Star of David shaped ceiling, carried on chunky concrete beams, survives, and was much

Belfast Hebrew Congregation, exterior (Nigel Corrie)

Current Belfast Hebrew Congregation, *hanukiah*
(Nigel Corrie)

imitated elsewhere. The minimalist but well-lit interior features a bronze *hanukiah* by *Nehemiah Azaz*. In the vestibule is preserved the consecration *inscription* from **Annesley Street** in the form of an Arts and Craft style copper *plaque*.

Consecration plaque (Nigel Corrie)

LOCATION: BT15 4DD is the postal address; BT15 3LH pinpoints the synagogue itself on Google maps.

OPENING HOURS: *Shabbat*, some weekday and festival services. Other times and groups by appointment: tel 028 9077 7974 (voicemail); www.belfastjewishcommunity.org.uk

Former **Belfast Hebrew Congregation**

4 Annesley Street, BT14 6AU

Young & Mackenzie (Belfast) with B S Jacobs (Hull), 1904, Grade II

The second purpose-built synagogue for Belfast's Jewish community (1864), which prospered largely from its involvement in the linen industry. Successor to Great Victoria Street (1871, demolished 1990s), designed in Venetian Gothic (a highly unusual choice for a synagogue) by *Francis Stirrat* (c 1833–95)[6] with interior by *N S Joseph* of London).[7] Here, conventional Romanesque, rather plain red brick and rough-cast render; double-height round-headed windows on the long street (north) wall. Closed 1964; it found a new use as the physiotherapy gym of the Mater Hospital.[8] The fine staircase, with heavy carved banister and original chequered floor, survives in the entrance hall, although the glazed tiled dado on the stairs has been painted over. Inside the downstairs clinic the slender iron columns supporting the gallery remained. Disused *mikveh* at rear.

The building was vacated on the opening of a brand new hospital after 2006. Spot the Stars of David in the doorway and windows, all of which retain their diamond leaded and coloured lights – fortunately protected by grilles. Situated just off the Crumlin Road, the former synagogue looked neglected and was covered in graffiti in 2014. At risk.

LOCATION: Just off Carlisle Circus.

Belfast City Cemetery, Jewish Section

The Falls Road, BT12 6EQ

1873

Acquired in January 1871, soon after the opening of the City Cemetery in 1869, laid out by *William Gay* of Bradford. The Jewish plot is bounded on the north by Whiterock Road. The earliest burials were located at the eastern end, closest to the now derelict buildings, one of which was once called Fox Lodge. The earliest interment was that of a stillborn child, HERSCHMAN, who died on 29 January 1873.[9] The central portion has few tombstones because, from 1884, it was reserved for pauper burials for which grave markers were prohibited – until this rule was revoked in 1929 when the rabbi protested. The last burial, of nearly 300 – over half of which were children – took place in 1964.

Situated in the Falls Road, a notorious centre of 'The Troubles' in the 1970s, this cemetery was for a long time a Site at Risk. The obelisk in memory of the German-born Jewish linen merchant DANIEL JOSEPH JAFFE (1809–1874), father of Otto Jaffe, twice Lord Mayor of Belfast, and much besides, was vandalised and the *ohel* destroyed. In the 2000s the whole site was rescued, largely on the initiative of the Sinn Fein Lord Mayor of Belfast Tom Hartley who is also a local historian. He documented the burials in the Jewish section, while a clean-up project was run by young people, across the city's sectarian divide, under the Heritage Lottery Fund's 'Young Roots' scheme. The Jaffe obelisk has been restored.

The stone gateway on Whiterock Street, with the Hebrew *inscription Bet HaHayim* on the lintel, remains bricked up.

LOCATION: The Jewish section is located along Whiterock Road.

ACCESS: Use the main gate on The Falls Road during general cemetery hours. On-site cemetery office: tel 028 9032 3112.

Carnmoney Jewish Cemetery

Church Road, Newtonabbey, County Antrim, BT36 6DJ

1912

The second cemetery of Belfast Jewry, in a scenic spot on the edge of suburbia, north of the city in rural Carnmoney. It dates from 1912, the *ohel* from 1924 as the leaded date-stone *inscription* records. The oldest tombstones are located closest to the main gate, the earliest being of ANNIE GROSS d 9 September 1912.

LOCATION: Opposite Carnmoney Parish Church, 75 Church Road, at postcode above. Note that the Jewish cemetery lies on the south side of the western *continuation* of Church Road, after it is interrupted by 'Prince Charles Way', which divides in two halves the extensive municipal cemetery nearby.

ACCESS: Keys c/o Robert Hart Memorials (stone masons), 65 O'Neil Road, Newtonabbey, BT36 6UN; tel 028 9085 4121.

Jaffe Memorial Fountain

Victoria Square Shopping Centre, 1 Victoria Square, BT1 4QG

1877, Grade II

Made by *George Smith & Co*'s Sun Foundry (Glasgow)[10] in 1877.[11] Helped by public funding for the Belfast Botanic Gardens in 2003, the rusting fountain was dismantled and shipped to England for restoration by *Eura Conservation Ltd* of Telford. It was then returned (2008) to its original site in Victoria Square as part of the Victoria Square regeneration scheme. Erected to the memory of DANIEL JOSEPH JAFFE, father of the Lord Mayor (who is

Carnmoney Jewish Cemetery (Nigel Corrie)

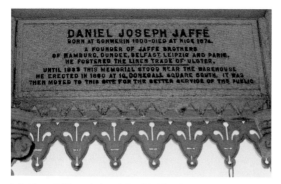

Jaffe Memorial Fountain, inscription (Nigel Corrie)

buried at the **Falls Road Cemetery**, *see* above), it had stood outside the family warehouse at 10 Donegall Square until 1938. The fountain's new home is immediately in front of the new shopping centre, the glass and steel dome of which makes an effective backdrop to the bright yellow octagonal ironwork canopy, which looks quite like a seaside bandstand. It stands on a stone plinth. The fancy finial on top is new, replacing a weather vane, now lost. *Inscription.*

The façade of the former Adelaide Road Synagogue (Nigel Corrie)

IRISH REPUBLIC

DUBLIN

Former **Dublin Hebrew Congregation**

36–7 Adelaide Road, D2

J J O'Callaghan 1892, extended 1925

This plain red-brick Romanesque façade, with stone, white-brick and terracotta dressings, is all that remains of the 'cathedral synagogue' of Ireland, shockingly demolished in 1999. It was replaced by an unremarkable block of flats.

Some of the (vast) proceeds were, it was understood at the time, to be spent on the redevelopment of the current **Terenure Hebrew Congregation** at 32A Rathfarnham Road, D6 (tel +353 (0)1 492 3751; www.jewishireland.org/). Fortunately, this plan never fully[12] materialised because Terenure, designed by Catholic architect *Wilfred Cantwell* in 1952–3, is itself not devoid of architectural interest, especially the sloping roof, the originality of the little window openings on the front, and large expanses of colourful abstract stained glass (a later addition). A new *mikveh* was built there to replace Adelaide Road's, which had been demolished along with the synagogue.

LOCATION: Near the eastern end of Adelaide Road, south side.

Former **Greenville Hall Synagogue**

228 South Circular Road, D8

Aubrey Vincent O'Rourke, 1924–5

Look carefully and you can still discern pockmarks on the cement render of what was dubbed 'Hitler's Synagogue'. The damage was inflicted by German aircraft in January 1941, notwithstanding the fact that Ireland was a neutral state during the Second World War. Compensation was subsequently paid out by the post-war German government for the repair of the classical building – the façade sports four giant unfluted Ionic columns under the pediment.

Former Greenville Hall Synagogue (Nigel Corrie)

It was actually the third synagogue on site, built 1924–5, for the 'United Dublin Hebrew Congregation', to act as a focus for the immigrant *hevrot* that clustered in the streets around South Circular Road, on the south side of the River Liffey – far away from **Adelaide Road**. The name 'Greenville Hall' came from the Victorian villa that stood on the site when it was acquired in 1913. Closed 1986 and, since 1989, the premises of scientific equipment suppliers Mason Technology, a family firm

that dates back to 1780. *Foundation stones.*

LOCATION: North side of road, near Dufferin Avenue.

Irish Jewish Museum
Former **Beth HaMedrash HaGadol Synagogue**

3 Walworth Road, D8

These two mid-terrace, mid 19th-century houses were combined to create a synagogue for a *hevrah* that functioned between 1917 until the mid 1970s. Note the matching doorways at either end. The furnishings of the upstairs prayer hall have been preserved and

Plaques on the Irish Jewish Museum (Nigel Corrie)

form part of the display of this small private museum founded in 1985. The building was restored with the assistance of the Irish Department of Labour. A treasure trove of artefacts salvaged from the lost synagogues and Jewish communities of Ireland. *Inscription:* 'Beth HaMedrash HaGodol'.

OPENING HOURS: Free admission. May to October: Sunday to Thursday 11.00 to 15.30; November to April: Sunday mornings

The Irish Jewish Museum (Nigel Corrie)

Synagogue interior at the Irish Jewish Museum (Nigel Corrie)

only. Other times and groups by appointment: tel +353 085 706 7357 (voicemail); +353 (0)1 453 1797 (office), www. jewishmuseum.ie

LOCATION: Off Victoria Street.

FURTHER INFORMATION: For a catalogue of holdings, see www.irishjewishroots. com

Former **Jewish Day School and Talmud Torah**

Bloomfield House, Bloomfield Avenue, D8

Rupert Jones, 1932–4

The school had started life at **Adelaide Road Synagogue** in 1893. The new building was made possible through a grant from the Irish Republic covering one-third of the cost (£12,000). *Rupert Jones* of *Dysert Jones*, formerly of the Board of Public Works, designed the mock Queen Anne institutional building in red brick, with a roof garden. The 'National Schools' were intended for children of 'primary school age, without distinction of sex or religion'.[13] Secular subjects were taught in the morning

and Hebrew in the Talmud Torah in the afternoon. Closed in 1980 and now used as offices. *Foundation stones* only semi-legible.

LOCATION: North end of Bloomfield Avenue (nearest to South Circular Road) and on west side of the street.

Ballybough Jewish Cemetery

rear of 67 Fairview Strand, Fairview, D3

1718

The oldest Jewish site on the island of Ireland. Owing to its proximity to Dublin Bay, the area

Datestone on caretaker's house (Nigel Corrie)

known as Ballybough (pronounced 'Ballyboc') was historically the poor immigrant quarter of the city, attracting Huguenots and Quakers as well as Jewish *conversos*. A 1,000-year lease was purchased by the Spanish and Portuguese Jews' Congregation at **Bevis Marks**, London, on behalf of their Irish brethren who were in debt to the landowner. The still extant 1748 lease refers to an earlier lost lease of 1718, thus dating the opening of the first Jewish burial ground in Ireland with precision.

Today, Ballybough is a tranquil and picturesque spot hidden from view behind a high stone wall on Fairview Strand. The cemetery is overhung with several mature trees and is effectively the big back garden of the Victorian **caretaker's house**, 67 Fairview Strand, whose narrow gable end faces the street. The Hebrew date stone in the shape of a shield bearing the English *inscription* BUILT IN THE YEAR 5618 may mystify passers-by, but translates as 1858.

The burial ground contains some 150 marked graves and many more are unmarked. Most of the earliest tombstones are illegible. By the early 19th century many tombstones had been plundered for secondary use when the Dublin Jewish community went into temporary decline. The burial registers are untraceable but Stuart Rosenblatt, founder of the Irish Jewish Genealogical Society, has compiled a database (2004).

LOCATION: North side.
ACCESS: Through caretaker's house.
Contact: Terenure Hebrew Congregation +353 (0)1 492 3751.

FURTHER INFORMATION: www.irishjewishroots.com

Dolphin's Barn Jewish Cemetery

Aughavanagh Road, D8

1898

A large suburban cemetery opened as successor to Ballybough for the Dublin Hebrew Congregation. The art deco *ohel*, with white paintwork and rounded corners, is probably genuine 1930s. It is unusually generous in size, comparable to those found particularly in the larger London Jewish cemeteries.

Lintel *inscription* in Hebrew: '*Ohel Bet Haim*' ('cemetery chapel'). The oldest tombstones are to be found near the *ohel*, close to the hedge that divides the old from the largely unused, though still in use, new section of the ground. The earliest tombstone and burial: ISAAC ZE'EV SON OF GEDALIYA LEVI GOLDRING d 6 September 1898, is inscribed, except for the date, in Hebrew. The records are incomplete but Stuart Rosenblatt compiled a database (2004).

ACCESS: Locked.
Contact: Terenure Hebrew Congregation +353 (0)1 492 3751.

FURTHER INFORMATION: www.irishjewishroots.com
NB Dublin Jewish Progressive Congregation (founded in 1946) (7 Leicester Avenue, Rathgar, Dublin, 6; www.djpcireland.com) has a plot at Woodtown Cemetery, Rathfarnham, D14, County Dublin; djpc@liberaljudaism.org or dublinjpc@gmail.com

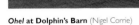
CORK

Jews from Lithuania began arriving in Cork in the 1880s and settled in **East Ville** in the streets around the gas works,

having travelled up from the port at Queenstown, the first point of arrival. The terraced streets of Cork's Jewish quarter, known as '**Jew Town**', have mostly been demolished, although the red-brick **Monerea Terrace** (pronounced 'Monrey'), with the rabbi's house on the far corner, where he killed kosher chickens, has survived. In 1989 the Irish Gas Board dedicated a new public space in the area, appropriately named **Shalom Park**, and bronze *plaques*, inscribed in English and Irish, were erected at either entrance to the park.

Cork Synagogue

10 South Terrace

Arthur Hill, 1914

A synagogue was opened on this site in 1893, probably in a Regency terraced house, and latterly used as an industrial 'ragged' school for the poor, but was very neglected by 1912. The Cork Jewish community was highly argumentative and faction-ridden. Rival *minyanim* met in East Ville and at South Terrace, and vied for the title of 'Cork Hebrew Congregation' and the official recognition of the Chief Rabbi in London. Eventually they amalgamated and the synagogue in South Terrace was completely rebuilt and reopened late in 1914. The architect was *Arthur Hill*, professor of architecture at University College, Cork. A simple street elevation set into the terrace, rendered and painted in a typically Irish pastel shade,

Ohel at Dolphin's Barn (Nigel Corrie)

Cork Synagogue (Nigel Corrie)

with a triple-arched entrance and just the hint of turrets above cornice level.

INTERIOR: Has much in common with small-scale purpose-built synagogues for immigrant communities in urban centres on mainland Britain in the late 19th century, especially those of the Federation of Synagogues in the East End of London: a plain rectangular prayer hall with gallery on three sides, traditional furnishings in a traditional Ashkenazi layout, all top-lit through a skylight.

The Cork Hebrew Congregation has almost ceased to function; its numbers peaked at about 400 before the First World War. The synagogue narrowly avoided closure in 2013; it is only used occasionally for a variety of styles of service.

NB There is some documentary evidence for a Georgian Jewish burial ground at **Kemp Street** (*c* 1796?) situated behind South Terrace, but any physical trace has long since disappeared. This may attest to the existence of a Sephardi community in Cork in the 18th century.

LOCATION: South side.
OPENING HOURS: Occasional. By appointment and groups: tel +353 (0)21 427 4280 or via Cork Tourist Office, Grand Parade, Cork City: tel +353 (0)21 425 5100.

Cork Jewish Cemetery

off Blarney Road, Curraghkippane
1887

An attractive and open rural site on a gently sloping hilltop with views into the distant Irish countryside. Acquired and the first burial took place in 1887; extended in 1914 and 1947. Many of the older graves at the far (south) end are either unmarked or collapsed. Notice here (south-east corner) the memorial to DAVID SAMUELS WHO WAS A VICTIM OF THE LUSITANIA DISASTER MAY 7TH 1915 AT THE AGE OF 36 YEARS, a poignant reminder of the torpedoing of this unarmed Cunard liner by a German submarine off the coast of Cork during the First World War. The old *ohel*, with slate pitched roof and rendered walls, was hard by the boundary between the old and new sections of the cemetery, and (in 2001) stood picturesquely derelict among the pines and other overhanging trees. It has since been demolished, the cemetery downsized (2006) and a new *ohel* built in a maintenance agreement with Cork City Council

Cork Synagogue, interior (Nigel Corrie)

LOCATION: North-west of the city of Cork to the south of Blarney Road. Take the (unnamed) south fork at Mackey's Cross. The cemetery is on the south side of the lane. Alternatively, north of the Lee Road.

ACCESS: Locked. Tel +353 (0)21 427 4280 or via Cork Tourist Office, Grand Parade, Cork City: tel +353 (0)21 425 5100.

FURTHER INFORMATION: WWW. irishjewishroots.com

The marble tablet in Limerick Ohel (Nigel Corrie)

Limerick Jewish Cemetery

Dublin Road, R[oute] 445, Newcastle

1902

Also known as Castletroy. The only physical remains testify to the fact that a Jewish community once existed in Limerick. Opened in 1902 and lovingly restored in 1990 by the Limerick Civic Trust, together with Limerick City Council, as a small public green space. The gravel path was laid through the middle to avoid any apparent burials. The cemetery contains only eight marked graves, the oldest dated 1914, and the latest (of the last rabbi in Limerick) 1944. The Hebrew *inscription* on the *Shemos* stone, beneath which sacred texts are buried, gives the date of the consecration of the ground, corresponding to November 1902. This date is also given on the marble tablet in the shape of *Luhot* inside the restored limestone *ohel*.

Limerick's Jews had mainly come from Lithuania in the 1880s, and the principal synagogue was in a house at 72 Colooney Street, now Wolf Tone Street, from 1904 (sold 1953), despite the toll taken in the so-called Limerick 'pogrom' of that year. In 2001 only one identifying Jew was known to live in Limerick. Inaccurate *plaque*.

LOCATION: By car follow the Dublin Road out of Limerick towards Dublin, as far as the thatched public house, 'The Hurlers', on the north side. Park, cross the road (to the south side) and walk back a few metres to an alleyway between houses and a Telecom station with satellite dish (on your left). This leads into the cemetery.

ACCESS: Open access. Limerick Civic Trust: tel +353 (0)61 313399.

FURTHER INFORMATION: www.irishjewishroots.com

Limerick Jewish Cemetery (Nigel Corrie)

Glossary

The following terms, unless otherwise indicated, are transliterations from the Hebrew. Local spellings are adopted in proper names.

Arba Minim 'Four species' of produce: date palm, willow, myrtle and citron used in the *Succot* ritual

Aron Kodesh, **Aron HaKodesh** Holy Ark, focal point of the synagogue in which the Scrolls of the Law are housed

Ashkenazi, pl. **Ashkenazim** Jews originating in central and eastern Europe, following the German or Polish rite

Bet Din, **Beth Din** Rabbinical court presided over by three judges or *dayanim*

Bet Knesset, **Bet HaKnesset** Hebrew name for synagogue

Bet Midrash, **Bet HaMidrash** Religious study hall often attached to a synagogue; locally spelled Beth HaMedrash

Bet Taharah Mortuary

Bimah Reading platform, traditionally centrally placed in Ashkenazi synagogues from where portions of the *Torah* are read aloud to the congregation during some services, especially on *Shabbat* morning

Cohen, pl **cohanim** By tradition, descendants of Aaron, the High Priest (*Cohen Gadol*) in Biblical times who today perform specific functions in the synagogue service. *Cohanim* are forbidden to enter cemeteries for reasons of ritual purity and a special area is often set aside for them at the entrance to the site or by the *ohel*. *Cohanim* are themselves often buried in a special plot set aside for them

Conversos Jews who converted to Catholicism under the Inquisition in late 15th-century Spain and Portugal

Dayan, pl **dayanim** Rabbinical court judge

Duhan Ark platform from where the congregation is blessed by the *Cohanim* during festival services

Edot Mizrakh Eastern or Oriental Jewish communities

Ehal See *Hehal*

Genizah Repository for used prayer books and other religious appurtenances, usually on synagogue premises

Haham Chief rabbi of the Spanish and Portuguese Jews' Congregation

Halakhah Orthodox Jewish law

Hanukiah See *Menorah*

Haredi Israeli term (adj) for strictly orthodox

Hasid, pl **Hasidim** Adherents of *Hasidut* (Hasidism), pietistic religious movement founded in eastern Europe in the 18th century and divided into various sects, each following a particular dynastic rabbinical leader or *rebbe* eg Lubavitch, Satmar, Sassov

Hehal Sephardi and Oriental term for Ark. Often pronounced *Ehal* in the Spanish and Portuguese community

Herem Ban on membership of the Jewish religious community

Hevrah, pl. **hevrot** (Hebrew) **hevros** (Yiddish) Prayer circle often functioning as a friendly society within east European immigrant communities

Hevrah kadisha Burial society; voluntary society which prepares the dead for burial and organises funerals

Hoshen Breastplate, part of the ceremonial robes of the Biblical High Priest as described in the Book of Exodus. Also the silver breastplate hung over the cover of a *Torah* scroll

Kehillah A self-governing religious community of Jews. Often used today simply to mean 'congregation'

Keter Decorative metalwork crown, often silver, placed on the handles of a Torah scroll, hence **Keter Torah** 'Crown of the Torah'

Kever, pl **kevorim** or **kevorot** Grave

Kollel Advanced religious seminary for married men

Landsmanschaft (*Yiddish*) Society of immigrants (*landsman* pl *landsleit*) originating from the same town in eastern Europe

Luhot Tablets of the Law, double-headed stone bearing abbreviated form of the Ten Commandments, often placed above the Ark in a synagogue and sometimes found on the front of the building

Lulav Palm branch shaken on the festival of Succot

Ma Tovu 'How goodly are thy tents, O Jacob, Thy dwelling places, O Israel': Bilaam's praise for the Camp of Israel, Numbers 24:5

Magen David (lit.) Shield of David. Star of David emblem

Mahamad Board of Management of the Spanish and Portuguese Jews' Congregation

Matzah, pl **matzot** Unleavened bread eaten at Passover

Matzevah, pl **matzevot** Tombstone

Mehitzah Partition in a synagogue between the men's and women's section. Often in the form of a latticed grille or fine curtain

Menorah, pl **menorot** Seven-branched candelabrum, which stood in the Temple in Jerusalem. Popularly used to refer to the nine-branched candelabrum (*hanukiah*) lit on the festival of *Hanukah*

Mezuzah Parchment scroll inscribed with scriptural verses placed in a container and affixed to doorposts and gates of Jewish homes and buildings

Mikveh, pl **mikvaot** Ritual bath. Sometimes found in the basement of a synagogue or as a separate outhouse

Minha Daily afternoon service

Minyan Quorum of 10 males, over the age of 13, required for collective worship

Mitnaged, pl **Mitnagdim**, **Misnagdish** (Yiddish adj) Opponents of Hasidism, mainly of Lithuanian origin, from the 18th century onwards

Mizrakh (lit) East. Direction for prayer facing Jerusalem, towards which synagogues are traditionally orientated *ie* the east or south-east in Britain and Europe. Also a decorative wall plaque or painting indicating the direction for prayer, often depicting a topographical or imaginary view of Jerusalem

Ner tamid Perpetual lamp hung over the Ark in a synagogue

Nusakh Specific form of the liturgy, especially musical

Nusakh Sephard A distinctive form of service practised by Hasidic (Ashkenazi) sects that is not identical with the Sephardi rite. *Nusakh Ari*, favoured by the Lubavitch (Chabad) sect, is the form of the liturgy attributed to the famous Kabbalist Rabbi Isaac Luria, called HaAri (the lion) (1534–72)

Ohel, pl **ohalim** Prayer hall or funerary chapel at a Jewish burial ground; a small walk-in memorial over the grave of a Hasidic rabbi

Omer calendar Notice board in the synagogue for *Sefirat HaOmer*, the counting of the 49 days between *Pesach* and *Shavuot*

Parohet, pl **Parohot** Embroidered curtain covering the *Torah* scrolls in a synagogue

Pesach Passover

Rebbe Hasidic rabbi, leader of Hasidic dynasty

Sefer Torah, pl **Sifrei Torah** Scrolls of the Law containing the Pentateuch, stored in the synagogue Ark and used in public worship

Sephardi, pl **Sephardim** Jews originating from the Iberian Peninsula

Shabbat The Jewish Sabbath, which lasts from sunset on Friday to nightfall on Saturday

Shavuot 'Festival of Weeks' or Pentecost

Shemos (Yiddish) or **Shemot** (Hebrew) (lit) 'Names'. Disused sacred texts and appurtenances containing *HaShem*, 'The Name' (of God), which are buried in a special plot in a Jewish cemetery. Sometimes confused with a *Genizah*

Shiviti Decorative inscription or wall plaque featuring the opening word from a verse in Psalm 16, 'I have set [the Lord always before me]'

Shofar Ram's horn blown to mark the Jewish New Year

Shtender (Yiddish) Lectern facing the Ark occupied by the prayer leader during services, especially in Hasidic synagogues. Called *Amud* in Hebrew, *Omud* in Yiddish

Shtiebl pl **Shtieblekh** (Yiddish) Small synagogue often in a private house, originally Hasidic

Shul/Shool (Yiddish) Synagogue

Sifrei Torah See *Sefer Torah*

Succah Temporary booth open to the sky erected to celebrate the festival of *Succot*, as a reminder of the nomadic existence of the Biblical Children of Israel in the desert

Succot Festival of 'Tabernacles' or 'Booths'

Talmud Torah Elementary religious school for boys

Tevah Sephardi and Oriental term for *bimah*

Tik, pl **tikim** Wooden case protecting Torah scrolls, often decorated with silver, used by North African and Oriental communities

Torah The Pentateuch; used generally to apply to the Jewish religious sources and tradition

Yahin and **Boaz** The names of the pair of columns at the entrance to Solomon's Temple (1 Kings 7:15–22)

Yahrzeit (Yiddish) Anniversary of a death, especially of a parent, according to the Hebrew calendar

Yeshivah, pl **yeshivot** Traditional religious seminary for young men

YKVK or **Yud Kay Vav Kay** The unspoken four letter name of God referred to by a variant of its Hebrew initials

Abbreviations

AP – Andrew Petersen
BB – Barbara Bowman
DCMS – Department for Culture, Media and Sport
JSCN – Jewish Small Communities Network
P & G – Parks and Gardens Register
RCAHMS – Royal Commission on the Ancient and Historical Monuments of Scotland

RCAHMW – Royal Commission on the Ancient and Historical Monuments of Wales
SJBH – Survey of the Jewish Built Heritage
SK – Sharman Kadish
VFM – Viorica Feler-Morgan

Notes

Preface to the Second Edition

1   *See* the explanation in the Introduction.
2   *Synagogues at Risk: A report based on the findings of a survey by Jewish Heritage* 2010. Swindon: English Heritage, available online from www.HistoricEngland.org.uk and reprinted in Kushner, T and Ewence, H (eds) 2010 *Whatever Happened to British Jewish Studies? Jewish Culture and History* **12**, 1 & 2 (summer/autumn 2010), 357–77.
3   In such cases, the primary source reference is given in a footnote if it has not been cited in my previous published research.
4   A joint project of JewishGen (www.jewishgen.org) and the Jewish Genealogical Society of Great Britain (www.jgsgb.org.uk).
5   Whose name was inadvertently omitted from the first edition.
6   For the rare exceptions to this rule, such as the Spitalfields Great Synagogue, *see* the Introduction.
7   Compare the two archive photographs in Williams, B 2008 *Jewish Manchester: An Illustrated History*. Manchester: Breedon Books: 62, top (mislabelled) of the Salem Chapel and part of the building next door, and 186, bottom, of the former *Beth HaMedrash* building.
8   Alterations were made to the interior to turn it into the Beth HaMedrash. It is not known whether the plan to include a 'Mikvah and communal baths' on the site was carried out; *Jewish Chronicle*, 23 June 1899.
9   *See* first edition, p 214 note 3; for photographs taken by English Heritage, *see* Kadish, S 2011 *The Synagogues of Britain and Ireland*. New Haven and London: Yale University Press, 216–17.
10 Note that the Channel Islands and Isle of Man have been absorbed into related English regions, the South and North-West respectively.
11 Shortlisted by the College Art Association (USA) for the Society of Historians of British Art Prize 2013.
12 Nigel and Barbara also collaborated on the companion guide *Jewish Heritage in Gibraltar*, *see* p 280.

Acknowledgements for the First Edition

1   Fishman, W J 1979 *The Streets of East London*. London: Duckworth.
2   Usually, unless the Jewish New Year intervenes.

Introduction

1   Perhaps from 1660–1 in Ireland.
2   For slight editorial variations between the first and second editions, *see* the Preface.
3   For example *Jtrails* online and in print: Kolsky, R and Rawson, R 2012 *Jewish London*, London: New Holland Publishers, that appeared after the first edition of this guidebook.
4   According to the latest statistics, see Graham D December 2013 '2011 Census Results: Thinning and Thickening: Geographical Change in the UK's Jewish Population, 2001–2011'. London: Institute for Jewish Policy Research. Available on the JRS's website. Revised upwards to 271,295, *Jewish Chronicle*, 6 March 2015. Plus *c* 2,000 Jews in Ireland, *see* p 258.

Notes for Visitors

1 Posted in 2009.
2 This changed hands after the appearance of the first edition, and became known as '1701', the historic year in which the synagogue opened. In February 2015 it closed.
3 There were two in 2006.
4 The Jewish Small Communities Network (www.jscn.org.uk) is a useful umbrella for many of them.
5 On technological developments in mapping, *see* the Preface.
6 Ditto for more on online resources.
7 Kadish, S 2005 'Bet Hayim: An Introduction to Jewish Funerary Art and Architecture in Britain' *Transactions of the Ancient Monuments Society* **49**, 31–58; Kadish, S 2011 'Jewish Funerary Architecture in Britain and Ireland since 1656' *Jewish Historical Studies* **43**, 59–88.
8 The vast majority of the synagogues listed in this guidebook are Orthodox. Very few Reform or Liberal synagogues in Britain were opened before the Second World War.

London

1 A breakdown, kindly supplied by Dr David Graham, is: Greater London Authority (ie within the London Boroughs) 148,602; Hertfordshire 21,345; Essex 6,662; Surrey 3,055 (by email, 31 December 2013).
2 Also of interest opposite, in the tiny cul de sac called Frederick's Place, stands a well-appointed Georgian house that was the office of the young future prime minister, Benjamin Disraeli, in 1821–4 (*blue plaque*). *See* p 8.
3 In the Ward of Portsoken, which was just outside the walls, but fell within the jurisdiction of the City of London.
4 The postcode of the synagogue house at the rear on Heneage Lane.
5 For more comparative information on the two buildings and architectural drawings, see Kadish, S 2011 *The Synagogues of Britain and Ireland: An Architectural and Social History*, chapter 1; a site guide, Kadish, S 2001 *Bevis Marks Synagogue 1701–2001*, was published by English Heritage to mark the tercentenary.
6 An adaptation of *Pirkei Avot* (*Ethics of the Fathers* derived from the *Mishnah*) 3:1 combined with *Babylonian Talmud, Tractate Berahot* 28b.
7 Not to be confused with St Botolph's, Bishopsgate 1727–9, which is also by *George Dance the Elder*, working as a mason with his father-in-law *James Gould*.

St Botolph was the patron saint of travellers, hence the occurrence of churches dedicated to him close to city gates and town limits.

8 *Jewish Chronicle*, 9 September 1870.
9 Jack Gilbert, oral testimony, 18 June 2009.
10 *Jewish Chronicle*, 30 July, 6 August 1858; 22 November 1861.
11 *Jewish Chronicle*, 27 November, 4 December 1885.
12 For example, vestiges in the kitchen behind the Indian restaurant at 89 Fieldgate Street.
13 *Jewish Chronicle*, 2, 9 March 1934, architect not named.
14 *Jewish Chronicle*, 4 April 1873.
15 *See* Preface on 'Mother Levy's' and above on Basil Henriques, p 21.
16 The 'Lying-in Hospital', that is, the maternity hospital, is not to be confused with the 'Jews Hospital' (founded 1795) that operated from substantial premises in Mile End. Contemporary engravings from 1806 to 1807, much reproduced, show that that institution was a plain three-storey building, perhaps extended and given a pedimented neo-classical façade in *c* 1818. Its full name, emblazoned across the pediment and under the cornice was: *Neve Tsedek* ('The dwelling place of Justice'): 'Jews' Hospital for Aged Poor and the Education and Employment of Youth'. This was the hospital that moved to Norwood in 1863. *See* p 68.
17 Drawings of both tablets are in Hyamson, A M 1951 *The Sephardim of England*. London: Methuen & Co., 321 and 325.
18 As remarked upon in the English Heritage inspector's report: David Garrard 2014 'The Novo Cemetery' unpublished, with acknowledgements.
19 A study based on the extant burial register and a few photographs was published by the congregation: Rodrigues-Pereira, M and Loewe, C 1997 *Bevis Marks Records, Part VI: The Burial Register (1733–1918) of the Novo (New) Cemetery of the Spanish & Portuguese Jews' Congregation*. London: The Congregation.
20 Westman, A 2007 and 2008 *Walls of the New Cemetery (Bethahaim Novo) of the Spanish & Portuguese Jewish Congregation, Queen Mary, University of London 331–333 Mile End Road E1*. London: Museum of London Archaeology Service (MOLAS archaeology reports); Lipman, C 2012 *The Sephardic Jewish Cemeteries at Queen Mary, University of London*. London: Queen Mary, University of London; and email from Dr Caron

Lipman, 9 July 2012. Thanks to Ken Worpole for drawing my attention to her work and to Andrew Abdulezer of Seth Stein Architects.

21 New research (2013) by Charles Tucker in the United Synagogue Minute Books in the London Metropolitan Archives, including a letter from N S Joseph dated 15 April 1890.

22 *Jewish Chronicle*, 18 March 1870. The builder was A M Cohen.

23 *See* the entry in the first edition, p 31.

24 The fourth one was stolen while the building was redundant.

25 *Jewish Chronicle*, 29 June, 14 September 1923.

26 *Jewish Chronicle*, 18 September 1857.

27 He gave his agreement on 12 June 1958, having consulted with Chief Rabbi Israel Herzog of Israel, *Jewish Chronicle*, 18 July 1958.

28 Glasgow's Garnethill Synagogue is Scottish A-listed, the equivalent to the English Grade I.

29 Post-dating liturgical innovations at Hampstead and Hammersmith, both supposedly 'Orthodox' synagogues under the auspices of the United Synagogue.

30 *See* photograph of the interior taken in 2001 in Kadish, *The Synagogues of Britain and Ireland*, 129.

31 Gailani, F 2000 *The Mosques of London*, Henstridge, Elm Grove, 42.

32 His father was Rabbi Samuel Isaac Hillman, minister of Glasgow's South Portland Street Synagogue (*see* p 242) and afterwards a *dayan* on the London Beth Din.

33 His studio was in the top of the family home at 91 Priory Road, West Hampstead.

34 Executed by his studio after Hillman's death in 1974.

35 Apparently a heavily remodelled Nonconformist chapel, 1957–91. The building is now a Seventh Day Adventist church.

36 Some of the other windows here are clearly not Hillman's work, judging by their inferior quality.

37 His son Walter Landor left for California and made his fortune as a pioneer of corporate design. He designed the *Coca-Cola* logo.

38 *See* photograph of the exterior taken in 1996 in Kadish, *Synagogues of Britain and Ireland*, 214.

39 In fact, this sculpture was originally intended for the grave of Hedwig Elkan (d 1959) but was placed in the new 'Rose Garden', where there are no burials, thanks to scruples on the part of the Liberal Ministers' Conference.

40 *See* online resources *Kunstlexikon Saar* (www.kunstlexikonsaar.de), entry for 'Völklingen' and *MuseumsplattformNRW* (www.nrw-museum.de), entry for 'Benno Elkan'.

41 *The Times*, 16 May 2012.

42 Visible from the A41 Edgware Way. The distinctive curved roof utilised trusses left over from the 1951 Festival of Britain.

43 *Jewish Chronicle*, 14 December 1956.

44 In 1973 the Spanish and Portuguese sold off 1.46 acres for housing in Temple Fortune Lane. New information here based on Epstein, J and Jacobs, D 2006 *Rabbis and Teachers Buried at Hoop Lane Cemetery*. London: Reform Judaism.

Information provided in 2011 from Liberal Jewish Synagogue correspondence files 1960–3 by LJS Archivist Bryan Diamond, and see his note 'Re: Benno Elkan' in *JHSE Newsletter*, September 2011, 3, available at www.jhse.org

South-East England

1 Postcodes for Honeysuckle Road, odd (8AA) and even (8AB) sides.

2 But see below for other vestiges of the Montefiores in Ramsgate.

3 Not counting George Basevi (1794–1845), a first cousin of Prime Minister Benjamin Disraeli on his father's side, and who was also a pupil of Soane. Basevi's mother's identity is unknown, thus putting his Jewish status into question and, in any case, it seems that the family became Christians. He married outside the Jewish faith.

4 So I am informed by Mark Samuel PhD FSA MIFA, via Mark Negin of Ramsgate Montefiore Heritage (email 4 October 2012). Dr Samuel states that it is 'large crystal "Imperial" porphyry, an igneous rock from the eastern desert of Egypt.' He thinks that the unfinished Roman column was probably reused later in a Byzantine building. He concludes: 'There is no reason to suppose the column did not come from the Holy Land, perhaps via several buildings on the way.'

5 'Flushed with architectural status' *Jewish Chronicle* 19 September 2003, front page.

6 His eldest grandson, *Manuel Nunes Castello*, was architect-surveyor to the Spanish and Portuguese Jews' Congregation in the early years of the 20th century, *see* p 29.

7 The building has no house number. There are two postcodes for King Street. The postal address is c/o the King's School, CT1 2ES.

8   Kadish, S 2011 *Synagogues of Britain and Ireland*. New Haven and London: Yale University Press, 73–4.
9   Gollop, A G 2009 'Former Halletts Garage 21–24 St Dunstan's Street. Canterbury, Kent', Archaeological Evaluation Report, Canterbury Archaeological Trust, February. Courtesy of the author, Adrian Gollop.
10   Decapitated by the Puritans but afterwards restored.

The South of England

1   *Jewish Chronicle*, 19 August 1887. This reference was found following a lead supplied by Gordon Franks. The Westlake pieces installed in 1887 were paid for by the three sons of Flora Sassoon.
2   I am informed that the second member of the family who was 'interred' in the mausoleum, Sir Edward Albert Sassoon (1856–1912), was, in fact, cremated; letter from Godfrey Gould, 22 March 2007. However, his memorial stone is in the Liberal Jewish Cemetery (see www.cemeteryscribes.com). The final resting place of his father, Sir Albert, has not been located.
3   According to local historian Godfrey Gould, letter 29 April 2007.
4   *Architectural Review*, January 1939, 36–7, with acknowledgements to Nick Antram, co-author of the *Brighton & Hove Pevsner Architectural Guide* (2008) for this reference.
5   Especially those influenced by Charles Chipiez's Temple reconstructions (1889), see Kadish S 2011 'Jewish funerary architecture in Britain and Ireland since 1656' *Jewish Historical Studies* 43, 84–5; Kravtsov, S R 2008 'Reconstruction of the Temple by Charles Chipiez and its Applications in Architecture', *Ars Judaica* IV, 25–42.
6   *Jewish Chronicle*, 5 August 1864.
7   Email correspondence with Michael Woolfson of Fleet, Hampshire, with genealogical research by Gaby Laws, August 2009.
8   Acquired 1969; first burial 1982. *Ohel*.
9   Due for completion in 2015. Compare with description in first edition.

The West Country

1   A series of studies by Dr Helen Fry includes: *Jewish Cemeteries of Devon; The Jews of Exeter: An illustrated history; The Jews of Plymouth: An illustrated history*, all Somerset: Halsgrove. *See* www.helen-fry.com and www.cemeteryscribes.com

2   Research in synagogue archives by Jerry Sibley, telephone communication 9 December 2013.
3   *See* Jamilly, E 1999 *The Georgian Synagogue*. London: Working Party on Jewish Monuments in the UK and Ireland, Jewish Memorial Council.
4   As pointed out by the late Rabbi Dr Bernard Susser.
5   A gift of £300 was given by the corporation in compensation for the compulsory purchase of the old *mikveh* and Hebrew school in 1834; information from Jerry Sibley.
6   The statutory status of nos.1 and 2 New Street and of the synagogue at the rear remained ambiguous at time of revision (2015). This explains the destruction of the synagogue interior some time between 1984 and 1987. Steps are now being taken to rectify this unsatisfactory situation in order to prevent any further damage: see Soyinka S 2014 'Penzance Synagogue: A Brief History', unpublished ms, posted (June 2014) on www.jewishgen.org/jcr-uk under Penzance, with acknowledgements to Susan Soyinka.
7   New research by Susan Soyinka (ibid.) has shown that an arched passageway once ran through no. 1 New Street, providing direct access to the synagogue behind. Alternative access from a narrow alley on New Street is also blocked off; it now serves as the entrance to a cycle centre.
8   *See* Soyinka (ibid.), 7 for a photograph of the original lease, which is now in private hands.
9   The enlarged synagogue was reconsecrated in 1840; *The Penzance Gazette*, 30 September 1840, as quoted by Soyinka (ibid.), 10.
10   On the north-west and south-west sides (opposite the Ark), as shown in plans (1958 and 1984) reproduced in Soyinka (ibid), 14 and 17.
11   Two brass Moorish gas lamps found in an antique shop in Penryn are probably from Penzance Synagogue (gas was installed *c* 1869–70). These can also now be seen at the Jewish Museum; *London Jewish News* 9 January 2004 and Soyinka (ibid.), 27–30.
12   *See* plate 11 in Friedlander, E et al 2000 *The Jews of Devon and Cornwall: Essays and Exhibition Catalogue*. Bristol: Redcliffe.
13   According to Godfrey Simmons, *see* Soyinka (ibid.), 10.

14 *See* Pearce, K and Fry, H (eds) 2000 *The Lost Jews of Cornwall*. Bristol: Redcliffe and revised and enlarged edn. Pearce, K 2014 *The Jews of Cornwall: A History, Tradition and Settlement to 1913*. Somerset: Halsgrove.

15 Unpublished research, jointly by Godfrey Simmons and Rabbi Dr Bernard Susser, 1990s, now in University of Southampton Archives; Godfrey Simmons' note on 'The Jewish Cemetery, Truro', in Pearce, K and Fry, H (eds) 2000 *The Lost Jews of Cornwall*. Bristol: Redcliffe, 155–6.

16 Emanuel, R R and Ponsford, M W 1994 'Jacob's Well, Bristol, Britain's only known Medieval Jewish Ritual Bath (*Mikveh*)', *Transactions of the Bristol & Gloucestershire Archaeological Society* **112**, 73–86.

17 Not 25 January 1814, as stated by Tobias.

18 Of Rueben [*sic*] Somers, great grandfather of Denise Chantrey, email 29 June 2007.

Lincoln and East Anglia

1 Identified by Cecil Roth.

2 Pevsner, N and Harris, J 1989 *Lincolnshire*, rev. edn. London: Penguin, 518–19.

3 Wood, M 1965 *The English Medieval House*. London and New York: Harper & Row.

4 Pevsner referred to the building simply as the Music House in his first Norfolk volume in 1962, completely ignoring and ignorant of its Jewish associations: *North East Norfolk and Norwich*. Harmondsworth: Penguin, 272. Corrected in the revised edition: Pevsner, N and Wilson, B 1997 *Norfolk: 1, Norwich and North-East*. London: Penguin, 274–5.

5 Discovered by architect Barbara Bowman in research for the Survey of the Jewish Built Heritage.

6 A single archive photograph is known, *see* Kadish S 2011 *The Synagogues of Britain and Ireland*. New Haven and London: Yale University Press, 71, and online at www.norwichsynagogue.org.uk.

7 Formal trusteeship pending (2014).

8 Pevsner, N and Wilson, B 1999 *Norfolk: 2, North-West and South*. London: Penguin, 474. The Jewish identity of the site is not mentioned.

9 Formal trusteeship pending (2014).

10 Kadish, *The Synagogues of Britain and Ireland* 43–4, with acknowledgements to Alan Coleman.

11 Formal trusteeship pending (2014).

12 Drawn to my attention in 2011 by Sarah Margittai of Pardes Hanna, Israel.

13 Still the case in 1999.

The Midlands

1 *See* Kadish S 2011 *The Synagogues of Britain and Ireland*. New Haven and London: Yale University Press, 279–81.

2 For images taken by English Heritage for SJBH see www.centralshul.com.

3 *Manchester Jewish Telegraph* 22 August 2014, 20; information on Children's (Middlemore) Emigration Homes from Peter Higginbotham's website at www.childrenshomes.org.uk/, accessed 24 August 2014.

4 Compare with the archive image in Kadish, *The Synagogues of Britain and Ireland*, 160.

5 According to the *Jewish Chronicle*, 5 February 1904.

6 Durham, B *et al* (1992). *Oxoniensia* 56, 17–74.

7 The practice of Spence, Bonnington & Collins, 1968–70, largely the work of Sir Basil's son John Urwin Spence.

North-West England

1 *Jewish Chronicle*, 2 August 1996.

2 Located at no. 29 Pembroke Place (Grade II), derelict. Developers of the site, Liverpool School of Tropical Hygiene proposed (2014) to remove the ceramic and iron façade and incorporate it into a freestanding sculpture nearby commemorating Liverpool's Jewish heritage.

3 Largely attributable to the high birth rate in North Manchester neighbourhoods of Broughton Park and Prestwich. Localised net population increase is also occurring in certain London districts containing significant *Haredi* or strictly Orthodox Jewish communities.

4 *Jewish Chronicle*, 11 September 1874.

5 Pevsner, N 1969 *Lancashire: Liverpool and the South West*. Harmondsworth: Penguin, 245–6.

6 Compare with a sketch dated 1854 reproduced in Ettinger, P 1930 '*Hope Place' in Liverpool Jewry*. Liverpool: T Lyon, fig 4, opposite 31.

7 A photograph appears in Ettinger, P 1930 '*Hope Place' in Liverpool Jewry*, 68.

8 Not spotted by our original site survey, but extant in 2013. Image provided by Arnold Lewis who carried out a field survey, email 18 December 2013.

9 *Jewish Chronicle*, 5 July 1929. Acknowledgements to Arnold Lewis for drawing this to my attention.

10 He was actually buried on 2 July 1930 according to the general burial registers held at LRO, email from archivist Roger Hull, 2 June 2014.

11   See discussion in Kadish, S 2011 The Synagogues of Britain and Ireland. New Haven and London: Yale University Press, 100-103.

12   Compare with archive photograph of 1903 reproduced in Kadish, Synagogues of Britain and Ireland, 191, fig 158.

13   The name of the firm, likewise written over the doorway, had been covered over by a new sign (August 2012).

14   See Preface.

15   Email correspondence with Tony Hayden's son David Hayden, June 2011. Thanks to Alex Klein for putting us in touch.

16   Manchester City News, 5 October 1929, 8, with thanks to Neil Darlington.

17   There was apparently no architect. I am informed by Harry Johnston that the building was finished by his firm TLC Building Contractors Ltd, after the original contractors, Medlock Builders, went bankrupt, in conversation 3 September 2013.

18   British Architect, 20 February 1914, 157–8.

19   See first edition, pp 155–6.

20   Slated for demolition in 2011.

21   See Kadish, Synagogues of Britain and Ireland, chapter 12.

22   The Georgian Raikes Hall (Grade II) itself survives as a hotel and public house.

23   Rebuilt at Kinloss by Downton & Hurst in 1965–7 – so the dating fits. Unresolved questions about the evolution of this building may be answered by a study of the congregational minute books, currently in London (2015).

24   Compare with the description in first edition, p 160.

25   According to local resident Carol Jempson: 'Isle of Man community struggles', Jewish Telegraph (Manchester edn), 24 January 2014, 28.

Yorkshire and Humberside

1   Only a tiny handful of Reform synagogues existed prior to the First World War. West London Synagogue is the only other survivor. See Kadish, S 2011 The Synagogues of Britain and Ireland. New Haven and London: Yale University Press, chapter 9, 'The Anglo-Jewish Reformation'.

2   Jewish Chronicle, 1 April 1881.

3   This synagogue, in Springhurst Road, BD18 3DN (Basil Gillinson, 1970), closed in May 2013.

4   Visible in 1998.

5   Building, 27 February 1998, 57–60.

6   See Kadish, The Synagogues of Britain and Ireland, 243–5.

7   See first edition, p 173. Burials remain at Rodmoor that seems to have been consecrated ground, a rabbi being present at the funeral of August Bright in 1880. The two sites are located respectively to the north and south of the A57 Manchester Road, westbound out of Sheffield. Addresses are Rodmoor: on land to the north-east, only accessible via Crawshaw Lodge, Rodside, Sheffield, S6 6GN; Moscar: 1 Moscar Cross Cottages, S6 6JG, in a large private garden, behind an iron gate on the road. Unmarked.

8   Later published: Lilley, J M et al 1994 The Jewish Burial Ground at Jewbury. York Archaeological Trust and Council for British Archaeology.

9   Planning permission was granted but work on site had not begun by August 2014.

10   Extant in 1999. See entry in first edition, p 176.

North-East England

1   See entry below.

2   A total of about 3,000 individuals were counted in Gateshead according to the 2011 Census, compared with only 670 in Newcastle.

3   Pevsner, N 1983 County Durham 2nd rev. edn by Elizabeth Williamson. Harmondsworth: Penguin, 452.

4   See entries for both Clapton and Sunderland in the first edition, which was published late in 2006, p 31, pp 182–5.

5   Quoted in Levy, A 1956 A History of the Sunderland Jewish Community. London: Macdonald, 147.

6   Psalm 118:19, 'Open for me the gates of righteousness …'; see entry in first edition, p 31.

7   Sunniside Conservation Area: Character Appraisal and Management Strategy, October 2009. Sunderland City Council, 38, 51.

8   Jewish Chronicle, 1 December 1899. See also Taylor, D and Davis, H 2010 The Sunderland Beth HaMedrash 1899–1999. Suffolk: Arima Publishing.

9   Information from Rabbi Shlomo Katanka and Rabbi Nathaniel Lieberman.

10   Jewish Chronicle, 10 January 1936 (mikveh), 11 February 1938 (Mowbray Road); Sunderland Echo, 5, 7 February 1938 (Mowbray Road).

11   Such windows and the 'broad-house' plan used in Gateshead also feature in new synagogues being built for strictly Orthodox communities (both Hasidic and Mitnagdic today, for example in north

Manchester, see Kadish, S 2011 *The Synagogues of Britain and Ireland*. New Haven and London: Yale University Press, chapter 21 'Current Trends', esp. 289–91, and Cohen-Mushlin, A, Kravtsov, S, Levin, V 2010–2 *Synagogues in Lithuania: A Catalogue*. Vilnius: Vilnius Academy of Arts Press.

12 Compare with the photograph in first edition, p 189.

13 *See* first edition, p 191.

14 The original burial register gives the name Louie Levey, d 1876 aged 56; information provided by Martin Levinson, trustee, 2002. A photograph posted online of the earliest tombstone gives the English spelling as Louis Levy. The rest of the inscription, in Hebrew, not entirely legible and including a chronogram, apparently gives death date as 7th? day of Passover 5636 (= 1876); survey by Bernard Bookey (2001–2), *see* www.kmbro.weebly.com

15 *Jewish Chronicle*, 13, 20 October 1871, 8, 15 November 1872; 'Consecration of the New Synagogue, West Hartlepool … Tuesday 5 November 1872', printed, Southampton University Archives ms 162; 'Order of Service at the celebration of the Jubilee of the Synagogue of the West Hartlepool Hebrew Congregation, Whitby Street. Wednesday, 13th December, 5683–1922', printed, Middlesbrough Reference Library, Local History Collection, Olsover Archive.

16 This was the very first site visited by the Survey of the Jewish Built Heritage, on 20 July 1998, when it was also photographed in black and white by Bob Skingle for Historic England Archives.

Scotland

1 The actual necropolis lies across Waterloo Place and contains some interesting memorials dating from the mid-18th century.

2 Identified by Historic Scotland, *see* revised list description available online.

3 The address used to be 2–4 Falloch Road, G42 9QX.

4 Not Baron Bercott, wrongly credited in Kadish, S 2011 *The Synagogues of Britain and Ireland*. New Haven and London: Yale University Press, 250, based on oral testimony disproved by subsequent research in the synagogue's archives. In fact, the architects were Norman Bailey Samuels & Partners, who also worked for the United Synagogue. Baron Bercott carried out repairs after a fire in the 1970s.

5 I am grateful to Paul O'Cuinn for the new information contained in this entry. For the preparation of a Craigton Cemetery heritage trail (due out 2014), he studied the records of the Craigton Cemetery Co that were not previously available. His *Sandymount Heritage Trail* was published in 2012 (*see* entry).

6 The earliest burial listed in the damaged registers kept down the road at Glenduffhill (inspected back in 1999) was that of baby Bessie Chitterer, died aged 8 months on 11th and buried on the 12th January 1908. The oldest stone found on site was that of Lazarus Fell d 22 Jan 1908 aged 44. It had toppled over.

7 *Sandymount Cemetery Heritage Trail* 2012 Glasgow City Council, 48. Author Paul O'Cuinn confirmed that his information came from a copy of the burial records, email 19 December 2013, with acknowledgements.

8 Documented by Bobbie Smith of NADFAS (2013) for the Scottish Stained Glass Symposium, a project undertaken in collaboration with RCAHMS. It has not been possible to identify the designers of the rest of the windows.

9 Double and triple Arks are a feature of synagogues in some Sephardi and Oriental Jewish communities, such as parts of north Africa. Perhaps the architect was influenced by trends in Israeli synagogue design, but this is uncertain.

10 *See* Sebak, P K 2004 *Titanic's Predecessor: The SS Norge Disaster of 1904*. Laksevaag, Norway: Seaward.

Wales

1 See Kadish, S 'The Jewish Presence in Wales: Image and Material Reality' in O'Kane, M and Morgan-Guy, J (eds) 2010 *Biblical Art from Wales*. Sheffield: Sheffield Phoenix Press, 272–89.

2 As interpreted by the Demographic Unit of the Board of Deputies of British Jews. I calculated a total of 2,064 from the unit's figures presented in a downloadable spreadsheet, broken down by local authority in England and Wales, available from www.bod.org.uk/ accessed 14 November 2013.

3 In 2006 an online North Wales Jewish Network was set up (www.northwalesjewishnetwork.org). Succeeded by a short-lived 'North Wales Jewish Community' 'Google' site in 2014.

4 The wooden Ark (1923) from upstairs is now in Gateshead, where it has been in use by the Yeshivah Ketana (L'Zeirim) in

Gladstone Terrace, NE8 4EF, information from Rabbi Shlomo Katanka, Rabbi Nathaniel Lieberman and Dovid Pruim.

5 Contrary to Jewish law, it must be said.

6 I am grateful to Professor Harold Pollins for confirming the continued existence of Brynmawr Synagogue, in 2008. No traces of Neath Synagogue (1867–8), also purpose-built, architect unknown, have been found.

7 *Jewish Chronicle*, 21, 28 June 1901.

8 Judge Anthony Morris (living in Golders Green) who came forward with this information by telephone, 30 April 2007. He also held minute books of the congregation, 1905–60.

9 Courtesy of Ken Davies of the Tredegar History and Archive Society, email correspondence, May 2014. I am also grateful to Michael Spitzer, a student at Sha'are Torah Yeshivah in Manchester, for first drawing my attention to the existence of the building in Morgan Street. Its former use as a synagogue has been confirmed by the present owners.

10 New research (2013) by Cai Parry-Jones (PhD student at University of Bangor), kindly shared with me. Sources: *The Cambrian*, 23 May 1818; *Sundays in Wales: Visits to the Places of Worship of the Quakers, the Unitarians, the Roman Catholics and the Jews by a Week-Day Preacher* 1859. Swansea and London: Pearse & Brown, 29–42 (copy in Swansea University Library).

11 The late Harry Sherman, who identified the building for the Survey of the Jewish Built Heritage (10 June 1999). He also recalled that there was a gallery on the north wall and a schoolroom at the back.

Ireland

1 The figure of 1,984 people, quoted online, is in fact an increase on previous estimates. However, there was no option to identify as Jewish either by religion or ethnicity in the last Irish Census (2011), unlike in the UK (since 2001). There are an unknown number of temporary workers, mainly Israelis, resident in the Republic, who do not participate in any form of communal life.

2 *c* 380 with the Orthodox community and *c* 180 with the Progressives (Reform), according to Stuart Rosenblatt, email 18 December 2013.

3 *c* 85 being members of the congregation, information from Stuart Rosenblatt, *ibid.*

4 At least the Ark and pulpit were salvaged and eventually installed in Kehillat Ahavat Tzion in Ramat Beit Shemesh, a new-build synagogue (2008) in Israel patronised by Irish Jews, see www.old.ahavat-tzion.com

5 Hence meriting an entry in this 'heritage' guide, one of only two post-war synagogues I have included (the other being Carmel College, *see* p 154).

6 A Scotsman who had an office in Belfast in the 1860s–1870s, *see* entry in the online *Dictionary of Scottish Architects*.

7 *Jewish Chronicle*, 29 September 1871 (laying of foundation stone) and 27 September 1872, where it is stated that the building was 'dedicated just at the close of last year.'

8 When visited by our Survey in 1999.

9 We failed to locate the burial records back in 1999. The new information in this entry is based on Tom Hartley's research, *see* Hartley T 2006 *Written in Stone: The History of Belfast City Cemetery*. Belfast: Brehon Press. See also: www.belfastcity. gov.uk/city cemetery/jewishburialground. asp accessed 28 August 2011, where the date of burial of baby Herschman was given as 2 February 1873. However, the online database of burial records compiled by Belfast City Council gives 31 January 1873; *see* under 'cemeteries' and 'burial records' on www.belfastcity. gov.uk/community

10 According to *Belfast Telegraph*, 12 February 2008, quoted at http://alaninbelfast.blogspot.com, entry for 14 February 2008, accessed 26 April 2009. This was probably accurate because this firm of art metal workers specialised in ornamental canopied drinking fountains for parks and gardens. They were Glasgow based and had offices in other cities, including London and Dublin, *see* www.glasgowsculpture.com

11 Many sources give 1874, the year recorded on the inscription when Daniel Jaffe died.

12 *See* Kadish, S 2011 *The Synagogues of Britain and Ireland*. New Haven and London: Yale University Press, 241–2.

13 *Jewish Chronicle* 16 February 1934.

Jewish Heritage in Gibraltar
An Architectural Guide
Sharman Kadish

The Rock of Gibraltar has been a haven for Jews for over 300 years, since its capture by the British in 1704, Catholic Spain having expelled them from its shores in 1492. By the mid-18th century, about a third of the population of Gibraltar was Jewish, adding to the richly cosmopolitan mix of the free port. Today Christians, Muslims, Jews and Hindus, from England, Spain, Portugal, Italy, North Africa and India live side by side in Gibraltar. Now the Gibraltar Jewish community, Sephardim mostly from Morocco, is some 600 strong and its four historic synagogues are all still in use, a rare legacy in Europe, untouched by the ravages of the Second World War.

Discover *Jewish Heritage in Gibraltar* with this first-ever authoritative guidebook featuring full-colour photographs, drawings and an architectural heritage trail.

Written by **Sharman Kadish**, Director of Jewish Heritage UK, with maps and drawings by architect **Barbara Bowman** and specially commissioned photography by **Nigel Corrie** formerly of English Heritage.

80pp paperback ISBN 978-1-904965-12-1
Published by Spire Books at £9.95

Sole Distributors:
In the UK: Jewish Heritage UK www.jewish-heritage-uk.org

In Gibraltar: Gibraltar Heritage Trust, stockist for all bookshops on the Rock www.gibraltarheritagetrust.org.gi

DISCOUNT for orders online

Index of Sites and Places

Page numbers in **bold** refer to illustrations.

Fulham and West Kensington Synagogue and Talmud Torah, London 51

Garnethill Synagogue, Glasgow 92, 234, **236**, 237–8, **237**, **238**
Gateshead 218–19
Gateshead Synagogue 229, **229**
Giffnock Old Synagogue, Glasgow 239
Gifford Place Jewish Cemetery, Plymouth 116
Gildersome Jewish Cemetery, Leeds 206–7
Gilroes Cemetery, Jewish Section, Leicester 157–8
Glasgow xxi, 234–5
Glasgow Eastern Necropolis, Jewish Section 241
Glasgow Necropolis, Jews' Enclosure xxi, 241
Glenduffhill Jewish Cemetery, Glasgow 243
Gloucester 123
Glyntaff Cemetery, Jewish Section, Pontypridd 253
Golders Green, London xxii, xxv, 3
Golders Green Jewish Cemetery, London 30, 67, **67**
Golders Green Synagogue, London 64–5, **65**
Goldsmid Family Estate, Somerhill 80–1
Great Garden Street Synagogue, London 16
Great Yarmouth 127, 135–7, **136**
Great Yarmouth Old Cemetery, Jewish Section 136
Great Yarmouth Old Jews' Burial Ground 135–6
Green Lane Jewish Cemetery, Liverpool 170
Greenock Cemetery, Jewish Section 244
Greenville Hall Synagogue, Dublin 264–5, **265**
Grimsby Jewish Cemetery 217
Grimsby Synagogue 215–17, **215**, **216**, **217**
Grove Cemetery, Jewish Section, Aberdeen 246–7
Guernsey 106
Guildford Medieval Synagogue 85–6, **85**
Guildhall, London xxx
Guildhall Yard, London xxx

Hackney, Borough of, London 34–9
Hackney Jewish Cemetery 34–5
Hackney Synagogue 34
Hammersmith and Fulham, Borough of, London 51–2
Hammersmith and West Kensington Synagogue, London 51
Hammond Memorial, Alderney 106
Hampstead Synagogue, London 52, **54**, 55–6, **56**
Hardy Street Jewish Cemetery, Nottingham 158–9
Hartlepool Jewish Cemetery 232, **232**
Harton Cemetery, Jewish Section, South Shields 230
Hazlerigg (Hazelrigg) Jewish Cemetery, Newcastle 222, 228
Hendon Synagogue, London 61, 66, **66**, 185
Hertford Cemetery, Jewish Section 86
Highams Park and Chingford Synagogue, Essex 41
Higher Crumpsall Synagogue, Manchester 182–4, **183**, 186
Highfield Road Old Jewish Cemetery, Cardiff 255–6, **255**
Hill Top Jewish Cemetery, Leeds 207
Holland Park Synagogue, London 50–1, **51**
Holy Law Synagogue, Manchester 185
Hoop Lane, *see* Golders Green 30
Houndsditch, London 1
Hove 88
Hove Hebrew Congregation, Brighton 97, **97**, 222
Hull 145, 198, 212–15, **213**
Hull 'New' Jewish Cemetery 213–14
Hull Old Hebrew Congregation 212

Imperial War Museum, London 55
Imperial Waterproof Co, Manchester **177 (map)**
Inge Court Back-to-Backs, Birmingham **147 (map)**
Inverness 234, 247
Ipswich 127

Ipswich Old Cemetery, Jewish Section 138
Irish Jewish Museum, Dublin 265, **265**, **266**
Isle of Man 196–7, **196**, **197**
Isle of Sheppey Cemetery, Jewish Section 85
Islington, Borough of, London 39, **39**

Jacob Cohen warehouse, Manchester **177 (map)**
Jacob's Well, Bristol 121–2, **122**
Jaffe Memorial Fountain, Belfast 263–4, **264**
Jersey 106–7, **107**
Jersey Jewish Cemetery, St Helier 106
Jersey Synagogue 106
Jesmond Synagogue, Newcastle 221, **223**, 227, **227**, 228
Jew Street Synagogue, Brighton 94, **96 (map)**
Jewish Board of Guardians offices, London **10 (map)**
Jewish Day School and Talmud Torah, Dublin 266
Jewish Model Dwellings, London 17
Jewish Museum, London 1, 54, 117, 118
Jewish Museum, Manchester xxii, xxvi, 189
Jewish Soup Kitchen, London **10 (map)**, 13, **13**
Jewish Soup Kitchen, Manchester **177 (map)**, 178, **178**
Jewry Wall, Leicester 155–6
Jews' House and Jews' Court, Lincoln **128**, 129–30, **130**
Jews' Infant School, London **10 (map)**, 17
Jubbergate, York 211
Jurnet the Jew's House, Norwich 132–3, **132**

Katz shop front, London **10 (map)**
Kensington and Chelsea, Borough of, London 50–1
Kingfield Synagogue, Sheffield 208
King's Lynn 127, 135
Kingston Cemetery, Jewish Section, Portsmouth 103
Kingston upon Hull 212–15, **213**
Kingston upon Thames 3